250
Poems
A Portable Anthology
Second Edition

Edited by

PETER SCHAKEL
Hope College

JACK RIDL
Hope College

Bedford/St. Martin's   BOSTON   ◆   NEW YORK

For Bedford/St. Martin's
Executive Editor: Stephen A. Scipione
Production Editor: Annette Pagliaro Sweeney
Production Supervisor: Sarah Ulicny
Marketing Manager: Adrienne Petsick
Editorial Assistant: Marisa Feinstein
Copyeditor: Paula Woolley
Text Design: Sandra Rigney
Cover Design: Donna Lee Dennison
Cover Art: Godfrey Frankel, *Chatham Square, New York, 1946*
Composition: TexTech International
Printing and Binding: Haddon Craftsmen, Inc., an RR Donnelley & Sons
   Company

President: Joan E. Feinberg
Editor in Chief: Karen S. Henry
Director of Marketing: Karen R. Soeltz
Director of Editing, Design, and Production: Marcia Cohen
Assistant Director of Editing, Design, and Production: Elise S. Kaiser
Managing Editor: Elizabeth M. Schaaf

Library of Congress Control Number: 2008925890

Manufactured in the United States of America

3 2 1 0 9
f e d c b

For information, write: Bedford/St. Martin's, 75 Arlington Street,
Boston, MA 02116 (617-399-4000)

ISBN-10: 0–312–46616–1
ISBN-13: 978–0–312–46616–9

Preface for Instructors

250 Poems: A Portable Anthology is a compact, inexpensive collection of poems, classic and contemporary, that is rewarding to teach and enjoyable to read. In preparing this volume, we sought to include many canonical poets along with poets writing since 1950 who have received considerable critical attention. We also included some poets who are deserving of such attention but who have been by and large undervalued, as well as recent poets we think will receive critical recognition in the future. We recognize, of course, that prognostication in any art is hazardous and realize that we have, reluctantly but necessarily, left out many poets worthy of inclusion. We tried to represent a wide variety of poetic strategies and forms in order to illustrate the diversity of approaches to the art. And we chose a range of poems that reveals the impact of ethnic diversity on poetry written in English.

The poems are arranged chronologically by birth date of the authors, to guide readers toward a sense of the historical development of poetry in English and the influence of earlier poets and poems on later ones. The dates given below the poems indicate earliest publication in a book, preceded in some cases by the probable date of composition, in *italics*, where that information seems useful. We have kept the apparatus in the book to a minimum. Glosses are provided for vocabulary that cannot be found readily in a current dictionary. Annotation is added to clarify lines that draw on ideas requiring specialized knowledge or practices not readily familiar in our time or outside a specific culture. We include a brief introduction to reading poetry and, following the anthology, biographical sketches for every poet in the book, a selective index of poems by form and type, and a glossary of poetic terms.

NEW TO THE SECOND EDITION

A survey of instructors who chose the first edition of *250 Poems* revealed that the book was being assigned in introductory literature or poetry classes and in creative writing courses. Accordingly, we have tried to make the second edition more useful for students in both types of courses. For introductory courses we have increased the number of poems by certain canonical authors (including Emily Dickinson, William Butler Yeats, Robert Frost, and Langston Hughes) to encourage a study of their work in some depth. For creative writing courses we have slightly increased the number of poems by contemporary writers, including work by Kim Addonizio, Denise Duhamel, Lucia Perillo, Donald Revell, Bob Hicok, and Honorée Fanonne Jeffers, among others. We hope our new introduction, "How to Read a Poem — and Why," and our new appendix, providing a selective list of poems in the anthology by form and type, will be helpful to students and instructors in both types of courses.

ADDITIONAL RESOURCES

The companion Web site at bedfordstmartins.com/250poems offers further materials for working with this anthology, and with literature in general. LitLinks presents concise annotations and links to hundreds of Web sites that contain useful biographical information about the poets included in this anthology. Links to the Academy of American Poets and Modern American Poetry Web sites provide further biographical information. VirtuaLit, an interactive poetry tutorial, offers exercises designed to promote close readings of poems. A substantial list of poems grouped by subject matter and theme is also available on the Web site.

ACKNOWLEDGMENTS

For assistance in selecting and annotating particular poets presented in this anthology, we are indebted to several Hope College colleagues: Susan Atefat Peckham, Marla Lunderberg, Jesse Montaño, and William Pannapacker. We are grateful to Charles Huttar, who provided valuable assistance with the biographical sketches, glossary, glosses, and annotations. Myra Kohsel, office manager for the Department of English at Hope College, helped us in a variety of ways with her usual graciousness, patience, and competence.

We would like to thank the reviewers of the first edition for their helpful suggestions: Jessica Baldanzi, Indiana University; Earl S. Braggs, University of Tennessee, Chattanooga; Julie A. Chappell, Tarleton State University; Heather Comfort, James Madison University; Alex Dick, University of British Columbia; Paul T. Gallagher, Red Rocks Community College; John Meredith Hill, University of Scranton; Margaret E. Johnson, Idaho State University; Roberta Kramer, Nassau Community College; Jessica Lang, George Mason University; Cate Marvin, College of Staten Island, CUNY; Adam McKible, John Jay College of Criminal Justice; Erin O'Neal, Asheville-Buncombe Tech; Mary Soliday, City College of New

York; Tom Zimmerman, Washtenaw Community College; and Aliesa Zoecklein, Santa Fe Community College.

We also want to express our appreciation to those at Bedford/St. Martin's who helped make the second edition possible, including Joan Feinberg, Denise Wydra, and Karen Henry. Steve Scipione helped us to develop the book with wise counsel on how to shape the revision, and Marisa Feinstein gracefully handled numerous tasks including the review program and Web site updating. We thank Elizabeth Schaaf and Annette Pagliaro Sweeney for smoothly overseeing the production of the book, Paula Woolley for her deft copyediting, and Sandy Schechter for clearing permissions.

Contents

How to Read
a Poem—and Why

WHAT IS POETRY? What is this thing we call poetry? We can usually tell someone what a novel, a play, or an essay is, but a poem can be baffling to explain. It can't be defined as writing that has meter: A lot of poetry, especially modern poetry, is nonmetrical. It's not confined to writing that rhymes, for many poems do not use rhyme. And though most poetry is written in lines, prose poems don't have line divisions. Much poetry uses figurative language and is intense and emotionally complex—but the same is true of powerful prose. Whatever characteristics one tries to apply are neither typical of all poetry nor exclusive to poetry. So, what can we say that poetry is?

Those who we'd think ought to know—poets themselves—usually offer subjective responses: E. E. Cummings said that poetry is "dancing on your own grave." Ezra Pound purportedly stated it is "what poets write." Emily Dickinson describes poetry by its effect: "If I read a book [and] it makes my whole body so cold no fire ever can warm me, I know THAT is poetry. If I feel physically as if the top of my head were taken off, I know THAT is poetry. These are the only ways I know it. Is there any other way?"

Poetry arises when some deep impulse needs expression, and no other form of writing can express it. The poem comes from a sense of urgency; it feels it must be "let out," shared, given, offered up. Poet Lucille Clifton once imagined, "Poetry began when somebody walked off a savanna or out of a cave and looked up at the sky with wonder and said, 'Ah-h-h!' *That* was the first poem. The urge toward 'Ah-h-h' is very human, it's in everybody." Every day, each of us feels that impulse, and we go "Ah-h-h!" or "Wow!" or "Oh no!" or simply sigh.

WHAT DOES POETRY DO? Maybe a better question than "What is poetry?" is "What does poetry do?" Poetry can do a lot of things.

• *Poetry makes connections.* We are all citizens in the culture of joy, pain, anger, love, fear, despair, and hope. Every one of us carries the same emotions as everyone else. Our situations, stories, and conflicts may differ, but the news from the heart comes to each of us. And though we can't claim, "I know just how you feel," we can say with confidence, "I, too, have known that feeling."

• *Poetry gives voice.* In our day-to-day lives, voices come at us — from the Internet, news media, sales pitches, cell phones, movies — creating information overload. It often seems our own voices are not heard. Poetry offers a chance to speak, and to speak from the deepest part of our selves. Whether we write it or read it, poetry lets us feel liberated and in touch with our selves, and with others. The words are our words; the rhythms are our rhythms; the clumsiness and sophistication of phrasings are ours; the sounds, tones, even the attempts to be artful are ours.

• *Poetry tells stories.* We read poems as we do other stories, to discover what happened and why. We read them to feel part of a larger world, where we encounter experiences we might otherwise never have, and where we may discover that our experiences are not unique but are shared by others.

• *Poetry describes.* Poems may describe a person, a relationship, a city street, a scene in nature, or almost anything else — using vivid, precise language that enables readers to conjure up clear images. Descriptive poetry enables us to see the world more precisely, more vividly. More often than not, a poem, like most great art, will give us new perceptions, fresh ways of seeing what is around us.

• *Poetry reflects.* Poetry sometimes puts readers right into a poet's head, allowing us to share the poet's thoughts and feelings. Lyric poems often convey meditations triggered by an object, idea, person, place, or event. Such a poem can lead you to reconnect with something from your own life, moving you deeply and stimulating your own reflections.

• *Poetry remembers.* Poet William Butler Yeats called memory the wellspring of all poetry. In one sense, a poem can come from nowhere else but the past. Poems can be acts of preservation, saving forever what has gone by, what will never happen in quite the same way again.

• *Poetry expresses, embodies, and kindles emotions.* In reading poetry, you may find a companion, someone who also has felt what you have felt. Poems can touch you and connect you to what is best in you, whether it be it outrage at injustice, sorrow for another's loss, or joy for another's good fortune.

• *Poetry celebrates language.* Poets live in language. Words are as real to them as a cup of coffee. They use language to draw us *past* the words themselves and into the mystery of experience. Yet poets also draw our attention *to* language by uncommon uses of words and phrases. Poets recognize that we spend much of our adult lives in what poet William Stafford called "language events" — talking, reading, listening, writing things down, sending and receiving e-mail messages, and so on. Poets seek to create works that enrich and invigorate our experiences in and with language.

The essence of poetry — both what it is and what it does — is elusive. There is no one way to pin it down. Though that elusiveness may challenge and perplex us, it is also part of the appeal, part of the seductiveness, of poetry. We enter the world of a poem not really knowing what to expect. And whenever we enter something new — whether an unfamiliar city, or a new job, or a new relationship — we tend to feel uncertain. We have to look around. We have to be attentive. We have to be open and flexible. So it is with approaching poems. We simply have to take the plunge and start reading.

HOW DO YOU START? What is the best way to approach a poem? Here are some practical tips:

- **Look at the poem.** Start by simply looking at the poem, at its shape and the way it appears on the page. Poems can have a visual effect in addition to the effects created by language, sounds, and ideas. Poets use lines and stanzas but also the white space around and throughout a poem to invite a reader to enter. Linger for a moment to absorb the poem visually.
- *Read straight through.* Go straight through a poem the first time you read it. Just wander through, stopping for a bit along the way to wonder about or savor a word or a line. Then keep going. Get a feel for the poem without worrying about what you don't know or understand.
- *Slow down and reread.* Slow down as you reread so you can really hear the poem. Slow reading is a genuine pleasure. You shouldn't speed-read a poem any more than you would speed up your favorite song. Reread poems you like several times, until the poem becomes a part of you. Focus on something different each time you read it.
- *Read aloud.* Most poems are meant to be heard as well as read on the page. Their sounds and rhythms need to be read aloud. So, read the poem out loud at least once, or listen to someone else read it. Find a private place if you are worried that someone will laugh at you.
- *Hear the "music."* Poems work with the musicality of language, blending the sounds and rhythms of words and word connections. Think of song lyrics set to music; in poetry, the poem makes its own music through the sounds and rhythms of language.
- *Open yourself to the poem.* Reading a poem differs from reading a newspaper or an e-mail message or a textbook. You usually read those to

glean information or ideas, without entering the work imaginatively or emotionally. Though many poems also impart information and ideas, they can do other things, too: They can lead us to feel intensely, to experience deeply, to perceive freshly, to understand experiences different from our own, and to affirm our own ideas, feelings, and experiences. To receive these things from a poem, you need to read experientially.

• *Focus on what catches your attention.* You might be drawn to a particular image that alters your usual perception of something. Maybe you like the sounds of the language, or the way the rhythm shifts or remains regular in every line. Maybe the poem is funny or poignant or both. You don't have to have a masterly grasp of the whole poem to be able to notice things within it or to wonder about it or to begin talking about it. Paying passionate attention to what is actually in a poem is a wise starting place.

• *Watch the words.* At some point, start paying attention to what the words say — not what the whole poem *means,* but what the words *say.* Don't be overly eager to figure out a poem's "meaning." When you walk through the woods, you don't keep asking, "What does that tree mean?" or "What does that stone represent?" You accept them for what they are. So it should be with poetry: Look at the words, listen for what they say, and understand them as best you can. And if at first you don't understand all that much, don't worry — there are many things in a poem that you can experience even before you "get" it.

• *Follow the sentences.* The sentences in the poem may be broken up into lines, but they are still sentences. Get their sense correct. If the order of words in a sentence is inverted, it's important to pay attention to cues that identify what is subject and what is object. If a poet uses incomplete sentences, or "fragments," try to figure out their purpose. After working out where sentences start and stop, focus on the lines: begin noticing what the line divisions and line breaks add to the experience of the sentence.

• *Ask questions.* You can, of course, ask what a poem means, but you don't need to start with that question. Instead, try asking questions such as, What is happening in this poem? What is this poem doing? Why am I drawn to that phrase or line? What is the poem connecting me with or challenging me about? How is the poem shifting my usual way of seeing things and leading me to reconsider the ways I've thought and felt?

• *Let the poem be itself.* You may have heard people talk about "interpreting a poem" or finding its "hidden meaning." But poetry isn't a foreign language that needs to be translated. Poets do not hide or bury meanings so that readers need special abilities or insights to get at them;

poets want their works to be accessible, not inscrutable. So, begin by trusting the literal. If a poem says it's about stopping in the woods on a snowy evening, trust what it says. Some readers may argue that it's also about something more than that, and that's okay. But if you only enjoy it as a richly descriptive poem that lets you appreciate the beauty of life more fully, that's still a very good way to read a poem.

Former poet laureate Rita Dove has stated, "[I want] to help people see that poetry is not something above them or somehow distant; it's part of their very lives. I would like to remind people that we *have* an interior life — even if we don't talk about it because it's not expedient, because it's not cool, because it's potentially embarrassing — and without that interior life, we are shells, we are nothing." Approaching poems that way, as a part of ourselves, paradoxically opens us to a wider life. Critic and poet C. S. Lewis once wrote that when we read, we become a thousand others, and we are never more ourselves than when we do. Read poems to feel connected to the things that you are pulled away from, things you cherish and need in your life. Read them to recover what you have lost or to hold on to what you have. Read to be challenged. Read to be shaken. Read for fun. Read to see new things or to see things in new ways. Read to be comforted or understood.

Poems can be friends, best friends, honest and trustworthy friends. As critic Helen Vendler has put it, "The strangest experience in reading poetry, as in writing it, is to find yourself in it, to be yourself in it. . . . We sometimes speak of this as finding a 'favorite poet.' . . . The important thing is to feel companioned, as you go through life, by a host of poems." We hope that you find many such friends in this anthology and that it will lead you to feel at home in the vast world of poems that lies outside it.

ANONYMOUS

Lord Randal

1

"O where ha' you been, Lord Randal, my son?
And where ha' you been, my handsome young man?"
"I ha' been at the greenwood; mother, mak my bed soon,
For I'm wearied wi' huntin', and fain wad° lie down."   *gladly would*

2

"And wha° met ye there, Lord Randal, my son?   *who*   5
And wha met you there, my handsome young man?"
"O I met wi' my true-love; mother, mak my bed soon,
For I'm wearied wi' huntin', and fain wad lie down."

3

"And what did she give you, Lord Randal, my son?
And what did she give you, my handsome young man?"   10
"Eels fried in a pan; mother, mak my bed soon,
For I'm wearied wi' huntin', and fain wad lie down."

4

"And wha gat your leavin's, Lord Randal, my son?
And wha gat your leavin's, my handsome young man?"
"My hawks and my hounds; mother, mak my bed soon,   15
For I'm wearied wi' huntin', and fain wad lie down."

5

"And what becam of them, Lord Randal, my son?
And what becam of them, my handsome young man?"
"They stretched their legs out and died; mother, mak my bed soon,
For I'm wearied wi' huntin', and fain wad lie down."   20

6

"O I fear you are poisoned, Lord Randal, my son!
I fear you are poisoned, my handsome young man!"
"O yes, I am poisoned; mother, mak my bed soon,
For I'm sick at the heart, and I fain wad lie down."

7

"What d' ye leave to your mother, Lord Randal, my son?   25
What d' ye leave to your mother, my handsome young man?"
"Four and twenty milk kye;° mother, mak my bed soon,   *cows*
For I'm sick at the heart, and I fain wad lie down."

8

"What d' ye leave to your sister, Lord Randal, my son?
What d' ye leave to your sister, my handsome young man?"   30
"My gold and my silver; mother, mak my bed soon,
For I'm sick at the heart, and I fain wad lie down."

9

"What d' ye leave to your brother, Lord Randal, my son?
What d' ye leave to your brother, my handsome young man?"
"My houses and my lands; mother, mak my bed soon,   35
For I'm sick at the heart, and I fain wad lie down."

10

"What d' ye leave to your true-love, Lord Randal, my son?
What d' ye leave to your true-love, my handsome young man?"
"I leave her hell and fire; mother, mak my bed soon,
For I'm sick at the heart, and I fain wad lie down."   40

[1803]

SIR THOMAS WYATT   [1503–1542]

They flee from me

They flee from me, that sometime did me seek,
With naked foot stalking in my chamber.
I have seen them, gentle, tame, and meek,
That now are wild, and do not remember
That sometime they put themselves in danger   5
To take bread at my hand; and now they range,
Busily seeking with a continual change.

Thankèd be fortune it hath been otherwise,
Twenty times better; but once in special,
In thin array, after a pleasant guise,°   *manner of dress* 10

When her loose gown from her shoulders did fall,
And she me caught in her arms long and small,°   *slender*
Therewithall sweetly did me kiss
And softly said, "Dear heart,° how like you this?"

It was no dream, I lay broad waking.   15
But all is turned, thorough° my gentleness,   *through*
Into a strange fashion of forsaking;
And I have leave to go, of° her goodness,   *out of (motivated by)*
And she also to use newfangleness.
But since that I so kindly° am served,   20
I fain would know what she hath deserved.

[from an undated manuscript]

14. Dear heart (pun): Heart, and hart (deer).
20. kindly (pun): Graciously (ironic), and "in kind"; i.e., in a way typical of female nature.

QUEEN ELIZABETH I   [1533–1603]

When I was fair and young

When I was fair and young, and favor graced me,
Of many was I sought, their mistress for to be;
But I did scorn them all, and answered them therefore,
    "Go, go, go seek some otherwhere,
        Importune me no more!"   5

How many weeping eyes I made to pine with woe,
How many sighing hearts, I have no skill to show;
Yet I the prouder grew, and answered them therefore,
    "Go, go, go seek some otherwhere,
        Importune me no more!"   10

Then spake fair Venus' son,° that proud victorious boy,   *Cupid*
And said: "Fine dame, since that you be so coy,
I will so pluck your plumes that you shall say no more,
    'Go, go, go seek some otherwhere,
        Importune me no more!'"   15

When he had spake these words, such change grew in my breast
That neither night nor day since that, I could take any rest.
Then lo! I did repent that I had said before,
    "Go, go, go seek some otherwhere,
           Importune me no more!"   20

                      [*c. 1580s*]

EDMUND SPENSER   [1552–1599]

One day I wrote her name upon the strand

One day I wrote her name upon the strand,
But came the waves and washèd it away:
Again I wrote it with a second hand,
But came the tide, and made my pains his prey.
"Vain man," said she, "that dost in vain assay,   5
A mortal thing so to immortalize,
For I myself shall like to this decay,
And eek° my name be wipèd out likewise."   *also*
"Not so," quod° I, "let baser things devise,   *quoth (said)*
To die in dust, but you shall live by fame: 10
My verse your virtues rare shall eternize,
And in the heavens write your glorious name.
Where whenas death shall all the world subdue,
Our love shall live, and later life renew."

                      [1595]

SIR PHILIP SIDNEY   [1554–1586]

Loving in truth, and fain in verse my love to show

Loving in truth, and fain° in verse my love to show,   *eager*
That the dear she might take some pleasure of my pain,
Pleasure might cause her read, reading might make her know,
Knowledge might pity win, and pity grace obtain,
    I sought fit words to paint the blackest face of woe: 5
Studying inventions fine, her wits to entertain,
Oft turning others' leaves, to see if thence would flow

Some fresh and fruitful showers upon my sunburned brain.
   But words came halting forth, wanting° Invention's stay;°
Invention, Nature's child, fled step-dame Study's blows,   10
And others' feet still seemed but strangers in my way.
Thus great with child to speak, and helpless in my throes,
   Biting my truant pen, beating myself for spite,
   "Fool," said my Muse to me, "look in thy heart and write."

                                                            [1582]

9. wanting: Lacking; **stay:** Support.

MARY (SIDNEY) HERBERT, COUNTESS OF PEMBROKE   [1561–1621]

Psalm 100 *Jubilate Deo*

O all you lands, the treasures of your joy
   In merry shout upon the Lord bestow:
Your service cheerfully on him employ,
   With triumph song into his presence go.
Know first that he is God; and after know   5
   This God did us, not we ourselves create:
We are his flock, for us his feedings grow:
   We are his folk, and he upholds our state.
With thankfulness O enter then his gate:
   Make through each porch of his your praises ring,   10
All good, all grace, of his high name relate,
   He of all grace and goodness is the spring.
Time in no terms his mercy comprehends,
From age to age his truth itself extends.

                                                      [c. 1595; 1823]

MICHAEL DRAYTON   [1563–1631]

Since there's no help, come let us kiss and part

Since there's no help, come let us kiss and part;
Nay, I have done, you get no more of me,
And I am glad, yea glad with all my heart

That thus so cleanly I myself can free;
Shake hands forever, cancel all our vows,   5
And when we meet at any time again,
Be it not seen in either of our brows
That we one jot of former love retain.
Now at the last gasp of love's latest breath,
When, his pulse failing, passion speechless lies,   10
When faith is kneeling by his bed of death,
And innocence is closing up his eyes,
    Now if thou wouldst, when all have given him over,
    From death to life thou mightst him yet recover.

                                              [1619]

CHRISTOPHER MARLOWE   [1564–1593]

The Passionate Shepherd to His Love

Come live with me and be my love,
And we will all the pleasures prove
That valleys, groves, hills, and fields,
Woods, or steepy mountain yields.

And we will sit upon the rocks,   5
Seeing the shepherds feed their flocks,
By shallow rivers, to whose falls
Melodious birds sing madrigals.

And I will make thee beds of roses
And a thousand fragrant posies,   10
A cap of flowers, and a kirtle
Embroidered all with leaves of myrtle.

A gown made of the finest wool
Which from our pretty lambs we pull,
Fair lined slippers for the cold,   15
With buckles of the purest gold.

A belt of straw and ivy buds,
With coral clasps and amber studs,
And if these pleasures may thee move,
Come live with me, and be my love.   20

The shepherd swains shall dance and sing
For thy delight each May morning.
If these delights thy mind may move,
Then live with me and be my love.

[1599]

WILLIAM SHAKESPEARE   [1564–1616]

Sonnet 18

Shall I compare thee to a summer's day?
Thou art more lovely and more temperate:
Rough winds do shake the darling buds of May,
And summer's lease° hath all too short a date;°   *allotted time/duration*
Sometimes too hot the eye of heaven shines,   5
And often is his gold complexion dimmed;
And every fair° from fair° sometimes declines,   *beautiful thing/beauty*
By chance or nature's changing course untrimmed;°   *stripped of its beauty*
But thy eternal summer shall not fade,
Nor lose possession of that fair thou ow'st;°   *beauty you own*   10
Nor shall death brag thou wand'rest in his shade,
When in eternal lines° to time thou grow'st:°
   So long as men can breathe, or eyes can see,
   So long lives this,° and this gives life to thee.   *this sonnet*

[1609]

12. **lines:** (Of poetry); **grow'st:** You are grafted to time.

WILLIAM SHAKESPEARE   [1564–1616]

Sonnet 73

That time of year thou mayst in me behold
When yellow leaves, or none, or few, do hang
Upon those boughs which shake against the cold,
Bare ruined choirs,° where late° the sweet birds sang.   *choir stalls/lately*
In me thou seest the twilight of such day   5

As after sunset fadeth in the west,
Which by and by black night doth take away,
Death's second self, that seals up all in rest.
In me thou seest the glowing of such fire
That on the ashes of his youth doth lie,   10
As the deathbed whereon it must expire,
Consumed with that which it was nourished by.
   This thou perceiv'st, which makes thy love more strong,
   To love that well which thou must leave ere long.

[1609]

WILLIAM SHAKESPEARE   [1564–1616]
Sonnet 116

Let me not to the marriage of true minds
Admit impediments. Love is not love
Which alters when it alteration finds,
Or bends with the remover to remove.
O, no, it is an ever-fixèd mark   5
That looks on tempests and is never shaken;
It is the star to every wandering bark,
Whose worth's unknown, although his height be taken.°   *is measured*
Love's not time's fool, though rosy lips and cheeks
Within his bending sickle's compass come;   10
Love alters not with his brief hours and weeks,
But bears it out even to the edge of doom.°   *Judgment Day*
   If this be error and upon me proved,
   I never writ, nor no man ever loved.

[1609]

WILLIAM SHAKESPEARE   [1564–1616]
Sonnet 130

My mistress' eyes are nothing like the sun;
Coral is far more red than her lips' red;
If snow be white, why then her breasts are dun;°   *dull grayish brown*
If hairs be wires, black wires grow on her head.
I have seen roses damasked,° red and white,   *variegated*   5

But no such roses see I in her cheeks;
And in some perfumes is there more delight
Than in the breath that from my mistress reeks.
I love to hear her speak, yet well I know
That music hath a far more pleasing sound.   10
I grant I never saw a goddess go;°   *walk*
My mistress, when she walks, treads on the ground.
   And yet, by heaven, I think my love as rare
   As any she° belied° with false compare.   *woman/misrepresented*

[1609]

JOHN DONNE   [1572–1631]

A Valediction: Forbidding Mourning

As virtuous men pass mildly away,
   And whisper to their souls to go,
Whilst some of their sad friends do say
   The breath goes now, and some say, No;

So let us melt, and make no noise,   5
   No tear-floods, nor sigh-tempests move;
'Twere profanation of our joys
   To tell the laity our love.

Moving of th' earth brings harms and fears,
   Men reckon what it did and meant;   10
But trepidation of the spheres,
   Though greater far, is innocent.°

Dull sublunary° lovers' love   *under the moon; hence, inconstant*
   (Whose soul is sense) cannot admit
Absence, because it doth remove   15
   Those things which elemented° it.   *composed*

But we, by a love so much refined
   That our selves know not what it is,
Inter-assurèd of the mind,
   Care less, eyes, lips, and hands to miss.   20

9–12. Moving . . . innocent: Earthquakes cause damage and were taken as portending further changes or dangers. Trepidation (an oscillating motion of the eighth or ninth sphere, in the Ptolemaic cosmological system) is greater than an earthquake, but not harmful or ominous.

Our two souls therefore, which are one,
  Though I must go, endure not yet
A breach, but an expansion,
  Like gold to airy thinness beat.

If they be two, they are two so   25
  As stiff twin compasses° are two;   *drawing compasses*
Thy soul, the fixed foot, makes no show
  To move, but doth, if th' other do.

And though it in the center sit,
  Yet when the other far doth roam,   30
It leans and hearkens after it,
  And grows erect, as that comes home.

Such wilt thou be to me, who must,
  Like th' other foot, obliquely run;
Thy firmness makes my circle just,   35
  And makes me end where I begun.

                                                        [1633]

JOHN DONNE   [1572–1631]

The Flea°

Mark but this flea, and mark in this,
How little that which thou deny'st me is;
Me it sucked first, and now sucks thee,
And in this flea, our two bloods mingled be;°
Confess it, this cannot be said°   *called*   5
A sin, or shame, or loss of maidenhead,°   *virginity*
  Yet this enjoys before it woo,°
  And pampered swells with one blood made of two,°
  And this, alas, is more than we would do.

Oh stay,° three lives in one flea spare,   10
Where we almost, nay more than married are.

The Flea: Fleas were used frequently in European erotic poems during the Renaissance, as a lover envies the liberties the insect takes with his lady.
4. two bloods mingled be: Renaissance medical theory held that blood was
mingled during intercourse, the "little" act the lady is denying the speaker (l. 2).
7. enjoys before it woo: Takes liberties without wooing the lady.
8. swells with one blood made of two: The flea's swelling suggests pregnancy.
10. stay: Stop; refrain from killing the flea. "Die" and "kill" were Renaissance slang
terms for orgasm (the sexual act was believed to reduce the length of a man's life).

This flea is you and I, and this
Our marriage bed, and marriage temple is;
Though parents grudge, and you, we are met,
And cloistered in these living walls of jet.°   15
   Though use° make you apt to kill me,   *habit*
   Let not to this, self murder added be,
   And sacrilege, three sins in killing three.°

Cruel and sudden, hast thou since
Purpled thy nail, in blood of innocence?   20
In what could this flea guilty be,
Except in that drop which it sucked from thee?
Yet thou triumph'st, and say'st that thou
Find'st not thyself, nor me the weaker now;
   'Tis true, then learn how false, fears be;   25
   Just so much honour, when thou yield'st to me,
   Will waste, as this flea's death took life from thee.

[1633]

15. jet: Black marble (describing the flea's body).
18. three sins: Murder (by denying him sexual gratification—l. 16), suicide, and
sacrilege (destroying a "marriage temple").

JOHN DONNE   [1572–1631]

Death, be not proud

Death, be not proud, though some have callèd thee
Mighty and dreadful, for thou art not so;
For those whom thou think'st thou dost overthrow
Die not, poor Death, nor yet canst thou kill me.
From rest and sleep, which but thy pictures be,   5
Much pleasure; then from thee much more must flow,
And soonest our best men with thee do go,
Rest of their bones, and soul's delivery.
Thou art slave to fate, chance, kings, and desperate men,
And dost with poison, war, and sickness dwell,   10
And poppy° or charms can make us sleep as well   *opium*

And better than thy stroke; why swell'st° thou then?   *(with pride)*
One short sleep past, we wake eternally
And death shall be no more; Death, thou shalt die.

[1633]

BEN JONSON   [1572–1637]

On My First Son

Farewell, thou child of my right hand,° and joy;
My sin was too much hope of thee, loved boy:
Seven years thou'wert lent to me, and I thee pay,
Exacted by thy fate, on the just day.
O could I lose all father now! for why   5
Will man lament the state he should envy,
To have so soon 'scaped world's and flesh's rage,
And, if no other misery, yet age?
Rest in soft peace, and asked, say, "Here doth lie
Ben Jonson his best piece of poetry."   10
For whose sake henceforth all his° vows be such   *(the father's)*
As what he loves may never like° too much.

[1616]

1. **child . . . hand:** A literal translation of the Hebrew name "Benjamin." The
boy, named for his father, was born in 1596 and died on his birthday ("the [exact]
day" — that on which the loan came due) in 1603.
12. **like:** Archaic meaning "please."

LADY MARY WROTH   [c. 1587–c. 1651]

My pain, still smothered in my grievèd breast

My pain, still smothered in my grievèd breast,
    Seeks for some ease, yet cannot passage find
    To be discharged of this unwelcome guest:
    When most I strive, most fast his burdens bind,

Like to a ship on Goodwin's° cast by wind,   5
   The more she strives, more deep in sand is pressed,
   Till she be lost; so am I, in this kind,°   *manner*
   Sunk, and devoured, and swallowed by unrest,
Lost, shipwrecked, spoiled, debarred of smallest hope,
   Nothing of pleasure left; save thoughts have scope,   10
   Which wander may. Go then, my thoughts, and cry
"Hope's perished, love tempest-beaten, joy lost:
   Killing despair hath all these blessings crossed."
   Yet faith still cries, "love will not falsify."

[1621]

5. **Goodwin's:** Goodwin Sands, a ten-mile-long sandbar off the east coast of
England, on which many ships have been wrecked.

ROBERT HERRICK   [1591–1674]

To the Virgins, to Make Much of Time

Gather ye rosebuds while ye may,
   Old time is still a-flying;
And this same flower that smiles today
   Tomorrow will be dying.

The glorious lamp of heaven, the sun,   5
   The higher he's a-getting,
The sooner will his race be run,
   And nearer he's to setting.

That age is best which is the first,
   When youth and blood are warmer;   10
But being spent, the worse, and worst
   Times still succeed the former.

Then be not coy, but use your time,
   And while ye may, go marry;
For having lost but once your prime,   15
   You may forever tarry.

[1648]

GEORGE HERBERT   [1593–1633]

Easter-wings°

Lord, who createdst man in wealth and store,°
Though foolishly he lost the same,°
Decaying more and more
Till he became
Most poor: 5
    With thee
    O let me rise
    As larks, harmoniously,
    And sing this day thy victories:
Then shall the fall further the flight in me.   10

My tender age in sorrow did begin:
And still with sicknesses and shame
Thou didst so punish sin,
That I became
Most thin.   15
    With thee
    Let me combine,
    And feel thy victory;
For, if I imp° my wing on thine,
Affliction shall advance the flight in me.   20

[1633]

Easter-wings: Originally the stanzas were printed on facing pages, lines 1–10 on the left page, to be read first, then lines 11–20 on the right page.
1. store: Abundance.
2. lost the same: Through the Fall in the Garden of Eden. Early editions include the words "this day" in line 18 (perhaps repeated by mistake from line 9); they do not appear in the only surviving manuscript and are not required for the meter.
19. imp: A term from falconry — to graft additional feathers onto the wings of a hawk to improve its flight.

GEORGE HERBERT   [1593–1633]

The Pulley

When God at first made man,
Having a glass of blessings standing by,
"Let us," said he, "pour on him all we can.
Let the world's riches, which dispersèd lie,
    Contract into a span."   5

So strength first made a way;
Then beauty flowed, then wisdom, honor, pleasure.
When almost all was out, God made a stay,
Perceiving that, alone of all his treasure,
   Rest in the bottom lay.   10

"For if I should," said he,
"Bestow this jewel also on my creature,
He would adore my gifts instead of me,
And rest in Nature, not the God of Nature;
   So both should losers be.   15

"Yet let him keep the rest,
But keep them with repining restlessness.
Let him be rich and weary, that at least,
If goodness lead him not, yet weariness
   May toss him to my breast."   20

[1633]

JOHN MILTON   [1608–1674]

When I consider how my light is spent

When I consider how my light is spent°
   Ere half my days, in this dark world and wide,
   And that one talent which is death to hide
   Lodged with me useless, though my soul more bent
To serve therewith my Maker, and present   5
   My true account, lest he returning chide.
   "Doth God exact day-labor, light denied?"
   I fondly ask; but patience to prevent
That murmur, soon replies, "God doth not need
   Either man's work or his own gifts; who best   10
   Bear his mild yoke, they serve him best. His state
Is kingly. Thousands at his bidding speed
   And post o'er land and ocean without rest:
   They also serve who only stand and wait."

[c. 1652; 1673]

---

1. When . . . spent: Milton went blind in 1652. Lines 1–2 allude to Matthew
25:1–13; line 3, to Matthew 25:14–30; and line 11, to Matthew 11:30.

JOHN MILTON   [1608–1674]

Lycidas

In this monody° the author bewails a learned friend, unfortunately drowned in his passage from Chester on the Irish Seas, 1637. And by occasion foretells the ruin of our corrupted clergy, then in their height.

Yet once more, O ye laurels,° and once more,	
Ye myrtles brown,° with ivy never sere,	*dark*
I come to pluck your berries harsh and crude,°	*unripe*
And with forced fingers rude	
Shatter your leaves before the mellowing year.	5
Bitter constraint, and sad occasion dear,	
Compels me to disturb your season due:	
For Lycidas is dead, dead ere his prime,	
Young Lycidas, and hath not left his peer.	
Who would not sing for Lycidas? He knew	10
Himself to sing, and build the lofty rhyme.	
He must not float upon his watery bier	
Unwept, and welter° to the parching wind,	*roll about*
Without the meed° of some melodious tear.	*reward*
Begin then, sisters of the sacred well°	15
That from beneath the seat of Jove doth spring,	
Begin, and somewhat loudly sweep the string.	
Hence with denial vain, and coy° excuse,	*reticent*
So may some gentle Muse	
With lucky words favor my destined urn,	20
And as he passes turn,	
And bid fair peace be to my sable° shroud.	*black*
For we were nursed upon the self-same hill,	
Fed the same flock, by fountain, shade, and rill.	
Together both, ere the high lawns° appeared	*pastures* 25
Under the opening eyelids of the morn,	

monody: A monody is an elegy or dirge sung by a single voice. The poem draws on the traditions of the pastoral elegy. It appeared in a collection of poems published as a tribute to Edward King, Milton's "learned friend" and fellow student at Cambridge.
1. ye laurels: Laurel, sacred to Apollo, was the emblem of poetic achievement. Myrtle is the crown of Venus and ivy of Bacchus. All three are evergreen, thus "never sere" (dry, withered).
15. sisters . . . well: The muses; the well sacred to them was Aganippe near Mount Helicon.

We drove afield, and both together heard
What time the grey-fly winds° her sultry horn,   *blows*
Battening° our flocks with the fresh dews of night,   *fattening*
Oft till the star that rose, at evening, bright   30
Toward heaven's descent had sloped his westering wheel.
Meanwhile the rural ditties were not mute,
Tempered to the oaten flute;°
Rough satyrs danced, and fauns with cloven heel
From the glad sound would not be absent long,   35
And old Damaetas° loved to hear our song.
   But O the heavy change, now thou art gone,
Now thou art gone, and never must return!
Thee, shepherd, thee the woods and desert caves,
With wild thyme and the gadding° vine o'ergrown,   *wandering* 40
And all their echoes mourn.
The willows and the hazel copses° green   *thickets*
Shall now no more be seen
Fanning their joyous leaves to thy soft lays.
As killing as the canker° to the rose,   *cankerworm* 45
Or taint-worm to the weanling herds that graze,
Or frost to flowers, that their gay wardrobe wear,
When first the white-thorn blows;°   *hawthorn blossoms*
Such, Lycidas, thy loss to shepherd's ear.
   Where were ye, nymphs, when the remorseless deep   50
Closed o'er the head of your loved Lycidas?
For neither were ye playing on the steep
Where your old bards, the famous Druids, lie,
Nor on the shaggy top of Mona high,
Nor yet where Deva spreads her wizard stream.°   55
Ay me, I fondly° dream,   *foolishly*
Had ye been there! — for what could that have done?
What could the Muse herself that Orpheus bore,
The Muse herself,° for her enchanting son
Whom universal nature did lament,   60

---

33. oaten flute: Instrument symbolic of pastoral poetry.
36. Damaetas: A pastoral name, referring probably to a Cambridge tutor.
55. Deva . . . stream: The River Dee in Cheshire, "wizard" because it was said to be able to change the size and position of its channel. "Mona" is the island of Anglesey, in northwest Wales. Both are in the west country near where King died.
59. The Muse herself: Calliope. Her son Orpheus was torn apart by a mob ("rout") of screaming Thracian women (Bacchantes). His bloody head floated down the river Hebrus, across the Aegean to the island of Lesbos.

When by the rout that made the hideous roar
His gory visage down the stream was sent,
Down the swift Hebrus to the Lesbian shore?
    Alas! what boots° it with uncessant care   *profits*
To tend the homely slighted shepherd's trade,   65
And strictly meditate the thankless Muse?
Were it not better done as others use,
To sport with Amaryllis in the shade,
Or with the tangles of Neaera's hair?°
Fame is the spur that the clear spirit doth raise   70
(That last infirmity of noble mind)
To scorn delights, and live laborious days;
But the fair guerdon° when we hope to find,   *reward*
And think to burst out into sudden blaze,
Comes the blind Fury with the abhorrèd shears,°   75
And slits the thin-spun life. "But not the praise,"
Phoebus replied, and touched my trembling ears:
"Fame is no plant that grows on mortal soil,
Nor in the glistering foil°
Set off to the world, nor in broad rumor lies,   80
But lives and spreads aloft by those pure eyes
And perfect witness of all-judging Jove;
As he pronounces lastly on each deed,
Of so much fame in heaven expect thy meed.'
    O fountain Arethuse,° and thou honored flood,   85
Smooth-sliding Mincius,° crowned with vocal reeds,
That strain I heard was of a higher mood.
But now my oat proceeds,
And listens to the herald of the sea°
That came in Neptune's plea.   90
He asked the waves, and asked the felon winds,

68–69. Amaryllis, Neaera: Conventional names for shepherdesses.
75. Fury: Atropos, one of the three Fates in Greek mythology, used her scissors to cut the thread of human life, after it had been spun and measured by her sisters. For the Greeks and Romans the Furies had a different role, but even in classical literature "Fury" and "Fate" were often used interchangeably.
79. glistering foil: Gold or silver leaf set under jewels to increase their brilliance.
85. Arethuse: A fountain in Sicily associated with the pastoral poetry of Theocritus.
86. Mincius: A river in Lombardy associated with the *Eclogues* of Virgil.
89. herald of the sea: The merman Triton, who pleads Neptune's innocence in Lycidas's death.

What hard mishap hath doomed this gentle swain?
And questioned every gust of rugged wings
That blows from off each beakèd promontory —
They knew not of his story,   95
And sage Hippotades° their answer brings,
That not a blast was from his dungeon strayed;
The air was calm, and on the level brine
Sleek Panope° with her all sisters played.
It was that fatal and perfidious bark,   100
Built in the eclipse, and rigged with curses dark,
That sunk so low that sacred head of thine.
   Next Camus,° reverend sire, went footing slow,
His mantle hairy, and his bonnet sedge,°   *plants growing near water*
Inwrought with figures dim, and on the edge   105
Like to that sanguine flower° inscribed with woe.
"Ah, who hath reft," quoth he, "my dearest pledge?"°   *child (hopefulness)*
Last came, and last did go,
The Pilot° of the Galilean lake;
Two massy keys he bore of metals twain   110
(The golden opes, the iron shuts amain).°   *with force*
He shook his mitred locks, and stern bespake:
"How well could I have spared for thee, young swain,
Enow° of such as for their bellies' sake   *enough*
Creep and intrude and climb into the fold!°   115
Of other care they little reckoning make
Than how to scramble at the shearers' feast,
And shove away the worthy bidden guest.
Blind mouths!° that scarce themselves know how to hold
A sheep-hook, or have learned aught else the least   120

---

96. Hippotades: Aeolus, the wind god, son of Hippotas.
99. Panope: The greatest of the Nereids (sea nymphs).
103. Camus: God of the river Cam, representing the ancient University of Cambridge.
106. sanguine flower: The blood-colored hyacinth; marks on its leaves supposedly are the Greek letters AIAI, expressing woe.
109. The Pilot: Saint Peter, Galilean fisherman, first bishop of the church (thus his "mitred" locks — entitled to wear a bishop's mitre); to him Christ promised "the keys of the kingdom" (Matthew 16:19) to open and close the gates of heaven.
115. Creep . . . fold: Alluding to John 10:1 — "Anyone who does not enter the sheepfold by the gate but climbs in by another way is a thief and a bandit."
119. Blind mouths!: A reference to the greed of the bishops: a bishop *(episcopus)* is one who oversees, and a pastor is one who feeds his flock.

That to the faithful herdman's art belongs!
What recks° it them? What need they? They are sped;°
And when they list,° their lean and flashy songs   *want*
Grate on their scrannel° pipes of wretched straw   *thin, feeble*
The hungry sheep look up, and are not fed,   125
But swoln with wind, and the rank mist they draw,
Rot inwardly, and foul contagion spread,
Besides what the grim wolf° with privy paw
Daily devours apace, and nothing said;
But that two-handed engine° at the door   130
Stands ready to smite once, and smite no more."
    Return, Alpheus,° the dread voice is past
That shrunk thy streams; return, Sicilian Muse,
And call the vales, and bid them hither cast
Their bells and flowerets of a thousand hues.   135
Ye valleys low where the mild whispers use°   *frequent (verb)*
Of shades and wanton winds and gushing brooks,
On whose fresh lap the swart star° sparely looks,   *Sirius*
Throw hither all your quaint enamelled eyes,
That on the green turf suck the honied showers,   140
And purple all the ground with vernal flowers.
Bring the rathe° primrose that forsaken dies,   *early*
The tufted crowtoe, and pale jessamine,
The white pink, and the pansy freaked° with jet,   *flecked*
The glowing violet,   145
The musk-rose, and the well-attired woodbine,
With cowslips wan that hang the pensive head,
And every flower that sad embroidery wears.
Bid amaranthus all his beauty shed,
And daffadillies fill their cups with tears,   150
To strew the laureate hearse where Lycid lies.
For so to interpose a little ease,
Let our frail thoughts dally with false surmise;
Ay me! whilst thee the shores and sounding seas
Wash far away, where'er thy bones are hurled,   155

---

122. recks: Matters to them; **are sped:** Have more than enough.
128. grim wolf: The Roman Catholic Church, secretly ("privy") opposing Protestantism.
130. two-handed engine: An apocalyptic instrument of revenge against clergy who neglect their responsibilities.
132. Alpheus: The reference to this river god who fell in love with the nymph Arethusa brings the poem back to the pastoral mode.

Whether beyond the stormy Hebrides,
Where thou perhaps under the whelming° tide   *engulfing*
Visit'st the bottom of the monstrous world;
Or whether thou, to our moist vows° denied,   *tearful prayers*
Sleep'st by the fable of Bellerus° old,   160
Where the great vision of the guarded mount°
Looks toward Namancos and Bayona's hold:°
Look homeward, Angel,° now, and melt with ruth;°
And, O ye dolphins,° waft the hapless youth.
     Weep no more, woeful shepherds, weep no more,   165
For Lycidas your sorrow is not dead,
Sunk though he be beneath the watery floor;
So sinks the day-star° in the ocean bed,   *the sun*
And yet anon repairs° his drooping head,   *returns (raises)*
And tricks° his beams, and with new-spangled ore   *plays tricks with* 170
Flames in the forehead of the morning sky:
So Lycidas sunk low, but mounted high,
Through the dear might of him that walked the waves,°   *(Christ)*
Where, other groves and other streams along,
With nectar pure his oozy locks he laves,°   *bathes*   175
And hears the unexpressive° nuptial song   *inexpressible*
In the blest kingdoms meek of joy and love.
There entertain him all the saints above,
In solemn troops and sweet societies
That sing, and singing in their glory move,   180
And wipe the tears for ever from his eyes.
Now, Lycidas, the shepherds weep no more;
Henceforth thou art the Genius of the Shore,
In thy large recompense, and shalt be good
To all that wander in that perilous flood.   185
     Thus sang the uncouth° swain to the oaks and rills,   *uneducated*
While the still morn went out with sandals grey;
He touched the tender stops of various quills,

160. Bellerus: A fabulous giant for whom Land's End (the southwestern tip of Cornwall) was called Bellerium in Roman times.
161. the guarded mount: Saint Michael's Mount, in Cornwall.
162. Namancos and Bayona: A mountain range and a fortress on the coast of northern Spain.
163. Angel: The archangel Michael, patron of mariners, imagined as standing on Saint Michael's Mount, looking southward; **ruth:** Pity.
164. ye dolphins: Dolphins brought the Greek poet Arion safely to shore and carried Melicertes to land, where he was transformed to a sea god, Palaemon.

With eager thought warbling his Doric lay.°   *pastoral song*
And now the sun had stretched out all the hills,   190
And now was dropped into the western bay;
At last he rose, and twitched his mantle blue:
Tomorrow to fresh woods, and pastures new.

[1638]

ANNE BRADSTREET   [c. 1612–1672]

To My Dear and Loving Husband

If ever two were one, then surely we.
If ever man were loved by wife, then thee;
If ever wife was happy in a man,
Compare with me ye women if you can.
I prize thy love more than whole mines of gold,   5
Or all the riches that the East doth hold.
My love is such that rivers cannot quench,
Nor ought but love from thee give recompense.
Thy love is such I can no way repay;
The heavens reward thee manifold, I pray.   10
Then while we live, in love let's so persever,
That when we live no more we may live ever.

[1678]

RICHARD LOVELACE   [1618–1657]

To Lucasta, Going to the Wars

Tell me not, Sweet, I am unkind,
    That from the nunnery
Of thy chaste breast and quiet mind
    To war and arms I fly.

True, a new mistress now I chase,   5
    The first foe in the field;
And with a stronger faith embrace
    A sword, a horse, a shield.

Yet this inconstancy is such
  As you too shall adore;   10
I could not love thee, dear, so much,
  Loved I not honor more.

[1649]

ANDREW MARVELL   [1621–1678]

To His Coy Mistress°

  Had we but world enough, and time,
This coyness, lady, were no crime.
We would sit down, and think which way
To walk, and pass our long love's day.
Thou by the Indian Ganges' side   5
Shouldst rubies find; I by the tide
Of Humber would complain.° I would
Love you ten years before the Flood,
And you should, if you please, refuse
Till the conversion of the Jews.°   10
My vegetable° love should grow   *living and growing*
Vaster than empires, and more slow;
An hundred years should go to praise
Thine eyes, and on thy forehead gaze;
Two hundred to adore each breast,   15
But thirty thousand to the rest;
An age at least to every part,
And the last age should show your heart.
For, lady, you deserve this state,°   *dignity*
Nor would I love at lower rate.   20
  But at my back I always hear
Time's wingèd chariot hurrying near;
And yonder all before us lie

Coy: In the seventeenth century, "coy" could carry its older meaning, "shy," or the modern sense of "coquettish." "Mistress" then could still mean "a woman loved and courted by a man; a female sweetheart."
5–7. Indian Ganges', Humber: The Ganges River in India, with its distant, romantic associations, contrasts with the Humber River, running through Hull in northeast England, Marvell's home town.
10. conversion . . . Jews: An occurrence foretold, in some traditions, as one of the concluding events of human history.

Deserts of vast eternity.
Thy beauty shall no more be found,   25
Nor, in thy marble vault, shall sound
My echoing song; then worms shall try
That long-preserved virginity,
And your quaint honor turn to dust,
And into ashes all my lust: 30
The grave's a fine and private place,
But none, I think, do there embrace.
    Now therefore, while the youthful hue
Sits on thy skin like morning dew,
And while thy willing soul transpires°   *breathes forth*   35
At every pore with instant fires,°   *urgent passion*
Now let us sport us while we may,
And now, like amorous birds of prey,
Rather at once our time devour
Than languish in his slow-chapped° power.   40
Let us roll all our strength and all
Our sweetness up into one ball,
And tear our pleasures with rough strife
Thorough° the iron gates of life;   *through*
Thus, though we cannot make our sun   45
Stand still,° yet we will make him run.

                                                    [*c. 1650;* 1681]

40. slow-chapped: Slow-jawed, devouring slowly.
45–46. make our sun stand still: An allusion to Joshua 10:12. In answer to
Joshua's prayer, God made the sun stand still, to prolong the day and give the
Israelites more time to defeat the Amorites.

EDWARD TAYLOR   [c. 1642–1729]

Housewifery

Make me, O Lord, thy spinning wheel complete.°
    Thy holy word my distaff make for me.
Make mine affections thy swift flyers neat,

1. spinning wheel complete: In a spinning wheel, the distaff holds the raw wool
or flax to be spun; the flyers twist and guide the thread; the thread is wound onto
the spool as it is spun; and the reel receives the finished thread.

And make my soul thy holy spool to be.
My conversation make to be thy reel,   5
And reel the yarn thereon spun on thy wheel.

Make me thy loom then, knit therein this twine;
   And make thy holy spirit, Lord, wind quills.°
Then weave the web thyself. The yarn is fine.
   Thine ordinances make my fulling mills.   10
   Then dye the same in heavenly colors choice,
   All pinked° with varnished° flowers of paradise.   *ornamented / lustrous*

Then clothe therewith mine understanding, will,
   Affections, judgment, conscience, memory,
My words, and actions, that their shine may fill   15
   My ways with glory and thee glorify.
   Then mine apparel shall display before ye
   That I am clothed in holy robes for glory.

[*1682–1683;* 1939]

8. quills: The spools of a loom.

JONATHAN SWIFT   [1667–1745]

A Description of the Morning

Now hardly here and there a hackney-coach
Appearing, showed the ruddy morn's approach.
Now Betty from her master's bed had flown,
And softly stole to discompose her own;
The slip-shod 'prentice from his master's door   5
Had pared the dirt and sprinkled round the floor.
Now Moll had whirled her mop with dext'rous airs,
Prepared to scrub the entry and the stairs.
The youth with broomy stumps° began to trace   *worn broom*
The kennel-edge,° where wheels had worn the place.   *gutter*   10
The small-coal man° was heard with cadence deep,   *coal vendor*
Till drowned in shriller notes of chimney-sweep:
Duns° at his lordship's gate began to meet;   *debt collectors*
And brickdust Moll° had screamed through half the street.

14. brickdust Moll: Woman selling powdered brick.

The turnkey° now his flock° returning sees,   *jailer/(inmates)*   15
Duly let out a-nights to steal for fees:°
The watchful bailiffs take their silent stands,
And schoolboys lag with satchels in their hands.

[1709]

16. fees: Payments for food and better treatment.

ALEXANDER POPE   [1688–1744]

From An Essay on Criticism, *Part 2*°

But most by numbers° judge a poet's song,   *versification*
And smooth or rough, with them, is right or wrong.
In the bright Muse though thousand charms conspire,
Her voice is all these tuneful fools admire,   340
Who haunt Parnassus but to please their ear,
Not mend their minds; as some to church repair,
Not for the doctrine, but the music there.
These equal syllables alone require,°
Though oft the ear the open vowels tire,   345
While expletives° their feeble aid do join,
And ten low words oft creep in one dull line:
While they ring round the same unvaried chimes,
With sure returns of still expected rhymes;
Where'er you find "the cooling western breeze,"   350
In the next line, it "whispers through the trees";
If crystal streams "with pleasing murmurs creep,"
The reader's threatened (not in vain) with "sleep";
Then, at the last and only couplet fraught

An Essay on Criticism: An Essay on Criticism is a verse epistle addressed to literary critics. In it Pope satirizes the pedantic judgments of inferior literary critics
(as he does in lines 337–61, on critics who care only about the way a poem sounds
and thus praise poets who produce rhyme and meter mechanically); he points out
the characteristics of excellent poetry (ll. 362–83); and he offers advice to critics
on how to critique literature sensibly and helpfully (ll. 384–93).
344–57. These . . . along: In alternating lines Pope describes, then illustrates
satirically, the kinds of metrics or diction these critics advocate ("these . . . require"). **equal syllables:** Mechanically regular accents.
346. expletives: Unnecessary words added to give a line the number of syllables
its meter requires, like *do* in this line.

With some unmeaning thing they call a thought,   355
A needless Alexandrine° ends the song,
That, like a wounded snake, drags its slow length along.
Leave such to tune their own dull rhymes, and know
What's roundly smooth or languishingly slow;
And praise the easy vigor of a line   360
Where Denham's strength and Waller's sweetness join.°
True ease in writing comes from art, not chance,
As those move easiest who have learned to dance.
'Tis not enough no harshness gives offense,
The sound must seem an echo to the sense.°   365
Soft is the strain when Zephyr° gently blows,   *the West Wind*
And the smooth stream in smoother numbers flows;
But when loud surges lash the sounding shore,
The hoarse, rough verse should like the torrent roar.
When Ajax° strives some rock's vast weight to throw,   370
The line too labors, and the words move slow;
Not so, when swift Camilla° scours the plain,
Flies o'er the unbending corn, and skims along the main.
Hear how Timotheus'° varied lays surprise,
And bid alternate passions fall and rise!   375
While at each change the son of Libyan Jove°
Now burns with glory, and then melts with love;
Now his fierce eyes with sparkling fury glow,
Now sighs steal out, and tears begin to flow:
Persians and Greeks like turns of nature° found   380
And the world's victor stood subdued by sound!

356. Alexandrine: A metrical line with six iambic feet, illustrated in the following line.
361. Denham's . . . join: Combine the qualities attributed to two important
shapers of the late-seventeenth-century heroic couplet: the "strength" (concise-
ness and emphasis on content) of Sir John Denham (1615–1669) and the "sweetness" (smoothness and musical qualities) of Edmund Waller (1606–1687).
365. sound . . . sense: Lines 366–83 provide examples of the precept that sound
should echo sense in poetry.
370. Ajax: The rough hero in Homer's *Iliad* 12.378–86.
372. Camilla: The female warrior in Virgil's *Aeneid* (see especially 7.808ff).
374. Timotheus': A Theban musician in the court of Alexander the Great, whose
music had powerful emotional effects. Lines 374–83 sum up the story told in John
Dryden's ode "Alexander's Feast" (1697).
376. Libyan Jove: Alexander the Great.
380. like turns of nature: Similar alternations of feelings.

The power of music all our hearts allow,
And what Timotheus was, is Dryden° now.
    Avoid extremes; and shun the fault of such
Who still° are pleased too little or too much.   *always* 385
At every trifle scorn to take offense:
That always shows great pride, or little sense.
Those heads, as stomachs, are not sure the best,
Which nauseate all, and nothing can digest.
Yet let not each gay turn° thy rapture move;   390
For fools admire,° but men of sense approve:°
As things seem large which we through mists descry,
Dullness is ever apt to magnify.

[1711]

383. **Dryden:** John Dryden (1631–1700) was the dominant poet in England from 1660 until his death.
390. **gay turn:** Apt and pleasing turn of phrase.
391. **admire:** Marvel; **approve:** Commend thoughtfully as good.

THOMAS GRAY   [1716–1771]

Elegy Written in a Country Churchyard

The curfew° tolls the knell of parting day,   *evening bell*
    The lowing herd wind slowly o'er the lea,
The plowman homeward plods his weary way,
    And leaves the world to darkness and to me.

Now fades the glimmering landscape on the sight,   5
    And all the air a solemn stillness holds,
Save where the beetle wheels his droning flight,
    And drowsy tinklings lull the distant folds;

Save that from yonder ivy-mantled tower
    The moping owl does to the moon complain   10
Of such, as wandering near her secret bower,
    Molest her ancient solitary reign.

Beneath those rugged elms, that yew tree's shade,
    Where heaves the turf in many a moldering heap,
Each in his narrow cell forever laid,   15
    The rude forefathers° of the hamlet sleep.   *humble ancestors*

The breezy call of incense-breathing morn,
   The swallow twittering from the straw-built shed,
The cock's shrill clarion, or the echoing horn,°   *(of a hunter)*
   No more shall rouse them from their lowly bed.   20

For them no more the blazing hearth shall burn,
   Or busy housewife ply her evening care;
No children run to lisp their sire's return,
   Or climb his knees the envied kiss to share.

Oft did the harvest to their sickle yield,   25
   Their furrow oft the stubborn glebe° has broke;   *soil*
How jocund did they drive their team afield!
   How bowed the woods beneath their sturdy stroke!

Let not Ambition mock their useful toil,
   Their homely joys, and destiny obscure;   30
Nor Grandeur hear with a disdainful smile
   The short and simple annals of the poor.

The boast of heraldry,° the pomp of power,   *noble ancestry*
   And all that beauty, all that wealth e'er gave,
Awaits alike the inevitable hour.   35
   The paths of glory lead but to the grave.

Nor you, ye proud, impute to these the fault,
   If memory o'er their tomb no trophies° raise,   *memorials*
Where through the long-drawn aisle and fretted° vault   *ornamented*
   The pealing anthem swells the note of praise.   40

Can storied° urn or animated° bust   *decorated/lifelike*
   Back to its mansion call the fleeting breath?
Can Honor's voice provoke° the silent dust,   *call forth*
   Or Flattery soothe the dull cold ear of Death?

Perhaps in this neglected spot is laid   45
   Some heart once pregnant with celestial fire;
Hands that the rod of empire might have swayed,
   Or waked to ecstasy the living lyre.

But Knowledge to their eyes her ample page
   Rich with the spoils of time did ne'er unroll;   50
Chill Penury repressed their noble rage,
   And froze the genial current of the soul.

Full many a gem of purest ray serene,
   The dark unfathomed caves of ocean bear:
Full many a flower is born to blush unseen,   55
   And waste its sweetness on the desert air.

Some village Hampden,° that with dauntless breast
   The little tyrant of his fields withstood;
Some mute inglorious Milton here may rest,
   Some Cromwell guiltless of his country's blood.   60

The applause of listening senates to command,
   The threats of pain and ruin to despise,
To scatter plenty o'er a smiling land,
   And read their history in a nation's eyes,

Their lot forbade: nor° circumscribed alone   *not* 65
   Their growing virtues, but their crimes confined;
Forbade to wade through slaughter to a throne,
   And shut the gates of mercy on mankind,

The struggling pangs of conscious truth to hide,
   To quench the blushes of ingenuous shame,   70
Or heap the shrine of Luxury and Pride
   With incense kindled at the Muse's flame.

Far from the madding crowd's ignoble strife,
   Their sober wishes never learned to stray;
Along the cool sequestered vale of life   75
   They kept the noiseless tenor of their way.

Yet even these bones from insult to protect
   Some frail memorial° still erected nigh,   *(simple tombstone)*
With uncouth rhymes and shapeless sculpture decked,
   Implores the passing tribute of a sigh.   80

Their name, their years, spelt by the unlettered Muse,
   The place of fame and elegy supply:
And many a holy text around she strews,
   That teach the rustic moralist to die.

For who to dumb Forgetfulness a prey,   85
   This pleasing anxious being e'er resigned,
Left the warm precincts of the cheerful day,
   Nor cast one longing lingering look behind?

On some fond breast the parting soul relies,
   Some pious drops° the closing eye requires;   *tears* 90
Even from the tomb the voice of Nature cries,
   Even in our ashes live their wonted fires.

57–60. Hampden, Cromwell: John Hampden (1594–1643) refused to pay a special tax imposed in 1636 and led a defense of the people's rights in Parliament.
Oliver Cromwell (1599–1658) was a rebel leader in the English Civil War.

For thee,° who mindful of the unhonored dead   *(the poet himself)*
    Dost in these lines their artless tale relate;
If chance, by lonely contemplation led,   95
    Some kindred spirit shall inquire thy fate,

Haply° some hoary-headed swain° may say,   *perhaps/elderly shepherd*
    "Oft have we seen him° at the peep of dawn   *the poet*
Brushing with hasty steps the dews away
    To meet the sun upon the upland lawn.   100

"There at the foot of yonder nodding beech
    That wreathes its old fantastic roots so high,
His listless length at noontide would he stretch,
    And pore upon the brook that babbles by.

"Hard by yon wood, now smiling as in scorn,   105
    Muttering his wayward fancies he would rove,
Now drooping, woeful wan, like one forlorn,
    Or crazed with care, or crossed in hopeless love.

"One morn I missed him on the customed hill,
    Along the heath and near his favorite tree;   110
Another° came; nor yet beside the rill,   *(another day)*
    Nor up the lawn, nor at the wood was he;

"The next with dirges due in sad array
    Slow through the churchway path we saw him borne.
Approach and read (for thou canst read) the lay,   115
    Graved on the stone beneath yon aged thorn."

THE EPITAPH

Here rests his head upon the lap of Earth
    A youth to fortune and to Fame unknown.
Fair Science° frowned not on his humble birth,   *learning*
    And Melancholy marked him for her own.   120

Large was his bounty, and his soul sincere,
    Heaven did a recompense as largely send:
He gave to Misery all he had, a tear,
    He gained from Heaven ('twas all he wished) a friend.

No farther seek his merits to disclose,   125
    Or draw his frailties from their dread abode
(There they alike in trembling hope repose),
    The bosom of his Father and his God.

[1751]

CHRISTOPHER SMART   [1722–1771]

From Jubilate Agno°

For I will consider my Cat Jeoffry.
For he is the servant of the Living God, duly and daily serving him.
For at the first glance of the glory of God in the East he worships
  in his way.
For is this done by wreathing his body seven times round with elegant
  quickness.
For then he leaps up to catch the musk, which is the blessing of God
  upon his prayer.   5
For he rolls upon prank° to work it in.   *prankishly*
For having done duty and received blessing he begins to consider himself.
For this he performs in ten degrees.
For first he looks upon his forepaws to see if they are clean.
For secondly he kicks up behind to clear away there.   10
For thirdly he works it upon stretch with the forepaws extended.
For fourthly he sharpens his paws by wood.
For fifthly he washes himself.
For sixthly he rolls upon wash.
For seventhly he fleas himself, that he may not be interrupted
  upon the beat.°   15
For eighthly he rubs himself against a post.
For ninthly he looks up for his instructions.
For tenthly he goes in quest of food.
For having considered God and himself he will consider his neighbor.
For if he meets another cat he will kiss her in kindness.   20
For when he takes his prey he plays with it to give it a chance.
For one mouse in seven escapes by his dallying.
For when his day's work is done his business more properly begins.
For he keeps the Lord's watch in the night against the adversary.
For he counteracts the powers of darkness by his electrical skin and
  glaring eyes.   25
For he counteracts the Devil, who is death, by brisking about the life.
For in his morning orisons he loves the sun and the sun loves him.

Jubilate Agno: "Rejoice in the Lamb" (Latin); i.e., in Jesus, the Lamb of God. The poem was written while Smart was confined for madness from 1759 to 1763. It is influenced by the form of Hebrew poetry, particularly the biblical psalms. The best-known section is that concerning his cat Jeoffry, his companion during his confinement.
15. that . . . beat: Not need to stop to scratch while on his daily rounds of hunting.

For he is of the tribe of Tiger.

For the Cherub Cat is a term of the Angel Tiger.°

For he has the subtlety and hissing of a serpent, which in goodness
he suppresses.   30

For he will not do destruction if he is well-fed, neither will he spit
without provocation.

For he purrs in thankfulness when God tells him he's a good Cat.

For he is an instrument for the children to learn benevolence upon.

For every house is incomplete without him, and a blessing is lacking
in the spirit.

For the Lord commanded Moses concerning the cats at the departure
of the Children of Israel from Egypt.   35

For every family had one cat at least in the bag.°

For the English Cats are the best in Europe.

For he is the cleanest in the use of his forepaws of any quadruped.

For the dexterity of his defense is an instance of the love of God to him
exceedingly.

For he is the quickest to his mark of any creature.   40

For he is tenacious of his point.

For he is a mixture of gravity and waggery.

For he knows that God is his Savior.

For there is nothing sweeter than his peace when at rest.

For there is nothing brisker than his life when in motion.   45

For he is of the Lord's poor, and so indeed is he called by benevolence
perpetually — Poor Jeoffry! poor Jeoffry! the rat has bit thy throat.

For I bless the name of the Lord Jesus that Jeoffry is better.

For the divine spirit comes about his body to sustain it in complete cat.

For his tongue is exceeding pure so that it has in purity what
it wants° in music.   *lacks*

For he is docile and can learn certain things.   50

For he can sit up with gravity, which is patience upon approbation.

For he can fetch and carry, which is patience in employment.

For he can jump over a stick, which is patience upon proof positive.

For he can spraggle upon waggle° at the word of command.

For he can jump from an eminence into his master's bosom.   55

For he can catch the cork and toss it again.

29. Cherub . . . Tiger: As a cherub is a small angel, so a cat is like a small tiger.
36. cat . . . bag: No cats are mentioned in the biblical account of the Exodus, but
Smart may have been aware that images of cats were among the Egyptian gods
and may be speculating that cats were among the jewelry of silver and gold the
Egyptians gave the Israelites as they left (Exodus 12:35–36).
54. spraggle upon waggle: Sprawl when his master waggles a finger.

For he is hated by the hypocrite and miser.
For the former is afraid of detection.
For the latter refuses the charge.
For he camels his back to bear the first notion of business.   60
For he is good to think on, if a man would express himself neatly.
For he made a great figure in Egypt for his signal services.
For he killed the Ichneumon° rat, very pernicious by land.
For his ears are so acute that they sting again.
For from this proceeds the passing quickness of his attention.   65
For by stroking of him I have found out electricity.
For I perceived God's light about him both wax and fire.
For the electrical fire is the spiritual substance which God sends from
    heaven to sustain the bodies both of man and beast.
For God has blessed him in the variety of his movements.
For, though he cannot fly, he is an excellent clamberer.   70
For his motions upon the face of the earth are more than any other
    quadruped.
For he can tread to all the measures upon the music.
For he can swim for life.
For he can creep.

                                                      [*c. 1760;* 1939]

63. Ichneumon: Egyptian species of mongoose that somewhat resembles a large
rat. It is, however, regarded as beneficial and was domesticated by the ancient
Egyptians.

WILLIAM BLAKE   [1757–1827]

The Lamb

Little Lamb, who made thee?
  Dost thou know who made thee?
Gave thee life & bid thee feed,
By the stream & o'er the mead;
Gave thee clothing of delight,   5
Softest clothing wooly bright;
Gave thee such a tender voice,
Making all the vales rejoice!
  Little Lamb who made thee?
  Dost thou know who made thee?   10

Little Lamb I'll tell thee,
Little Lamb I'll tell thee!
He is callèd by thy name,
For he calls himself a Lamb:
He is meek & he is mild,   15
He became a little child:
I a child & thou a lamb,
We are callèd by his name.
   Little Lamb God bless thee.
   Little Lamb God bless thee.   20

[1789]

WILLIAM BLAKE   [1757–1827]

The Tyger

Tyger, Tyger, burning bright
In the forests of the night,
What immortal hand or eye
Could frame thy fearful symmetry?

In what distant deeps or skies   5
Burnt the fire of thine eyes?
On what wings dare he aspire?
What the hand, dare seize the fire?

And what shoulder, & what art,
Could twist the sinews of thy heart?   10
And when thy heart began to beat,
What dread hand? & what dread feet?

What the hammer? what the chain?
In what furnace was thy brain?
What the anvil? what dread grasp   15
Dare its deadly terrors clasp?

When the stars threw down their spears
And water'd heaven with their tears,
Did he smile his work to see?
Did he who made the Lamb make thee?   20

Tyger, Tyger, burning bright
In the forests of the night,
What immortal hand or eye
Dare frame thy fearful symmetry?

[1794]

WILLIAM BLAKE   [1757–1827]

London

I wander through each chartered street,
Near where the chartered Thames does flow,
And mark in every face I meet
Marks of weakness, marks of woe.

In every cry of every man,   5
In every infant's cry of fear,
In every voice, in every ban,
The mind-forged manacles I hear.

How the chimney-sweeper's cry
Every black'ning church appalls;   10
And the hapless soldier's sigh
Runs in blood down palace walls.

But most through midnight streets I hear
How the youthful harlot's curse
Blasts the new-born infant's tear,   15
And blights with plagues the marriage hearse.

[1794]

ROBERT BURNS   [1759–1796]

A Red, Red Rose

O my luve's like a red, red rose,
   That's newly sprung in June;
O my luve's like the melodie
   That's sweetly played in tune.

As fair art thou, my bonnie lass,   5
    So deep in luve am I;
And I will luve thee still, my dear,
    Till a' the seas gang dry.

Till a' the seas gang dry, my dear,
    And the rocks melt wi' the sun: 10
O I will love thee still, my dear,
    While the sands o' life shall run.

And fare thee weel, my only luve,
    And fare thee weel awhile!
And I will come again, my luve,   15
    Though it were ten thousand mile.

                          [1796]

WILLIAM WORDSWORTH   [1770–1850]

I wandered lonely as a cloud

I wandered lonely as a cloud
That floats on high o'er vales and hills,
When all at once I saw a crowd,
A host, of golden daffodils;
Beside the lake, beneath the trees,   5
Fluttering and dancing in the breeze.

Continuous as the stars that shine
And twinkle on the milky way,
They stretched in never-ending line
Along the margin of a bay: 10
Ten thousand saw I at a glance,
Tossing their heads in sprightly dance.

The waves beside them danced; but they
Outdid the sparkling waves in glee:
A poet could not but be gay,   15
In such a jocund company:
I gazed — and gazed — but little thought
What wealth the show to me had brought:

For oft, when on my couch I lie
In vacant or in pensive mood,   20

They flash upon that inward eye
Which is the bliss of solitude;
And then my heart with pleasure fills,
And dances with the daffodils.

[1807]

WILLIAM WORDSWORTH   [1770–1850]

Lines

Composed a Few Miles above Tintern Abbey°
on Revisiting the Banks of the Wye
During a Tour. July 13, 1798

Five years have passed; five summers, with the length
Of five long winters! and again I hear
These waters, rolling from their mountain-springs
With a soft inland murmur. Once again
Do I behold these steep and lofty cliffs,   5
That on a wild secluded scene impress
Thoughts of more deep seclusion; and connect
The landscape with the quiet of the sky.
The day is come when I again repose
Here, under this dark sycamore, and view   10
These plots of cottage ground, these orchard tufts,
Which at this season, with their unripe fruits,
Are clad in one green hue, and lose themselves
'Mid groves and copses. Once again I see
These hedgerows, hardly hedgerows, little lines   15
Of sportive wood run wild; these pastoral farms,
Green to the very door; and wreaths of smoke
Sent up, in silence, from among the trees!
With some uncertain notice, as might seem
Of vagrant dwellers in the houseless woods,   20
Or of some Hermit's cave, where by his fire
The Hermit sits alone.

Tintern Abbey: The ruins of a medieval abbey that Wordsworth had visited in
August 1793. Wordsworth says that he composed the poem in his head in four or
five hours as he walked from Tintern to Bristol in 1798, and then wrote it down
without revisions.

                    These beauteous forms,
Through a long absence, have not been to me
As is a landscape to a blind man's eye;
But oft, in lonely rooms, and 'mid the din   25
Of towns and cities, I have owed to them,
In hours of weariness, sensations sweet,
Felt in the blood, and felt along the heart;
And passing even into my purer mind,
With tranquil restoration—feelings too   30
Of unremembered pleasure; such, perhaps,
As have no slight or trivial influence
On that best portion of a good man's life,
His little, nameless, unremembered, acts
Of kindness and of love. Nor less, I trust,   35
To them I may have owed another gift,
Of aspect more sublime; that blessed mood,
In which the burthen of the mystery,
In which the heavy and the weary weight
Of all this unintelligible world,   40
Is lightened—that serene and blessed mood,
In which the affections gently lead us on—
Until, the breath of this corporeal frame
And even the motion of our human blood
Almost suspended, we are laid asleep   45
In body, and become a living soul;
While with an eye made quiet by the power
Of harmony, and the deep power of joy,
We see into the life of things.

                                    If this
Be but a vain belief, yet, oh! how oft—   50
In darkness and amid the many shapes
Of joyless daylight; when the fretful stir
Unprofitable, and the fever of the world,
Have hung upon the beatings of my heart—
How oft, in spirit, have I turned to thee,   55
O sylvan° Wye! thou wanderer through the woods,   *wooded*
How often has my spirit turned to thee!

    And now, with gleams of half-extinguished thought,
With many recognitions dim and faint,
And somewhat of a sad perplexity,   60
The picture of the mind revives again;
While here I stand, not only with the sense

Of present pleasure, but with pleasing thoughts
That in this moment there is life and food
For future years. And so I dare to hope,   65
Though changed, no doubt, from what I was when first
I came among these hills; when like a roe
I bounded o'er the mountains, by the sides
Of the deep rivers, and the lonely streams,
Wherever nature led — more like a man   70
Flying from something that he dreads than one
Who sought the thing he loved. For nature then
(The coarser pleasures of my boyish days,
And their glad animal movements all gone by)
To me was all in all. — I cannot paint   75
What then I was. The sounding cataract
Haunted me like a passion; the tall rock,
The mountain, and the deep and gloomy wood,
Their colors and their forms, were then to me
An appetite; a feeling and a love,   80
That had no need of a remoter charm,
By thought supplied, nor any interest
Unborrowed from the eye. — That time is past,
And all its aching joys are now no more,
And all its dizzy raptures. Not for this   85
Faint° I, nor mourn nor murmur; other gifts   *become discouraged*
Have followed; for such loss, I would believe,
Abundant recompense. For I have learned
To look on nature, not as in the hour
Of thoughtless youth; but hearing oftentimes   90
The still, sad music of humanity,
Nor harsh nor grating, though of ample power
To chasten and subdue. And I have felt
A presence that disturbs me with the joy
Of elevated thoughts; a sense sublime   95
Of something far more deeply interfused,
Whose dwelling is the light of setting suns,
And the round ocean and the living air,
And the blue sky, and in the mind of man:
A motion and a spirit, that impels   100
All thinking things, all objects of all thought,
And rolls through all things. Therefore am I still
A lover of the meadows and the woods,
And mountains; and of all that we behold
From this green earth; of all the mighty world   105

Of eye, and ear—both what they half create,
And what perceive; well pleased to recognize
In nature and the language of the sense
The anchor of my purest thoughts, the nurse,
The guide, the guardian of my heart, and soul   110
Of all my moral being.

               Nor perchance,
If I were not thus taught, should I the more
Suffer my genial spirits° to decay: *creative powers*
For thou art with me here upon the banks
Of this fair river; thou my dearest Friend,°   115
My dear, dear Friend; and in thy voice I catch
The language of my former heart, and read
My former pleasures in the shooting lights
Of thy wild eyes. Oh! yet a little while
May I behold in thee what I was once,   120
My dear, dear Sister! and this prayer I make,
Knowing that Nature never did betray
The heart that loved her; 'tis her privilege,
Through all the years of this our life, to lead
From joy to joy: for she can so inform   125
The mind that is within us, so impress
With quietness and beauty, and so feed
With lofty thoughts, that neither evil tongues,
Rash judgments, nor the sneers of selfish men,
Nor greetings where no kindness is, nor all   130
The dreary intercourse of daily life,
Shall e'er prevail against us, or disturb
Our cheerful faith, that all which we behold
Is full of blessings. Therefore let the moon
Shine on thee in thy solitary walk;   135
And let the misty mountain winds be free
To blow against thee: and, in after years,
When these wild ecstasies shall be matured
Into a sober pleasure; when thy mind
Shall be a mansion for all lovely forms,   140
Thy memory be as a dwelling place
For all sweet sounds and harmonies; oh! then,
If solitude, or fear, or pain, or grief

115. Friend: Wordsworth's sister Dorothy, who is made to sound younger by
more than the year and a half that separated them.

Should be thy portion, with what healing thoughts
Of tender joy wilt thou remember me,   145
And these my exhortations! Nor, perchance —
If I should be where I no more can hear
Thy voice, nor catch from thy wild eyes these gleams
Of past existence — wilt thou then forget
That on the banks of this delightful stream   150
We stood together; and that I, so long
A worshiper of Nature, hither came
Unwearied in that service; rather say
With warmer love — oh! with far deeper zeal
Of holier love. Nor wilt thou then forget,   155
That after many wanderings, many years
Of absence, these steep woods and lofty cliffs,
And this green pastoral landscape, were to me
More dear, both for themselves and for thy sake!

                                                              [1798]

WILLIAM WORDSWORTH   [1770–1850]

Ode

*Intimations of Immortality from Recollections
of Early Childhood*

> *The Child is father of the Man;
> And I could wish my days to be
> Bound each to each by natural piety.*°

1

There was a time when meadow, grove, and stream,
The earth, and every common sight,
        To me did seem
        Appareled in celestial light,
The glory and the freshness of a dream.   5
It is not now as it hath been of yore —
        Turn whereso'er I may,
        By night or day,
The things which I have seen I now can see no more.

Epigraph: The final lines of Wordsworth's "My Heart Leaps Up."

2

The Rainbow comes and goes,   10
   And lovely is the Rose,
   The Moon doth with delight
Look round her when the heavens are bare,
    Waters on a starry night
    Are beautiful and fair;   15
  The sunshine is a glorious birth;
  But yet I know, where'er I go,
That there hath passed away a glory from the earth.

3

Now, while the birds thus sing a joyous song,
   And while the young lambs bound   20
    As to the tabor's° sound,
To me alone there came a thought of grief:
A timely utterance gave that thought relief,
    And I again am strong:
The cataracts blow their trumpets from the steep;   25
No more shall grief of mine the season wrong;
I hear the Echoes through the mountains throng,
The Winds come to me from the fields of sleep,
    And all the earth is gay;
      Land and sea   30
    Give themselves up to jollity,
     And with the heart of May
    Doth every Beast keep holiday —
     Thou Child of Joy,
Shout round me, let me hear thy shouts, thou happy Shepherd-boy!   35

4

Ye blessèd Creatures, I have heard the call
  Ye to each other make; I see
The heavens laugh with you in your jubilee;
   My heart is at your festival,
    My head hath its coronal,°   40
The fullness of your bliss, I feel — I feel it all.
    Oh, evil day! if I were sullen
    While Earth herself is adorning,

21. tabor: A small drum, used chiefly as an accompaniment to the pipe or trumpet.
40. coronal: A wreath of flowers or leaves for the head; a garland.

This sweet May morning,
And the Children are culling   45
   On every side,
In a thousand valleys far and wide,
Fresh flowers; while the sun shines warm,
And the Babe leaps up on his Mother's arm—
   I hear, I hear, with joy I hear!   50
   — But there's a Tree, of many, one,
A single Field which I have looked upon,
Both of them speak of something that is gone:
   The Pansy at my feet
   Doth the same tale repeat: 55
Whither is fled the visionary gleam?
Where is it now, the glory and the dream?

        5

Our birth is but a sleep and a forgetting:
The Soul that rises with us, our life's Star,
   Hath had elsewhere its setting,   60
   And cometh from afar:
   Not in entire forgetfulness,
   And not in utter nakedness,
But trailing clouds of glory do we come
   From God, who is our home: 65
Heaven lies about us in our infancy!
Shades of the prison-house begin to close
   Upon the growing Boy
     But he
Beholds the light, and whence it flows,   70
   He sees it in his joy;
The Youth, who daily farther from the east
   Must travel, still is Nature's Priest,
   And by the vision splendid
   Is on his way attended;   75
At length the Man perceives it die away,
And fade into the light of common day.°

---

77. Lines 58–77 reflect Plato's belief that human souls inhabit "a pre-existent state" (in Wordsworth's terms) before being born into this world. Though imprisoned in a physical body and the material world, the soul of the infant has recollections of and longs to return to the perfect world of ideas. As the child grows older, those memories begin to fade, though reminders of that primal glory recur (usually from experiences with things in nature). By adulthood, such glimpses become rare and the adult becomes reconciled to the material world and its values.

6

Earth fills her lap with pleasures of her own;
Yearnings she hath in her own natural kind,
And, even with something of a Mother's mind,   80
    And no unworthy aim,
    The homely° Nurse doth all she can   *simple, kindly*
To make her foster child, her Inmate Man,
    Forget the glories he hath known,
And that imperial palace whence he came.   85

7

Behold the Child among his newborn blisses,
A six-years' Darling of a pygmy size!
See, where 'mid work of his own hand he lies,
Fretted° by sallies of his mother's kisses,   *annoyed*
With light upon him from his father's eyes!   90
See, at his feet, some little plan or chart,
Some fragment from his dream of human life,
Shaped by himself with newly-learnèd art;
    A wedding or a festival,
    A mourning or a funeral;   95
      And this hath now his heart,
      And unto this he frames his song;
      Then will he fit his tongue
To dialogues of business, love, or strife;
      But it will not be long   100
      Ere this be thrown aside,
      And with new joy and pride
The little Actor cons° another part;   *learns*
Filling from time to time his "humorous stage"°
With all the Persons,° down to palsied Age,   *dramatis personae* 105
That Life brings with her in her equipage;°
      As if his whole vocation
      Were endless imitation.

104. "humorous stage": Quoted from a sonnet by the Elizabethan poet Samuel
Daniel: the varied temperaments (humors) of characters represented on the stage.
Lines 103–05 echo Jaques's "All the world's a stage" speech in Shakespeare's
As You Like It (2.7.138–65), with its description of the "seven ages" in the life of a
person.
105–06. all . . . equipage: All that is needed for a military operation, a journey,
or a domestic establishment.

8

Thou, whose exterior semblance doth belie
    Thy Soul's immensity;   110
Thou best Philosopher, who yet dost keep
Thy heritage, thou Eye among the blind,
That, deaf and silent, read'st the eternal deep,
Haunted forever by the eternal mind —
    Mighty Prophet! Seer blest!   115
    On whom those truths do rest,
Which we are toiling all our lives to find,
In darkness lost, the darkness of the grave;
Thou, over whom thy Immortality
Broods like the Day, a Master o'er a Slave,   120
A Presence which is not to be put by;
Thou little Child, yet glorious in the might
Of heaven-born freedom on thy being's height,
Why with such earnest pains dost thou provoke
The years to bring the inevitable yoke,   125
Thus blindly with thy blessedness at strife?
Full soon thy Soul shall have her earthly freight,
And custom lie upon thee with a weight,
Heavy as frost, and deep almost as life!

9

    O joy! that in our embers   130
    Is something that doth live,
    That nature yet remembers
    What was so fugitive!
The thought of our past years in me doth breed
Perpetual benediction: not indeed   135
For that which is most worthy to be blest;
Delight and liberty, the simple creed
Of Childhood, whether busy or at rest,
With new-fledged hope still fluttering in his breast —
    Not for these I raise   140
    The song of thanks and praise;
   But for those obstinate questionings
   Of sense and outward things,
   Fallings from us, vanishings;
   Blank misgivings of a Creature   145
Moving about in worlds not realized,°   *not seeming real*
High instincts before which our mortal Nature

Did tremble like a guilty Thing surprised;
     But for those first affections,
     Those shadowy recollections, 150
    Which, be they what they may,
Are yet the fountain light of all our day,
Are yet a master light of all our seeing;
    Uphold us, cherish, and have power to make
Our noisy years seem moments in the being 155
Of the eternal Silence: truths that wake,
     To perish never;
Which neither listlessness, nor mad endeavor,
     Nor Man nor Boy,
Nor all that is at enmity with joy, 160
Can utterly abolish or destroy!
    Hence in a season of calm weather
    Though inland far we be,
Our Souls have sight of that immortal sea
    Which brought us hither, 165
    Can in a moment travel thither,
And see the Children sport upon the shore,
And hear the mighty waters rolling evermore.

10

Then sing, ye Birds, sing, sing a joyous song!
    And let the young Lambs bound 170
    As to the tabor's sound!
We in thought will join your throng,
    Ye that pipe and ye that play,
    Ye that through your hearts today
    Feel the gladness of the May! 175
What though the radiance which was once so bright
Be now forever taken from my sight,
    Though nothing can bring back the hour
Of splendor in the grass, of glory in the flower;
    We will grieve not, rather find 180
    Strength in what remains behind;
    In the primal sympathy
    Which having been must ever be;
    In the soothing thoughts that spring
    Out of human suffering; 185
    In the faith that looks through death,
In years that bring the philosophic mind.

11

And O, ye Fountains, Meadows, Hills, and Groves,
Forebode not any severing of our loves!
Yet in my heart of hearts I feel your might;   190
I only have relinquished one delight
To live beneath your more habitual sway.
I love the Brooks which down their channels fret,°   *move in agitated waves*
Even more than when I tripped lightly as they;
The innocent brightness of a newborn Day   195
      Is lovely yet;
The clouds that gather round the setting sun
Do take a sober coloring from an eye
That hath kept watch o'er man's mortality;
Another race hath been, and other palms° are won.   *symbols of victory* 200
Thanks to the human heart by which we live,
Thanks to its tenderness, its joys, and fears,
To me the meanest° flower that blows° can give   *most ordinary/blooms*
Thoughts that do often lie too deep for tears.

[1807]

WILLIAM WORDSWORTH   [1770–1850]

The world is too much with us

The world is too much with us; late and soon,
Getting and spending, we lay waste our powers;
Little we see in Nature that is ours;
We have given our hearts away, a sordid boon!°   *gift*
This Sea that bares her bosom to the moon,   5
The winds that will be howling at all hours,
And are up-gathered now like sleeping flowers,
For this, for everything, we are out of tune;
It moves us not. — Great God! I'd rather be
A Pagan suckled in a creed outworn;   10
So might I, standing on this pleasant lea,°   *open meadow*
Have glimpses that would make me less forlorn;

Have sight of Proteus° rising from the sea;
Or hear old Triton° blow his wreathèd° horn.

[1807]

13. Proteus: In Greek mythology, a sea god who could change his own form or appearance at will.
14. Triton: A Greek sea god with the head and upper body of a man and the tail of a fish, usually pictured as playing on a conch-shell trumpet; **wreathèd:** Curved.

SAMUEL TAYLOR COLERIDGE   [1772–1834]

Kubla Khan

Or, a Vision in a Dream. A Fragment°

In Xanadu did Kubla Khan
A stately pleasure dome decree:°
Where Alph,° the sacred river, ran
Through caverns measureless to man
    Down to a sunless sea.   5
So twice five miles of fertile ground
With walls and towers were girdled round:
And there were gardens bright with sinuous rills,
Where blossomed many an incense-bearing tree;
And here were forests ancient as the hills,   10
Enfolding sunny spots of greenery.

But oh! that deep romantic chasm which slanted
Down the green hill athwart a cedarn cover!
A savage place! as holy and enchanted
As e'er beneath a waning moon was haunted   15
By woman wailing for her demon lover!

Or, a Vision . . . A Fragment: Coleridge stated in a preface that this poem composed itself in his mind during "a profound sleep" (actually an opium-induced reverie); that he began writing it down immediately upon waking but was interrupted by a caller; and that when he returned to his room an hour later he could not complete it.
1–2. In . . . decree: "In Xamdu did Cublai Can build a stately Palace, encompassing sixteene miles of plaine ground with a wall" (Samuel Purchas, *Purchas his Pilgrimage* [1613]). The historical Kublai Khan (1215–1294) was the founder of the Yüan dynasty of China and overlord of the Mongol Empire.
3. Alph: Probably derived from the name of the River Alpheus in southern Greece, which according to mythology ran under the sea and emerged at Syracuse (Italy) in the fountain of Arethusa.

And from this chasm, with ceaseless turmoil seething,
As if this earth in fast thick pants were breathing,
A mighty fountain momently was forced:
Amid whose swift half-intermitted burst   20
Huge fragments vaulted like rebounding hail,
Or chaffy grain beneath the thresher's flail:
And 'mid these dancing rocks at once and ever
It flung up momently the sacred river.
Five miles meandering with a mazy motion   25
Through wood and dale the sacred river ran,
Then reached the caverns measureless to man,
And sank in tumult to a lifeless ocean:
And 'mid this tumult Kubla heard from far
Ancestral voices prophesying war!   30
   The shadow of the dome of pleasure
   Floated midway on the waves;
   Where was heard the mingled measure
   From the fountain and the caves.
It was a miracle of rare device,   35
A sunny pleasure dome with caves of ice!

   A damsel with a dulcimer
   In a vision once I saw:
   It was an Abyssinian maid,
   And on her dulcimer she played,   40
   Singing of Mount Abora.°
   Could I revive within me
   Her symphony and song,
   To such a deep delight 'twould win me,
That with music loud and long,   45
I would build that dome in air,
That sunny dome! those caves of ice!
And all who heard should see them there,
And all should cry, Beware! Beware!
His flashing eyes, his floating hair!   50
Weave a circle round him thrice,
And close your eyes with holy dread,
For he on honey-dew hath fed,
And drunk the milk of Paradise.

[*c. 1797–1798;* 1813]

39–41. Abyssinian . . . Abora: See *Paradise Lost* 4.280–82: "where Abassin Kings
their issue Guard, / Mount Amara, though this by some supposed / True Paradise
under the Ethiop Line."

GEORGE GORDON, LORD BYRON   [1788–1824]

She walks in beauty

1

She walks in beauty, like the night
    Of cloudless climes and starry skies;
And all that's best of dark and bright
    Meet in her aspect and her eyes:
Thus mellowed to that tender light   5
    Which heaven to gaudy day denies.

2

One shade the more, one ray the less,
    Had half impaired the nameless grace
Which waves in every raven tress,
    Or softly lightens o'er her face;   10
Where thoughts serenely sweet express
    How pure, how dear their dwelling place.

3

And on that cheek, and o'er that brow,
    So soft, so calm, yet eloquent,
The smiles that win, the tints that glow,   15
    But tell of days in goodness spent,
A mind at peace with all below,
    A heart whose love is innocent!

[1815]

PERCY BYSSHE SHELLEY   [1792–1822]

Ozymandias°

I met a traveler from an antique land
Who said: Two vast and trunkless legs of stone
Stand in the desert. Near them, on the sand,
Half sunk, a shattered visage lies, whose frown,
And wrinkled lip, and sneer of cold command,   5

Ozymandias: The Greek name for Ramses II of Egypt (thirteenth century B.C.E.),
who erected the largest statue in Egypt as a memorial to himself.

Tell that its sculptor well those passions read
Which yet survive, stamped on these lifeless things,
The hand that mocked them, and the heart that fed:
And on the pedestal these words appear:
"My name is Ozymandias, king of kings: 10
Look on my works, ye Mighty, and despair!"
Nothing beside remains. Round the decay
Of that colossal wreck, boundless and bare
The lone and level sands stretch far away.

[1818]

PERCY BYSSHE SHELLEY   [1792–1822]

Ode to the West Wind

1

O wild West Wind, thou breath° of Autumn's being,
Thou, from whose unseen presence the leaves dead
Are driven, like ghosts from an enchanter fleeing,

Yellow, and black, and pale, and hectic red,
Pestilence-stricken multitudes: O thou,   5
Who chariotest to their dark wintry bed

The wingèd seeds, where they lie cold and low,
Each like a corpse within its grave, until
Thine azure sister of the Spring shall blow

Her clarion o'er the dreaming earth, and fill   10
(Driving sweet buds like flocks to feed in air)
With living hues and odors plain and hill:

Wild Spirit, which art moving everywhere;
Destroyer and preserver; hear, oh, hear!

---

1. breath: In many ancient languages, the words for *breath, wind, soul,* and *inspiration* are the same or closely related: in Latin, *spiritus.* Shelley uses this word to interconnect nature and artistic inspiration (poetry) in his poem.

2

Thou on whose stream, mid the steep sky's commotion,   15
Loose clouds like earth's decaying leaves are shed,
Shook from the tangled boughs of Heaven and Ocean,

Angels of rain and lightning: there are spread
On the blue surface of thine airy surge,
Like the bright hair uplifted from the head   20

Of some fierce Maenad,° even from the dim verge
Of the horizon to the zenith's height,
The locks of the approaching storm. Thou dirge

Of the dying year, to which this closing night
Will be the dome of a vast sepulcher,   25
Vaulted with all thy congregated might

Of vapors, from whose solid atmosphere
Black rain, and fire, and hail will burst: oh, hear!

3

Thou who didst waken from his summer dreams
The blue Mediterranean, where he lay,   30
Lulled by the coil of his crystàlline streams,

Beside a pumice° isle in Baiae's bay,°
And saw in sleep old palaces° and towers
Quivering within the wave's intenser day,

All overgrown with azure moss and flowers   35
So sweet, the sense faints picturing them! Thou
For whose path the Atlantic's level powers

Cleave themselves into chasms, while far below
The sea-blooms and the oozy woods which wear
The sapless foliage of the ocean, know   40

Thy voice, and suddenly grow gray with fear,
And tremble and despoil themselves: oh, hear!

21. Maenad: A female votary of Dionysus, Greek god of wine and vegetation, who took part in the wild, orgiastic rites that characterize his worship.
32. pumice: Porous volcanic stone; **Baiae's bay:** West of Naples, Italy.
33. old palaces: Villas built by the Roman emperors.

4

If I were a dead leaf thou mightest bear;
If I were a swift cloud to fly with thee;
A wave to pant beneath thy power, and share   45

The impulse of thy strength, only less free
Than thou, O uncontrollable! If even
I were as in my boyhood, and could be

The comrade of thy wanderings over Heaven,
As then, when to outstrip thy skyey speed   50
Scarce seemed a vision; I would ne'er have striven

As thus with thee in prayer in my sore need.
Oh, lift me as a wave, a leaf, a cloud!
I fall upon the thorns of life! I bleed!

A heavy weight of hours has chained and bowed   55
One too like thee: tameless, and swift, and proud.

5

Make me thy lyre,° even as the forest is:
What if my leaves are falling like its own!
The tumult of thy mighty harmonies

Will take from both a deep, autumnal tone,   60
Sweet though in sadness. Be thou, Spirit fierce,
My spirit! Be thou me, impetuous one!

Drive my dead thoughts over the universe
Like withered leaves to quicken a new birth!
And, by the incantation of this verse,   65

Scatter, as from an unextinguished hearth
Ashes and sparks, my words among mankind!
Be through my lips to unawakened earth

The trumpet of a prophecy! O Wind,
If Winter comes, can Spring be far behind?   70

[1820]

---

57. lyre: An Aeolian harp, whose strings produce a sequence of rising and falling harmonies as air blows over them.

JOHN KEATS   [1795–1821]

When I have fears
that I may cease to be

When I have fears that I may cease to be
  Before my pen has gleaned my teeming brain,
Before high piled books, in charactry,°   *writing*
  Hold like rich garners the full ripened grain;
When I behold, upon the night's starred face,   5
  Huge cloudy symbols of a high romance,
And think that I may never live to trace
  Their shadows, with the magic hand of chance;
And when I feel, fair creature of an hour,
  That I shall never look upon thee more,   10
Never have relish in the fairy power
  Of unreflecting love; — then on the shore
Of the wide world I stand alone, and think
Till love and fame to nothingness do sink.

[*1818;* 1848]

JOHN KEATS   [1795–1821]

La Belle Dame sans Merci°

O what can ail thee, Knight at arms,
  Alone and palely loitering?
The sedge° has withered from the Lake   *rushes*
  And no birds sing!

O what can ail thee, Knight at arms,   5
  So haggard, and so woebegone?
The squirrel's granary is full
  And the harvest's done.

I see a lily on thy brow
  With anguish moist and fever dew,   10
And on thy cheeks a fading rose
  Fast withereth too.

La Belle Dame sans Merci: "The beautiful lady without pity" (French). This version, first published in 1888, is earlier than the one Keats published in 1820, and is generally the preferred version.

"I met a Lady in the Meads,°   *meadows*
    Full beautiful, a faery's child,
Her hair was long, her foot was light   15
    And her eyes were wild.

"I made a Garland for her head,
    And bracelets too, and fragrant Zone;°   *girdle*
She looked at me as she did love
    And made sweet moan.   20

"I set her on my pacing steed
    And nothing else saw all day long,
For sidelong would she bend and sing
    A faery's song.

"She found me roots of relish sweet,   25
    And honey wild, and manna dew,
And sure in language strange she said
    'I love thee true.'

"She took me to her elfin grot°   *grotto, cave*
    And there she wept and sighed full sore,
And there I shut her wild wild eyes   30
    With kisses four.

"And there she lulléd me asleep,
    And there I dreamed, Ah Woe betide!
The latest° dream I ever dreamt   *last*   35
    On the cold hill side.

"I saw pale Kings, and Princes too,
    Pale warriors, death-pale were they all;
They cried, 'La belle dame sans merci
    Hath thee in thrall!'   40

"I saw their starved lips in the gloom°   *twilight*
    With horrid warning gapéd wide,
And I awoke, and found me here
    On the cold hill's side.

"And this is why I sojourn here,   45
    Alone and palely loitering;
Though the sedge is withered from the Lake
    And no birds sing."

                                             [*1819;* 1888]

JOHN KEATS   [1795–1821]

Ode on a Grecian Urn

1

Thou still unravished bride of quietness,
   Thou foster child of silence and slow time,
Sylvan historian, who canst thus express
   A flowery tale more sweetly than our rhyme:
What leaf-fringed legend haunts about thy shape   5
   Of deities or mortals, or of both,
      In Tempe or the dales of Arcady?°
   What men or gods are these? What maidens loath?
What mad pursuit? What struggle to escape?
      What pipes and timbrels? What wild ecstasy?   10

2

Heard melodies are sweet, but those unheard
   Are sweeter; therefore, ye soft pipes, play on;
Not to the sensual ear,° but, more endeared,
   Pipe to the spirit ditties of no tone:
Fair youth, beneath the trees, thou canst not leave   15
   Thy song, nor ever can those trees be bare;
      Bold lover, never, never canst thou kiss,
Though winning near the goal—yet, do not grieve;
      She cannot fade, though thou hast not thy bliss,
      Forever wilt thou love, and she be fair!   20

3

Ah, happy, happy boughs! that cannot shed
   Your leaves, nor ever bid the spring adieu;
And, happy melodist, unwearièd,
   Forever piping songs forever new;
More happy love! more happy, happy love!   25
   Forever warm and still to be enjoyed,
      Forever panting, and forever young;
All breathing human passion far above,
      That leaves a heart high-sorrowful and cloyed,
      A burning forehead, and a parching tongue.   30

7. Tempe, Arcady: Tempe, a valley in Greece, and Arcadia ("Arcady"), a region of ancient Greece, represent ideal pastoral landscapes.
13. not . . . ear: Not to the ear of the senses, but to the imagination.

4

Who are these coming to the sacrifice?
　To what green altar, O mysterious priest,
Lead'st thou that heifer lowing at the skies,
　　And all her silken flanks with garlands dressed?
What little town by river or sea shore,　　　　　　　　　　35
　　Or mountain-built with peaceful citadel,
　　　Is emptied of this folk, this pious morn?
And, little town, thy streets forevermore
　　Will silent be; and not a soul to tell
　　　Why thou art desolate, can e'er return.　　　　　　　40

5

O Attic° shape! Fair attitude! with brede°
　Of marble men and maidens overwrought,
With forest branches and the trodden weed;
　　Thou, silent form, dost tease us out of thought
As doth eternity: Cold Pastoral!　　　　　　　　　　　　45
　　When old age shall this generation waste,
　　　Thou shalt remain, in midst of other woe
Than ours, a friend to man, to whom thou say'st,
　"Beauty is truth, truth beauty,"° — that is all
　　Ye know on earth, and all ye need to know.　　　　　50

[1820]

---

41. Attic: Greek, specifically Athenian; **brede:** Interwoven pattern.
49. "Beauty . . . beauty": The quotation marks around this phrase were found in its earliest printing, in an 1820 volume of poetry by Keats, but not in a printing later that year or in written transcripts. This discrepancy has led to considerable critical controversy concerning the last two lines. Critics disagree whether "Beauty is truth, truth beauty" is spoken by the urn (and thus perhaps expressing a limited perspective not to be taken at face value) or by the speaker in the poem, or whether the last two lines in their entirety are said by the urn (some recent editors enclose both lines in parentheses to make this explicit) or by the speaker.

JOHN KEATS   [1795–1821]

To Autumn

I

Season of mists and mellow fruitfulness,
   Close bosom-friend of the maturing sun;
Conspiring with him how to load and bless
   With fruit the vines that round the thatch-eves run;
To bend with apples the mossed cottage-trees,   5
   And fill all fruit with ripeness to the core;
      To swell the gourd, and plump the hazel shells
With a sweet kernel; to set budding more,
   And still more, later flowers for the bees,
   Until they think warm days will never cease,   10
      For Summer has o'er-brimmed their clammy cells.

II

Who hath not seen thee oft amid thy store?
   Sometimes whoever seeks abroad may find
Thee sitting careless on a granary floor,
   Thy hair soft-lifted by the winnowing wind;   15
Or on a half-reaped furrow sound asleep,
   Drowsed with the fume of poppies, while thy hook°   *scythe*
      Spares the next swath and all its twinèd flowers:
And sometimes like a gleaner thou dost keep
   Steady thy laden head across a brook;   20
   Or by a cider-press, with patient look,
      Thou watchest the last oozings hours by hours.

III

Where are the songs of Spring? Aye, where are they?
   Think not of them, thou hast thy music too, —
While barrèd clouds bloom the soft-dying day,   25
   And touch the stubble-plains with rosy hue;
Then in a wailful choir the small gnats mourn
   Among the river sallows,° borne aloft   *willows*
      Or sinking as the light wind lives or dies;
And full-grown lambs loud bleat from hilly bourn;°   *region* 30
   Hedge-crickets sing; and now with treble soft
   The red-breast whistles from a garden-croft;
      And gathering swallows twitter in the skies.

[1820]

ELIZABETH BARRETT BROWNING   [1806–1861]

How do I love thee?
Let me count the ways

How do I love thee? Let me count the ways.
I love thee to the depth and breadth and height
My soul can reach, when feeling out of sight
For the ends of Being and ideal Grace.
I love thee to the level of everyday's   5
Most quiet need, by sun and candlelight.
I love thee freely, as men strive for Right;
I love thee purely, as they turn from Praise.
I love thee with the passion put to use
In my old griefs, and with my childhood's faith.   10
I love thee with a love I seemed to lose
With my lost saints — I love thee with the breath,
Smiles, tears, of all my life! — and, if God choose,
I shall but love thee better after death.

[1850]

EDGAR ALLAN POE   [1809–1849]

To Helen

Helen,° thy beauty is to me
    Like those Nicéan barks° of yore,
That gently, o'er a perfumed sea,
    The weary, way-worn wanderer bore
        To his own native shore.   5

On desperate seas long wont to roam,
    Thy hyacinth° hair, thy classic face,
Thy Naiad° airs have brought me home
    To the glory that was Greece
And the grandeur that was Rome.   10

1. Helen: Daughter of Leda and Zeus, the most beautiful woman in the world; her abduction by Paris gave rise to the Trojan war.
2. barks: Small sailing boats; Poe probably invented "Nicéan" for its sound and suggestiveness.
7. hyacinth: "Raven-black" and "naturally curling" (from Poe's story "Ligeia").
8. Naiads: Fresh-water nymphs in classical myths.

Lo! in yon brilliant window-niche
   How statue-like I see thee stand,
   The agate lamp within thy hand!
Ah! Psyche, from the regions which
   Are Holy Land!   15

[*1823;* 1831]

EDGAR ALLAN POE   [1809–1849]

Annabel Lee

It was many and many a year ago,
   In a kingdom by the sea,
That a maiden there lived whom you may know
   By the name of Annabel Lee;
And this maiden she lived with no other thought   5
   Than to love and be loved by me.

She was a child and *I* was a child,
   In this kingdom by the sea,
But we loved with a love that was more than love—
   I and my Annabel Lee—   10
With a love that the wingèd seraphs° of Heaven   *angels of the highest order*
   Coveted her and me.

And this was the reason that, long ago,
   In this kingdom by the sea,
A wind blew out of a cloud by night   15
   Chilling my Annabel Lee;
So that her highborn kinsmen came
   And bore her away from me,
To shut her up in a sepulchre
   In this kingdom by the sea.   20

The angels, not half so happy in Heaven,
   Went envying her and me:
Yes! that was the reason (as all men know,
   In this kingdom by the sea)
That the wind came out of the cloud, chilling   25
   And killing my Annabel Lee.

But our love it was stronger by far than the love
   Of those who were older than we—

Of many far wiser than we —
And neither the angels in Heaven above   30
  Nor the demons down under the sea,
Can ever dissever my soul from the soul
  Of the beautiful Annabel Lee:

For the moon never beams without bringing me dreams
  Of the beautiful Annabel Lee;   35
And the stars never rise but I see the bright eyes
  Of the beautiful Annabel Lee;
And so, all the night-tide, I lie down by the side
Of my darling, my darling, my life and my bride,
  In her sepulchre there by the sea —   40
  In her tomb by the side of the sea.

[1849]

ALFRED, LORD TENNYSON   [1809–1892]

Ulysses°

It little profits that an idle king,
By this still hearth, among these barren crags,
Matched with an agèd wife, I mete and dole
Unequal laws unto a savage race,°
That hoard, and sleep, and feed, and know not me.   5

  I cannot rest from travel; I will drink
Life to the lees. All times I have enjoyed

Ulysses (the Roman form of Odysseus): The hero of Homer's epic *The Odyssey*,
which tells the story of Odysseus's adventures on his voyage back to Ithaca, the
small island of which he was king, after he and the other Greek heroes had
defeated Troy. It took Odysseus ten years to reach Ithaca, where his wife (Penelope) and son (Telemachus) had been waiting for him. Upon his return, he defeated the suitors who had been trying to marry the faithful Penelope, and he
resumed the kingship and his old ways of life. Here Homer's story ends, but in
Canto 26 of the *Inferno*, Dante extended the story: Odysseus eventually became
restless and dissatisfied with his settled life and decided to return to the sea and
sail west, into the unknown sea, and seek whatever adventures he might find
there. Tennyson's poem amplifies the speech delivered in Dante's poem as Ulysses
challenges his men to accompany him on this new voyage.
3–4. mete . . . race: Administer inadequate (unequal to what is needed) laws to a
still somewhat lawless race.

Greatly, have suffered greatly, both with those
That loved me, and alone; on shore, and when
Through scudding drifts° the rainy Hyades°   10
Vexed the dim sea. I am become a name;
For always roaming with a hungry heart
Much have I seen and known — cities of men
And manners, climates, councils, governments,
Myself not least, but honored of them all —   15
And drunk delight of battle with my peers,
Far on the ringing plains of windy Troy.
I am a part of all that I have met;
Yet all experience is an arch wherethrough
Gleams that untraveled world whose margin fades   20
Forever and forever when I move.
How dull it is to pause, to make an end,
To rust unburnished, not to shine in use!
As though to breathe were life! Life piled on life
Were all too little, and of one to me   25
Little remains; but every hour is saved
From that eternal silence, something more,
A bringer of new things; and vile it were
For some three suns° to store and hoard myself,   *years*
And this gray spirit yearning in desire   30
To follow knowledge like a sinking star,
Beyond the utmost bound of human thought.

    This is my son, mine own Telemachus,
To whom I leave the scepter and the isle —
Well-loved of me, discerning to fulfill   35
This labor, by slow prudence to make mild
A rugged people, and through soft degrees
Subdue them to the useful and the good.
Most blameless is he, centered in the sphere
Of common duties, decent not to fail   40
In offices of tenderness, and pay
Meet adoration to my household gods,
When I am gone. He works his work, I mine.

    There lies the port; the vessel puffs her sail;
There gloom the dark, broad seas. My mariners,   45
Souls that have toiled, and wrought, and thought with me —

10. scudding drifts: Wind-driven spray; **Hyades:** Five stars in the constellation
Taurus whose rising was assumed to be followed by rain.

That ever with a frolic welcome took
The thunder and the sunshine, and opposed
Free hearts, free foreheads — you and I are old;
Old age hath yet his honor and his toil.   50
Death closes all; but something ere the end,
Some work of noble note, may yet be done,
Not unbecoming men that strove with Gods.
The lights begin to twinkle from the rocks;
The long day wanes; the slow moon climbs; the deep   55
Moans round with many voices. Come, my friends,
'Tis not too late to seek a newer world.
Push off, and sitting well in order smite
The sounding furrows; for my purpose holds
To sail beyond the sunset, and the baths°   60
Of all the western stars, until I die.
It may be that the gulfs will wash us down;
It may be we shall touch the Happy Isles,°
And see the great Achilles,° whom we knew.
Though much is taken, much abides; and though   65
We are not now that strength which in old days
Moved earth and heaven, that which we are, we are —
One equal temper of heroic hearts,
Made weak by time and fate, but strong in will
To strive, to seek, to find, and not to yield.   70

[1833]

60. baths: The outer river or ocean surrounding the flat earth, in Greek cosmology, into which the stars descended upon setting.
63. Happy Isles: The Islands of the Blessed, or Elysian Fields, in Greek myth, which lay in the western seas beyond the Strait of Gibraltar and were the abode of heroes after death.
64. Achilles: The hero of the Greeks, and Odysseus's comrade, in Homer's *Iliad*.

ALFRED, LORD TENNYSON   [1809–1892]

The Lady of Shalott

PART I

On either side the river lie
Long fields of barley and of rye,
That clothe the wold° and meet the sky;   *plain*
And through the field the road runs by

To many towered Camelot;°   5
And up and down the people go,
Gazing where the lilies blow°   *bloom*
Round an island there below,
   The island of Shalott.

Willows whiten, aspens quiver,   10
Little breezes dusk and shiver
Through the wave that runs for ever
By the island in the river
   Flowing down to Camelot.
Four gray walls, and four gray towers,   15
Overlook a space of flowers,
And the silent isle imbowers
   The Lady of Shalott.

By the margin, willow-veiled,
Slide the heavy barges trailed
By slow horses; and unhailed   20
The shallop° flitteth silken-sailed   *small boat*
   Skimming down to Camelot:
But who hath seen her wave her hand?
Or at the casement seen her stand?   25
Or is she known in all the land,
   The Lady of Shalott?

Only reapers, reaping early
In among the bearded barley,
Hear a song that echoes cheerly   30
From the river winding clearly,
   Down to towered Camelot:
And by the moon the reaper weary,
Piling sheaves in uplands airy,
Listening, whispers "'Tis the fairy   35
   Lady of Shalott."

PART II

There she weaves by night and day
A magic web with colors gay.
She has heard a whisper say,
A curse is on her if she stay°   *pause*   40
   To look down to Camelot.

---

5. Camelot: King Arthur's castle.

She knows not what the curse may be,
And so she weaveth steadily,
And little other care hath she,
    The Lady of Shalott.   45

And moving through a mirror clear°
That hangs before her all the year,
Shadows of the world appear.
There she sees the highway near
    Winding down to Camelot: 50
There the river eddy whirls,
And there the surly village-churls,°   *peasants*
And the red cloaks of market girls,
    Pass onward from Shalott.

Sometimes a troop of damsels glad,   55
An abbot on an ambling pad,°   *easy-paced horse*
Sometimes a curly shepherd-lad,
Or long-haired page in crimson clad,
    Goes by to towered Camelot;
And sometimes through the mirror blue   60
The knights come riding two and two:
She hath no loyal knight and true,
    The Lady of Shalott.

But in her web she still delights
To weave the mirror's magic sights,   65
For often through the silent nights
A funeral, with plumes and lights
    And music, went to Camelot;
Or when the moon was overhead,
Came two young lovers lately wed;   70
"I am half sick of shadows," said
    The Lady of Shalott.

PART III

A bow-shot from her bower-eaves,
He rode between the barley-sheaves,
The sun came dazzling through the leaves,   75
And flamed upon the brazen greaves°
    Of bold Sir Lancelot.
A red-cross knight for ever kneeled

46. mirror clear: Weavers placed mirrors facing their looms to watch the progress of their work.
76. brazen greaves: Brass armor for the leg below the knee.

To a lady in his shield,
That sparkled on the yellow field,   80
   Beside remote Shalott.

The gemmy bridle glittered free,
Like to some branch of stars we see
Hung in the golden Galaxy.
The bridle bells rang merrily   85
   As he rode down to Camelot:
And from his blazoned° baldric° slung
A mighty silver bugle hung,
And as he rode his armor rung,
   Beside remote Shalott.   90

All in the blue unclouded weather
Thick-jewelled shone the saddle-leather,
The helmet and the helmet-feather
Burned like one burning flame together,
   As he rode down to Camelot.   95
As often through the purple night,
Below the starry clusters bright,
Some bearded meteor, trailing light,
   Moves over still Shalott.

His broad clear brow in sunlight glowed;   100
On burnished hooves his war-horse trode;
From underneath his helmet flowed
His coal-black curls as on he rode,
   As he rode down to Camelot.
From the bank and from the river   105
He flashed into the crystal mirror,
"Tirra lirra," by the river
   Sang Sir Lancelot.

She left the web, she left the loom,
She made three paces through the room,   110
She saw the water-lily bloom,
She saw the helmet and the plume,
   She looked down to Camelot.
Out flew the web and floated wide;
The mirror cracked from side to side;   115
"The curse is come upon me," cried
   The Lady of Shalott.

87. blazoned: Painted with a heraldic device; **baldric:** Belt worn diagonally
from the shoulder to the opposite hip to support a sword or bugle.

PART IV

In the stormy east-wind straining,
The pale yellow woods were waning,
The broad stream in his banks complaining.   120
Heavily the low sky raining
    Over towered Camelot;
Down she came and found a boat
Beneath a willow left afloat,
And round about the prow she wrote   125
    The Lady of Shalott.

And down the river's dim expanse
Like some bold seer in a trance,
Seeing all his own mischance —
With a glassy countenance   130
    Did she look to Camelot.
And at the closing of the day
She loosed the chain, and down she lay;
The broad stream bore her far away,
    The Lady of Shalott.   135

Lying, robed in snowy white
That loosely flew to left and right —
The leaves upon her falling light —
Through the noises of the night
    She floated down to Camelot: 140
And as the boat-head wound along
The willowy hills and fields among,
They heard her singing her last song,
    The Lady of Shalott.

Heard a carol, mournful, holy,   145
Chanted loudly, chanted lowly,
Till her blood was frozen slowly,
And her eyes were darkened wholly,
    Turned to towered Camelot.
For ere she reached upon the tide   150
The first house by the water-side,
Singing in her song she died,
    The Lady of Shalott.

Under tower and balcony,
By garden-wall and gallery,   155
A gleaming shape she floated by,
Dead-pale between the houses high,

Silent into Camelot.
Out upon the wharfs they came,
Knight and burgher, lord and dame,   160
And round the prow they read her name,
    The Lady of Shalott.

Who is this? and what is here?
And in the lighted palace near
Died the sound of royal cheer;   165
And they crossed themselves for fear,
    All the knights at Camelot:
But Lancelot mused a little space;
He said, "She has a lovely face;
God in his mercy lend her grace,   170
    The Lady of Shalott."

[1832]

ALFRED, LORD TENNYSON   [1809–1892]

Crossing the Bar

Sunset and evening star,
    And one clear call for me!
And may there be no moaning of the bar,°
    When I put out to sea,

But such a tide as moving seems asleep,   5
    Too full for sound and foam,
When that which drew from out the boundless deep
    Turns again home.

Twilight and evening bell,
    And after that the dark!   10
And may there be no sadness of farewell,
    When I embark;

For though from out our bourne of Time and Place
    The flood may bear me far,
I hope to see my Pilot face to face   15
    When I have crossed the bar.

[1889]

3. **moaning of the bar:** The mournful sound of waves crashing against a sand
bar at the mouth of a river or harbor at low tide.

ROBERT BROWNING [1812–1889]

Home-Thoughts, from Abroad

1

Oh, to be in England
Now that April's there,
And whoever wakes in England
Sees, some morning, unaware,
That the lowest boughs and the brushwood sheaf   5
Round the elm-tree bole are in tiny leaf,
While the chaffinch sings on the orchard bough
In England—now!

2

And after April, when May follows,
And the whitethroat builds, and all the swallows!   10
Hark, where my blossomed pear-tree in the hedge
Leans to the field and scatters on the clover
Blossoms and dewdrops—at the bent spray's edge—
That's the wise thrush; he sings each song twice over,
Lest you should think he never could recapture   15
The first fine careless rapture!
And though the fields look rough with hoary dew
All will be gay when noontide wakes anew
The buttercups, the little children's dower
—Far brighter than this gaudy melon-flower!   20

[1845]

ROBERT BROWNING [1812–1889]

My Last Duchess

Ferrara°

That's my last Duchess° painted on the wall,
Looking as if she were alive. I call

Ferrara: The poem is based on events that occurred in the life of Alfonso II, duke of Ferrara in Italy, in the sixteenth century.
1. last Duchess: Ferrara's first wife, Lucrezia, died in 1561 at age seventeen after three years of marriage.

That piece a wonder, now: Frà Pandolf's° hands
Worked busily a day, and there she stands.
Will't please you sit and look at her? I said   5
"Frà Pandolf" by design, for never read
Strangers like you that pictured countenance,
The depth and passion of its earnest glance,
But to myself they turned (since none puts by
The curtain I have drawn for you, but I)   10
And seemed as they would ask me, if they durst,
How such a glance came there; so, not the first
Are you to turn and ask thus. Sir, 'twas not
Her husband's presence only, called that spot
Of joy into the Duchess' cheek: perhaps   15
Frà Pandolf chanced to say "Her mantle laps
Over my lady's wrist too much," or "Paint
Must never hope to reproduce the faint
Half-flush that dies along her throat": such stuff
Was courtesy, she thought, and cause enough   20
For calling up that spot of joy. She had
A heart—how shall I say?—too soon made glad,
Too easily impressed; she liked whate'er
She looked on, and her looks went everywhere.
Sir, 'twas all one! My favor at her breast,   25
The dropping of the daylight in the West,
The bough of cherries some officious fool
Broke in the orchard for her, the white mule
She rode with round the terrace—all and each
Would draw from her alike the approving speech,   30
Or blush, at least. She thanked men,—good! but thanked
Somehow—I know not how—as if she ranked
My gift of a nine-hundred-years-old name
With anybody's gift. Who'd stoop to blame
This sort of trifling? Even had you skill   35
In speech—(which I have not)—to make your will
Quite clear to such an one, and say, "Just this
Or that in you disgusts me; here you miss,
Or there exceed the mark"—and if she let
Herself be lessoned so, nor plainly set   40
Her wits to yours, forsooth, and made excuse,
—E'en then would be some stooping; and I choose
Never to stoop. Oh sir, she smiled, no doubt,

3. Frà Pandolf: Brother Pandolf, a fictional painter.

Whene'er I passed her; but who passed without
Much the same smile? This grew; I gave commands;   45
Then all smiles stopped together. There she stands
As if alive. Will't please you rise? We'll meet
The company below, then. I repeat,
The Count your master's known munificence
Is ample warrant that no just pretence   50
Of mine for dowry will be disallowed;
Though his fair daughter's self, as I avowed
At starting, is my object. Nay, we'll go
Together down, sir. Notice Neptune, though,
Taming a sea-horse, thought a rarity,   55
Which Claus of Innsbruck° cast in bronze for me!

[1842]

56. **Claus of Innsbruck:** A fictional sculptor.

WALT WHITMAN   [1819–1892]

From Song of Myself°

1

I celebrate myself, and sing myself,
And what I assume you shall assume,
For every atom belonging to me as good belongs to you.

I loafe and invite my soul,
I lean and loafe at my ease observing a spear of summer grass.   5

Song of Myself: The poem was first published in 1855 as an untitled section of *Leaves of Grass.* It was a rough, rude, and vigorous example of antebellum American cultural politics and free verse experimentation. The version used here, from the sixth edition (1891–1892), is much longer, more carefully crafted, and more conventionally punctuated. Sections 1–3 introduce the persona and the scope and method of the poem; section 6 explains grass as a symbol; sections 7–10, examples of Whitman's dynamic panoramic miniatures, are also of historical significance regarding Native and African Americans; section 14 extends the outward sweep of 7–10; section 21 develops Whitman's theme of sex and nature; section 24 extends the handling of the poem's persona; sections 46 and 48 recapitulate the major themes of the poem; sections 51 and 52 deal with the absorption of the poet's persona into the converted reader.

My tongue, every atom of my blood, form'd from this soil, this air,
Born here of parents born here from parents the same, and their
   parents the same,
I, now thirty-seven years old in perfect health begin,
Hoping to cease not till death.

Creeds and schools in abeyance,   10
Retiring back a while sufficed at what they are, but never
   forgotten,
I harbor for good or bad, I permit to speak at every hazard,
Nature without check with original energy.

2

Houses and rooms are full of perfumes, the shelves are crowded with
   perfumes,
I breathe the fragrance myself and know it and like it,   15
The distillation would intoxicate me also, but I shall not let it.

The atmosphere is not a perfume, it has no taste of the distillation,
   it is odorless,
It is for my mouth forever, I am in love with it,
I will go to the bank by the wood and become undisguised and naked,
I am mad for it to be in contact with me.   20

The smoke of my own breath,
Echoes, ripples, buzz'd whispers, love-root, silk-thread, crotch and
   vine,
My respiration and inspiration, the beating of my heart, the passing of
   blood and air through my lungs,
The sniff of green leaves and dry leaves, and of the shore and
   dark-color'd sea-rocks, and of hay in the barn,
The sound of the belch'd words of my voice loos'd to the eddies of the
   wind,   25
A few light kisses, a few embraces, a reaching around of arms,
The play of shine and shade on the trees as the supple boughs wag,
The delight alone or in the rush of the streets, or along the fields and
   hill-sides,
The feeling of health, the full-noon trill, the song of me rising from bed
   and meeting the sun.

Have you reckon'd a thousand acres much? have you reckon'd the earth
   much?   30
Have you practis'd so long to learn to read?
Have you felt so proud to get at the meaning of poems?

Stop this day and night with me and you shall possess the origin of all
    poems,
You shall possess the good of the earth and sun, (there are millions of
    suns left,)
You shall no longer take things at second or third hand, nor look
    through the eyes of the dead, nor feed on the spectres in books,   35
You shall not look through my eyes either, nor take things from me,
You shall listen to all sides and filter them from your self.

3

I have heard what the talkers were talking, the talk of the beginning
    and the end,
But I do not talk of the beginning or the end.

There was never any more inception than there is now,   40
Nor any more youth or age than there is now,
And will never be any more perfection than there is now,
Nor any more heaven or hell than there is now.
Urge and urge and urge,
Always the procreant urge of the world.   45

Out of the dimness opposite equals advance, always substance and
    increase, always sex,
Always a knit of identity, always distinction, always a breed of life.

To elaborate is no avail, learn'd and unlearn'd feel that it is so.

Sure as the most certain sure, plumb in the uprights, well entretied,°
    braced in the beams,
Stout as a horse, affectionate, haughty, electrical,   50
I and this mystery here we stand.

Clear and sweet is my soul, and clear and sweet is all that is not my soul.

Lack one lacks both, and the unseen is proved by the seen,
Till that becomes unseen and receives proof in its turn.

Showing the best and dividing it from the worst age vexes age,   55
Knowing the perfect fitness and equanimity of things, while they discuss
    I am silent, and go bathe and admire myself.

Welcome is every organ and attribute of me, and of any man hearty and
    clean,
Not an inch nor a particle of an inch is vile, and none shall be less
    familiar than the rest.

49. entretied: Cross-braced, as between two joists in carpentry.

I am satisfied — I see, dance, laugh, sing;
As the hugging and loving bed-fellow sleeps at my side through the
    night, and withdraws at the peep of the day with stealthy tread,   60
Leaving me baskets cover'd with white towels swelling the house with
    their plenty,
Shall I postpone my acceptation and realization and scream at my eyes,
That they turn from gazing after and down the road,
And forthwith cipher and show me to a cent,
Exactly the value of one and exactly the value of two, and which is
    ahead?   65

• • •

6

A child said *What is the grass?* fetching it to me with full hands;
How could I answer the child? I do not know what it is any more
    than he.   100

I guess it must be the flag of my disposition, out of hopeful green stuff
    woven.

Or I guess it is the handkerchief of the Lord,
A scented gift and remembrancer designedly dropt,
Bearing the owner's name someway in the corners, that we may see and
    remark, and say *Whose?*

Or I guess the grass is itself a child, the produced babe of the vegetation. 105

Or I guess it is a uniform hieroglyphic,
And it means, Sprouting alike in broad zones and narrow zones,
Growing among black folks as among white,
Kanuck,° Tuckahoe,° Congressman, Cuff,° I give them the same,
    I receive them the same.

And now it seems to me the beautiful uncut hair of graves.   110

Tenderly will I use you curling grass,
It may be you transpire from the breasts of young men,
It may be if I had known them I would have loved them,
It may be you are from old people, or from offspring taken soon out of
    their mothers' laps,
And here you are the mothers' laps.   115

109. Kanuck: A French Canadian; **Tuckahoe:** A Virginian living in the tidewa-
ter region and eating tuckahoe, a fungus; **Cuff:** A black person.

This grass is very dark to be from the white heads of old mothers,
Darker than the colorless beards of old men,
Dark to come from under the faint red roofs of mouths.

O I perceive after all so many uttering tongues,
And I perceive they do not come from the roofs of mouths for nothing.   120

I wish I could translate the hints about the dead young men and women,
And the hints about old men and mothers, and the offspring taken soon
    out of their laps.
What do you think has become of the young and old men?
And what do you think has become of the women and children?

They are alive and well somewhere,   125
The smallest sprout shows there is really no death,
And if ever there was it led forward life, and does not wait at the end to
    arrest it,
And ceas'd the moment life appear'd.

All goes onward and outward, nothing collapses,
And to die is different from what any one supposed, and luckier.   130

7

Has any one supposed it lucky to be born?
I hasten to inform him or her it is just as lucky to die, and I know it.

I pass death with the dying and birth with the new-wash'd babe, and am
    not contain'd between my hat and boots,
And peruse manifold objects, no two alike and every one good,
The earth good and the stars good, and their adjuncts all good.   135

I am not an earth nor an adjunct of an earth,
I am the mate and companion of people, all just as immortal and
    fathomless as myself,
(They do not know how immortal, but I know.)

Every kind for itself and its own, for me mine male and female,
For me those that have been boys and that love women,   140
For me the man that is proud and feels how it stings to be slighted,
For me the sweet-heart and the old maid, for me mothers and the
    mothers of mothers,
For me lips that have smiled, eyes that have shed tears,
For me children and the begetters of children.

Undrape! you are not guilty to me, nor stale nor discarded,   145
I see through the broadcloth and gingham whether or no,
And am around, tenacious, acquisitive, tireless, and cannot be
    shaken away.

8

The little one sleeps in its cradle,
I lift the gauze and look a long time, and silently brush away flies with
    my hand.

The youngster and the red-faced girl turn aside up the bushy hill,   150
I peeringly view them from the top.

The suicide sprawls on the bloody floor of the bedroom,
I witness the corpse with its dabbled hair, I note where the pistol has
    fallen.

The blab of the pave, tires of carts, sluff of boot-soles, talk of the
    promenaders,
The heavy omnibus, the driver with his interrogating thumb, the clank
    of the shod horses on the granite floor,   155
The snow-sleighs, clinking, shouted jokes, pelts of snow-balls,
The hurrahs for popular favorites, the fury of rous'd mobs,
The flap of the curtain'd litter, a sick man inside borne to the
    hospital,
The meeting of enemies, the sudden oath, the blows and fall,
The excited crowd, the policeman with his star quickly working his
    passage to the centre of the crowd,   160
The impassive stones that receive and return so many echoes,
What groans of over-fed or half-starv'd who fall sunstruck
    or in fits,
What exclamations of women taken suddenly who hurry home and give
    birth to babes,
What living and buried speech is always vibrating here, what howls
    restrain'd by decorum,
Arrests of criminals, slights, adulterous offers made, acceptances,
    rejections with convex lips,   165
I mind them or the show or resonance of them — I come and I depart.

9

The big doors of the country barn stand open and ready,
The dried grass of the harvest-time loads the slow-drawn
    wagon,
The clear light plays on the brown gray and green intertinged,
The armfuls are pack'd to the sagging mow.   170

I am there, I help, I came stretch'd atop of the load,
I felt its soft jolts, one leg reclined on the other,
I jump from the cross-beams and seize the clover and timothy,
And roll head over heels and tangle my hair full of wisps.

10

Alone far in the wilds and mountains I hunt,   175
Wandering amazed at my own lightness and glee,
In the late afternoon choosing a safe spot to pass the night,
Kindling a fire and broiling the fresh-kill'd game,
Falling asleep on the gather'd leaves with my dog and gun by my side.

The Yankee clipper is under her sky-sails, she cuts the sparkle and scud,   180
My eyes settle the land, I bend at her prow or shout joyously from the
    deck.

The boatmen and clam-diggers arose early and stopt for me,
I tuck'd my trowser-ends in my boots and went and had a good time;
You should have been with us that day round the chowder-kettle.

I saw the marriage of the trapper in the open air in the far west, the
    bride was a red girl,   185
Her father and his friends sat near cross-legged and dumbly smoking,
    they had moccasins to their feet and large thick blankets hanging
    from their shoulders,
On a bank lounged the trapper, he was drest mostly in skins, his
    luxuriant beard and curls protected his neck, he held his bride by the
    hand,
She had long eyelashes, her head was bare, her coarse straight locks
    descended upon her voluptuous limbs and reach'd to her feet.

The runaway slave came to my house and stopt outside,
I heard his motions crackling the twigs of the woodpile,
Through the swung half-door of the kitchen I saw him limpsy and   190
    weak,
And went where he sat on a log and led him in and assured him,
And brought water and fill'd a tub for his sweated body and bruis'd feet,
And gave him a room that enter'd from my own, and gave him some
    coarse clean clothes,
And remember perfectly well his revolving eyes and his awkwardness,   195
And remember putting plasters on the galls of his neck and ankles;
He staid with me a week before he was recuperated and pass'd north,
I had him sit next me at table, my fire-lock lean'd in the corner.

14

The wild gander leads his flock through the cool night,   245
Ya-honk he says, and sounds it down to me like an invitation,
The pert may suppose it meaningless, but I listening close,
Find its purpose and place up there toward the wintry sky.

The sharp-hoof'd moose of the north, the cat on the house-sill, the
   chickadee, the prairie-dog,
The litter of the grunting sow as they tug at her teats,   250
The brood of the turkey-hen and she with her half-spread wings,
I see in them and myself the same old law.

The press of my foot to the earth springs a hundred affections,
They scorn the best I can do to relate them.

I am enamour'd of growing out-doors,   255
Of men that live among cattle or taste of the ocean or woods,
Of the builders and steerers of ships and the wielders of axes and mauls,
   and the drivers of horses,
I can eat and sleep with them week in and week out.

What is commonest, cheapest, nearest, easiest, is Me,
Me going in for my chances, spending for vast returns,   260
Adorning myself to bestow myself on the first that will take me,
Not asking the sky to come down to my good will,
Scattering it freely forever.

21

I am the poet of the Body and I am the poet of the Soul,
The pleasures of heaven are with me and the pains of hell are with me,
The first I graft and increase upon myself, the latter I translate into a
   new tongue.

I am the poet of the woman the same as the man,   425
And I say it is as great to be a woman as to be a man,
And I say there is nothing greater than the mother of men.

I chant the chant of dilation or pride,
We have had ducking and deprecating about enough,
I show that size is only development.   430

Have you outstript the rest? are you the President?
It is a trifle, they will more than arrive there every one, and still
   pass on.

I am he that walks with the tender and growing night,
I call to the earth and sea half-held by the night.

Press close bare-bosom'd night — press close magnetic nourishing
   night!   435
Night of south winds — night of the large few stars!
Still nodding night — mad naked summer night.

Smile O voluptuous cool-breath'd earth!
Earth of the slumbering and liquid trees!
Earth of departed sunset — earth of the mountains misty-topt!   440
Earth of the vitreous pour of the full moon just tinged with blue!
Earth of shine and dark mottling the tide of the river!
Earth of the limpid gray of clouds brighter and clearer for my sake!
Far-swooping elbow'd earth — rich apple-blossom'd earth!
Smile, for your lover comes.   445

Prodigal, you have given me love — therefore I to you give love!
O unspeakable passionate love.

24

Walt Whitman, a kosmos, of Manhattan the son,
Turbulent, fleshy, sensual, eating, drinking and breeding,
No sentimentalist, no stander above men and women or apart from them,
No more modest than immodest.   500

Unscrew the locks from the doors!
Unscrew the doors themselves from their jambs!

Whoever degrades another degrades me,
And whatever is done or said returns at last to me.

Through me the afflatus° surging and surging, through me the current
    and index.   505

I speak the pass-word primeval, I give the sign of democracy,
By God! I will accept nothing which all cannot have their counterpart
    of on the same terms.

Through me many long dumb voices,
Voices of the interminable generations of prisoners and slaves,
Voices of the diseas'd and despairing and of thieves and dwarfs,   510
Voices of cycles of preparation and accretion,
And of the threads that connect the stars, and of wombs and of the
    father-stuff,
And of the rights of them the others are down upon,
Of the deform'd, trivial, flat, foolish, despised,
Fog in the air, beetles rolling balls of dung.   515

Through me forbidden voices,
Voices of sexes and lusts, voices veil'd and I remove the veil,
Voices indecent by me clarified and transfigur'd.

---

505. afflatus: Inspiration (from the Latin for "to blow on").

I do not press my fingers across my mouth,
I keep as delicate around the bowels as around the head and heart,   520
Copulation is no more rank to me than death is.

I believe in the flesh and the appetites,
Seeing, hearing, feeling, are miracles, and each part and tag of me is a
     miracle.

Divine am I inside and out, and I make holy whatever I touch or am
     touch'd from,
The scent of these arm-pits aroma finer than prayer,   525
This head more than churches, bibles, and all the creeds.

If I worship one thing more than another it shall be the spread of my
     own body, or any part of it,
Translucent mould of me it shall be you!
Shaded ledges and rests it shall be you!
Firm masculine colter° it shall be you!   530
Whatever goes to the tilth° of me it shall be you!
You my rich blood! your milky stream pale strippings of my life!
Breast that presses against other breasts it shall be you!
My brain it shall be your occult convolutions!
Root of wash'd sweet-flag! timorous pond-snipe! nest of guarded
     duplicate eggs! it shall be you!   535
Mix'd tussled hay of head, beard, brawn, it shall be you!
Trickling sap of maple, fibre of manly wheat, it shall be you!
Sun so generous it shall be you!
Vapors lighting and shading my face it shall be you!
You sweaty brooks and dews it shall be you!   540
Winds whose soft-tickling genitals rub against me it shall be you!
Broad muscular fields, branches of live oak, loving lounger in my
     winding paths, it shall be you!
Hands I have taken, face I have kiss'd, mortal I have ever touch'd, it shall
     be you.

46

I know I have the best of time and space, and was never measured and
     never will be measured.

I tramp a perpetual journey, (come listen all!)
My signs are a rain-proof coat, good shoes, and a staff cut from the woods,
No friend of mine takes his ease in my chair,

530. colter: Blade or disk on a plow for cutting the earth.
531. tilth: Cultivation of land.

I have no chair, no church, no philosophy,   1205
I lead no man to a dinner-table, library, exchange,
But each man and each woman of you I lead upon a knoll,
My left hand hooking you round the waist,
My right hand pointing to landscapes of continents and the public road.

Not I, not any one else can travel that road for you,   1210
You must travel it for yourself.

It is not far, it is within reach,
Perhaps you have been on it since you were born and did not know,
Perhaps it is everywhere on water and on land.

Shoulder your duds dear son, and I will mine, and let us hasten forth,   1215
Wonderful cities and free nations we shall fetch as we go.

If you tire, give me both burdens, and rest the chuff° of your hand
    on my hip,
And in due time you shall repay the same service to me,
For after we start we never lie by again.

This day before dawn I ascended a hill and look'd at the crowded
    heaven,   1220
And I said to my spirit *When we become the enfolders of those orbs, and
    the pleasure and knowledge of every thing in them, shall we be fill'd and
    satisfied then?*
And my spirit said *No, we but level that lift to pass and continue beyond.*

You are also asking me questions and I hear you,
I answer that I cannot answer, you must find out for yourself.

Sit a while dear son,   1225
Here are biscuits to eat and here is milk to drink,
But as soon as you sleep and renew yourself in sweet clothes, I kiss you
    with a good-by kiss and open the gate for your egress hence.

Long enough have you dream'd contemptible dreams,
Now I wash the gum from your eyes,
You must habit yourself to the dazzle of the light and of every moment
    of your life.   1230

Long have you timidly waded holding a plank by the shore,
Now I will you to be a bold swimmer,
To jump off in the midst of the sea, rise again, nod to me, shout, and
    laughingly dash with your hair.

1217. chuff: Weight.

48

I have said that the soul is not more than the body,
And I have said that the body is not more than the soul,   1270
And nothing, not God, is greater to one than one's self is,
And whoever walks a furlong without sympathy walks to his own
    funeral drest in his shroud,
And I or you pocketless of a dime may purchase the pick of the earth,
And to glance with an eye or show a bean in its pod confounds the
    learning of all times,
And there is no trade or employment but the young man following it
    may become a hero,   1275
And there is no object so soft but it makes a hub for the wheel'd
    universe,
And I say to any man or woman, Let your soul stand cool and composed
    before a million universes.

And I say to mankind, Be not curious about God,
For I who am curious about each am not curious about God,
(No array of terms can say how much I am at peace about God and
    about death.)   1280

I hear and behold God in every object, yet understand God not in the
    least,
Nor do I understand who there can be more wonderful than myself.

Why should I wish to see God better than this day?
I see something of God each hour of the twenty-four, and each
    moment then,
In the faces of men and women I see God, and in my own face in the
    glass,   1285
I find letters from God dropt in the street, and every one is sign'd by
    God's name,
And I leave them where they are, for I know that wheresoe'er I go,
Others will punctually come for ever and ever.

51

The past and present wilt—I have fill'd them, emptied them,
And proceed to fill my next fold of the future.   1320

Listener up there! what have you to confide to me?
Look in my face while I snuff° the sidle° of evening,
(Talk honestly, no one else hears you, and I stay only a minute longer.)

1322. snuff: Snuff out; **sidle:** Sidewise or stealthy movement.

Do I contradict myself?
Very well then I contradict myself,   1325
(I am large, I contain multitudes.)

I concentrate toward them that are nigh, I wait on the door-slab.

Who has done his day's work? who will soonest be through with his
    supper?
Who wishes to walk with me?

Will you speak before I am gone? will you prove already too late?   1330

52

The spotted hawk swoops by and accuses me, he complains of my gab
    and my loitering.

I too am not a bit tamed, I too am untranslatable,
I sound my barbaric yawp over the roofs of the world.

The last scud of day holds back for me,
It flings my likeness after the rest and true as any on the shadow'd wilds, 1335
It coaxes me to the vapor and the dusk.

I depart as air, I shake my white locks at the runaway sun,
I effuse my flesh in eddies, and drift it in lacy jags.

I bequeath myself to the dirt to grow from the grass I love,
If you want me again look for me under your boot-soles.   1340

You will hardly know who I am or what I mean,
But I shall be good health to you nevertheless,
And filter and fibre your blood.

Failing to fetch me at first keep encouraged,
Missing me one place search another,   1345
I stop somewhere waiting for you.

[*1855*/1891–1892]

WALT WHITMAN   [1819–1892]

When Lilacs Last in the Dooryard Bloom'd°

1

When lilacs last in the dooryard bloom'd,
And the great star early droop'd in the western sky in the night,
I mourn'd, and yet shall mourn with ever-returning spring.

Ever-returning spring, trinity sure to me you bring,
Lilac blooming perennial and drooping star in the west,   5
And thought of him I love.

2

O powerful western fallen star!
O shades of night — O moody, tearful night!
O great star disappear'd — O the black murk that hides the star!
O cruel hands that hold me powerless — O helpless soul of me!   10
O harsh surrounding cloud that will not free my soul.

3

In the dooryard fronting an old farm-house near the white-wash'd
    palings,
Stands the lilac-bush tall-growing with heart-shaped leaves of rich
    green,
With many a pointed blossom rising delicate, with the perfume strong
    I love,
With every leaf a miracle — and from this bush in the dooryard,   15
With delicate-color'd blossoms and heart-shaped leaves of rich green,
A sprig with its flower I break.

4

In the swamp in secluded recesses,
A shy and hidden bird is warbling a song.
Solitary the thrush,   20
The hermit withdrawn to himself, avoiding the settlements,
Sings by himself a song.

When Lilacs Last in the Dooryard Bloom'd: This is one of four elegies written
by Whitman on the death of President Abraham Lincoln, 14 April 1865, and first
published as an addendum to *Drum-Taps* called "Sequel to *Drum-Taps*." Whitman
later added the *Drum-Taps* volume to *Leaves of Grass*. The version used here is
from the sixth edition of *Leaves of Grass* (1891–1892).

Song of the bleeding throat,
Death's outlet song of life, (for well dear brother I know,
If thou wast not granted to sing thou would'st surely die.)   25

5

Over the breast of the spring, the land, amid cities,
Amid lanes and through old woods, where lately the violets peep'd from
    the ground, spotting the gray debris,
Amid the grass in the fields each side of the lanes, passing the endless
    grass,
Passing the yellow-spear'd wheat, every grain from its shroud in the
    dark-brown fields uprisen,
Passing the apple-tree blows of white and pink in the orchards,   30
Carrying a corpse to where it shall rest in the grave,
Night and day journeys a coffin.

6

Coffin that passes through lanes and streets,°
Through day and night with the great cloud darkening the land,
With the pomp of the inloop'd flags with the cities draped in black,   35
With the show of the States themselves as of crape-veil'd women standing,
With processions long and winding and the flambeaus° of the night,
With the countless torches lit, with the silent sea of faces and the
    unbared heads,
With the waiting depot, the arriving coffin, and the sombre faces,
With dirges through the night, with the thousand voices rising strong
    and solemn,
With all the mournful voices of the dirges pour'd around the coffin,   40
The dim-lit churches and the shuddering organs — where amid these
    you journey,
With the tolling tolling bells' perpetual clang,
Here, coffin that slowly passes,
I give you my sprig of lilac.   45

7

(Nor for you, for one alone,
Blossoms and branches green to coffins all I bring,
For fresh as the morning, thus would I chant a song for you O sane and
    sacred death.

33. lanes and streets: President Lincoln's funeral procession traveled from
Washington to Springfield, Illinois, with stops at cities and towns to enable people
to honor their assassinated president.
37. flambeaus: Flaming torches.

All over bouquets of roses,
O death, I cover you over with roses and early lilies,   50
But mostly and now the lilac that blooms the first,
Copious I break, I break the sprigs from the bushes,
With loaded arms I come, pouring for you,
For you and the coffins all of you O death.)

8

O western orb sailing the heaven,   55
Now I know what you must have meant as a month since I walk'd,
As I walk'd in silence the transparent shadowy night,
As I saw you had something to tell as you bent to me night after
    night,
As you droop'd from the sky low down as if to my side, (while the other
    stars all look'd on,)
As we wander'd together the solemn night, (for something I know not
    what kept me from sleep,)   60
As the night advanced, and I saw on the rim of the west how full you
    were of woe,
As I stood on the rising ground in the breeze in the cool transparent
    night,
As I watch'd where you pass'd and was lost in the netherward black of
    the night,
As my soul in its trouble dissatisfied sank, as where you sad orb,
Concluded, dropt in the night, and was gone.   65

9

Sing on there in the swamp,
O singer bashful and tender, I hear your notes, I hear your call,
I hear, I come presently, I understand you,
But a moment I linger, for the lustrous star has detain'd me,
The star my departing comrade holds and detains me.   70

10

O how shall I warble myself for the dead one there I loved?
And how shall I deck my song for the large sweet soul that has gone?
And what shall my perfume be for the grave of him I love?

Sea-winds blown from east and west,
Blown from the Eastern sea and blown from the Western sea, till there
    on the prairies meeting,   75
These and with these and the breath of my chant,
I'll perfume the grave of him I love.

11

O what shall I hang on the chamber walls?
And what shall the pictures be that I hang on the walls,
To adorn the burial-house of him I love?   80

Pictures of growing spring and farms and homes,
With the Fourth-month eve at sundown, and the gray smoke lucid and
   bright,
With floods of the yellow gold of the gorgeous, indolent, sinking sun,
   burning, expanding the air,
With the fresh sweet herbage under foot, and the pale green leaves
   of the trees prolific,
In the distance the flowing glaze, the breast of the river, with a
   wind-dapple here and there,   85
With ranging hills on the banks, with many a line against the sky, and
   shadows,
And the city at hand with dwellings so dense, and stacks of
   chimneys,
And all the scenes of life and the workshops, and the workmen
   homeward returning.

12

Lo, body and soul — this land,
My own Manhattan with spires, and the sparkling and hurrying tides,
   and the ships,   90
The varied and ample land, the South and the North in the light, Ohio's
   shores and flashing Missouri,
And ever the far-spreading prairies cover'd with grass and corn.

Lo, the most excellent sun so calm and haughty,
The violet and purple morn with just-felt breezes,
The gentle soft-born measureless light,   95
The miracle spreading, bathing all, the fulfill'd noon,
The coming eve delicious, the welcome night and the stars,
Over my cities shining all, enveloping man and land.

13

Sing on, sing on you gray-brown bird,
Sing from the swamps, the recesses, pour your chant from the bushes,   100
Limitless out of the dusk, out of the cedars and pines.

Sing on dearest brother, warble your reedy song,
Loud human song, with voice of uttermost woe.

O liquid and free and tender!
O wild and loose to my soul — O wondrous singer!   105
You only I hear — yet the star holds me, (but will soon depart,)
Yet the lilac with mastering odor holds me.

14

Now while I sat in the day and look'd forth,
In the close of the day with its light and the fields of spring, and the
    farmers preparing their crops,
In the large unconscious scenery of my land with its lakes and forests,   110
In the heavenly aerial beauty, (after the perturb'd winds and the
    storms,)
Under the arching heavens of the afternoon swift passing, and the
    voices of children and women,
The many-moving sea-tides, and I saw the ships how they sail'd,
And the summer approaching with richness, and the fields all busy with
    labor,
And the infinite separate houses, how they all went on, each with its
    meals and minutia of daily usages,   115
And the streets how their throbbings throbb'd, and the cities pent — lo,
    then and there,
Falling upon them all and among them all, enveloping me with the rest,
Appear'd the cloud, appear'd the long black trail,
And I knew death, its thought, and the sacred knowledge of death.

Then with the knowledge of death as walking one side of me,   120
And the thought of death close-walking the other side of me,
And I in the middle as with companions, and as holding the hands of
    companions,
I fled forth to the hiding receiving night that talks not,
Down to the shores of the water, the path by the swamp in the dimness,
To the solemn shadowy cedars and ghostly pines so still.   125

And the singer so shy to the rest receiv'd me,
The gray-brown bird I know receiv'd us comrades three,
And he sang the carol of death, and a verse for him I love.

From deep secluded recesses,
From the fragrant cedars and the ghostly pines so still,   130
Came the carol of the bird.

And the charm of the carol rapt me,
As I held as if by their hands my comrades in the night,
And the voice of my spirit tallied the song of the bird.

Come lovely and soothing death,   135
Undulate round the world, serenely arriving, arriving,
In the day, in the night, to all, to each,
Sooner or later delicate death.

Prais'd be the fathomless universe,
For life and joy, and for objects and knowledge curious,
And for love, sweet love—but praise! praise! praise!   140
For the sure-enwinding arms of cool-enfolding death.

Dark mother always gliding near with soft feet,
Have none chanted for thee a chant of fullest welcome?
Then I chant it for thee, I glorify thee above all,   145
I bring thee a song that when thou must indeed come, come unfalteringly.

Approach strong deliveress,
When it is so, when thou hast taken them I joyously sing the dead,
Lost in the loving floating ocean of thee,
Laved in the flood of thy bliss O death.   150

From me to thee glad serenades,
Dances for thee I propose saluting thee, adornments and feastings for thee,
And the sights of the open landscape and the high-spread sky are fitting,
And life and the fields, and the huge and thoughtful night.

The night in silence under many a star,   155
The ocean shore and the husky whispering wave whose voice I know,
And the soul turning to thee O vast and well-veil'd death,
And the body gratefully nestling close to thee.

Over the tree-tops I float thee a song,
Over the rising and sinking waves, over the myriad fields and the
    prairies wide,   160
Over the dense-pack'd cities all and the teeming wharves and ways,
I float this carol with joy, with joy to thee O death.

15

To the tally of my soul,
Loud and strong kept up the gray-brown bird,
With pure deliberate notes spreading filling the night.   165

Loud in the pines and cedars dim,
Clear in the freshness moist and the swamp-perfume,
And I with my comrades there in the night.

While my sight that was bound in my eyes unclosed,
As to long panoramas of visions.   170

And I saw askant the armies,
I saw as in noiseless dreams hundreds of battle-flags,
Borne through the smoke of the battles and pierc'd with missiles I
    saw them,
And carried hither and yon through the smoke, and torn and bloody,
And at last but a few shreds left on the staffs, (and all in silence,)   175
And the staffs all splinter'd and broken.

I saw battle-corpses, myriads of them,
And the white skeletons of young men, I saw them,
I saw the debris and debris of all the slain soldiers of the war,
But I saw they were not as was thought,   180
They themselves were fully at rest, they suffer'd not,
The living remain'd and suffer'd, the mother suffer'd,
And the wife and the child and the musing comrade suffer'd,
And the armies that remain'd suffer'd.

16

Passing the visions, passing the night,   185
Passing, unloosing the hold of my comrades' hands,
Passing the song of the hermit bird and the tallying song of my soul,
Victorious song, death's outlet song, yet varying ever-altering song,
As low and wailing, yet clear the notes, rising and falling, flooding
    the night,
Sadly sinking and fainting, as warning and warning, and yet again
    bursting with joy,   190
Covering the earth and filling the spread of the heaven,
As that powerful psalm in the night I heard from recesses,
Passing, I leave thee lilac with heart-shaped leaves,
I leave thee there in the door-yard, blooming, returning with spring.

I cease from my song for thee,   195
From my gaze on thee in the west, fronting the west, communing
    with thee,
O comrade lustrous with silver face in the night.

Yet each to keep and all, retrievements out of the night,
The song, the wondrous chant of the gray-brown bird,
And the tallying chant, the echo arous'd in my soul,   200
With the lustrous and drooping star with the countenance full
    of woe,
With the holders holding my hand nearing the call of the bird,
Comrades mine and I in the midst, and their memory ever to keep, for
    the dead I loved so well,

For the sweetest, wisest soul of all my days and lands — and this for his
    dear sake,
Lilac and star and bird twined with the chant of my soul,   205
There in the fragrant pines and the cedars dusk and dim.

                        [1865; 1891–92]

WALT WHITMAN   [1819–1892]

A Noiseless Patient Spider

A noiseless patient spider,
I mark'd where on a little promontory it stood isolated,
Mark'd how to explore the vacant vast surrounding,
It launch'd forth filament, filament, filament, out of itself,
Ever unreeling them, ever tirelessly speeding them.   5

And you O my soul where you stand,
Surrounded, detached, in measureless oceans of space,
Ceaselessly musing, venturing, throwing, seeking the spheres to connect
    them,
Till the bridge you will need be form'd, till the ductile anchor hold,
Till the gossamer thread you fling catch somewhere, O my soul.   10

                        [1868–1881]

MATTHEW ARNOLD   [1822–1888]

Dover Beach

The sea is calm tonight.
The tide is full, the moon lies fair
Upon the straits; on the French coast the light
Gleams and is gone; the cliffs of England stand,
Glimmering and vast, out in the tranquil bay.   5
Come to the window, sweet is the night-air!
Only, from the long line of spray
Where the sea meets the moon-blanched land,
Listen! you hear the grating roar

Of pebbles which the waves draw back, and fling,   10
At their return, up the high strand,
Begin, and cease, and then again begin,
With tremulous cadence slow, and bring
The eternal note of sadness in.

Sophocles long ago   15
Heard it on the Aegean, and it brought
Into his mind the turbid ebb and flow
Of human misery; we
Find also in the sound a thought,
Hearing it by this distant northern sea.   20

The Sea of Faith
Was once, too, at the full, and round earth's shore
Lay like the folds of a bright girdle furled.
But now I only hear
Its melancholy, long, withdrawing roar,   25
Retreating, to the breath
Of the night-wind, down the vast edges drear
And naked shingles° of the world.   *pebble-covered beaches*

Ah, love, let us be true
To one another! for the world, which seems   30
To lie before us like a land of dreams,
So various, so beautiful, so new,
Hath really neither joy, nor love, nor light,
Nor certitude, nor peace, nor help for pain;
And we are here as on a darkling plain   35
Swept with confused alarms of struggle and flight,
Where ignorant armies clash by night.

                                                                    [*c. 1851;* 1867]

EMILY DICKINSON   [1830–1886]

Wild Nights—Wild Nights!

Wild Nights — Wild Nights!
Were I with thee
Wild Nights should be
Our luxury!

Futile — the Winds —   5
To a Heart in port —
Done with the Compass —
Done with the Chart!

Rowing in Eden —
Ah, the Sea!   10
Might I but moor — Tonight —
In Thee!

[*c. 1861;* 1891]

EMILY DICKINSON   [1830–1886]

I felt a Funeral, in my Brain

I felt a Funeral, in my Brain,
And Mourners to and fro
Kept treading — treading — till it seemed
That Sense was breaking through —

And when they all were seated,   5
A Service, like a Drum —
Kept beating — beating — till I thought
My Mind was going numb —

And then I heard them lift a Box
And creak across my Soul   10
With those same Boots of Lead, again,
Then Space — began to toll,

As all the Heavens were a Bell,
And Being, but an Ear,
And I, and Silence, some strange Race   15
Wrecked, solitary, here —

And then a Plank in Reason, broke,
And I dropped down, and down —
And hit a World, at every plunge,
And Finished knowing — then —   20

[*c. 1861;* 1896]

EMILY DICKINSON   [1830–1886]

Much Madness is divinest Sense

Much Madness is divinest Sense —
To a discerning Eye —
Much Sense — the starkest Madness —
'Tis the Majority
In this, as All, prevail —   5
Assent — and you are sane —
Demur — you're straightway dangerous —
And handled with a Chain —

[c. 1862; 1890]

EMILY DICKINSON   [1830–1886]

I heard a Fly buzz — when I died

I heard a Fly buzz — when I died —
The Stillness in the Room
Was like the Stillness in the Air —
Between the Heaves of Storm —

The Eyes around — had wrung them dry —   5
And Breaths were gathering firm
For that last Onset — when the King
Be witnessed — in the Room —

I willed my Keepsakes — Signed away
What portion of me be   10
Assignable — and then it was
There interposed a Fly —

With Blue — uncertain stumbling Buzz —
Between the light — and me —
And then the Windows failed — and then   15
I could not see to see —

[c. 1862; 1890]

EMILY DICKINSON   [1830–1886]

I like to see it lap the Miles

I like to see it lap the Miles—
And lick the Valleys up—
And stop to feed itself at Tanks—
And then—prodigious step

Around a Pile of Mountains—   5
And supercilious peer
In Shanties—by the sides of Roads—
And then a Quarry pare

To fit its Ribs
And crawl between   10
Complaining all the while
In horrid—hooting stanza—
Then chase itself down Hill—

And neigh like Boanerges°—
Then—punctual as a Star   15
Stop—docile and omnipotent
At its own stable door—

[*c. 1862;* 1891]

14. like Boanerges: As loud as thunder. *Boanerges* is the surname given by Jesus to James and John in Mark 3:17, translated there as "the sons of thunder."

EMILY DICKINSON   [1830–1886]

Because I could not stop for Death

Because I could not stop for Death—
He kindly stopped for me—
The Carriage held but just Ourselves—
And Immortality.

We slowly drove—He knew no haste   5
And I had put away
My labor and my leisure too,
For His Civility—

We passed the School, where Children strove
At Recess — in the Ring —   10
We passed the Fields of Gazing Grain —
We passed the Setting Sun —

Or rather — He passed Us —
The Dews drew quivering and chill —
For only Gossamer, my Gown —   15
My Tippet° — only Tulle° —   *scarf/silk net*

We paused before a House that seemed
A Swelling of the Ground —
The Roof was scarcely visible —
The Cornice — in the Ground —   20

Since then —'tis Centuries — and yet
Feels shorter than the Day
I first surmised the Horses' Heads
Were toward Eternity —

[*c. 1863;* 1890]

CHRISTINA ROSSETTI   [1830–1894]

Song

When I am dead, my dearest,
    Sing no sad songs for me;
Plant thou no roses at my head,
    Nor shady cypress tree:
Be the green grass above me   5
    With showers and dewdrops wet;
And if thou wilt, remember,
    And if thou wilt, forget.

I shall not see the shadows,
    I shall not feel the rain;   10
I shall not hear the nightingale
    Sing on, as if in pain:
And dreaming through the twilight
    That doth not rise nor set,
Haply I may remember,   15
    And haply may forget.

[1862]

THOMAS HARDY   [1840–1928]

The Convergence of the Twain

Lines on the Loss of the Titanic°

1

In a solitude of the sea
Deep from human vanity,
And the Pride of Life that planned her, stilly couches she.

2

Steel chambers, late the pyres
Of her salamandrine° fires,   5
Cold currents thrid,° and turn to rhythmic tidal lyres.   *thread*

3

Over the mirrors meant
To glass the opulent
The sea-worm crawls — grotesque, slimed, dumb, indifferent.

4

Jewels in joy designed   10
To ravish the sensuous mind
Lie lightless, all their sparkles bleared and black and blind.

5

Dim moon-eyed fishes near
Gaze at the gilded gear
And query: "What does this vaingloriousness down here?"   15

6

Well: while was fashioning
This creature of cleaving wing,
The Immanent Will that stirs and urges everything

Titanic: A famous luxury ocean liner, largest of its time and considered unsink-
able. It collided with an iceberg on its maiden voyage, 15 April 1912, and sank. Of
some 2,200 people aboard, more than 1,500 were lost.
5. salamandrine: Fierce, inextinguishable (the lizardlike salamander supposedly
is able to resist or live in fire).

7

Prepared a sinister mate
For her — so gaily great —
A Shape of Ice, for the time far and dissociate.   20

8

And as the smart ship grew
In stature, grace, and hue,
In shadowy silent distance grew the Iceberg too.

9

Alien they seemed to be: 25
No mortal eye could see
The intimate welding of their later history,

10

Or sign that they were bent
By paths coincident
On being anon twin halves of one august event,   30

11

Till the Spinner of the Years
Said "Now!" And each one hears,
And consummation comes, and jars two hemispheres.

[1912]

GERARD MANLEY HOPKINS   [1844–1889]

God's Grandeur

The world is charged with the grándeur of God.
  It will flame out, like shining from shook foil;°   *shaken gold foil*
  It gathers to a greatness, like the ooze of oil°   *(from olives)*
Crushed. Why do men then now not reck° his rod°?   *recognize / discipline*
Génerátions have trod, have trod, have trod;   5
  And all is seared with trade; bleared, smeared, with toil;
  And wears man's smudge and shares man's smell: the soil
Is bare now, nor can foot feel, being shod.

Ánd, for° all this, náture is never spent;   *despite*
  There lives the dearest freshness deep down things;   10
And though the last lights off the black West went
  Oh, morning, at the brown brink eastward, springs—
Because the Holy Ghost óver the bent
  World broods with warm breast and with ah! bright wings.

[*1877;* 1918]

GERARD MANLEY HOPKINS   [1844–1889]

Pied° Beauty   *multicolored, variegated*

Glóry be to God for dappled things—
  For skies of couple-colour as a brinded° cow;   *streaked*
    For rose-moles all in stipple upon trout that swim;
Fresh-firecoal chestnut-fálls; fínches' wings;
  Lándscape plotted and pieced—fold, fallow, and plough;   5
    And áll trádes, their gear and tackle and trim.

All things counter, original, spáre, stránge;
  Whatever is fickle, freckled (who knows how?)
    With swift, slow; sweet, sour; adazzle, dim;
He fathers-forth whose beauty is pást chánge: 10
              Práise hím.

[*1877;* 1918]

GERARD MANLEY HOPKINS   [1844–1889]

Spring and Fall

to a young child

Márgarét, áre you gríeving
Over Goldengrove unleaving?
Leáves, líke the things of mán, you
With your fresh thoughts care for, can you?
Áh! ás the héart grows ólder   5
It will come to such sights colder
By and by, nor spare a sigh

Though worlds of wanwood leafmeal° lie;
And yet you *will* weep and know why.
Now no matter, child, the name: 10
Sórrow's spríngs áre the sáme.
Nor mouth had, no nor mind, expressed
What héart héard of, ghóst° guéssed: *spirit*
It ís the blíght man was bórn for,
It is Margaret you mourn for.   15

[*1880;* 1918]

8. **wanwood leafmeal:** Colorless forest with scattered leaves.

A. E. HOUSMAN   [1859–1936]

Loveliest of trees, the cherry now

Loveliest of trees, the cherry now
Is hung with bloom along the bough,
And stands about the woodland ride
Wearing white for Eastertide.

Now, of my threescore years and ten,   5
Twenty will not come again,
And take from seventy springs a score,
It only leaves me fifty more.

And since to look at things in bloom
Fifty springs are little room,   10
About the woodlands I will go
To see the cherry hung with snow.

[1896]

A. E. HOUSMAN   [1859–1936]

To an Athlete Dying Young

The time you won your town the race
We chaired you through the market-place;
Man and boy stood cheering by,
And home we brought you shoulder-high.

To-day, the road all runners come,   5
Shoulder-high we bring you home,
And set you at your threshold down,
Townsman of a stiller town.

Smart lad, to slip betimes away
From fields where glory does not stay   10
And early though the laurel grows
It withers quicker than the rose.

Eyes the shady night has shut
Cannot see the record cut,°   *broken*
And silence sounds no worse than cheers   15
After earth has stopped the ears:

Now you will not swell the rout
Of lads that wore their honours out,
Runners whom renown outran
And the name died before the man.   20

So set, before its echoes fade,
The fleet foot on the sill of shade,
And hold to the low lintel up
The still-defended challenge-cup.

And round that early-laurelled head   25
Will flock to gaze the strengthless dead,
And find unwithered on its curls
The garland briefer than a girl's.

[1896]

WILLIAM BUTLER YEATS   [1865–1939]

The Lake Isle of Innisfree

I will arise and go now, and go to Innisfree,
And a small cabin build there, of clay and wattles made:
Nine bean-rows will I have there, a hive for the honey-bee,
And live alone in the bee-loud glade.

And I shall have some peace there, for peace comes dropping slow,   5
Dropping from the veils of the morning to where the cricket sings;
There midnight's all a glimmer, and noon a purple glow,
And evening full of the linnet's wings.

I will arise and go now, for always night and day
I hear lake water lapping with low sounds by the shore;   10
While I stand on the roadway, or on the pavements grey,
I hear it in the deep heart's core.

[1892]

WILLIAM BUTLER YEATS   [1865–1939]

The Second Coming°

Turning and turning in the widening gyre
The falcon cannot hear the falconer;
Things fall apart; the centre cannot hold;
Mere anarchy is loosed upon the world,
The blood-dimmed tide is loosed, and everywhere   5
The ceremony of innocence is drowned;
The best lack all conviction, while the worst
Are full of passionate intensity.

Surely some revelation is at hand;
Surely the Second Coming is at hand.   10
The Second Coming! Hardly are those words out
When a vast image out of *Spiritus Mundi*°
Troubles my sight: somewhere in sands of the desert
A shape with lion body and the head of a man,
A gaze blank and pitiless as the sun,   15
Is moving its slow thighs, while all about it
Reel shadows of the indignant desert birds.

The Second Coming: Alludes to Matthew 24:3–44, on the return of Christ at the
end of the present age. Yeats viewed history as a series of 2,000-year cycles
(imaged as gyres, cone-shaped motions). The birth of Christ in Bethlehem
brought to an end the cycle that ran from the Babylonians through the Greeks and
Romans. The approach of the year 2000, then, anticipated for Yeats the end of
another era (the Christian age). Yeats wrote this poem shortly after the Russian
Revolution of 1917 (lines 4–8), which may have confirmed his sense of imminent
change and of a new beginning of an unpredictable nature (Yeats expected the
new era to be violent and despotic).
12. *Spiritus Mundi:* Latin, "the spirit of the universe." Yeats believed in a Great
Memory, a universal storehouse of symbolic images from the past. Individuals,
drawing on it for images, are put in touch with the soul of the universe.

The darkness drops again; but now I know
That twenty centuries of stony sleep
Were vexed to nightmare by a rocking cradle,   20
And what rough beast, its hour come round at last,
Slouches towards Bethlehem to be born?

[1921]

WILLIAM BUTLER YEATS   [1865–1939]

Leda and the Swan°

A sudden blow: the great wings beating still
Above the staggering girl, her thighs caressed
By the dark webs, her nape caught in his bill,
He holds her helpless breast upon his breast.

How can those terrified vague fingers push   5
The feathered glory from her loosening thighs?
And how can body, laid in that white rush,
But feel the strange heart beating where it lies?

A shudder in the loins engenders there
The broken wall, the burning roof and tower   10
And Agamemnon dead.
                              Being so caught up,
So mastered by the brute blood of the air,
Did she put on his knowledge with his power
Before the indifferent beak could let her drop?   15

[1928]

Leda and the Swan: In Greek mythology, Leda was seduced (or raped) by Zeus, who approached her in the form of a swan. She gave birth to Helen, whose abduction by Paris gave rise to the Trojan War (referred to in line 10). The Greek forces were headed by Agamemnon, who was killed (line 11) upon his return to Greece by his wife Clytemnestra, daughter of Leda by her husband, Tyndareus. Yeats regarded Zeus's visit as a "violent annunciation" of the founding of Greek civilization, with parallels to the annunciation to Mary (Luke 1:26–38), 2,000 years later, of the coming of the Christian age. See the note to "The Second Coming" for Yeats's view of historical eras (p. 103).

WILLIAM BUTLER YEATS   [1865–1939]

Among School Children°

1

I walk through the long schoolroom questioning;
A kind old nun in a white hood replies;
The children learn to cipher° and to sing,   *do arithmetic*
To study reading-books and history,
To cut and sew, be neat in everything   5
In the best modern way — the children's eyes
In momentary wonder stare upon
A sixty-year-old smiling public man.

2

I dream of a Ledaean° body, bent
Above a sinking fire, a tale that she   10
Told of a harsh reproof, or trivial event
That changed some childish day to tragedy —
Told, and it seemed that our two natures blent
Into a sphere from youthful sympathy,
Or else, to alter Plato's parable,   15
Into the yolk and white of the one shell.°

3

And thinking of that fit of grief or rage
I look upon one child or t'other there
And wonder if she stood so at that age —

Among School Children: In February 1926, Yeats visited a Montessori school as
part of his duties as a senator. In March he wrote in his diary the following topic
for a poem: "School children and the thought that life will waste them, perhaps
that no possible life can fulfill their own dreams or even their teacher's hope.
Bring in the old thought that life prepares for what never happens."
9. Ledaean: Helen-like (referring to Helen, daughter of Leda — see the note to
"Leda and the Swan," page 104). Here and in lines 19–28 Yeats was thinking of
Maud Gonne, a beautiful actress and Irish nationalist whom he loved desperately
for many years but who refused to marry him.
16. Into . . . shell: To explain love, in Plato's *Symposium*, Aristophanes describes
primeval humans as round with "four hands and four feet, back and sides forming
a circle, one head with two faces." Fearful of their power, Zeus cut them in two, as
one would divide an egg. After separation, each half desired to be reunited with its
opposite: "Each of us is . . . but the half of a human being, . . . forever seeking his
missing half."

For even daughters of the swan can share   20
Something of every paddler's heritage—
And had that colour upon cheek or hair,
And thereupon my heart is driven wild:
She stands before me as a living child.

4

Her present image floats into the mind—   25
Did Quattrocento° finger fashion it
Hollow of cheek as though it drank the wind
And took a mess of shadows for its meat?
And I though never of Ledaean kind
Had pretty plumage once—enough of that,   30
Better to smile on all that smile, and show
There is a comfortable kind of old scarecrow.

5

What youthful mother, a shape upon her lap
Honey of generation had betrayed,°
And that must sleep, shriek, struggle to escape   35
As recollection or the drug decide,
Would think her son, did she but see that shape
With sixty or more winters on its head,
A compensation for the pang of his birth,
Or the uncertainty of his setting forth?   40

6

Plato thought nature but a spume that plays
Upon a ghostly paradigm of things;°

---

26. Quattrocento: The fifteenth century, as a period in Italian art and literature.
34. Honey . . . betrayed: Yeats wrote in a note, "I have taken the 'honey of generation' from Porphyry's essay on 'The Cave of the Nymphs' but find no warrant in Porphyry for considering it the 'drug' that destroys the 'recollection' of pre-natal freedom." Porphyry (a third-century Neoplatonic philosopher) described the sweetness of honey as allegorically representing "the pleasure arising from copulation." For Yeats, however, the honey of generation seems to blot out the memory of prenatal happiness, thus "betraying" an infant into consenting to be born into this world.
41–42. but . . . things: Plato thought that the world of nature is merely an appearance ("spume") that covers the world of ideal, spiritual and mathematical realities ("ghostly paradigm").

Solider Aristotle played the taws
Upon the bottom of a king of kings;°
World-famous golden-thighed Pythagoras°   45
Fingered upon a fiddle-stick or strings
What a star sang and careless Muses heard:
Old clothes upon old sticks to scare a bird.°

7

Both nuns and mothers worship images,°
But those the candles light are not as those   50
That animate a mother's reveries,
But keep a marble or a bronze repose.
And yet they too break hearts — O Presences
That passion, piety or affection knows,
And that all heavenly glory symbolize —   55
O self-born mockers of man's enterprise;

8

Labour is blossoming or dancing where
The body is not bruised to pleasure soul,
Nor beauty born out of its own despair,
Nor blear-eyed wisdom out of midnight oil.   60
O chestnut-tree, great-rooted blossomer,
Are you the leaf, the blossom or the bole?°   *trunk*
O body swayed to music, O brightening glance,
How can we know the dancer from the dance?

[1928]

43–44. Solider . . . kings: Aristotle, who was tutor to Alexander the Great and presumably disciplined him by whippings ("played the taws"), was "solider" than Plato in that he believed that nature itself had reality.
45. Pythagoras: Greek philosopher (6th century B.C.E.) whose study of mathematics and music supposedly led to his discovery of the music of the spheres, the harmonies that hold the universe in order.
48. Old . . . bird: Yeats's dismissal of the three philosophers just named.
49. nuns . . . images: Nuns worship religious images; mothers worship mental images of their own children.

WILLIAM BUTLER YEATS   [1865–1939]

Sailing to Byzantium°

1

That is no country for old men. The young
In one another's arms, birds in the trees
— Those dying generations — at their song,
The salmon-falls, the mackerel-crowded seas,
Fish, flesh, or fowl, commend all summer long   5
Whatever is begotten, born, and dies.
Caught in that sensual music all neglect
Monuments of unaging intellect.

2

An aged man is but a paltry thing,
A tattered coat upon a stick, unless   10
Soul clap its hands and sing, and louder sing
For every tatter in its mortal dress,
Nor is there singing school but studying
Monuments of its own magnificence;
And therefore I have sailed the seas and come   15
To the holy city of Byzantium.

3

O sages standing in God's holy fire
As in the gold mosaic of a wall,
Come from the holy fire, perne in a gyre,°

Sailing to Byzantium: Yeats wrote in *A Vision* (1925): "I think if I could be given
a month of Antiquity and leave to spend it where I chose, I would spend it in
Byzantium [modern Istanbul] a little before Justinian [ruled 527 to 565] opened
St. Sophia and closed the Academy of Plato. . . . I think that in early Byzantium,
and maybe never before or since in recorded history, religious, aesthetic and practical life were one, and that architect and artificers . . . spoke to the multitude and
the few alike. The painter and the mosaic worker, the worker in gold and silver, the
illuminator of Sacred Books were almost impersonal, almost perhaps without
the consciousness of individual design, absorbed in their subject matter and that
the vision of a whole people" (3.3). Byzantium becomes for Yeats a symbol of eternity, a place of perfection where the growth and change that characterize nature
and physical life do not occur.
19. gyre: Whirl in a spiral motion (a *perne* is a spool or bobbin on which something is wound; a *gyre* is a spiral).

And be the singing-masters of my soul.   20
Consume my heart away; sick with desire
And fastened to a dying animal
It knows not what it is; and gather me
Into the artifice of eternity.

4

Once out of nature I shall never take   25
My bodily form from any natural thing,
But such a form as Grecian goldsmiths make
Of hammered gold and gold enamelling
To keep a drowsy Emperor awake;°
Or set upon a golden bough to sing   30
To lords and ladies of Byzantium
Of what is past, or passing, or to come.

[1928]

25–29. Yeats wrote in a note, "I have read somewhere that in the Emperor's palace at Byzantium was a tree made of gold and silver, and artificial birds that sang." He may have been thinking of Hans Christian Andersen's *The Emperor's Nightingale.*

EDWIN ARLINGTON ROBINSON   [1869–1935]

Richard Cory

Whenever Richard Cory went down town,
We people on the pavement looked at him:
He was a gentleman from sole to crown,
Clean favored, and imperially slim.

And he was always quietly arrayed,   5
And he was always human when he talked;
But still he fluttered pulses when he said,
"Good-morning," and he glittered when he walked.

And he was rich — yes, richer than a king —
And admirably schooled in every grace: 10
In fine, we thought that he was everything
To make us wish that we were in his place.

So on we worked, and waited for the light,
And went without the meat, and cursed the bread;

And Richard Cory, one calm summer night,   15
Went home and put a bullet through his head.

[1897]

STEPHEN CRANE   [1871–1900]

Do not weep, maiden, for war is kind

Do not weep, maiden, for war is kind.
Because your lover threw wild hands toward the sky
And the affrighted steed ran on alone,
Do not weep.
War is kind.   5

    Hoarse, booming drums of the regiment,
    Little souls who thirst for fight,
    These men were born to drill and die.
    The unexplained glory flies above them,
    Great is the Battle-God, great, and his Kingdom—   10
    A field where a thousand corpses lie.

Do not weep, babe, for war is kind.
Because your father tumbled in the yellow trenches,
Raged at his breast, gulped and died,
Do not weep.   15
War is kind.

    Swift blazing flag of the regiment,
    Eagle with crest of red and gold,
    These men were born to drill and die.
    Point for them the virtue of slaughter,   20
    Make plain to them the excellence of killing
    And a field where a thousand corpses lie.

Mother whose heart hung humble as a button
On the bright splendid shroud of your son,
Do not weep.   25
War is kind.

[1899]

PAUL LAURENCE DUNBAR   [1872–1906]

We Wear the Mask

We wear the mask that grins and lies,
It hides our cheeks and shades our eyes, —
This debt we pay to human guile;
With torn and bleeding hearts we smile,
And mouth with myriad subtleties.   5

Why should the world be over-wise,
In counting all our tears and sighs?
Nay, let them only see us, while
   We wear the mask.

We smile, but, O great Christ, our cries   10
To thee from tortured souls arise.
We sing, but oh the clay is vile
Beneath our feet, and long the mile;
But let the world dream otherwise,
   We wear the mask!   15

[1896]

ROBERT FROST   [1874–1963]

After Apple-Picking

My long two-pointed ladder's sticking through a tree
Toward heaven still,
And there's a barrel that I didn't fill
Beside it, and there may be two or three
Apples I didn't pick upon some bough.   5
But I am done with apple-picking now.
Essence of winter sleep is on the night,
The scent of apples: I am drowsing off.
I cannot rub the strangeness from my sight
I got from looking through a pane of glass   10
I skimmed this morning from the drinking trough
And held against the world of hoary grass.
It melted, and I let it fall and break.
But I was well

Upon my way to sleep before it fell,   15
And I could tell
What form my dreaming was about to take.
Magnified apples appear and disappear,
Stem end and blossom end,
And every fleck of russet showing clear.   20
My instep arch not only keeps the ache,
It keeps the pressure of a ladder-round.
I feel the ladder sway as the boughs bend.
And I keep hearing from the cellar bin
The rumbling sound   25
Of load on load of apples coming in.
For I have had too much
Of apple-picking: I am overtired
Of the great harvest I myself desired.
There were ten thousand thousand fruit to touch,   30
Cherish in hand, lift down, and not let fall.
For all
That struck the earth,
No matter if not bruised or spiked with stubble,
Went surely to the cider-apple heap   35
As of no worth.
One can see what will trouble
This sleep of mine, whatever sleep it is.
Were he not gone,
The woodchuck could say whether it's like his   40
Long sleep, as I describe its coming on,
Or just some human sleep.

[1914]

ROBERT FROST   [1874–1963]

The Road Not Taken

Two roads diverged in a yellow wood,
And sorry I could not travel both
And be one traveler, long I stood
And looked down one as far as I could
To where it bent in the undergrowth;   5

Then took the other, as just as fair,
And having perhaps the better claim,

Because it was grassy and wanted wear;
Though as for that, the passing there
Had worn them really about the same,   10

And both that morning equally lay
In leaves no step had trodden black.
Oh, I kept the first for another day!
Yet knowing how way leads on to way,
I doubted if I should ever come back.   15

I shall be telling this with a sigh
Somewhere ages and ages hence:
Two roads diverged in a wood, and I —
I took the one less traveled by,
And that has made all the difference.   20

[1916]

ROBERT FROST   [1874–1963]

Birches

When I see birches bend to left and right
Across the lines of straighter darker trees,
I like to think some boy's been swinging them.
But swinging doesn't bend them down to stay
As ice storms do. Often you must have seen them   5
Loaded with ice a sunny winter morning
After a rain. They click upon themselves
As the breeze rises, and turn many-colored
As the stir cracks and crazes their enamel.
Soon the sun's warmth makes them shed crystal shells   10
Shattering and avalanching on the snow crust —
Such heaps of broken glass to sweep away
You'd think the inner dome of heaven had fallen.
They are dragged to the withered bracken by the load,
And they seem not to break; though once they are bowed   15
So low for long, they never right themselves:
You may see their trunks arching in the woods
Years afterwards, trailing their leaves on the ground
Like girls on hands and knees that throw their hair
Before them over their heads to dry in the sun.   20
But I was going to say when Truth broke in

With all her matter of fact about the ice storm,
I should prefer to have some boy bend them
As he went out and in to fetch the cows —
Some boy too far from town to learn baseball,   25
Whose only play was what he found himself,
Summer or winter, and could play alone.
One by one he subdued his father's trees
By riding them down over and over again
Until he took the stiffness out of them,   30
And not one but hung limp, not one was left
For him to conquer. He learned all there was
To learn about not launching out too soon
And so not carrying the tree away
Clear to the ground. He always kept his poise   35
To the top branches, climbing carefully
With the same pains you use to fill a cup
Up to the brim, and even above the brim.
Then he flung outward, feet first, with a swish,
Kicking his way down through the air to the ground.   40
So was I once myself a swinger of birches.
And so I dream of going back to be.
It's when I'm weary of considerations,
And life is too much like a pathless wood
Where your face burns and tickles with the cobwebs   45
Broken across it, and one eye is weeping
From a twig's having lashed across it open.
I'd like to get away from earth awhile
And then come back to it and begin over.
May no fate willfully misunderstand me   50
And half grant what I wish and snatch me away
Not to return. Earth's the right place for love:
I don't know where it's likely to go better.
I'd like to go by climbing a birch tree,
And climb black branches up a snow-white trunk   55
Toward heaven, till the tree could bear no more,
But dipped its top and set me down again.
That would be good both going and coming back.
One could do worse than be a swinger of birches.

[1916]

ROBERT FROST   [1874–1963]

"Out, Out —"

The buzz saw snarled and rattled in the yard
And made dust and dropped stove-length sticks of wood,
Sweet-scented stuff when the breeze drew across it.
And from there those that lifted eyes could count
Five mountain ranges one behind the other   5
Under the sunset far into Vermont.
And the saw snarled and rattled, snarled and rattled,
As it ran light, or had to bear a load.
And nothing happened: day was all but done.
Call it a day, I wish they might have said   10
To please the boy by giving him the half hour
That a boy counts so much when saved from work.
His sister stood beside them in her apron
To tell them "Supper." At the word, the saw,
As if to prove saws knew what supper meant,   15
Leaped out at the boy's hand, or seemed to leap —
He must have given the hand. However it was,
Neither refused the meeting. But the hand!
The boy's first outcry was a rueful laugh,
As he swung toward them holding up the hand,   20
Half in appeal, but half as if to keep
The life from spilling. Then the boy saw all —
Since he was old enough to know, big boy
Doing a man's work, though a child at heart —
He saw all spoiled. "Don't let him cut my hand off —   25
The doctor, when he comes. Don't let him, sister!"
So. But the hand was gone already.
The doctor put him in the dark of ether.
He lay and puffed his lips out with his breath.
And then — the watcher at his pulse took fright.   30
No one believed. They listened at his heart.
Little — less — nothing! — and that ended it.
No more to build on there. And they, since they
Were not the one dead, turned to their affairs.

[1916]

ROBERT FROST   [1874–1963]

Stopping by Woods on a Snowy Evening

Whose woods these are I think I know.
His house is in the village, though;
He will not see me stopping here
To watch his woods fill up with snow.

My little horse must think it queer   5
To stop without a farmhouse near
Between the woods and frozen lake
The darkest evening of the year.

He gives his harness bells a shake
To ask if there is some mistake.   10
The only other sound's the sweep
Of easy wind and downy flake.

The woods are lovely, dark, and deep,
But I have promises to keep,
And miles to go before I sleep,   15
And miles to go before I sleep.

[1923]

ROBERT FROST   [1874–1963]

Design

I found a dimpled spider, fat and white,
On a white heal-all, holding up a moth
Like a white piece of rigid satin cloth —
Assorted characters of death and blight
Mixed ready to begin the morning right,   5
Like the ingredients of a witches' broth —
A snow-drop spider, a flower like a froth,
And dead wings carried like a paper kite.

What had that flower to do with being white,
The wayside blue and innocent heal-all?   10
What brought the kindred spider to that height,
Then steered the white moth thither in the night?
What but design of darkness to appall? —
If design govern in a thing so small.

[1936]

GERTRUDE STEIN   [1874–1946]

Susie Asado

Sweet sweet sweet sweet sweet tea.
   Susie Asado.
Sweet sweet sweet sweet sweet tea.
   Susie Asado.
Susie Asado which is a told tray sure.   5
A lean on the shoe this means slips slips hers.
When the ancient light grey is clean it is yellow, it is a silver seller.
This is a please this is a please there are the saids to jelly. These are
the wets these say the sets to leave a crown to Incy.
   Incy is short for incubus.
A pot. A pot is a beginning of a rare bit of trees. Trees tremble, the
old vats are in bobbles, bobbles which shade and shove and render
clean, render clean must.   10
    Drink pups.
   Drink pups drink pups lease a sash hold, see it shine and a bobolink
has pins. It shows a nail.
   What is a nail. A nail is unison.
   Sweet sweet sweet sweet sweet tea.

[1913]

WALLACE STEVENS   [1879–1955]

The Emperor of Ice-Cream

Call the roller of big cigars,
The muscular one, and bid him whip
In kitchen cups concupiscent curds.
Let the wenches dawdle in such dress
As they are used to wear, and let the boys   5
Bring flowers in last month's newspapers.
Let be be finale of seem.
The only emperor is the emperor of ice-cream.

Take from the dresser of deal,°
Lacking the three glass knobs, that sheet   10
On which she embroidered fantails once

9. **deal:** Fir or pine wood.

And spread it so as to cover her face.
If her horny feet protrude, they come
To show how cold she is, and dumb.
Let the lamp affix its beam.   15
The only emperor is the emperor of ice-cream.

[1923]

WALLACE STEVENS   [1879–1955]

Disillusionment of Ten O'Clock

The houses are haunted
By white night-gowns.
None are green,
Or purple with green rings,
Or green with yellow rings,   5
Or yellow with blue rings.
None of them are strange,
With socks of lace
And beaded ceintures.°   *girdles*
People are not going   10
To dream of baboons and periwinkles.
Only, here and there, an old sailor,
Drunk and asleep in his boots,
Catches tigers
In red weather.   15

[1923]

WALLACE STEVENS   [1879–1955]

Sunday Morning

I

Complacencies of the peignoir,° and late   *negligee*
Coffee and oranges in a sunny chair,
And the green freedom of a cockatoo
Upon a rug mingle to dissipate
The holy hush of ancient sacrifice.   5
She dreams a little, and she feels the dark

Encroachment of that old catastrophe,
As a calm darkens among water-lights.
The pungent oranges and bright, green wings
Seem things in some procession of the dead,   10
Winding across wide water, without sound.
The day is like wide water, without sound,
Stilled for the passing of her dreaming feet
Over the seas, to silent Palestine,
Dominion of the blood and sepulchre.   15

II

Why should she give her bounty to the dead?
What is divinity if it can come
Only in silent shadows and in dreams?
Shall she not find in comforts of the sun,
In pungent fruit and bright, green wings, or else   20
In any balm or beauty of the earth,
Things to be cherished like the thought of heaven?
Divinity must live within herself:
Passions of rain, or moods in falling snow;
Grievings in loneliness, or unsubdued   25
Elations when the forest blooms; gusty
Emotions on wet roads on autumn nights;
All pleasures and all pains, remembering
The bough of summer and the winter branch.
These are the measures destined for her soul.   30

III

Jove in the clouds had his inhuman birth.
No mother suckled him, no sweet land gave
Large-mannered motions to his mythy mind
He moved among us, as a muttering king,
Magnificent, would move among his hinds,   35
Until our blood, commingling, virginal,
With heaven, brought such requital to desire
The very hinds discerned it, in a star.
Shall our blood fail? Or shall it come to be
The blood of paradise? And shall the earth   40
Seem all of paradise that we shall know?
The sky will be much friendlier then than now,
A part of labor and a part of pain,
And next in glory to enduring love,
Not this dividing and indifferent blue.   45

IV

She says, "I am content when wakened birds,
Before they fly, test the reality
Of misty fields, by their sweet questionings;
But when the birds are gone, and their warm fields
Return no more, where, then, is paradise?"   50
There is not any haunt of prophecy,
Nor any old chimera of the grave,
Neither the golden underground, nor isle
Melodious, where spirits gat° them home,   *got*
Nor visionary south, nor cloudy palm   55
Remote on heaven's hill, that has endured
As April's green endures; or will endure
Like her remembrance of awakened birds,
Or her desire for June and evening, tipped
By the consummation of the swallow's wings.   60

V

She says, "But in contentment I still feel
The need of some imperishable bliss."
Death is the mother of beauty; hence from her,
Alone, shall come fulfilment to our dreams
And our desires. Although she strews the leaves   65
Of sure obliteration on our paths,
The path sick sorrow took, the many paths
Where triumph rang its brassy phrase, or love
Whispered a little out of tenderness,
She makes the willow shiver in the sun   70
For maidens who were wont to sit and gaze
Upon the grass, relinquished to their feet.
She causes boys to pile new plums and pears
On disregarded plate. The maidens taste
And stray impassioned in the littering leaves.   75

VI

Is there no change of death in paradise?
Does ripe fruit never fall? Or do the boughs
Hang always heavy in that perfect sky,
Unchanging, yet so like our perishing earth,
With rivers like our own that seek for seas   80
They never find, the same receding shores
That never touch with inarticulate pang?
Why set the pear upon those river-banks

Or spice the shores with odors of the plum?
Alas, that they should wear our colors there,   85
The silken weavings of our afternoons,
And pick the strings of our insipid lutes!
Death is the mother of beauty, mystical,
Within whose burning bosom we devise
Our earthly mothers waiting, sleeplessly.   90

VII

Supple and turbulent, a ring of men
Shall chant in orgy on a summer morn
Their boisterous devotion to the sun,
Not as a god, but as a god might be,
Naked among them, like a savage source.   95
Their chant shall be a chant of paradise,
Out of their blood, returning to the sky;
And in their chant shall enter, voice by voice,
The windy lake wherein their lord delights,
The trees, like serafin,° and echoing hills,   *seraphim* 100
That choir among themselves long afterward.
They shall know well the heavenly fellowship
Of men that perish and of summer morn.
And whence they came and whither they shall go
The dew upon their feet shall manifest.   105

VIII

She hears, upon that water without sound,
A voice that cries, "The tomb in Palestine
Is not the porch of spirits lingering.
It is the grave of Jesus, where he lay."
We live in an old chaos of the sun,   110
Or old dependency of day and night,
Or island solitude, unsponsored, free,
Of that wide water, inescapable.
Deer walk upon our mountains, and the quail
Whistle about us their spontaneous cries;   115
Sweet berries ripen in the wilderness;
And, in the isolation of the sky,
At evening, casual flocks of pigeons make
Ambiguous undulations as they sink,
Downward to darkness, on extended wings.   120

[1923]

WILLIAM CARLOS WILLIAMS   [1883–1963]

The Red Wheelbarrow

so much depends
upon

a red wheel
barrow

glazed with rain   5
water

beside the white
chickens.

[1923]

WILLIAM CARLOS WILLIAMS   [1883–1963]

Spring and All

By the road to the contagious hospital
under the surge of the blue
mottled clouds driven from the
northeast — a cold wind. Beyond, the
waste of broad, muddy fields   5
brown with dried weeds, standing and fallen

patches of standing water
the scattering of tall trees

All along the road the reddish
purplish, forked, upstanding, twiggy   10
stuff of bushes and small trees
with dead, brown leaves under them
leafless vines —

Lifeless in appearance, sluggish
dazed spring approaches —   15

They enter the new world naked,
cold, uncertain of all
save that they enter. All about them
the cold, familiar wind —

Now the grass, tomorrow   20
the stiff curl of wildcarrot leaf

One by one objects are defined —
It quickens: clarity, outline of leaf

But now the stark dignity of
entrance — Still, the profound change   25
has come upon them: rooted, they
grip down and begin to awaken

[1923]

WILLIAM CARLOS WILLIAMS   [1883–1963]

This Is Just to Say

I have eaten
the plums
that were in
the icebox

and which   5
you were probably
saving
for breakfast

Forgive me
they were delicious   10
so sweet
and so cold

[1934]

EZRA POUND   [1885–1972]

The River-Merchant's Wife: A Letter

While my hair was still cut straight across my forehead
I played about the front gate, pulling flowers.
You came by on bamboo stilts, playing horse,
You walked about my seat, playing with blue plums.
And we went on living in the village of Chokan: 5
Two small people, without dislike or suspicion.

At fourteen I married My Lord you.
I never laughed, being bashful.
Lowering my head, I looked at the wall.
Called to, a thousand times, I never looked back.   10

At fifteen I stopped scowling,
I desired my dust to be mingled with yours
Forever and forever and forever.
Why should I climb the look out?

At sixteen you departed,   15
You went into far Ku-to-yen, by the river of swirling eddies,
And you have been gone five months.
The monkeys make sorrowful noise overhead.

You dragged your feet when you went out.
By the gate now, the moss is grown, the different mosses,   20
Too deep to clear them away!
The leaves fall early this autumn, in wind.
The paired butterflies are already yellow with August
Over the grass in the West garden;
They hurt me. I grow older.   25
If you are coming down through the narrows of the river Kiang,
Please let me know beforehand,
And I will come out to meet you
                    As far as Cho-fu-Sa.

By Rihaku°

[1915]

By Rihaku: An adaptation of a Chinese poem by the famous poet Li Po (701–762
C.E.), whose Japanese name is Rihaku.

H. D. [HILDA DOOLITTLE]   [1886–1961]

Garden

I

You are clear
O rose, cut in rock,
hard as the descent of hail.

I could scrape the colour
from the petals   5
like spilt dye from a rock.

If I could break you
I could break a tree.

If I could stir
I could break a tree —   10
I could break you.

II

O wind, rend open the heat,
cut apart the heat,
rend it to tatters.

Fruit cannot drop   15
through this thick air —
fruit cannot fall into heat
that presses up and blunts
the points of pears
and rounds the grapes.   20

Cut the heat —   -
plough through it,
turning it on either side
of your path.

                                                       [1916]

MARIANNE MOORE   [1887–1972]

Poetry

I, too, dislike it: there are things that are important beyond all this fiddle.
    Reading it, however, with a perfect contempt for it, one discovers in
    it after all, a place for the genuine.
        Hands that can grasp, eyes
        that can dilate, hair that can rise
            if it must, these things are important not because a   5

high-sounding interpretation can be put upon them but because they are
    useful. When they become so derivative as to become unintelligible,
    the same thing may be said for all of us, that we
        do not admire what   10

    we cannot understand: the bat
      holding on upside down or in quest of something to

eat, elephants pushing, a wild horse taking a roll, a tireless wolf under
  a tree, the immovable critic twitching his skin like a horse that feels a
                     flea, the base-

  ball fan, the statistician —   15
      nor is it valid
         to discriminate against "business documents and

school-books"; all these phenomena are important. One must make a
                              distinction
  however: when dragged into prominence by half poets, the result is
                         not poetry,

  nor till the poets among us can be   20
      "literalists of
      the imagination" — above
         insolence and triviality and can present

for inspection, "imaginary gardens with real toads in them," shall we
                       have
  it. In the meantime, if you demand on the one hand,   25
  the raw material of poetry in
    all its rawness and
    that which is on the other hand
      genuine, you are interested in poetry.

                                  [1921]

EDITH SITWELL   [1887–1964]

Lullaby

Though the world has slipped and gone,
Sounds my loud discordant cry
Like the steel birds' song on high:
"Still one thing is left — the Bone!"
Then out danced the Babioun.°   *baboon* 5

She sat in the hollow of the sea —
A socket whence the eye's put out —
She sang to the child a lullaby
(The steel birds' nest was thereabout).

"Do, do, do, do —   10
Thy mother's hied to the vaster race:
The Pterodactyl made its nest
And laid a steel egg in her breast —
Under the Judas-colored sun.
She'll work no more, nor dance, nor moan,   15
And I am come to take her place
Do, do.

There's nothing left but earth's low bed —
(The Pterodactyl fouls its nest):
But steel wings fan thee to thy rest,   20
And wingless truth and larvae lie
And eyeless hope and handless fear —
All these for thee as toys are spread,
Do — do —

Red is the bed of Poland, Spain,   25
And thy mother's breast, who has grown wise
In that fouled nest. If she could rise.
Give birth again,
In wolfish pelt she'd hide thy bones
To shield thee from the world's long cold,   30
And down on all fours shouldst thou crawl
For thus from no height canst thou fall —
Do, do.

She'd give no hands: there's nought to hold
And nought to make: there's dust to sift,   35
But no food for the hands to lift.
Do, do.

Heed my ragged lullaby,
Fear not living, fear not chance;
All is equal — blindness, sight,
There is no depth, there is no height: 40
Do, do.

The Judas-colored sun is gone,
And with the Ape thou art alone —
Do,   45
    Do."

[1942]

ROBINSON JEFFERS   [1887–1962]

Hurt Hawks

I

The broken pillar of the wing jags from the clotted shoulder,
The wing trails like a banner in defeat,
No more to use the sky forever but live with famine
And pain a few days: cat nor coyote
Will shorten the week of waiting for death, there is game without talons.   5
He stands under the oak-bush and waits
The lame feet of salvation; at night he remembers freedom
And flies in a dream, the dawns ruin it.
He is strong and pain is worse to the strong, incapacity is worse.
The curs of the day come and torment him   10
At distance, no one but death the redeemer will humble that head,
The intrepid readiness, the terrible eyes.
The wild God of the world is sometimes merciful to those
That ask mercy, not often to the arrogant.
You do not know him, you communal people, or you have forgotten him;   15
Intemperate and savage, the hawk remembers him;
Beautiful and wild, the hawks, and men that are dying, remember him.

II

I'd sooner, except the penalties, kill a man than a hawk; but the great
    redtail
Had nothing left but unable misery
From the bone too shattered for mending, the wing that trailed under
    his talons when he moved.   20
We had fed him six weeks, I gave him freedom,
He wandered over the foreland hill and returned in the evening, asking
    for death,
Not like a beggar, still eyed with the old
Implacable arrogance. I gave him the lead gift in the twilight. What fell
    was relaxed,   25
Owl-downy, soft feminine feathers; but what
Soared: the fierce rush: the night-herons by the flooded river cried fear
    at its rising
Before it was quite unsheathed from reality.

[1928]

T. S. ELIOT   [1888–1965]

The Love Song of J. Alfred Prufrock

S'io credesse che mia risposta fosse
A persona che mai tornasse al mondo,
Questa fiamma staria senza piu scosse.
Ma perciocche giammai di questo fondo
Non torno vivo alcun, s'i'odo il vero,
Senza tema d'infamia ti rispondo.°

Let us go then, you and I,
When the evening is spread out against the sky
Like a patient etherised upon a table;
Let us go, through certain half-deserted streets,
The muttering retreats   5
Of restless nights in one-night cheap hotels
And sawdust restaurants with oyster-shells:
Streets that follow like a tedious argument
Of insidious intent
To lead you to an overwhelming question . . .   10
Oh, do not ask, "What is it?"
Let us go and make our visit.

    In the room the women come and go
Talking of Michelangelo.

    The yellow fog that rubs its back upon the window-panes,   15
The yellow smoke that rubs its muzzle on the window-panes
Licked its tongue into the corners of the evening,
Lingered upon the pools that stand in drains,
Let fall upon its back the soot that falls from chimneys,
Slipped by the terrace, made a sudden leap,   20

Epigraph: "If I thought that my answer were being made to someone who would ever return to earth, this flame would remain without further movement; but since no one has ever returned alive from this depth, if what I hear is true, I answer you without fear of infamy" (Dante, *Inferno* 27.61–66). Dante encounters Guido de Montefeltro in the eighth circle of hell, where souls are trapped within flames (tongues of fire) as punishment for giving evil counsel. Guido tells Dante details about his evil life only because he assumes that Dante is on his way to an even deeper circle in hell and will never return to earth and be able to repeat what he has heard.

And seeing that it was a soft October night,
Curled once about the house, and fell asleep.

   And indeed there will be time
For the yellow smoke that slides along the street,
Rubbing its back upon the window-panes;   25
There will be time, there will be time
To prepare a face to meet the faces that you meet;
There will be time to murder and create,
And time for all the works and days° of hands
That lift and drop a question on your plate;   30
Time for you and time for me,
And time yet for a hundred indecisions,
And for a hundred visions and revisions,
Before the taking of a toast and tea.

   In the room the women come and go   35
Talking of Michelangelo.

   And indeed there will be time
To wonder, "Do I dare?" and, "Do I dare?"
Time to turn back and descend the stair,
With a bald spot in the middle of my hair—   40
[They will say: "How his hair is growing thin!"]
My morning coat, my collar mounting firmly to the chin,
My necktie rich and modest, but asserted by a simple pin—
[They will say: "But how his arms and legs are thin!"]
Do I dare   45
Disturb the universe?
In a minute there is time
For decisions and revisions which a minute will reverse.

   For I have known them all already, known them all:—
Have known the evenings, mornings, afternoons,   50
I have measured out my life with coffee spoons;
I know the voices dying with a dying fall°
Beneath the music from a farther room.
   So how should I presume?

---

29. works and days: *Works and Days* is the title of a didactic poem about farming by the Greek poet Hesiod (eighth century B.C.E.) that includes instruction
about doing each task at the proper time.
52. a dying fall: An allusion to Shakespeare's *Twelfth Night* (1.1.4): "That strain
[of music] again! It had a dying fall" (a cadence that falls away).

And I have known the eyes already, known them all —   55
The eyes that fix you in a formulated phrase,
And when I am formulated, sprawling on a pin,
When I am pinned and wriggling on the wall,
Then how should I begin
To spit out all the butt-ends of my days and ways?   60
    And how should I presume?

    And I have known the arms already, known them all —
Arms that are braceleted and white and bare
[But in the lamplight, downed with light brown hair!]
Is it perfume from a dress   65
That makes me so digress?
Arms that lie along a table, or wrap about a shawl.
    And should I then presume?
    And how should I begin?

                    •   •   •

Shall I say, I have gone at dusk through narrow streets   70
And watched the smoke that rises from the pipes
Of lonely men in shirt-sleeves, leaning out of windows? . . .

    I should have been a pair of ragged claws
Scuttling across the floors of silent seas.

                    •   •   •

And the afternoon, the evening, sleeps so peacefully!   75
Smoothed by long fingers,
Asleep . . . tired . . . or it malingers,
Stretched on the floor, here beside you and me.
Should I, after tea and cakes and ices,
Have the strength to force the moment to its crisis?   80
But though I have wept and fasted, wept and prayed,
Though I have seen my head [grown slightly bald] brought in upon a
            platter,°
I am no prophet — and here's no great matter;
I have seen the moment of my greatness flicker,
And I have seen the eternal Footman hold my coat, and snicker,   85
And in short, I was afraid.

82. head . . . platter: As a reward for dancing before King Herod, Salome, his
stepdaughter, asked for the head of John the Baptist to be presented to her on a
platter (Matthew 14:1–12; Mark 6:17–28).

And would it have been worth it, after all,
After the cups, the marmalade, the tea,
Among the porcelain, among some talk of you and me,
Would it have been worth while,   90
To have bitten off the matter with a smile,
To have squeezed the universe into a ball
To roll it toward some overwhelming question,
To say: "I am Lazarus,° come from the dead,
Come back to tell you all, I shall tell you all" —   95
If one, settling a pillow by her head,
   Should say: "That is not what I meant at all.
   That is not it, at all."

   And would it have been worth it, after all,
Would it have been worth while,   100
After the sunsets and the dooryards and the sprinkled streets,
After the novels, after the teacups, after the skirts that trail along the
        floor—
And this, and so much more?—
It is impossible to say just what I mean!
But as if a magic lantern threw the nerves in patterns on a screen: 105
Would it have been worth while
If one, settling a pillow or throwing off a shawl,
And turning toward the window, should say:
"That is not it at all,
That is not what I meant, at all."   110

         •   •   •

No! I am not Prince Hamlet, nor was meant to be;
Am an attendant lord, one that will do
To swell a progress,° start a scene or two,
Advise the prince; no doubt, an easy tool,
Deferential, glad to be of use,   115
Politic, cautious, and meticulous;
Full of high sentence,° but a bit obtuse;   *sententiousness*
At times, indeed, almost ridiculous—
Almost, at times, the Fool.

   I grow old . . . I grow old . . .   120
I shall wear the bottoms of my trousers rolled.°   *turned up, with cuffs*

94. Lazarus: Either the beggar Lazarus, who in Luke 16:19–31 did not return
from the dead, or Jesus' friend Lazarus, who did (John 11:1–44).
113. progress: Ceremonial journey made by a royal court.

Shall I part my hair behind? Do I dare to eat a peach?
I shall wear white flannel trousers, and walk upon the beach.
I have heard the mermaids singing, each to each.

I do not think that they will sing to me.   125

I have seen them riding seaward on the waves
Combing the white hair of the waves blown back
When the wind blows the water white and black.

We have lingered in the chambers of the sea
By sea-girls wreathed with seaweed red and brown   130
Till human voices wake us, and we drown.

[1917]

T. S. ELIOT   [1888–1965]

Preludes

I

The winter evening settles down
With smell of steaks in passageways.
Six o'clock.
The burnt-out ends of smoky days.
And now a gusty shower wraps   5
The grimy scraps
Of withered leaves about your feet
And newspapers from vacant lots;
The showers beat
On broken blinds and chimney-pots,   10
And at the corner of the street
A lonely cab-horse steams and stamps.
And then the lighting of the lamps.

II

The morning comes to consciousness
Of faint stale smells of beer   15
From the sawdust-trampled street
With all its muddy feet that press
To early coffee-stands.
With the other masquerades

That time resumes,   20
One thinks of all the hands
That are raising dingy shades
In a thousand furnished rooms.

III

You tossed a blanket from the bed,
You lay upon your back, and waited;   25
You dozed, and watched the night revealing
The thousand sordid images
Of which your soul was constituted;
They flickered against the ceiling.
And when all the world came back   30
And the light crept up between the shutters
And you heard the sparrows in the gutters,
You had such a vision of the street
As the street hardly understands;
Sitting along the bed's edge, where   35
You curled the papers from your hair,
Or clasped the yellow soles of feet
In the palms of both soiled hands.

IV

His soul stretched tight across the skies
That fade behind a city block,   40
Or trampled by insistent feet
At four and five and six o'clock;
And short square fingers stuffing pipes,
And evening newspapers, and eyes
Assured of certain certainties,   45
The conscience of a blackened street
Impatient to assume the world.

   I am moved by fancies that are curled
Around these images, and cling:
The notion of some infinitely gentle   50
Infinitely suffering thing.

   Wipe your hand across your mouth, and laugh;
The worlds revolve like ancient women
Gathering fuel in vacant lots.

                                          [1917]

JOHN CROWE RANSOM   [1888–1974]

Bells for John Whiteside's Daughter

There was such speed in her little body,
And such lightness in her footfall,
It is no wonder her brown study°
Astonishes us all.

Her wars were bruited in our high window.   5
We looked among orchard trees and beyond
Where she took arms against her shadow,
Or harried unto the pond

The lazy geese, like a snow cloud
Dripping their snow on the green grass,   10
Tricking and stopping, sleepy and proud,
Who cried in goose, Alas,

For the tireless heart within the little
Lady with rod that made them rise
From their noon apple-dreams and scuttle   15
Goose-fashion under the skies!

But now go the bells, and we are ready,
In one house we are sternly stopped
To say we are vexed at her brown study,
Lying so primly propped.   20

[1924]

3. brown study: Being deeply absorbed in one's thoughts; reverie.

CLAUDE McKAY   [1890–1948]

America

Although she feeds me bread of bitterness,
And sinks into my throat her tiger's tooth,
Stealing my breath of life, I will confess
I love this cultured hell that tests my youth!
Her vigor flows like tides into my blood,   5
Giving me strength erect against her hate.

Her bigness sweeps my being like a flood.
Yet as a rebel fronts a king in state,
I stand within her walls with not a shred
Of terror, malice, not a word of jeer.   10
Darkly I gaze into the days ahead,
And see her might and granite wonders there,
Beneath the touch of Time's unerring hand,
Like priceless treasures sinking in the sand.

[1922]

EDNA ST. VINCENT MILLAY   [1892–1950]

Wild Swans

I looked in my heart while the wild swans went over.
And what did I see I had not seen before?
Only a question less or a question more;
Nothing to match the flight of wild birds flying.
Tiresome heart, forever living and dying,   5
House without air, I leave you and lock your door.
Wild swans, come over the town, come over
The town again, trailing your legs and crying!

[1921]

WILFRED OWEN   [1893–1918]

Dulce et Decorum Est

Bent double, like old beggars under sacks,
Knock-kneed, coughing like hags, we cursed through sludge,
Till on the haunting flares we turned our backs
And towards our distant rest began to trudge.
Men marched asleep. Many had lost their boots   5
But limped on, blood-shod. All went lame; all blind;
Drunk with fatigue; deaf even to the hoots
Of tired, outstripped Five-Nines° that dropped behind.

8. Five-Nines: 5.9-inch caliber shells.

Gas! GAS! Quick, boys! — An ecstasy of fumbling,
Fitting the clumsy helmets just in time;   10
But someone still was yelling out and stumbling
And flound'ring like a man in fire or lime . . .
Dim, through the misty panes° and thick green light,   *of a gas mask*
As under a green sea, I saw him drowning.

In all my dreams, before my helpless sight,   15
He plunges at me, guttering, choking, drowning.

If in some smothering dreams you too could pace
Behind the wagon that we flung him in,
And watch the white eyes writhing in his face,
His hanging face, like a devil's sick of sin;   20
If you could hear, at every jolt, the blood
Come gargling from the froth-corrupted lungs,
Obscene as cancer, bitter as the cud
Of vile, incurable sores on innocent tongues, —
My friend, you would not tell with such high zest   25
To children ardent for some desperate glory,
The old Lie: Dulce et decorum est
Pro patria mori.°

[1920]

27–28. Dulce . . . mori: It is sweet and fitting / to die for one's country (Horace, *Odes* 3.12.13).

E. E. CUMMINGS   [1894–1962]

in Just-

in Just-
spring   when the world is mud-
luscious the little
lame balloonman

whistles   far   and wee   5

and eddieandbill come
running from marbles and

piracies and it's
spring

when the world is puddle-wonderful   10

the queer
old balloonman whistles
far   and   wee
and bettyandisbel come dancing

from hop-scotch and jump-rope and   15

it's
spring
and
    the

        goat-footed   20

balloonMan   whistles
far
and
wee

                                                     [1923]

E. E. CUMMINGS   [1894–1962]

pity this busy monster,manunkind

pity this busy monster,manunkind,

not. Progress is a comfortable disease:
your victim(death and life safely beyond)

plays with the bigness of his littleness
— electrons deify one razorblade   5
into a mountainrange;lenses extend

unwish through curving wherewhen till unwish
returns on its unself.

                    A world of made
is not a world of born — pity poor flesh   10

and trees,poor stars and stones,but never this
fine specimen of hypermagical

ultraomnipotence. We doctors know

a hopeless case if—listen:there's a hell
of a good universe next door;let's go   15

[1944]

JEAN TOOMER   [1894–1967]

Reapers

Black reapers with the sound of steel on stones
Are sharpening scythes. I see them place the hones
In their hip-pockets as a thing that's done.
And start their silent swinging, one by one.
Black horses drive a mower through the weeds.   5
And there, a field rat, startled, squealing bleeds.
His belly close to ground. I see the blade,
Blood-stained, continue cutting weeds and shade.

[1923]

LOUISE BOGAN   [1897–1970]

Women

Women have no wilderness in them,
They are provident instead,
Content in the tight hot cell of their hearts
To eat dusty bread.

They do not see cattle cropping red winter grass,   5
They do not hear
Snow water going down under culverts
Shallow and clear.

They wait, when they should turn to journeys,
They stiffen, when they should bend.   10
They use against themselves that benevolence
To which no man is friend.

They cannot think of so many crops to a field
Or of clean wood cleft by an axe.
Their love is an eager meaninglessness   15
Too tense, or too lax.

They hear in every whisper that speaks to them
A shout and a cry.
As like as not, when they take life over their door-sills
They should let it go by.   20

[1923]

HART CRANE   [1899–1932]

My Grandmother's Love Letters

There are no stars tonight
But those of memory.
Yet how much room for memory there is
In the loose girdle of soft rain.

There is even room enough   5
For the letters of my mother's mother,
Elizabeth,
That have been pressed so long
Into a corner of the roof
That they are brown and soft,   10
And liable to melt as snow.

Over the greatness of such space
Steps must be gentle.
It is all hung by an invisible white hair.
It trembles as birch limbs webbing the air.   15

And I ask myself:

"Are your fingers long enough to play
Old keys that are but echoes:
Is the silence strong enough
To carry back the music to its source   20
And back to you again
As though to her?"

Yet I would lead my grandmother by the hand
Through much of what she would not understand;

And so I stumble. And the rain continues on the roof   25
With such a sound of gently pitying laughter.

[1926]

STERLING A. BROWN   [1901–1989]

Riverbank Blues

A man git his feet set in a sticky mudbank,
A man git dis yellow water in his blood,
No need for hopin', no need for doin',
Muddy streams keep him fixed for good.

Little Muddy, Big Muddy, Moreau and Osage,   5
Little Mary's, Big Mary's, Cedar Creek,
Flood deir muddy water roundabout a man's roots,
Keep him soaked and stranded and git him weak.

Lazy sun shinin' on a little cabin,
Lazy moon glistenin' over river trees;   10
Ole river whisperin', lappin' 'gainst de long roots:
"Plenty of rest and peace in these. . . ."

Big mules, black loam, apple and peach trees,
But seems lak de river washes us down
Past de rich farms, away from de fat lands,   15
Dumps us in some ornery riverbank town.

Went down to the river, sot me down an' listened,
Heard de water talkin' quiet, quiet lak an' slow:
"Ain' no need fo' hurry, take yo' time, take yo' time. . . ."
Heard it sayin'—*"Baby, hyeahs de way life go. . . ."*   20

Dat is what it tole me as I watched it slowly rollin',
But somp'n way inside me rared up an' say,
"Better be movin' . . . better be travelin' . . .
Riverbank'll git you ef you stay. . . ."

Towns are sinkin' deeper, deeper in de riverbank,   25
Takin' on de ways of deir sulky Ole Man—
Takin' on his creepy ways, takin' on his evil ways,
"Bes' git way, a long way . . . whiles you can.

"Man got his sea too lak de Mississippi
Ain't got so long for a whole lot longer way,   30

Man better move some, better not git rooted
Muddy water fool you, ef you stay. . . ."

[1932]

LANGSTON HUGHES   [1902–1967]

The Negro Speaks of Rivers

I've known rivers:
I've known rivers ancient as the world and older than the flow of human
    blood in human veins.

My soul has grown deep like the rivers.

I bathed in the Euphrates when dawns were young.
I built my hut near the Congo and it lulled me to sleep.   5
I looked upon the Nile and raised the pyramids above it.
I heard the singing of the Mississippi when Abe Lincoln went down to
    New Orleans, and I've seen its muddy bosom turn all golden in the
    sunset.

I've known rivers:
Ancient, dusky rivers.

My soul has grown deep like the rivers.   10

[1926]

LANGSTON HUGHES   [1902–1967]

Theme for English B

The instructor said,

> *Go home and write*
> *a page tonight.*
> *And let that page come out of you —*
> *Then, it will be true.*   5

I wonder if it's that simple?
I am twenty-two, colored, born in Winston-Salem.
I went to school there, then Durham, then here

to this college on the hill above Harlem.
I am the only colored student in my class.   10
The steps from the hill lead down into Harlem,
through a park, then I cross St. Nicholas,
Eighth Avenue, Seventh, and I come to the Y,
the Harlem Branch Y, where I take the elevator
up to my room, sit down, and write this page: 15

It's not easy to know what is true for you or me
at twenty-two, my age. But I guess I'm what
I feel and see and hear, Harlem, I hear you:
hear you, hear me — we two — you, me, talk on this page.
(I hear New York, too.) Me — who?   20
Well, I like to eat, sleep, drink, and be in love.
I like to work, read, learn, and understand life.
I like a pipe for a Christmas present,
or records — Bessie,° bop, or Bach.
I guess being colored doesn't make me *not* like   25
the same things other folks like who are other races.
So will my page be colored that I write?
Being me, it will not be white.
But it will be
a part of you, instructor.   30
You are white —
yet a part of me, as I am a part of you.
That's American.
Sometimes perhaps you don't want to be a part of me.
Nor do I often want to be a part of you.   35
But we are, that's true!
As I learn from you,
I guess you learn from me —
although you're older — and white —
and somewhat more free.   40

This is my page for English B.

[1951]

---

24. Bessie: Bessie Smith (1895–1937), American blues singer.

LANGSTON HUGHES   [1902–1967]

Harlem

What happens to a dream deferred?

Does it dry up
like a raisin in the sun?
Or fester like a sore —
And then run?   5
Does it stink like rotten meat?
Or crust and sugar over —
like a syrupy sweet?

Maybe it just sags
like a heavy load.   10

Or does it explode?

[1951]

COUNTEE CULLEN   [1903–1946]

Incident

for Eric Walrond

Once riding in old Baltimore,
  Heart-filled, head-filled with glee,
I saw a Baltimorean
  Keep looking straight at me.

Now I was eight and very small,   5
  And he was no whit bigger,
And so I smiled, but he poked out
  His tongue, and called me, "Nigger."

I saw the whole of Baltimore
  From May until December;   10
Of all the things that happened there
  That's all that I remember.

[1925]

LORINE NIEDECKER   [1903–1970]

My Life by Water

My life
  by water—
    Hear

spring's
  first frog
    or board   5

out on the cold
  ground
    giving

Muskrats   10
  gnawing
    doors

to wild green
  arts and letters
    Rabbits   15

raided
  my lettuce
    One boat

two—
  pointed toward
    my shore   20

thru birdstart
  wingdrip
    weed-drift

of the soft   25
  and serious—
    Water

[1985]

LOUIS ZUKOFSKY   [1904–1978]

From "A" 15

An
   hinny
by
   stallion
out of   5
   she-ass

He neigh ha lie low h'who y'he gall mood
So roar cruel hire
Lo to achieve an eye leer rot off
Mass th'lo low o loam echo   10
How deal me many coeval yammer
Naked on face of white rock — sea.
Then I said: Liveforever my nest
Is arable hymn
Shore she root to water   15
Dew anew to branch.

Wind: Yahweh° at Iyyob°   *Israel's deity/Job*
Mien His roar "Why yammer
Measly make short hates oh
By milling bleat doubt?   20
Eye sore gnaw key heaver haul its core
Weigh as I lug where hide any?
If you — had you towed beside the roots?
How goad Him — you'd do it by now —
My sum My made day a key to daw?   25
O Me not there allheal — a cave.

All mouth deny hot bough?
O Me you're raw — Heaven pinned Dawn stars
Brine I heard choir and weigh by care —
Why your ear would call by now Elohim:°   *Hebrew for "God"* 30
Where was soak — bid lot tie in hum —
How would you have known to hum
How would you all oats rose snow lay
Assáy how'd a rock light rollick ore
Had the rush in you curb, ah bay,   35
Bay the shophar yammer *heigh horse"*

Wind: Yahweh at Iyyob "Why yammer,"
Wind: Iyyob at Yahweh, "Why yammer
How cold the mouth achieved echo."
Wind: Yahweh at Iyyob "Why yammer   40
Ha neigh now behēmoth° and share I see see your make   *beast*
Giddy pair — stones — whose rages go
Weigh raw all gay where how spill lay who"
Wind: Iyyob
"Rain without sun hated? *hurt no one*   45
In two we shadow, how hide any."

The traffic below,
sound of it a wind
eleven stories
below: *The Parkway*   50
no parking there ever:
the deaths as
after it might be said
"ordered," the one
the two old   55
songsters would not
live to see —
the death of
the young man,
who had possibly   60
alleviated
the death of
the oldest
vagrantly back he
might have thought   65
from vying culturally
with the Russian
Puritan Bear —
to vagary of
Bear hug and King   70
Charles° losing his head —   *Charles I of England*
and the other
a decade younger
never international
emissary   75
at least not
for his President,
aged in a suburb
dying maundering

the language —   80
American — impatient now
sometimes extreme clarity —
to hurrȳ
his compost
to the hill   85
his grave —
(distance
   a gastank)

he would
miss   90
living thru the
assassination

[1978]

STANLEY KUNITZ   [1905–2006]

Father and Son

Now in the suburbs and the falling light
I followed him, and now down sandy road
Whiter than bone-dust, through the sweet
Curdle of fields, where the plums
Dropped with their load of ripeness, one by one.   5
Mile after mile I followed, with skimming feet,
After the secret master of my blood,
Him, steeped in the odor of ponds, whose indomitable love
Kept me in chains. Strode years; stretched into bird;
Raced through the sleeping country where I was young,   10
The silence unrolling before me as I came,
The night nailed like an orange to my brow.

How should I tell him my fable and the fears,
How bridge the chasm in a casual tone,
Saying, "The house, the stucco one you built,   15
We lost. Sister married and went from home,
And nothing comes back, it's strange, from where she goes.
I lived on a hill that had too many rooms:
Light we could make, but not enough of warmth,
And when the light failed, I climbed under the hill.   20

The papers are delivered every day;
I am alone and never shed a tear."

At the water's edge, where the smothering ferns lifted
Their arms, "Father!" I cried, "Return! You know
The way. I'll wipe the mudstains from your clothes;   25
No trace, I promise, will remain. Instruct
Your son, whirling between two wars,
In the Gemara° of your gentleness,
For I would be a child to those who mourn
And brother to the foundlings of the field   30
And friend of innocence and all bright eyes.
O teach me how to work and keep me kind."

Among the turtles and the lilies he turned to me
The white ignorant hollow of his face.

[1944]

28. Gemara: The second division of the Talmud; it is a commentary on Jewish
civil and religious laws.

W. H. AUDEN   [1907–1973]

As I Walked Out One Evening

As I walked out one evening,
    Walking down Bristol Street,
The crowds upon the pavement
    Were fields of harvest wheat.

And down by the brimming river   5
    I heard a lover sing
Under an arch of the railway:
    "Love has no ending.

"I'll love you, dear, I'll love you
    Till China and Africa meet,   10
And the river jumps over the mountain
    And the salmon sing in the street,

"I'll love you till the ocean
    Is folded and hung up to dry

And the seven stars° go squawking   15
   Like geese about the sky.

The years shall run like rabbits,
   For in my arms I hold
The Flower of the Ages,
   And the first love of the world."   20

But all the clocks in the city
   Began to whirr and chime:
"O let not Time deceive you,
   You cannot conquer Time.

"In the burrows of the Nightmare   25
   Where Justice naked is,
Time watches from the shadow
   And coughs when you would kiss.

"In headaches and in worry
   Vaguely life leaks away,   30
And Time will have his fancy
   To-morrow or to-day.

"Into many a green valley
   Drifts the appalling snow;
Time breaks the threaded dances   35
   And the diver's brilliant bow.

"O plunge your hands in water,
   Plunge them in up to the wrist;
Stare, stare in the basin
   And wonder what you've missed.   40

"The glacier knocks in the cupboard,
   The desert sighs in the bed,
And the crack in the tea-cup opens
   A lane to the land of the dead.

"Where the beggars raffle the banknotes°   45
   And the Giant° is enchanting to Jack,

15. the seven stars: An echo of the traditional counting song "Green Grow the Rushes, O": "What are your seven, O? / Seven for the seven stars in the sky."
45–48. "Where the beggars . . .": This stanza alludes to and — through social satire and sexual innuendo — inverts the milieu of nursery rhymes and a counting song.
46. Giant: From the fairy tale "Jack the Giant-Killer."

And the Lily-white Boy° is a Roarer,°
And Jill° goes down on her back.

"O look, look in the mirror,
    O look in your distress;   50
Life remains a blessing
    Although you cannot bless.

"O stand, stand at the window
    As the tears scald and start;
You shall love your crooked neighbour   55
    With your crooked heart."°

It was late, late in the evening,
    The lovers they were gone;
The clocks had ceased their chiming,
    And the deep river ran on.   60

                                            [1937]

47. Lily-white Boy: Echoing "Green Grow the Rushes, O": "What are your two, O? / Two, two the lily-white boys / Clothed all in green, O"; **Roarer:** Hell raiser.
48. Jill: From the nursery rhyme "Jack and Jill."
55–56. "You . . . heart.": Perhaps a distorted conflation of Matthew 22:37 and 22:39: "Thou shalt love the Lord thy God with all thy heart . . . [and] thy neighbor as thyself."

W. H. AUDEN   [1907–1973]

Musée des Beaux Arts°

About suffering they were never wrong,
The Old Masters: how well they understood
Its human position; how it takes place
While someone else is eating or opening a window or just walking dully
    along;
How, when the aged are reverently, passionately waiting   5
For the miraculous birth, there always must be
Children who did not specially want it to happen, skating
On a pond at the edge of the wood:
They never forgot

Musée des Beaux Arts: The painting *Landscape with the Fall of Icarus* by Pieter Brueghel the Elder, on which the poem is based, is in the Musées Royaux des Beaux-Arts in Brussels.

Brueghel, *Landscape with the Fall of Icarus*

That even the dreadful martyrdom must run its course   10
Anyhow in a corner, some untidy spot
Where the dogs go on with their doggy life and the torturer's horse
Scratches its innocent behind on a tree.

In Brueghel's *Icarus*, for instance: how everything turns away
Quite leisurely from the disaster; the ploughman may   15
Have heard the splash, the forsaken cry,
But for him it was not an important failure; the sun shone
As it had to on the white legs disappearing into the green
Water; and the expensive delicate ship that must have seen
Something amazing, a boy falling out of the sky,   20
Had somewhere to get to and sailed calmly on.

[1940]

THEODORE ROETHKE   [1908–1963]

My Papa's Waltz

The whiskey on your breath
Could make a small boy dizzy;
But I hung on like death:
Such waltzing was not easy.

We romped until the pans   5
Slid from the kitchen shelf;
My mother's countenance
Could not unfrown itself.

The hand that held my wrist
Was battered on one knuckle;   10
At every step you missed
My right ear scraped a buckle.

You beat time on my head
With a palm caked hard by dirt,
Then waltzed me off to bed   15
Still clinging to your shirt.

[1948]

ELIZABETH BISHOP   [1911–1979]

The Fish

I caught a tremendous fish
and held him beside the boat
half out of water, with my hook
fast in a corner of his mouth.
He didn't fight.   5
He hadn't fought at all.
He hung a grunting weight,
battered and venerable
and homely. Here and there
his brown skin hung in strips   10
like ancient wallpaper,
and its pattern of darker brown
was like wallpaper:
shapes like full-blown roses
stained and lost through age.   15
He was speckled with barnacles,
fine rosettes of lime,
and infested
with tiny white sea-lice,
and underneath two or three   20
rags of green weed hung down.
While his gills were breathing in

the terrible oxygen
— the frightening gills,
fresh and crisp with blood,   25
that can cut so badly —
I thought of the coarse white flesh
packed in like feathers,
the big bones and the little bones,
the dramatic reds and blacks   30
of his shiny entrails,
and the pink swim-bladder
like a big peony.
I looked into his eyes
which were far larger than mine   35
but shallower, and yellowed,
the irises backed and packed
with tarnished tinfoil
seen through the lenses
of old scratched isinglass.°   *transparent sheet of mica*   40
They shifted a little, but not
to return my stare.
— It was more like the tipping
of an object toward the light.
I admired his sullen face,   45
the mechanism of his jaw,
and then I saw
that from his lower lip
— if you could call it a lip —
grim, wet, and weaponlike,   50
hung five old pieces of fish-line,
or four and a wire leader
with the swivel still attached,
with all their five big hooks
grown firmly in his mouth.   55
A green line, frayed at the end
where he broke it, two heavier lines,
and a fine black thread
still crimped from the strain and snap
when it broke and he got away.   60
Like medals with their ribbons
frayed and wavering,
a five-haired beard of wisdom
trailing from his aching jaw.

I stared and stared   65
and victory filled up
the little rented boat,
from the pool of bilge
where oil had spread a rainbow
around the rusted engine   70
to the bailer rusted orange,
the sun-cracked thwarts,
the oarlocks on their strings,
the gunnels — until everything
was rainbow, rainbow, rainbow!   75
And I let the fish go.

[1946]

ELIZABETH BISHOP   [1911–1979]

In the Waiting Room

In Worcester, Massachusetts,
I went with Aunt Consuelo
to keep her dentist's appointment
and sat and waited for her
in the dentist's waiting room.   5
It was winter. It got dark
early. The waiting room
was full of grown-up people,
arctics and overcoats,
lamps and magazines.   10
My aunt was inside
what seemed like a long time
and while I waited I read
the *National Geographic*
(I could read) and carefully   15
studied the photographs:
the inside of a volcano,
black, and full of ashes;
then it was spilling over
in rivulets of fire.   20
Osa and Martin Johnson°

21. **Osa and Martin Johnson:** Husband-and-wife explorers and naturalists.

dressed in riding breeches,
laced boots, and pith helmets.
A dead man slung on a pole
— "Long Pig,"° the caption said.   25
Babies with pointed heads
wound round and round with string;
black, naked women with necks
wound round and round with wire
like the necks of light bulbs.   30
Their breasts were horrifying.
I read it right straight through.
I was too shy to stop.
And then I looked at the cover:
the yellow margins, the date.   35
Suddenly, from inside,
came an *oh!* of pain
— Aunt Consuelo's voice —
not very loud or long.
I wasn't at all surprised;   40
even then I knew she was
a foolish, timid woman.
I might have been embarrassed,
but wasn't. What took me
completely by surprise   45
was that it was *me:*
my voice, in my mouth.
Without thinking at all
I was my foolish aunt,
I — we — were falling, falling,   50
our eyes glued to the cover
of the *National Geographic,*
February, 1918.

I said to myself: three days
and you'll be seven years old.   55
I was saying it to stop
the sensation of falling off
the round, turning world
into cold, blue-black space.
But I felt: you are an *I,*   60

25. **Long Pig:** Polynesian cannibals' name for a human carcass.

you are an *Elizabeth*,
you are one of *them*.
Why should you be one, too?
I scarcely dared to look
to see what it was I was.   65
I gave a sidelong glance
— I couldn't look any higher —
at shadowy gray knees,
trousers and skirts and boots
and different pairs of hands   70
lying under the lamps.
I knew that nothing stranger
had ever happened, that nothing
stranger could ever happen.
Why should I be my aunt,   75
or me, or anyone?
What similarities —
boots, hands, the family voice
I felt in my throat, or even
the *National Geographic*   80
and those awful hanging breasts —
held us all together
or made us all just one?
How — I didn't know any
word for it — how "unlikely" . . .   85
How had I come to be here,
like them, and overhear
a cry of pain that could have
got loud and worse but hadn't?

The waiting room was bright   90
and too hot. It was sliding
beneath a big black wave,
another, and another.

Then I was back in it.
The War was on. Outside,   95
in Worcester, Massachusetts,
were night and slush and cold,
and it was still the fifth
of February, 1918.

[1976]

ELIZABETH BISHOP   [1911–1979]

One Art

The art of losing isn't hard to master;
so many things seem filled with the intent
to be lost that their loss is no disaster.

Lose something every day. Accept the fluster
of lost door keys, the hour badly spent.   5
The art of losing isn't hard to master.

Then practice losing farther, losing faster:
places, and names, and where it was you meant
to travel. None of these will bring disaster.

I lost my mother's watch. And look! my last, or   10
next-to-last, of three loved houses went.
The art of losing isn't hard to master.

I lost two cities, lovely ones. And, vaster,
some realms I owned, two rivers, a continent.
I miss them, but it wasn't a disaster.   15

—Even losing you (the joking voice, a gesture
I love) I shan't have lied. It's evident
the art of losing's not too hard to master
though it may look like (*Write* it!) like disaster.

[1976]

JOHN FREDERICK NIMS   [1913–1999]

Love Poem

My clumsiest dear, whose hands shipwreck vases,
At whose quick touch all glasses chip and ring,
Whose palms are bulls in china, burs in linen,
And have no cunning with any soft thing

Except all ill-at-ease fidgeting people: 5
The refugee uncertain at the door
You make at home; deftly you steady
The drunk clambering on his undulant floor.

Unpredictable dear, the taxi drivers' terror,
Shrinking from far headlights pale as a dime   10
Yet leaping before red apoplectic streetcars —
Misfit in any space. And never on time.

A wrench in clocks and the solar system. Only
With words and people and love you move at ease;
In traffic of wit expertly maneuver   15
And keep us, all devotion, at your knees.

Forgetting your coffee spreading on our flannel,
Your lipstick grinning on our coat,
So gaily in love's unbreakable heaven
Our souls on glory of spilt bourbon float.   20

Be with me, darling, early and late. Smash glasses —
I will study wry music for your sake.
For should your hands drop white and empty
All the toys of the world would break.

[1947]

ROBERT HAYDEN   [1913–1980]

Those Winter Sundays

Sundays too my father got up early
and put his clothes on in the blueblack cold,
then with cracked hands that ached
from labor in the weekday weather made
banked fires blaze. No one ever thanked him.   5

I'd wake and hear the cold splintering, breaking.
When the rooms were warm, he'd call,
and slowly I would rise and dress,
fearing the chronic angers of that house,

Speaking indifferently to him,   10
who had driven out the cold
and polished my good shoes as well.
What did I know, what did I know
of love's austere and lonely offices?

[1962]

DUDLEY RANDALL   [1914–2000]

Ballad of Birmingham

On the bombing of a church in Birmingham, Alabama, 1963

"Mother dear, may I go downtown
Instead of out to play,
And march the streets of Birmingham
In a Freedom March today?"

"No, baby, no, you may not go,   5
For the dogs are fierce and wild,
And clubs and hoses, guns and jails
Aren't good for a little child."

"But, mother, I won't be alone.
Other children will go with me,   10
And march the streets of Birmingham
To make our country free."

"No, baby, no, you may not go,
For I fear those guns will fire.
But you may go to church instead   15
And sing in the children's choir."

She has combed and brushed her night-dark hair,
And bathed rose petal sweet,
And drawn white gloves on her small brown hands,
And white shoes on her feet.   20

The mother smiled to know her child
Was in the sacred place,
But that smile was the last smile
To come upon her face.

For when she heard the explosion,   25
Her eyes grew wet and wild.
She raced through the streets of Birmingham
Calling for her child.

She clawed through bits of glass and brick,
Then lifted out a shoe.   30
"Oh, here's the shoe my baby wore,
But, baby, where are you?"

[1969]

JOHN BERRYMAN [1914–1972]

Henry's Confession
from *The Dream Songs* 76

Nothin very bad happen to me lately.
How you explain that? — I explain that, Mr Bones,°   *minstrel figure*
terms o' your bafflin odd sobriety.
Sober as man can get, no girls, no telephones,
what could happen bad to Mr Bones?   5
— *If* life is a handkerchief sandwich,

in a modesty of death I join my father
who dared so long agone leave me.
A bullet on a concrete stoop
close by a smothering southern sea   10
spreadeagled on an island, by my knee.
— You is from hunger, Mr Bones,

I offers you this handkerchief, now set
your left foot by my right foot,
shoulder to shoulder, all that jazz,   15
arm in arm, by the beautiful sea,
hum a little, Mr Bones.
— I saw nobody coming, so I went instead.

[1964]

WILLIAM STAFFORD [1914–1995]

Traveling through the Dark

Traveling through the dark I found a deer
dead on the edge of the Wilson River road.
It is usually best to roll them into the canyon:
that road is narrow; to swerve might make more dead.

By glow of the tail-light I stumbled back of the car   5
and stood by the heap, a doe, a recent killing;
she had stiffened already, almost cold.
I dragged her off; she was large in the belly.

My fingers touching her side brought me the reason —
her side was warm; her fawn lay there waiting,
alive, still, never to be born.
Beside that mountain road I hesitated.   10

The car aimed ahead its lowered parking lights;
under the hood purred the steady engine.
I stood in the glare of the warm exhaust turning red;   15
around our group I could hear the wilderness listen.

I thought hard for us all — my only swerving —,
then pushed her over the edge into the river.

[1962]

DYLAN THOMAS   [1914–1953]

Fern Hill

Now as I was young and easy under the apple boughs
About the lilting house and happy as the grass was green,
   The night above the dingle° starry,   *small wooded valley*
    Time let me hail and climb
   Golden in the heydays of his eyes,   5
And honoured among wagons I was prince of the apple towns
And once below a time I lordly had the trees and leaves
    Trail with daisies and barley
   Down the rivers of the windfall light.

And as I was green and carefree, famous among the barns   10
About the happy yard and singing as the farm was home,
   In the sun that is young once only,
    Time let me play and be
   Golden in the mercy of his means,
And green and golden I was huntsman and herdsman, the calves   15
Sang to my horn, the foxes on the hills barked clear and cold,
    And the sabbath rang slowly
   In the pebbles of the holy streams.

All the sun long it was running, it was lovely, the hay
Fields high as the house, the tunes from the chimneys, it was air   20
   And playing, lovely and watery
    And fire green as grass.
   And nightly under the simple stars

As I rode to sleep the owls were bearing the farm away,
All the moon long I heard, blessed among stables, the nightjars   25
   Flying with the ricks, and the horses
      Flashing into the dark.

And then to awake, and the farm, like a wanderer white
With the dew, come back, the cock on his shoulder: it was all
   Shining, it was Adam and maiden,   30
     The sky gathered again
   And the sun grew round that very day.
So it must have been after the birth of the simple light
In the first, spinning place, the spellbound horses walking warm
   Out of the whinnying green stable   35
     On to the fields of praise.

And honoured among foxes and pheasants by the gay house
Under the new made clouds and happy as the heart was long,
   In the sun born over and over,
    I ran my heedless ways,
   My wishes raced through the house high hay   40
And nothing I cared, at my sky blue trades, that time allows
In all his tuneful turning so few and such morning songs
   Before the children green and golden
     Follow him out of grace,   45

Nothing I cared, in the lamb white days, that time would take me
Up to the swallow thronged loft by the shadow of my hand,
   In the moon that is always rising,
    Nor that riding to sleep
   I should hear him fly with the high fields   50
And wake to the farm forever fled from the childless land.
Oh as I was young and easy in the mercy of his means,
    Time held me green and dying
   Though I sang in my chains like the sea.

[1946]

DYLAN THOMAS   [1914–1953]

Do not go gentle into that good night

Do not go gentle into that good night,
Old age should burn and rave at close of day;
Rage, rage against the dying of the light.

Though wise men at their end know dark is right,
Because their words had forked no lightning they   5
Do not go gentle into that good night.

Good men, the last wave by, crying how bright
Their frail deeds might have danced in a green bay,
Rage, rage against the dying of the light.

Wild men who caught and sang the sun in flight,   10
And learn, too late, they grieved it on its way,
Do not go gentle into that good night.

Grave men, near death, who see with blinding sight
Blind eyes could blaze like meteors and be gay,   15
Rage, rage against the dying of the light.

And you, my father, there on the sad height,
Curse, bless, me now with your fierce tears, I pray.
Do not go gentle into that good night.
Rage, rage against the dying of the light.

[1952]

RANDALL JARRELL   [1914–1965]

The Death of the Ball Turret Gunner°

From my mother's sleep I fell into the State,
And I hunched in its belly till my wet fur froze.
Six miles from earth, loosed from its dream of life,
I woke to black flak and the nightmare fighters.
When I died they washed me out of the turret with a hose.   5

[1945]

Ball Turret Gunner: "A ball turret was a plexiglass sphere set into the belly of a B-17 or B-24, and inhabited by two .50 caliber machine-guns and one man, a short small man. When this gunner tracked with his machine guns a fighter attacking his bomber from below, he revolved with the turret; hunched upside-down in his little sphere, he looked like the foetus in the womb. The fighters that attacked him were armed with cannon-firing explosive shells. The hose was a steam hose" [Jarrell's note].

GWENDOLYN BROOKS   [1917–2000]

We Real Cool

The Pool Players.
Seven at the Golden Shovel.

We real cool. We
Left school. We

Lurk late. We
Strike straight. We

Sing sin. We   5
Thin gin. We

Jazz° June. We   *have sexual intercourse (with)*
Die soon.

[1960]

GWENDOLYN BROOKS   [1917–2000]

The Bean Eaters

They eat beans mostly, this old yellow pair.
Dinner is a casual affair.
Plain chipware on a plain and creaking wood,
Tin flatware.

Two who are Mostly Good.   5
Two who have lived their day,
But keep on putting on their clothes
and putting things away.

And remembering . . .
Remembering, with twinklings and twinges,   10
As they lean over the beans in their rented back room that
    is full of beads and receipts and dolls and cloths,
    tobacco crumbs, vases and fringes.

[1960]

ROBERT LOWELL   [1917–1978]

Skunk Hour

for Elizabeth Bishop

Nautilus Island's hermit
heiress still lives through winter in her Spartan cottage;
her sheep still graze above the sea.
Her son's a bishop. Her farmer
is first selectman in our village;   5
she's in her dotage.

Thirsting for
the hierarchic privacy
of Queen Victoria's century,
she buys up all   10
the eyesores facing her shore,
and lets them fall.

The season's ill —
we've lost our summer millionaire,
who seemed to leap from an L. L. Bean   15
catalogue. His nine-knot yawl
was auctioned off to lobstermen.
A red fox stain covers Blue Hill.

And now our fairy
decorator brightens his shop for fall;   20
his fishnet's filled with orange cork,
orange, his cobbler's bench and awl;
there is no money in his work,
he'd rather marry.

                                                                     25
One dark night,
my Tudor Ford climbed the hill's skull;
I watched for love-cars. Lights turned down,
they lay together, hull to hull,
where the graveyard shelves on the town. . . .
My mind's not right.   30

A car radio bleats,
"Love, O careless Love. . . ." I hear
my ill-spirit sob in each blood cell,
as if my hand were at its throat. . . .

I myself am hell;
nobody's here —   35

only skunks, that search
in the moonlight for a bite to eat.
They march on their soles up Main Street:
white stripes, moonstruck eyes' red fire
under the chalk-dry and spar spire   40
of the Trinitarian Church.

I stand on top
of our back steps and breathe the rich air —
a mother skunk with her column of kittens swills the garbage pail.
She jabs her wedge-head in a cup   45
of sour cream, drops her ostrich tail,
and will not scare.

[1963]

ROBERT DUNCAN   [1919–1988]

The Torso

Passages 18

Most beautiful!   the red-flowering eucalyptus,
        the madrone, the yew

    Is he . . .

So thou wouldst smile, and take me in thine arms
The sight of London to my exiled eyes   5
Is as Elysium° to a new-come soul   paradise

        If he be Truth
        I would dwell in the illusion of him

His hands unlocking from chambers of my male body

        such an idea in man's image   10

    rising tides that sweep me towards him

            . . . *homosexual?*

                and at the treasure of his mouth

pour forth my soul

his soul   commingling   15

I thought a Being more than vast, His body leading
    into Paradise,   his eyes
        quickening a fire in me,   a trembling

hieroglyph:°   At the root of the neck

the clavicle, for the neck is the stem of the great artery   20
    upward into his head that is beautiful

            At the rise of the pectoral muscle,

the nipples, for the breasts are like sleeping fountains
    of feeling in man, waiting above the beat of his heart,
    shielding the rise and fall of his breath, to be   25
    awakend

            At the axis of his mid hriff

the navel, for in the pit of his stomach the chord from
    which first he was fed has its temple

            At the root of the groin   30

the pubic hair, for the torso is the stem in which the man
    flowers forth and leads to the stamen of flesh in which
    his seed rises

a wave of need and desire over   taking me

            cried out my name   35

    (This was long ago.   It was another life)

                and said,

    What do you want of me?

I do not know, I said.   I have fallen in love.   He
    has brought me into heights and depths my heart   40
        would fear   without him.   His look

    pierces my side   •   fire eyes   •

    I have been waiting for you, he said:
        I know what you desire

        you do not yet know   but through me   •   45

19. hieroglyph: A picture or symbol representing a word or sound.

And I am with you everywhere.   In your falling

I have fallen from a high place.   I have raised myself

from darkness in your   rising

wherever you are

my hand in your hand   seeking   the locks, the keys   50

I am there.   Gathering me, you gather

your Self   •

For my Other is not a woman but a man

the King upon whose bosom let me lie.

[1968]

CHARLES BUKOWSKI   [1920–1994]

my old man

16 years old
during the depression
I'd come home drunk
and all my clothing—
shorts, shirts, stockings—   5
suitcase, and pages of
short stories
would be thrown out on the
front lawn and about the
street.   10

my mother would be
waiting behind a tree:
"Henry, Henry, don't
go in . . . he'll
kill you, he's read   15
your stories . . ."

"I can whip his
ass . . ."

"Henry, please take
this . . . and   20
find yourself a room."

but it worried him
that I might not
finish high school
so I'd be back   25
again.

one evening he walked in
with the pages of
one of my short stories
(which I had never submitted   30
to him)
and he said, "this is
a great short story."
I said, "o.k.,"
and he handed it to me   35
and I read it.
it was a story about
a rich man
who had a fight with
his wife and had   40
gone out into the night
for a cup of coffee
and had observed
the waitress and the spoons
and forks and the   45
salt and pepper shakers
and the neon sign
in the window
and then had gone back
to his stable   50
to see and touch his
favorite horse
who then
kicked him in the head
and killed him.   55

somehow
the story held
meaning for him
though
when I had written it   60
I had no idea
of what I was
writing about.

so I told him,
"o.k., old man, you can
have it."   65
and he took it
and walked out
and closed the door.
I guess that's
as close   70
as we ever got.

[1977]

RICHARD WILBUR   [b. 1921]

Love Calls Us to the Things
of This World

The eyes open to a cry of pulleys,
And spirited from sleep, the astounded soul
Hangs for a moment bodiless and simple
As false dawn.
                    Outside the open window
The morning air is all awash with angels.   5

Some are in bed-sheets, some are in blouses,
Some are in smocks: but truly there they are.
Now they are rising together in calm swells
Of halcyon feeling, filling whatever they wear
With the deep joy of their impersonal breathing;   10

Now they are flying in place, conveying
The terrible speed of their omnipresence, moving
And staying like white water; and now of a sudden
They swoon down into so rapt a quiet
That nobody seems to be there.
                              The soul shrinks   15

From all that it is about to remember,
From the punctual rape of every blessèd day,
And cries,
          "Oh, let there be nothing on earth but laundry,
Nothing but rosy hands in the rising steam
And clear dances done in the sight of heaven."   20

Yet, as the sun acknowledges
With a warm look the world's hunks and colors,
The soul descends once more in bitter love
To accept the waking body, saying now
In a changed voice as the man yawns and rises,   25

   "Bring them down from their ruddy gallows;
Let there be clean linen for the backs of thieves;
Let lovers go fresh and sweet to be undone,
And the heaviest nuns walk in a pure floating
Of dark habits,
                keeping their difficult balance."   30

                                            [1956]

PHILIP LARKIN   [1922–1985]

High Windows

When I see a couple of kids
And guess he's fucking her and she's
Taking pills or wearing a diaphragm,
I know this is paradise

Everyone old has dreamed of all their lives —   5
Bonds and gestures pushed to one side
Like an outdated combine harvester,
And everyone young going down the long slide

To happiness, endlessly. I wonder if
Anyone looked at me, forty years back,   10
And thought, *That'll be the life;*
No God any more, or sweating in the dark

About hell and that, or having to hide
What you think of the priest. He
And his lot will all go down the long slide   15
Like free bloody birds. And immediately

Rather than words comes the thought of high windows:
The sun-comprehending glass,
And beyond it, the deep blue air, that shows
Nothing, and is nowhere, and is endless.   20

                                            [1974]

DENISE LEVERTOV   [1923–1997]

In Thai Binh (Peace) Province

for Muriel and Jane

I've used up all my film on bombed hospitals,
bombed village schools, the scattered
lemon-yellow cocoons at the bombed silk-factory,

and for the moment all my tears too
are used up, having seen today   5
yet another child with its feet blown off,
       a girl, this one, eleven years old,
patient and bewildered in her home, a fragile
small house of mud bricks among rice fields.

So I'll use my dry burning eyes   10
to photograph within me
dark sails of the river boats,
warm slant of afternoon light
apricot on the brown, swift, wide river,
village towers — church and pagoda — on the far shore,   15
and a boy and small bird both
perched, relaxed, on a quietly grazing
buffalo.   Peace within the
        long war.

It is that life, unhurried, sure, persistent,   20
I must bring home when I try to bring
the war home.
        Child, river, light.

Here the future, fabled bird
that has migrated away from America,   25
nests, and breeds, and sings,

common as any sparrow.

[1975]

MAXINE KUMIN [b. 1925]

Credo

I believe in magic. I believe in the rights
of animals to leap out of our skins
as recorded in the Kiowa legend:
Directly there was a bear where the boy had been

as I believe in the resurrected wake-robin,   5
first wet knob of trillium to knock
in April at the underside of earth's door
in central New Hampshire where bears are

though still denned up at that early greening.
I believe in living on grateful terms   10
with the earth, with the black crumbles
of ancient manure that sift through my fingers

when I topdress the garden for winter. I believe
in the wet strings of earthworms aroused out of season
and in the bear, asleep now in the rock cave   15
where my outermost pasture abuts the forest.

I cede him a swale of chokecherries in August.
I give the sow and her cub as much yardage
as they desire when our paths intersect
as does my horse shifting under me   20

respectful but not cowed by our encounter.
I believe in the gift of the horse, which is magic,
their deep fear-snorts in play when the wind comes up,
the ballet of nip and jostle, plunge and crow hop.

I trust them to run from me, necks arched in a full   25
swan's S, tails cocked up over their backs
like plumes on a Cavalier's hat. I trust them
to gallop back, skid to a stop, their nostrils

level with my mouth, asking for my human breath
that they may test its intent, taste the smell of it.   30
I believe in myself as their sanctuary
and the earth with its summer plumes of carrots,

its clamber of peas, beans, masses of tendrils
as mine. I believe in the acrobatics of boy
into bear, the grace of animals   35
in my keeping, the thrust to go on.

[1992]

KENNETH KOCH   [1925–2002]

Thank You

Oh thank you for giving me the chance
Of being ship's doctor! I am sorry that I shall have to refuse —
But, you see, the most I know of medicine is orange flowers
Tilted in the evening light against a cashmere red
Inside which breasts invent the laws of light   5
And of night, where cashmere moors itself across the sea.
And thank you for giving me these quintuplets
To rear and make happy . . . My mind was on something else.

Thank you for giving me this battleship to wash,
But I have a rash on my hands and my eyes hurt,   10
And I know so little about cleaning a ship
That I should rather clean an island.
There one knows what one is about — sponge those palm trees, sweep
     up the sand a little, polish those coconuts;
Then take a rest for a while and it's time to trim the grass as well as
     separate it from each other where gummy substances have made
     individual blades stick together, forming an ugly bunch;
And then take the dead bark off the trees, and perfume these islands
     a bit with a song. . . . That's easy — but a battleship!   15
Where does one begin and how does one do? to batten the hatches?
     I would rather clean a million palm trees.

Now here comes an offer of a job for setting up a levee
In Mississippi. No thanks. Here it says *Rape or Worse.* I think they
     must want me to publicize this book.
On the jacket it says "Published in Boothbay Harbor, Maine" — what
     a funny place to publish a book!
I suppose it is some provincial publishing house   20
Whose provincial pages emit the odor of sails
And the freshness of the sea
Breeze. . . . But publicity!
The only thing I could publicize well would be my tooth,
Which I could say came with my mouth and in a most engaging manner   25
With my whole self, my body and including my mind,
Spirits, emotions, spiritual essences, emotional substances, poetry,
     dreams, and lords
Of my life, everything, all embraceleted with my tooth
In a way that makes one wish to open the windows and scream "Hi!"
     to the heavens,
And "Oh, come and take me away before I die in a minute!"   30

It is possible that the dentist is smiling, that he dreams of extraction
Because he believes that the physical tooth and the spiritual tooth
   are one.

Here is another letter, this one from a textbook advertiser;
He wants me to advertise a book on chopping down trees.
But how could I? I love trees! and I haven't the slightest sympathy
   with chopping them down, even though I know   35
We need their products for wood-fires, some houses, and maple syrup—
Still I like trees better
In their standing condition, when they sway at the beginning of
   evening . . .
And thank you for the pile of driftwood.
Am I wanted at the sea?   40

And thank you for the chance to run a small hotel
In an elephant stopover in Zambezi,
But I do not know how to take care of guests, certainly they would all
   leave soon
After seeing blue lights out the windows and rust on their iron beds—
   I'd rather own a bird-house in Jamaica:
Those people come in, the birds, they do not care how things are kept
   up . . .   45
It's true that Zambezi proprietorship would be exciting, with people
   getting off elephants and coming into my hotel,
But as tempting as it is I cannot agree.
And thank you for this offer of the post of referee
For the Danish wrestling championship — I simply do not feel
   qualified . . .

But the fresh spring air has been swabbing my mental decks   50
Until, although prepared for fight, still I sleep on land.
Thank you for the ostriches. I have not yet had time to pluck them,
But I am sure they will be delicious, adorning my plate at sunset,
My tremendous plate, and the plate
Of the offers to all my days. But I cannot fasten my exhilaration to
   the sun.   55

And thank you for the evening of the night on which I fell off my horse
   in the shadows. That was really useful.

[1962]

GERALD STERN   [b. 1925]

The Dog

What I was doing with my white teeth exposed
like that on the side of the road I don't know,
and I don't know why I lay beside the sewer
so that lover of dead things could come back
with his pencil sharpened and his piece of white paper.   5
I was there for a good two hours whistling
dirges, shrieking a little, terrifying
hearts with my whimpering cries before I died
by pulling the one leg up and stiffening.
There is a look we have with the hair of the chin   10
curled in mid-air, there is a look with the belly
stopped in the midst of its greed. The lover of dead things
stoops to feel me, his hand is shaking. I know
his mouth is open and his glasses are slipping.
I think his pencil must be jerking and the terror   15
of smell—and sight—is overtaking him;
I know he has that terrified faraway look
that death brings—he is contemplating. I want him
to touch my forehead once and rub my muzzle
before he lifts me up and throws me into   20
that little valley. I hope he doesn't use
his shoe for fear of touching me; I know,
or used to know, the grasses down there; I think
I knew a hundred smells. I hope the dog's way
doesn't overtake him, one quick push,   25
barely that, and the mind freed, something else,
some other thing, to take its place. Great heart,
great human heart, keep loving me as you lift me,
give me your tears, great loving stranger, remember
the death of dogs, forgive the yapping, forgive   30
the shitting, let there be pity, give me your pity.
How could there be enough? I have given
my life for this, emotion has ruined me, oh lover,
I have exchanged my wildness—little tricks
with the mouth and feet, with the tail, my tongue is a parrot's,   35
I am a rampant horse, I am a lion,
I wait for the cookie, I snap my teeth—
as you have taught me, oh distant and brilliant and lonely.

[1987]

FRANK O'HARA   [1926–1966]

The Day Lady° Died

It is 12:20 in New York a Friday
three days after Bastille day,° yes   *(July 14)*
it is 1959 and I go get a shoeshine
because I will get off the 4:19 in Easthampton
at 7:15 and then go straight to dinner   5
and I don't know the people who will feed me

I walk up the muggy street beginning to sun
and have a hamburger and a malted and buy
an ugly NEW WORLD WRITING to see what the poets
in Ghana are doing these days   10
                              I go on to the bank
and Miss Stillwagon (first name Linda I once heard)
doesn't even look up my balance for once in her life
and in the GOLDEN GRIFFIN I get a little Verlaine°   *French poet*
for Patsy with drawings by Bonnard° although I do   15
think of Hesiod,° trans. Richmond Lattimore or   *Greek poet*
Brendan Behan's° new play or *Le Balcon* or *Les Nègres*   *Irish playwright*
of Genet,° but I don't, I stick with Verlaine
after practically going to sleep with quandariness

and for Mike I just stroll into the PARK LANE   20
Liquor Store and ask for a bottle of Strega and
then I go back where I came from to 6th Avenue
and the tobacconist in the Ziegfeld Theatre and
casually ask for a carton of Gauloises° and a carton   *French cigarettes*
of Picayunes,° and a NEW YORK POST with her face on it *Southern cigarettes* 25

and I am sweating a lot by now and thinking of
leaning on the john door in the 5 SPOT
while she whispered a song along the keyboard
to Mal Waldron and everyone and I stopped breathing

                                                       [1964]

Lady: Jazz singer Billie Holliday.
15. Bonnard: French modernist painter.
18. Genet: French playwright and novelist.

ALLEN GINSBERG   [1926–1997]

A Supermarket in California

What thoughts I have of you tonight, Walt Whitman, for I walked down the sidestreets under the trees with a headache self-conscious looking at the full moon.

In my hungry fatigue, and shopping for images, I went into the neon fruit supermarket, dreaming of your enumerations!

What peaches and what penumbras! Whole families shopping at night! Aisles full of husbands! Wives in the avocados, babies in the tomatoes! — and you, García Lorca,° what were you doing down by the watermelons?

I saw you, Walt Whitman, childless, lonely old grubber, poking among the meats in the refrigerator and eyeing the grocery boys.

I heard you asking questions of each: Who killed the pork chops? What price bananas? Are you my Angel?   5

I wandered in and out of the brilliant stacks of cans following you, and followed in my imagination by the store detective.

We strode down the open corridors together in our solitary fancy tasting artichokes, possessing every frozen delicacy, and never passing the cashier.

Where are we going, Walt Whitman? The doors close in an hour. Which way does your beard point tonight?

(I touch your book and dream of our odyssey in the supermarket and feel absurd.)

Will we walk all night through solitary streets? The trees add shade to shade, lights out in the houses, we'll both be lonely.   10

Will we stroll dreaming of the lost America of love past blue automobiles in driveways, home to our silent cottage?

Ah, dear father, graybeard, lonely old courage-teacher, what America did you have when Charon° quit poling his ferry and you got out on a smoking bank and stood watching the boat disappear on the black waters of Lethe?°

Berkeley, 1955

[1956]

---

3. García Lorca: Spanish surrealist poet and playwright (1899–1936).
12. Charon: The boatman in Greek mythology who carried the dead across the river Styx to Hades; **Lethe:** River of Forgetfulness in Hades.

ROBERT CREELEY   [1926–2005]

Time

Moment to
moment the
body seems

to me to
be there: a   5
catch of

air, pattern
of space — Let's
walk today

all the way   10
to the beach,
let's think

of where we'll be
in two years'
time, of where   15

we *were.* Let
the days go.
Each moment is

of such paradoxical
definition — a   20
waterfall that would

flow backward
if it could. It
can? My time,

one thinks,   25
is drawing to
some close. This

feeling comes
and goes. No
measure ever serves   30

enough, enough —
so "finish it"
gets done, alone.

[1972]

JAMES MERRILL   [1926–1995]

The Pier: Under Pisces

The shallows, brighter,
Wetter than water,
Tepidly glitter with the fingerprint-
Obliterating feel of kerosene.

Each piling like a totem   5
Rises from rock bottom
Straight through the ceiling
Aswirl with suns, clear ones or pale bluegreen,

And beyond! where bubbles burst,
Sphere of their worst dreams,   10
If dream is what they do,
These floozy fish —

Ceramic-lipped in filmy
Peekaboo blouses,
Fluorescent body   15
Stockings, hot stripes,

Swayed by the hypnotic ebb and flow
Of supermarket Muzak,
Bolero° beat the undertow's   *a Spanish dance*
Pebble-filled gourds repeat;   20

Jailbait consumers of subliminal
Hints dropped from on high
In gobbets° none   *fragments, bits*
Eschews as minced kin;

Who, hooked themselves — bamboo diviner   25
Bent their way
Vigorously nodding
Encouragement —

Are one by one hauled kisswise, oh
Into some blinding hell   30
Policed by leathery ex-
Justices each

Minding his catch, if catch is what he can,
If mind is what one means —
The torn mouth   35
Stifled by newsprint, working still. If . . . if . . .

The little scales
Grow stiff. Dusk plugs her dryer in,
Buffs her nails, riffles through magazines,
While far and wide and deep   40

Rove the great sharkskin-suited criminals
And safe in this lit shrine
A boy sits. He'll be eight.
We've drunk our milk, we've eaten our stringbeans,

But left untasted on the plate   45
The fish. An eye, a broiled pearl, meeting mine,
I lift his fork . . .
The bite. The tug of fate.

[1985]

ROBERT BLY   [b. 1926]

Driving to Town Late to Mail a Letter

It is a cold and snowy night. The main street is deserted.
The only things moving are swirls of snow.
As I lift the mailbox door, I feel its cold iron.
There is a privacy I love in this snowy night.
Driving around, I will waste more time.   5

[1962]

W. S. MERWIN   [b. 1927]

The Nails

I gave you sorrow to hang on your wall
Like a calendar in one color.
I wear a torn place on my sleeve.
It isn't as simple as that.

Between no place of mine and no place of yours   5
You'd have thought I'd know the way by now
Just from thinking it over.

Oh I know
I've no excuse to be stuck here turning
Like a mirror on a string,   10
Except it's hardly credible how
It all keeps changing.
Loss has a wider choice of directions
Than the other thing.

As if I had a system   15
I shuffle among the lies
Turning them over, if only
I could be sure what I'd lost.
I uncover my footprints, I
Poke them till the eyes open.   20
They don't recall what it looked like.
When was I using it last?
Was it like a ring or a light
Or the autumn pond
Which chokes and glitters but   25
Grows colder?
It could be all in the mind. Anyway
Nothing seems to bring it back to me.

And I've been to see
Your hands as trees borne away on a flood,   30
The same film over and over,
And an old one at that, shattering its account
To the last of the digits, and nothing
And the blank end.

The lightning has shown me the scars of the future.   35

I've had a long look at someone
Alone like a key in a lock
Without what it takes to turn.

It isn't as simple as that.

Winter will think back to your lit harvest   40
For which there is no help, and the seed
Of eloquence will open its wings
When you are gone.
But at this moment
When the nails are kissing the fingers good-bye   45
And my only
Chance is bleeding from me,

When my one chance is bleeding,
For speaking either truth or comfort
I have no more tongue than a wound.   50

[1963]

JOHN ASHBERY   [b. 1927]

Worsening Situation

Like a rainstorm, he said, the braided colors
Wash over me and are no help. Or like one
At a feast who eats not, for he cannot choose
From among the smoking dishes. This severed hand
Stands for life, and wander as it will,   5
East or west, north or south, it is ever
A stranger who walks beside me. O seasons,
Booths, chaleur,° dark-hatted charlatans
On the outskirts of some rural fete,
The name you drop and never say is mine, mine!   10
Some day I'll claim to you how all used up
I am because of you but in the meantime the ride
Continues. Everyone is along for the ride,
It seems. Besides, what else is there?
The annual games? True, there are occasions   15
For white uniforms and a special language
Kept secret from the others. The limes
Are duly sliced. I know all this
But can't seem to keep it from affecting me,
Every day, all day. I've tried recreation,   20
Reading until late at night, train rides
And romance.
               One day a man called while I was out
And left this message: "You got the whole thing wrong
From start to finish. Luckily, there's still time
To correct the situation, but you must act fast.   25
See me at your earliest convenience. And please,
Tell no one of this. Much besides your life depends on it."
I thought nothing of it at the time. Lately

---

8. chaleur: (French) "heat," "warmth"; figuratively, "glow," "passion."

I've been looking at old-fashioned plaids, fingering   30
Starched white collars, wondering whether there's a way
To get them really white again. My wife
Thinks I'm in Oslo — Oslo, France, that is.

[1975]

GALWAY KINNELL   [b. 1927]

The Bear

1

In late winter
I sometimes glimpse bits of steam
coming up from
some fault in the old snow
and bend close and see it is lung-colored   5
and put down my nose
and know
the chilly, enduring odor of bear.

2

I take a wolf's rib and whittle
it sharp at both ends   10
and coil it up
and freeze it in blubber and place it out
on the fairway of the bears.

And when it has vanished
I move out on the bear tracks,   15
roaming in circles
until I come to the first, tentative, dark
splash on the earth.

And I set out
running, following the splashes   20
of blood wandering over the world.
At the cut, gashed resting places
I stop and rest,
at the crawl-marks
where he lay out on his belly   25

to overpass some stretch of bauchy° ice   *weak, thin*
I lie out
dragging myself forward with bear-knives in my fists.

3

On the third day I begin to starve,
at nightfall I bend down as I knew I would   30
at a turd sopped in blood,
and hesitate, and pick it up,
and thrust it in my mouth, and gnash it down,
and rise   35
and go on running.

4

On the seventh day,
living by now on bear blood alone,
I can see his upturned carcass far out ahead, a scraggled,
steamy hulk,
the heavy fur riffling in the wind.   40

I come up to him
and stare at the narrow-spaced, petty eyes,
the dismayed
face laid back on the shoulder, the nostrils
flared, catching   45
perhaps the first taint of me as he
died.

I hack
a ravine in his thigh, and eat and drink,
and tear him down his whole length   50
and open him and climb in
and close him up after me, against the wind,
and sleep.

5

And dream
of lumbering flatfooted   55
over the tundra,
stabbed twice from within,
splattering a trail behind me,
splattering it out no matter which way I lurch,

no matter which parabola of bear-transcendence,   60
which dance of solitude I attempt,
which gravity-clutched leap,
which trudge, which groan.

6

Until one day I totter and fall —
fall on this   65
stomach that has tried so hard to keep up,
to digest the blood as it leaked in,
to break up
and digest the bone itself: and now the breeze
blows over me, blows off   70
the hideous belches of ill-digested bear blood
and rotted stomach
and the ordinary, wretched odor of bear,

blows across
my sore, lolled tongue a song   75
or screech, until I think I must rise up
and dance. And I lie still.

7

I awaken I think. Marshlights
reappear, geese
come trailing again up the flyway.   80
In her ravine under old snow the dam-bear
lies, licking
lumps of smeared fur
and drizzly eyes into shapes
with her tongue. And one   85
hairy-soled trudge stuck out before me,
the next groaned out,
the next,
the next,
the rest of my days I spend   90
wandering: wondering
what, anyway,
was that sticky infusion, that rank flavor of blood, that poetry, by which
    I lived?

[1967]

JAMES WRIGHT   [1927–1980]

A Blessing

Just off the highway to Rochester, Minnesota,
Twilight bounds softly forth on the grass.
And the eyes of those two Indian ponies
Darken with kindness.
They have come gladly out of the willows   5
To welcome my friend and me.
We step over the barbed wire into the pasture
Where they have been grazing all day, alone.

They ripple tensely, they can hardly contain their happiness
That we have come.   10
They bow shyly as wet swans. They love each other.
There is no loneliness like theirs.
At home once more,
They begin munching the young tufts of spring in the darkness.
I would like to hold the slenderer one in my arms,   15
For she has walked over to me
And nuzzled my left hand.
She is black and white,
Her mane falls wild on her forehead,
And the light breeze moves me to caress her long ear   20
That is delicate as the skin over a girl's wrist.
Suddenly I realize
That if I stepped out of my body I would break
Into blossom.

[1963]

PHILIP LEVINE   [b. 1928]

What Work Is

We stand in the rain in a long line
waiting at Ford Highland Park. For work.
You know what work is — if you're
old enough to read this you know what
work is, although you may not do it.   5

Forget you. This is about waiting,
shifting from one foot to another.
Feeling the light rain falling like mist
into your hair, blurring your vision
until you think you see your own brother   10
ahead of you, maybe ten places.
You rub your glasses with your fingers,
and of course it's someone else's brother,
narrower across the shoulders than
yours but with the same sad slouch, the grin   15
that does not hide the stubbornness,
the sad refusal to give in to
rain, to the hours wasted waiting,
to the knowledge that somewhere ahead
a man is waiting who will say, "No,   20
we're not hiring today," for any
reason he wants. You love your brother,
now suddenly you can hardly stand
the love flooding you for your brother,
who's not beside you or behind or   25
ahead because he's home trying to
sleep off a miserable night shift
at Cadillac so he can get up
before noon to study his German.
Works eight hours a night so he can sing   30
Wagner, the opera you hate most,
the worst music ever invented.
How long has it been since you told him
you loved him, held his wide shoulders,
opened your eyes wide and said those words,   35
and maybe kissed his cheek? You've never
done something so simple, so obvious,
not because you're too young or too dumb,
not because you're jealous or even mean
or incapable of crying in   40
the presence of another man, no,
just because you don't know what work is.

[1991]

DONALD HALL   [b. 1928]

Names of Horses

All winter your brute shoulders strained against collars, padding
and steerhide over the ash hames, to haul
sledges of cordwood for drying through spring and summer,
for the Glenwood stove next winter, and for the simmering range.

In April you pulled cartloads of manure to spread on the fields,   5
dark manure of Holsteins, and knobs of your own clustered
    with oats.
All summer you mowed the grass in meadow and hayfield, the mowing
    machine
clacketing beside you, while the sun walked high in the morning;

and after noon's heat, you pulled a clawed rake through the
    same acres,
gathering stacks, and dragged the wagon from stack to stack,   10
and the built hayrack back, up hill to the chaffy barn,
three loads of hay a day, hanging wide from the hayrack.

Sundays you trotted the two miles to church with the light load
of a leather quartertop buggy, and grazed in the sound of hymns.
Generation on generation, your neck rubbed the window sill   15
of the stall, smoothing the wood as the sea smooths glass.

When you were old and lame, when your shoulders hurt bending
    to graze,
one October the man who fed you and kept you, and harnessed you
    every morning,
led you through corn stubble to sandy ground above Eagle Pond,
and dug a hole beside you where you stood shuddering in your skin,   20

and lay the shotgun's muzzle in the boneless hollow behind your ear,
and fired the slug into your brain, and felled you into your grave,
shoveling sand to cover you, setting goldenrod upright above you,
where by next summer a dent in the ground made your monument.

For a hundred and fifty years, in the pasture of dead horses,   25
roots of pine trees pushed through the pale curves of your ribs,
yellow blossoms flourished above you in autumn, and in winter
frost heaved your bones in the ground — old toilers, soil makers:

O Roger, Mackerel, Riley, Ned, Nellie, Chester, Lady Ghost.

[1978]

CONRAD HILBERRY   [b. 1928]

Player Piano

She was right: basement was the place for it.
Who wants a Pianola in the dining room?
It's not an instrument, not a household
object even, more a curiosity.

So with a rented dolly and four big friends   5
from work, he eased it down the cellar stairs,
across the concrete to its place against
the wall. Now he leans back on the bench

and pumps the Basement Rag. His youngest daughter
sits beside him on the bench within
the light of the gooseneck lamp, the dog curls   10
on the rug, and always the ghostly fingers move,

the left hand striding and the right hand climbing
down out of the high notes. Four of them,
father, daughter, dog, and piano player,
all in a circle of light, the roll unwinding   15

its dots and dashes, music clattering out,
and no one saying anything. "Hey,
Cosby's on,"° his wife calls down the stairs.
"Why not come on up?" And so they sit   20

in the kitchen, laughing at Rudy and the Cos.
Afterwards, homework and bed — and he drifts
back to the basement, back to the wooden music.
Gradually, his wife becomes sarcastic,

as if he were counterfeiting bills down there,   25
or dissecting cats. His daughter says she isn't
coming down. But he believes the piano
brings him closer to them all. It's something

he can count on, almost like a law
of nature, not needing praise or inspiration,   30
sticking to its version of the story.
The roll scrolling in front of him is

19. Cosby's on: *The Cosby Show* was a popular television situation comedy
(1984–1992) starring Bill Cosby and Phylicia Rashad.

Morse code talking to people in other basements
or in huts or lean-to's — Sarasota, Caracas,
up-country Liberia. The key taps out   35
news of high winds, the river rising, families

sheltered in the local school, news
of people he's never met, clicking in a voice
without inflection, neither speech
nor silence. The longs and shorts, the steady   40

white keys and the black must carry
through the studs of the house, he thinks,
easing the children into sleep.
He hears a pipe muttering

and knows his wife is drawing water for   45
a bath. It stops. She must be in the tub.
He taps a message on the pipe, binary,
the way nerves talk, signaling across

the gaps, need and love condensed to dots
and dashes. She must hear it as she steams   50
and lathers in the bath, metallic music
played by no one's fingers on the pipes.

[1999]

SAMUEL HAZO   [b. 1928]

For Fawzi in Jerusalem

Leaving a world too old to name
and too undying to forsake,
I flew the cold, expensive sea
toward Columbus' mistake
where life could never be the same   5

for me. In Jerash° on the sand
I saw the colonnades of Rome
bleach in the sun like skeletons.

6. **Jerash:** The ancient city of Gerasa, twenty-two miles north of Amman in
present-day Jordan. Called Jerash by the Romans who rebuilt it in 65 c.e., it is the
best-preserved Palestinian city of Roman times.

Behind a convalescent home,
armed soldiers guarded no man's land   10

between Jordanians and Jews.
Opposing sentries frowned and spat.
Fawzi, you mocked in Arabic
this justice from Jehoshophat°
before you shined my Pittsburgh shoes   15

for nothing. Why you never kept
the coins I offered you is still
your secret and your victory.
Saying you saw marauders kill
your father while Beershebans° wept   20

for mercy in their holy war,
you told me how you stole to stay
alive. You must have thought I thought
your history would make me pay
a couple of piastres more   25

than any shine was worth — and I
was ready to — when you said, "No,
I never take. I never want
America to think I throw
myself on you. I never lie."   30

I watched your young but old man's stare
demand the sword to flash again
in blood and flame from Jericho°
and leave the bones of these new men
of Judah bleaching in the air   35

like Roman stones upon the plain
of Jerash. Then you faced away.
Jerusalem, Jerusalem,
I asked myself if I could pray
for peace and not recall the pain   40

14. Jehoshophat: Hebrew king of Judah (c. 873–849 B.C.E.), the first to make a treaty with the neighboring kingdom of Israel.
20. Beershebans: Inhabitants of Beersheba, a city in southern Israel. Given to the Arabs in the partition of Palestine (1948), it was retaken by Israel in the Arab-Israeli war of 1948.
33. Jericho: Ancient city in biblical Palestine, in the Jordan valley north of the Dead Sea, captured from the Canaanites by Joshua and destroyed (Joshua 6:1–21).

you spoke. But what could praying do?
Today I live your loss in no
man's land but mine, and every time
I talk of fates not just but so,
Fawzi, my friend, I think of you.   45

                                                            [1968]

ANNE SEXTON   [1928–1974]

Cinderella

You always read about it:
the plumber with twelve children
who wins the Irish Sweepstakes.
From toilets to riches.
That story.   5

Or the nursemaid,
some luscious sweet from Denmark
who captures the oldest son's heart.
From diapers to Dior.°
That story.   10

Or a milkman who serves the wealthy,
eggs, cream, butter, yogurt, milk,
the white truck like an ambulance
who goes into real estate
and makes a pile.   15
From homogenized to martinis at lunch.

Or the charwoman
who is on the bus when it cracks up
and collects enough from the insurance.
    From mops to Bonwit Teller.°   20
    That story.

Once
the wife of a rich man was on her deathbed
and she said to her daughter Cinderella:

9. Dior: Fashions designed by the French house of Dior, established by Christian
Dior (1905–1957).
20. Bonwit Teller: A fashionable and expensive department store.

Be devout. Be good. Then I will smile   25
down from heaven in the seam of a cloud.
The man took another wife who had
two daughters, pretty enough
but with hearts like blackjacks.
Cinderella was their maid.   30
She slept on the sooty hearth each night
and walked around looking like Al Jolson.°
Her father brought presents home from town,
jewels and gowns for the other women
but the twig of a tree for Cinderella.   35
She planted that twig on her mother's grave
and it grew to a tree where a white dove sat.
Whenever she wished for anything the dove
would drop it like an egg upon the ground.
The bird is important, my dears, so heed him.   40

Next came the ball, as you all know.
It was a marriage market.
The prince was looking for a wife.
All but Cinderella were preparing
and gussying up for the big event.   45
Cinderella begged to go too.
Her stepmother threw a dish of lentils
into the cinders and said: Pick them
up in an hour and you shall go.
The white dove brought all his friends;   50
all the warm wings of the fatherland came,
and picked up the lentils in a jiffy.
No, Cinderella, said the stepmother,
you have no clothes and cannot dance.
That's the way with stepmothers.   55

Cinderella went to the tree at the grave
and cried forth like a gospel singer:
Mama! Mama! My turtledove,
send me to the prince's ball!
The bird dropped down a golden dress   60
and delicate little gold slippers.
Rather a large package for a simple bird.
So she went. Which is no surprise.

---

32. Al Jolson: American entertainer (1888–1950), known particularly for singing in blackface.

Her stepmother and sisters didn't
recognize her without her cinder face   65
and the prince took her hand on the spot
and danced with no other the whole day.

As nightfall came she thought she'd better
get home. The prince walked her home
and she disappeared into the pigeon house   70
and although the prince took an axe and broke
it open she was gone. Back to her cinders.
These events repeated themselves for three days.
However on the third day the prince
covered the palace steps with cobbler's wax   75
and Cinderella's gold shoe stuck upon it.

Now he would find whom the shoe fit
and find his strange dancing girl for keeps.
He went to their house and the two sisters
were delighted because they had lovely feet.   80
The eldest went into a room to try the slipper on
but her big toe got in the way so she simply
sliced it off and put on the slipper.
The prince rode away with her until the white dove
told him to look at the blood pouring forth.   85
That is the way with amputations.
They don't just heal up like a wish.
The other sister cut off her heel
but the blood told as blood will.
The prince was getting tired.   90
He began to feel like a shoe salesman.
But he gave it one last try.
This time Cinderella fit into the shoe
like a love letter into its envelope.

At the wedding ceremony   95
the two sisters came to curry favor
and the white dove pecked their eyes out.
Two hollow spots were left
like soup spoons.

Cinderella and the prince   100
lived, they say, happily ever after,
like two dolls in a museum case
never bothered by diapers or dust,
never arguing over the timing of an egg,

never telling the same story twice,
never getting a middle-aged spread,   105
their darling smiles pasted on for eternity.
Regular Bobbsey Twins.
That story.

[1971]

ADRIENNE RICH   [b. 1929]

Diving into the Wreck

First having read the book of myths,
and loaded the camera,
and checked the edge of the knife-blade,
I put on
the body-armor of black rubber   5
the absurd flippers
the grave and awkward mask.
I am having to do this
not like Cousteau° with his
assiduous team   10
aboard the sun-flooded schooner
but here alone.

There is a ladder.
The ladder is always there
hanging innocently
close to the side of the schooner.   15
We know what it is for,
we who have used it.
Otherwise
it's a piece of maritime floss
some sundry equipment.   20

I go down.
Rung after rung and still
the oxygen immerses me
the blue light   25

---

9. Cousteau: Jacques-Yves Cousteau (1910–1997), French underwater explorer,
photographer, and author.

the clear atoms
of our human air.
I go down.
My flippers cripple me,
I crawl like an insect down the ladder   30
and there is no one
to tell me when the ocean
will begin.

First the air is blue and then   35
it is bluer and then green and then
black I am blacking out and yet
my mask is powerful
it pumps my blood with power
the sea is another story   40
the sea is not a question of power
I have to learn alone
to turn my body without force
in the deep element.

And now: it is easy to forget   45
what I came for
among so many who have always
lived here
swaying their crenellated° fans
between the reefs   50
and besides
you breathe differently down here.

I came to explore the wreck.
The words are purposes.
The words are maps.   55
I came to see the damage that was done
and the treasures that prevail.
I stroke the beam of my lamp
slowly along the flank
of something more permanent   60
than fish or weed

the thing I came for:
the wreck and not the story of the wreck

48. crenellated: Notched; *crenels* are the open spaces between the solid portions
of a battlement.

the thing itself and not the myth
the drowned face° always staring
toward the sun   65
the evidence of damage
worn by salt and sway into this threadbare beauty
the ribs of the disaster
curving their assertion
among the tentative haunters.   70

This is the place.
And I am here, the mermaid whose dark hair
streams black, the merman in his armored body
We circle silently
about the wreck   75
we dive into the hold.
I am she: I am he

whose drowned face sleeps with open eyes
whose breasts still bear the stress
whose silver, copper, vermeil° cargo lies
obscurely inside barrels   80
half-wedged and left to rot
we are the half-destroyed instruments
that once held to a course
the water-eaten log
the fouled compass   85

We are, I am, you are
by cowardice or courage
the one who find our way
back to this scene
carrying a knife, a camera   90
a book of myths
in which
our names do not appear.

[1973]

64. **drowned face:** The ornamental female figurehead on the prow of an old sailing ship.
80. **vermeil:** Gilded silver, bronze, or copper.

GARY SNYDER   [b. 1930]

Hitch Haiku

They didn't hire him
        so he ate his lunch alone:
the noon whistle

      • • •

Cats shut down
        deer thread through
men all eating lunch

      • • •

Frying hotcakes in a dripping shelter
        Fu Manchu°
Queets Indian Reservation in the rain

      • • •

A truck went by
        three hours ago:
Smoke Creek desert

      • • •

Jackrabbit eyes all night
  breakfast in Elko.

      • • •

Old kanji° hid by dirt
on skidroad Jap town walls
        down the hill
to the Wobbly hall

                  Seattle

      • • •

Spray drips from the cargo-booms
a fresh-chipped winch
        spotted with red lead
young fir —
        soaking in summer rain

      • • •

8. **Fu Manchu:** Master criminal in a series of "Yellow Peril Thrillers" by Sax Rohmer (pen name of Arthur Henry Sarsfield Ward, 1883–1959) that were immensely popular in the first half of the twentieth century.
15. **kanji:** Japanese written characters, or ideographs, borrowed and adapted from Chinese ideographs.

Over the Mindanao Deep

Scrap bass
            dumpt off the fantail
falling six miles

. . .

[*The following two were written on classical
themes while traveling through Sappho, Washington.
The first is by Thomas L. Hoodlatch.*]

Moonlight on the burned-out temple —
            wooden horse shit.

Sunday dinner in Ithaca —
            the twang of a bowstring

. . .

After weeks of watching the roof leak
            I fixed it tonight
by moving a single board

. . .

*A freezing morning in October in the high
Sierra crossing Five Lakes Basin to the
Kaweahs with Bob Greensfelder and Claude Dalenburg*

Stray white mare
            neck rope dangling
forty miles from farms.

. . .

Back from the Kaweahs

Sundown, Timber Gap
            — sat down —
                        dark firs.
    dirty;   cold;
too tired to talk

. . .

Cherry blossoms at Hood river
            rusty sand near Tucson
mudflats of Willapa Bay

. . .

Pronghorn country

Steering into the sun
            glittering jewel-road
shattered obsidian

. . .

The mountain walks over the water!
Rain down from the mountain!
       high bleat of a
cow elk
     over blackberries
         • • •

A great freight truck
      lit like a town
through the dark stony desert
         • • •

Drinking hot saké
         toasting fish on coals
  the motorcycle
out   parked in the rain.
           • • •

Switchback

turn, turn,
and again,   hard-
scrabble
steep travel a-
head.

[1968]

DEREK WALCOTT   [b. 1930]

Sea Grapes

That sail which leans on light,
tired of islands,
a schooner beating up the Caribbean

for home, could be Odysseus,°
home-bound on the Aegean;
that father and husband's

5

4. Odysseus: For background, see page 62. Princess Nausicaa (line 8) fell in love with Odysseus when he was carried by a storm to Phaiacia; he could have married her and stayed there, but he chose to go home (responsibility) rather than to enjoy an indulgent life with her (obsession). Odysseus blinded Polyphemus (line 16), a giant one-eyed Cyclops, who held him prisoner; as Odysseus escaped, Polyphemus threw great rocks in front of his boat to wash it back to shore. The *Odyssey* was written in hexameter verse (line 17).

longing, under gnarled sour grapes, is
like the adulterer hearing Nausicaa's name
in every gull's outcry.

This brings nobody peace. The ancient war   10
between obsession and responsibility
will never finish and has been the same

for the sea-wanderer or the one on shore
now wriggling on his sandals to walk home,
since Troy sighed its last flame,   15

and the blind giant's boulder heaved the trough
from whose groundswell the great hexameters come
to the conclusions of exhausted surf.

The classics can console. But not enough.

[1976]

GEOFFREY HILL   [b. 1932]

In Memory of Jane Fraser

When snow like sheep lay in the fold
And winds went begging at each door,
And the far hills were blue with cold,
And a cold shroud lay on the moor,

She kept the siege. And every day   5
We watched her brooding over death
Like a strong bird above its prey.
The room filled with the kettle's breath.

Damp curtains glued against the pane
Sealed time away. Her body froze   10
As if to freeze us all, and chain
Creation to a stunned repose.

She died before the world could stir.
In March the ice unloosed the brook
And water ruffled the sun's hair.   15
Dead cones upon the alder shook.

[1959]

LINDA PASTAN   [b. 1932]

An Early Afterlife

> *. . . a wise man in time of peace, shall*
> *make the necessary preparations for war.*
> *— Horace*

Why don't we say goodbye right now
in the fallacy of perfect health
before whatever is going to happen
happens. We could perfect our parting,
like those characters in *On the Beach*   5
who said farewell in the shadow
of the bomb as we sat watching,
young and holding hands at the movies.
We could use the loving words
we otherwise might not have time to say.   10
We could hold each other for hours
in a quintessential dress rehearsal.

Then we would just continue
for however many years were left.
The ragged things that are coming next —   15
arteries closing like rivers silting over,
or rampant cells stampeding us to the exit —
would be like postscripts to our lives
and wouldn't matter. And we would bask
in an early afterlife of ordinary days,   20
impervious to the inclement weather
already in our long-range forecast.
Nothing could touch us. We'd never
have to say goodbye again.

[1995]

SYLVIA PLATH   [1932–1963]

Metaphors

I'm a riddle in nine syllables,
An elephant, a ponderous house,
A melon strolling on two tendrils.

O red fruit, ivory, fine timbers!
This loaf's big with its yeasty rising.
Money's new-minted in this fat purse.
I'm a means, a stage, a cow in calf.
I've eaten a bag of green apples,
Boarded the train there's no getting off.

[1960]

SYLVIA PLATH   [1932–1963]

Daddy

You do not do, you do not do
Any more, black shoe
In which I have lived like a foot
For thirty years, poor and white,
Barely daring to breathe or Achoo.   5

Daddy, I have had to kill you.
You died before I had time—
Marble-heavy, a bag full of God,
Ghastly statue with one grey toe
Big as a Frisco seal   10

And a head in the freakish Atlantic
Where it pours bean green over blue
In the waters off beautiful Nauset.
I used to pray to recover you.
Ach, du.°   *Oh, you (German)*   15

In the German tongue, in the Polish town
Scraped flat by the roller
Of wars, wars, wars.
But the name of the town is common.
My Polack friend   20

Says there are a dozen or two.
So I never could tell where you
Put your foot, your root,
I never could talk to you.
The tongue stuck in my jaw.   25

It stuck in a barb wire snare.
Ich, ich, ich, ich,°   *I (German)*

I could hardly speak.
I thought every German was you.
And the language obscene   30

An engine, an engine
Chuffing me off like a Jew.
A Jew to Dachau, Auschwitz, Belsen.°
I began to talk like a Jew.
I think I may well be a Jew.   35

The snows of the Tyrol,° the clear beer of Vienna
Are not very pure or true.
With my gypsy ancestress and my weird luck
And my Taroc pack and my Taroc pack
I may be a bit of a Jew.   40

I have always been scared of *you*,
With your Luftwaffe,° your gobbledygoo.
And your neat moustache
And your Aryan eye, bright blue.
Panzer°-man, panzer-man, O You—   45

Not God but a swastika
So black no sky could squeak through.
Every woman adores a Fascist,
The boot in the face, the brute
Brute heart of a brute like you.   50

You stand at the blackboard, daddy,
In the picture I have of you,
A cleft in your chin instead of your foot
But no less a devil for that, no not
Any less the black man who   55

Bit my pretty red heart in two.
I was ten when they buried you.
At twenty I tried to die
And get back, back, back to you.
I thought even the bones would do.   60

But they pulled me out of the sack,
And they stuck me together with glue.

33. Dachau, Auschwitz, Belsen: Nazi concentration camps.
36. the Tyrol: An alpine region in western Austria and northern Italy.
42. Luftwaffe: The Nazi air force in World War II.
45. Panzer: An armored unit in the German army in World War II.

And then I knew what to do.
I made a model of you,
A man in black with a Meinkampf° look   65

And a love of the rack and the screw.
And I said I do, I do.
So daddy, I'm finally through.
The black telephone's off at the root,
The voices just can't worm through.   70

If I've killed one man, I've killed two—
The vampire who said he was you
And drank my blood for a year,
Seven years, if you want to know.
Daddy, you can lie back now.   75

There's a stake in your fat black heart
And the villagers never liked you.
They are dancing and stamping on you.
They always *knew* it was you.
Daddy, daddy, you bastard, I'm through.   80

[1962]

65. *Mein Kampf:* *My Struggle,* the title of Adolf Hitler's autobiography.

ETHERIDGE KNIGHT   [1933–1991]

Hard Rock Returns to Prison from the Hospital for the Criminal Insane

Hard Rock / was / "known not to take no shit
From nobody," and he had the scars to prove it:
Split purple lips, lumbed ears, welts above
His yellow eyes, and one long scar that cut
Across his temple and plowed through a thick   5
Canopy of kinky hair.

The WORD / was / that Hard Rock wasn't a mean nigger
Anymore, that the doctors had bored a hole in his head,
Cut out part of his brain, and shot electricity
Through the rest. When they brought Hard Rock back,   10
Handcuffed and chained, he was turned loose,
Like a freshly gelded stallion, to try his new status.

And we all waited and watched, like a herd of sheep,
To see if the WORD was true.

As we waited we wrapped ourselves in the cloak   15
Of his exploits: "Man, the last time, it took eight
Screws° to put him in the Hole."° "Yeah, remember when he
Smacked the captain with his dinner tray?" "He set
The record for time in the Hole—67 straight days!"
"Ol Hard Rock! man, that's one crazy nigger."   20
And then the jewel of a myth that Hard Rock had once bit
A screw on the thumb and poisoned him with syphilitic spit.

The testing came, to see if Hard Rock was really tame.
A hillbilly called him a black son of a bitch
And didn't lose his teeth, a screw who knew Hard Rock   25
From before shook him down and barked in his face.
And Hard Rock did *nothing*. Just grinned and looked silly,
His eyes empty like knot holes in a fence.

And even after we discovered that it took Hard Rock
Exactly 3 minutes to tell you his first name,   30
We told ourselves that he had just wised up,
Was being cool; but we could not fool ourselves for long,
And we turned away, our eyes on the ground. Crushed.
He had been our Destroyer, the doer of things
We dreamed of doing but could not bring ourselves to do,   35
The fears of years, like a biting whip,
Had cut deep bloody grooves
Across our backs.

[1968]

17. Screws: Guards; **Hole:** Solitary confinement.

JIM BARNES   [b. 1933]

Return to La Plata, Missouri

The warping bandstand reminds you of the hard rage
you felt in the heart of the town the day you said goodbye
to the park, silver jet, and cicadas dead in the sage.

The town is basic red, although it browns. A cry
of murder, rape, or wrong will always bend the night   5
hard into the broken grass. You listen close for sighs

of lovers on the ground. The darkness gathers light
and throws it down: something glows that you cannot name,
something fierce, abstract, given time and space you might

on a journey leave behind, a stone to carve your fame   10
on, or a simple word like *love*. The sun is down
or always going down in La Plata, the same

sun. Same too the child's cry that turns the mother's frown
brittle as chalk or the town's face against the moon.
Same too the moan of dog and diesel circling the town   15

in an air so heavy with cloud that there is little room
for breath or moon. Strange: in a town so country, so
foreign, you never hear a song nor see a loom

pattern dark threads into a history you would know
and would not know. You think you see one silver star.   20
But the town offers only itself, and you must go.

[1982]

SONIA SANCHEZ   [b. 1934]

An Anthem

for the ANC° and Brandywine Peace Community

Our vision is our voice
we cut through the country
where madmen goosestep in tune to Guernica.°

we are people made of fire
we walk with ceremonial breaths   5
we have condemned talking mouths.

ANC: African National Congress.
3. Guernica: A town in northern Spain that was destroyed in 1937 by insurgents in the Spanish civil war, aided by German planes; the indiscriminate killing of women and children aroused world condemnation, and the bombing of Guernica made it a symbol of fascist brutality.

we run without legs
we see without eyes
loud laughter breaks over our heads.

give me courage so I can spread   10
it over my face and mouth.

we are secret rivers
with shaking hips and crests
come awake in our thunder
so that our eyes can see behind trees.   15

for the world is split wide open
and you hide your hands behind your backs
for the world is broken into little pieces
and you beg with tin cups for life.

are we not more than hunger and music?   20
are we not more than harlequins and horns?
are we not more than color and drums?
are we not more than anger and dance?
give me courage so I can spread it
over my face and mouth.   25

we are the shakers
walking from top to bottom in a day
we are like Shango°
involving ourselves in acts
that bring life to the middle   30
of our stomachs

we are coming towards you madmen
shredding your death talk
standing in front with mornings around our waist
we have inherited our prayers from   35
the rain
our eyes from the children of Soweto.°

28. Shango: One of the orishas, or gods, of the Yoruba tribe of western Nigeria. The legendary fourth king of the ancient kingdom of Oyo, he is lord of lightning, thunder, rain, and testicular fertility.
37. Soweto: A group of segregated townships inhabited by blacks near Johannesburg, South Africa. It was the scene of a massive uprising in 1976 against the policies of apartheid.

red rain pours over the land
and our fire mixes with the water.

give me courage so I can spread   40
it over my face and mouth.

[1987]

PAUL ZIMMER   [b. 1934]

Zimmer Imagines Heaven

for Merrill Leffler

I sit with Joseph Conrad in Monet's garden.
We are listening to Yeats chant his poems,
A breeze stirs through Thomas Hardy's moustache,
John Skelton has gone to the house for beer,
Wanda Landowska lightly fingers a harpsichord,   5
Along the spruce tree walk Roberto Clemente and
Thurman Munson whistle a baseball back and forth.
Mozart chats with Ellington in the roses.

Monet smokes and dabs his canvas in the sun,
Brueghel and Turner set easels behind the wisteria.   10
The band is warming up in the Big Studio:
Bean, Brute, Bird, and Serge on saxes,
Kai, Bill Harris, Lawrence Brown trombones,
Little Jazz, Clifford, Fats, Diz on trumpets,
Klook plays drums, Mingus bass, Bud the piano.   15
Later Madam Schuman-Heink will sing Schubert,
The monks of Benedictine Abbey will chant.
There will be more poems from Emily Dickinson,
James Wright, John Clare, Walt Whitman.
Shakespeare rehearses players for *King Lear*.   20

At dusk Alice Toklas brings out platters
Of sweetbreads, Salad Livonière,
And a tureen of Gazpacho of Málaga.
After the meal Brahms passes fine cigars.
God comes then, radiant with a bottle of cognac,   25
She pours generously into the snifters,
I tell Her I have begun to learn what
Heaven is about. She wants to hear.

It is, I say, being thankful for eternity.
Her smile is the best part of the day.   30

[1996]

Eating Poetry

Ink runs from the corners of my mouth.
There is no happiness like mine.
I have been eating poetry.

The librarian does not believe what she sees.   5
Her eyes are sad
and she walks with her hands in her dress.

The poems are gone.
The light is dim.
The dogs are on the basement stairs and coming up.

Their eyeballs roll,   10
their blond legs burn like brush.
The poor librarian begins to stamp her feet and weep.

She does not understand.
When I get on my knees and lick her hand,
she screams.   15

I am a new man.
I snarl at her and bark.
I romp with joy in the bookish dark.

[1968]

Coal

I   is the total black
being spoken
from the earth's inside.

There are many kinds of open
how a diamond comes   5
into a knot of flame
how sound comes into a word

colored
by who pays what for speaking.

Some words are open   10
diamonds on a glass window
singing out within the crash
of passing sun
other words are stapled wagers
in a perforated book   15
buy and sign and tear apart
and come whatever wills all chances
the stub remains
an ill-pulled tooth
with a ragged edge.   20

Some words live in my throat
breeding like adders
others
know sun
seeking like gypsies   25
over my tongue
to explode through my lips
like young sparrows
bursting from shell.

Some words   30
bedevil me.

Love is a word, another kind of open.
As the diamond comes
into a knot of flame
I am Black   35
because I come from the earth's inside
take my word for jewel
in the open light.

[1962; rev. 1992]

CHARLES WRIGHT   [b. 1935]

March Journal

—After the Rapture comes, and everyone goes away
Quicker than cream in a cat's mouth,
                              all of them gone

In an endless slipknot down the sky
                              and its pink tongue   5
Into the black hole of Somewhere Else,

What will we do, left with the empty spaces of our lives
Intact,
        the radio frequencies still unchanged,
The same houses up for sale,   10
Same books unread,
                all comfort gone and its comforting . . .

For us, the earth is a turbulent rest,
                            a different bed
Altogether, and kinder than that—   15
After the first death is the second,
A little fire in the afterglow,
                    somewhere to warm your hands.

—The clean, clear line, incised, unbleeding,
Sharp and declarative as a cut   20
                        the instant before the blood wells out . . .

—*March Blues*
The insides were blue, the color of Power Putty,
When Luke dissected the dogfish,
                        a plastic blue   25
In the whey
        sharkskin infenestrated:
Its severed tailfin bobbed like a wing nut in another pan
As he explained the dye job
                    and what connected with what,   30
Its pursed lips skewed and pointed straight-lined at the ceiling,
The insides so blue, so blue . . .

March gets its second wind,
                        starlings high shine in the trees
As dread puts its left foot down and then the other.   35
Buds hold their breaths and sit tight.
The weeping cherries
                lower their languorous necks and nibble the grass
Sprout ends that jump headfirst from the ground,
Magnolia drums blue weight   40
                    next door when the sun is right.

—Rhythm comes from the roots of the world,
                            rehearsed and expandable.

—After the ice storm a shower of crystal down from the trees

Shattering over the ground   45
              like cut glass twirling its rainbows,
Sunlight in flushed layers under the clouds,
Twirling and disappearing into the clenched March grass.

— Structure is binary, intent on a resolution,
Its parts tight but the whole loose   50
             and endlessly repetitious.
— And here we stand, caught
In the crucifixal noon
         with its bled, attendant bells,
And nothing to answer back with.   55
Forsythia purrs in its burning shell,
Jonquils, like Dante's angels, appear from their blue shoots.

How can we think to know of another's desire for darkness,
That low coo like a dove's
         insistent outside the heart's window?   60
How can we think to think this?
How can we sit here, crossing out line after line,
Such five-finger exercises
        up and down, learning our scales,

And say that all quartets are eschatological° *pertaining to the end times* 65
Heuristically
      when the willows swim like medusas through the trees,
Their skins beginning to blister into a thousand green welts?
How can we think to know these things,
Clouds like full suds in the sky   70
       keeping away, keeping away?

— Form is finite, an undestroyable hush over all things.

                       [1988]

MARY OLIVER   [b. 1935]

First Snow

The snow
began here
this morning and all day
continued, its white
rhetoric everywhere   5
calling us back to *why, how,*

whence such beauty and *what*
the meaning; such
an oracular fever! flowing
past windows, an energy it seemed   10
would never ebb, never settle
less than lovely! and only now,
deep into night,
it has finally ended.
The silence   15
is immense,
and the heavens still hold
a million candles; nowhere
the familiar things:
stars, the moon,   20
the darkness we expect
and nightly turn from. Trees
glitter like castles
of ribbons, the broad fields
smolder with light, a passing   25
creekbed lies
heaped with shining hills;
and though the questions
that have assailed us all day
remain — not a single   30
answer has been found —
walking out now
into the silence and the light
under the trees,
and through the fields,   35
feels like one.

[1983]

RUSSELL EDSON   [b. 1935]

The Sweet Twilight

By the use of centrifugal force streets are brought up into the sky.
Boulevards move unsupported through the stars. Promenades off these
circle moons and planets . . .

It is a marvelous age, and casual clothes are the fashion. At night
children are heard screaming in the alleys, their bodies being mined for
their organs. It is possible to live forever! And all manner of sweets are

being offered on the public thoroughfares; flavored ices, pastel choco-
lates and cherry soda aphrodisiacs. And oh, the strumming of ukuleles!
Casual clothes! Century-long summers in Alpha Centauri!

I love you, your gray hair spreading like a broken spider's web in
the Martian winds. Come spring and we'll gondola down through the
canals . . .

Space and desire meet, like emptiness and the desire for emptiness,
sucking each into the other, back and forth.

Having opened heaven for its jewelry — chandelier of galaxies, glass
gardens of the night! . . . Having opened ourselves to this opening of
heaven . . . in spite even of living forever in hearing of ukuleles strummed,
the flavored ices, your gray hair in the Martian winds, I felt empty,
emptied out of myself . . .

I hid on earth under my bed listening to the cries of children, and the
dry coughing of paper cups dropping on the boulevards . . .

[1985]

JAYNE CORTEZ   [b. 1936]

Into This Time

for Charles Mingus°

Into this time
of steel feathers blowing from hearts
into this turquoise flame time in the mouth
into this sonic boom time in the conch
into this musty stone-fly time sinking into   5
the melancholy buttocks of dawn
sinking into lacerated whelps
into gun holsters
into breast bones
into a manganese field of uranium nozzles   10
into a nuclear tube full of drunk rodents
into the massive vein of one interval
into one moment's hair plucked down into
the timeless droning fixed into
long pauses   15
fixed into a lash of ninety-eight minutes screeching into

Charles Mingus: An innovative American jazz bassist (1929–1979).

the internal heat of an ice ball melting time into
a configuration of commas on strike
into a work force armed with a calendar of green wings
into a collection of nerves   20
into magnetic mucus
into tongueless shrines
into water pus of a silver volcano
into the black granite face of Morelos°
into the pigeon toed dance of Mingus   25
into a refuge of air bubbles
into a cylinder of snake whistles
into clusters of slow spiders
into spade fish skulls
into rosin coated shadows of women wrapped in live iguanas   30
into coins into crosses into St. Martin De Porres°
into the pain of this place changing pitches beneath
fingers swelling into
night shouts
into day trembles   35
into month of precious bloods flowing into
this fiesta of sadness year
into this city of eternal spring
into this solo
on the road of young bulls   40
on the street of lost children
on the avenue of dead warriors
on the frisky horse tail fuzz zooming
into ears of every madman
stomping into every new composition   45
everyday of the blues
penetrating into this time

This time of loose strings in low tones
pulling boulders of Olmec heads into the sun
into tight wires uncoiling from body of a strip teaser on the table   50
into half-tones wailing between snap and click
of two castanets smoking into
scales jumping from tips of sacrificial flints
into frogs yodeling across grieving cults
yodeling up into word stuffed smell of flamingo stew   55

24. Morelos: José Maria Morelos (1765–1815), a Mexican revolutionary leader.
31. Martin De Porres: A seventeenth-century Peruvian saint.

into wind packed fuel of howling dog throats slit into
this January flare of aluminum dust falling into
laminated stomach of a bass violin rubbed into red ashes
rubbed into the time sequence of
this time of salmonella leaking from eyeballs of a pope   60
into this lavender vomit time in the chest into
this time plumage of dried bats in the brain into
this wallowing time weed of invisible wakes on cassettes into
this off-beat time syncopation in a leopard skin suit
into this radiated protrusion of time in the desert into   65
this frozen cheek time of dead infants in the cellar
into this time flying with the rotten bottoms of used tuxedos
into this purple   brown   grey   gold minus zero time trilling into
a lime stone crusted Yucatan belching
into fifty six medallions shaking   70
into armadillo drums thumping
into tambourines of fetishes rattling
into an oil slick of poverty symbols flapping
into flat-footed shuffle of two birds advancing
into back spine of luminous impulses tumbling   75
into metronomes of colossal lips ticking
into a double zigzag of callouses splitting
into foam of electric snow flashing into this time
of steel feathers blowing from hearts
into this turquoise flame time in the mouth into   80
this sonic boom time in the conch
into this musty stone fly time sinking into
the melancholy buttocks of dawn

[1991]

LUCILLE CLIFTON   [b. 1936]

at the cemetery,
walnut grove plantation,
south carolina, 1989

among the rocks
at walnut grove
your silence drumming

in my bones,
tell me your names.

nobody mentioned slaves
and yet the curious tools
shine with your fingerprints.
nobody mentioned slaves   10
but somebody did this work
who had no guide, no stone,
who moulders under rock.

tell me your names,
tell me your bashful names   15
and i will testify.

the inventory lists ten slaves
but only men were recognized.

among the rocks
at walnut grove   20
some of these honored dead
were dark
some of these dark
were slaves

some of these slaves   25
were women
some of them did this
honored work.
tell me your names
foremothers, brothers,   30
tell me your dishonored names.
here lies
here lies
here lies
here lies   35
hear

                                                    [1991]

NANCY WILLARD   [b. 1936]

Questions My Son Asked Me, Answers I Never Gave Him

1. Do gorillas have birthdays?
   Yes. Like the rainbow, they happen.
   Like the air, they are not observed.

2. Do butterflies make a noise?
   The wire in the butterfly's tongue
   hums gold. Some men hear butterflies   5
   even in winter.

3. Are they part of our family?
   They forgot us, who forgot how to fly.

4. Who tied my navel? Did God tie it?
   God made the thread: O man, live forever!   10
   Man made the knot: enough is enough.

5. If I drop my tooth in the telephone
   will it go through the wires and bite someone's ear?
   I have seen earlobes pierced by a tooth of steel.
   It loves what lasts.   15
   It does not love flesh.
   It leaves a ring of gold in the wound.

6. If I stand on my head
   will the sleep in my eye roll up into my head?
   Does the dream know its own father?   20
   Can bread go back to the field of its birth?

7. Can I eat a star?
   Yes, with the mouth of time
   that enjoys everything.   25

8. Could we Xerox the moon?
   This is the first commandment:
   I am the moon, thy moon.
   Thou shalt have no other moons before thee.

9. Who invented water?   30
   The hands of the air, that wanted to wash each other.

10. What happens at the end of numbers?
    I see three men running toward a field.
    At the edge of the tall grass, they turn into light.

11. Do the years ever run out?   35
    God said, I will break time's heart.
    Time ran down like an old phonograph.
    It lay flat as a carpet.
    At rest on its threads, I am learning to fly.

[1982]

MARGE PIERCY   [b. 1936]

Barbie Doll

This girlchild was born as usual
and presented dolls that did pee-pee
and miniature GE stoves and irons
and wee lipsticks the color of cherry candy.
Then in the magic of puberty, a classmate said: 5
You have a great big nose and fat legs.

She was healthy, tested intelligent,
possessed strong arms and back,
abundant sexual drive and manual dexterity.
She went to and fro apologizing.   10
Everyone saw a fat nose on thick legs.

She was advised to play coy,
exhorted to come on hearty,
exercise, diet, smile and wheedle.
Her good nature wore out   15
like a fan belt.
So she cut off her nose and her legs
and offered them up.

In the casket displayed on satin she lay
with the undertaker's cosmetics painted on,   20
a turned-up putty nose,
dressed in a pink and white nightie.
Doesn't she look pretty? everyone said.
Consummation at last.
To every woman a happy ending.   25

[1973]

CHARLES SIMIC   [b. 1938]

Begotten of the Spleen°

The Virgin Mother° walked barefoot
Among the land mines.
She carried an old man in her arms
Like a howling babe.

The earth was an old people's home.   5
Judas was the night nurse,
Emptying bedpans into the river Jordan,
Tying people on a dog chain.

The old man had two stumps for legs.
St. Peter came pushing a cart   10
Loaded with flying carpets.
They were not flying carpets.

They were piles of bloody diapers.
The Magi° stood around
Cleaning their nails with bayonets.   15
The old man gave little Mary Magdalene°

A broken piece of a mirror.
She hid in the church outhouse.
When she got thirsty she licked
the steam off the glass.   20

That leaves Joseph.° Poor Joseph,
Standing naked in the snow.
He only had a rat
To load his suitcases on.

The rat wouldn't run into its hole.   25
Even when the lights came on —
And the lights came on:
The floodlights in the guard towers.

[1980; 1999]

Spleen: Once believed to be the source in a person either of high spirit, courage,
and resolute mind or of ill-nature, ill-humor, and irritable or peevish temper.
1. The Virgin Mother: Mary, the mother of Jesus.
14. Magi: The wise men from the East who visited the baby Jesus.
16. Mary Magdalene: A follower of Jesus who was present at his crucifixion and
burial and who went to the tomb on Easter Sunday to anoint his body.
21. Joseph: The husband of Mary, the mother of Jesus.

MICHAEL S. HARPER   [b. 1938]

Nightmare Begins Responsibility

I place these numbed wrists to the pane
watching white uniforms whisk over
him in the tube-kept
prison
fear what they will do in experiment   5
watch my gloved stickshifting gasolined hands
breathe *boxcar-information-please* infirmary tubes
distrusting white-pink mending paperthin
silkened end hairs, distrusting tubes
shrunk in his *trunk-skincapped*   10
shaven head, in thighs
distrusting-white-hands-picking-baboon-light
on this son who will not make his second night
of this wardstrewn intensive airpocket
where his father's asthmatic   15
hymns of *night-train,* train done gone
his mother can only know that he has flown
up into essential calm unseen corridor
going boxscarred home, *mamaborn, sweetsonchild*
gonedowntown into *researchtestingwarehousebatteryacid*   20
mama-son-done-gone/me telling her 'nother
train tonight, no music, no breathstroked
heartbeat in my infinite distrust of them:

and of my distrusting self
white-doctor-who-breathed-for-him-all-night   25
say it for two sons gone,
say nightmare, say it loud
panebreaking heartmadness:
nightmare begins responsibility.

[1975]

SEAMUS HEANEY   [b. 1939]

Digging

Between my finger and my thumb
The squat pen rests; snug as a gun.

Under my window, a clean rasping sound
When the spade sinks into gravelly ground:
My father, digging. I look down   5

Till his straining rump among the flowerbeds
Bends low, comes up twenty years away
Stooping in rhythm through potato drills
Where he was digging.

The coarse boot nestled on the lug, the shaft   10
Against the inside knee was levered firmly.
He rooted out tall tops, buried the bright edge deep
To scatter new potatoes that we picked
Loving their cool hardness in our hands.

By God, the old man could handle a spade.   15
Just like his old man.

My grandfather cut more turf in a day
Than any other man on Toner's bog.
Once I carried him milk in a bottle
Corked sloppily with paper. He straightened up   20
To drink it, then fell to right away
Nicking and slicing neatly, heaving sods
Over his shoulder, going down and down
For the good turf. Digging.

The cold smell of potato mould, the squelch and slap 25
Of soggy peat, the curt cuts of an edge
Through living roots awaken in my head.
But I've no spade to follow men like them.

Between my finger and my thumb
The squat pen rests.   30
I'll dig with it.

[1966]

MARGARET ATWOOD   [b. 1939]

True Stories

I

Don't ask for the true story;
why do you need it?

It's not what I set out with
or what I carry.

What I'm sailing with,   5
a knife, blue fire,

luck, a few good words
that still work, and the tide.

II

The true story was lost
on the way down to the beach, it's something   10

I never had, that black tangle
of branches in a shifting light,

my blurred footprints
filling with salt

water, this handful   15
of tiny bones, this owl's kill;

a moon, crumpled papers, a coin,
the glint of an old picnic,

the hollows made by lovers
in sand a hundred   20

years ago: no clue.

III

The true story lies
among the other stories,

a mess of colours, like jumbled clothing
thrown off or away,   25

like hearts on marble, like syllables, like
butchers' discards.

The true story is vicious
and multiple and untrue

after all. Why do you   30
need it? Don't ever

ask for the true story.

[1981]

TED KOOSER   [b. 1939]

Old Cemetery

Somebody has been here this morning
to cut the grass, coming and going unseen
but leaving tracks, probably driving a pickup
with a low mower trailer that bent down
the weeds in the lane from the highway,   5
somebody paid by the job, not paid enough,
and mean and peevish, too hurried
to pull the bindweed that weaves up
into the filigreed iron crosses
or to trim the tall red prairie grass   10
too close to the markers to mow
without risking the blade. Careless
and reckless, too, leaving green paint
scraped from the deck of the mower
on the cracked concrete base of a marker.   15
The dead must have been overjoyed
to have their world back to themselves,
to hear the creak of trailer springs
under the weight of the cooling mower
and to hear the pickup turn over and over   20
and start at last, and drive away,
and then to hear the soft ticking of weeds
springing back, undeterred, in the lane
that leads nowhere the dead want to go.

[2004]

AL YOUNG   [b. 1939]

A Dance for Ma Rainey

I'm going to be just like you, Ma
Rainey this monday morning
clouds puffing up out of my head
like those balloons
that float above the faces of white people   5
in the funnypapers
I'm going to hover in the corners
of the world, Ma
& sing from the bottom of hell
up to the tops of high heaven   10
& send out scratchless waves of yellow
& brown & that basic black honey
misery

I'm going to cry so sweet
& so low   15
& so dangerous,
Ma,
that the message is going to reach you
back in 1922
where you shimmer   20
snaggle-toothed
perfumed &
powdered
in your bauble beads

hair pressed & tied back   25
throbbing with that sick pain
I know
& hide so well
that pain that blues
jives the world with   30
aching to be heard
that downness
that bottomlessness
first felt by some stolen delta nigger
swamped under with redblooded american agony;   35
reduced to the sheer shit
of existence

that bred
& battered us all,
Ma,
the beautiful people   40
our beautiful brave black people
who no longer need to jazz
or sing to themselves in murderous vibrations
or play the veins of their strong tender arms   45
with needles
to prove we're still here

[1969]

JAMES WELCH   [b. 1940]

Christmas Comes to Moccasin Flat

Christmas comes like this: Wise men
unhurried, candles bought on credit (poor price
for calves), warriors face down in wine sleep.
Winds cheat to pull heat from smoke.

Friends sit in chinked cabins, stare out
plastic windows and wait for commodities.   5
Charlie Blackbird, twenty miles from church
and bar, stabs his fire with flint.

When drunks drain radiators for love
or need, chiefs eat snow and talk of change,
an urge to laugh pounding their ribs.   10
Elk play games in high country.

Medicine Woman, clay pipe and twist tobacco,
calls each blizzard by name and predicts
five o'clock by spitting at her television.   15
Children lean into her breath to beg a story:

Something about honor and passion,
warriors back with meat and song,
a peculiar evening star, quick vision of birth.
Blackbird feeds his fire. Outside, a quick 30 below.   20

[1976]

NELLIE WONG   [b. 1940]

Grandmother's Song

Grandmothers sing their song
Blinded by the suns' rays
Grandchildren for whom they long
For pomelo°-golden days   *grapefruit*

Blinded by the sun's rays   5
Gold bracelets, opal rings
For pomelo-golden days
Tiny fingers, ancient things

Gold bracelets, opal rings   10
Sprinkled with Peking dust
Tiny fingers, ancient things
So young they'll never rust

Sprinkled with Peking dust
To dance in fields of mud   15
So young they'll never rust
Proud as if of royal blood

To dance in fields of mud
Or peel shrimp for pennies a day
Proud as if of royal blood   20
Coins and jade to put away

Or peel shrimp for pennies a day
Seaweed washes up the shore
Coins and jade to put away
A camphor chest is home no more

Seaweed washes up the shore   25
Bound feet struggle to loosen free
A camphor chest is home no more
A foreign tongue is learned at three

Bound feet struggle to loosen free   30
Grandchildren for whom they long
A foreign tongue is learned at three
Grandmothers sing their song

[1977]

ROBERT PINSKY   [b. 1940]

Shirt

The back, the yoke, the yardage. Lapped seams,
The nearly invisible stitches along the collar
Turned in a sweatshop by Koreans or Malaysians

Gossiping over tea and noodles on their break
Or talking money or politics while one fitted
This armpiece with its overseam to the band   5

Of cuff I button at my wrist. The presser, the cutter,
The wringer, the mangle. The needle, the union,
The treadle, the bobbin. The code. The infamous blaze

At the Triangle Factory° in nineteen-eleven.   *(in New York City)*   10
One hundred and forty-six died in the flames
On the ninth floor, no hydrants, no fire escapes—

The witness in a building across the street
Who watched how a young man helped a girl to step
Up to the windowsill, then held her out   15

Away from the masonry wall and let her drop.
And then another. As if he were helping them up
To enter a streetcar, and not eternity.

A third before he dropped her put her arms
Around his neck and kissed him. Then he held   20
Her into space, and dropped her. Almost at once

He stepped to the sill himself, his jacket flared
And fluttered up from his shirt as he came down,
Air filling up the legs of his gray trousers—

Like Hart Crane's Bedlamite, "shrill shirt ballooning."   25
Wonderful how the pattern matches perfectly
Across the placket and over the twin bar-tacked

Corners of both pockets, like a strict rhyme
Or a major chord. Prints, plaids, checks,
Houndstooth, Tattersall, Madras. The clan tartans   30

Invented by mill-owners inspired by the hoax of Ossian,°
To control their savage Scottish workers, tamed
By a fabricated heraldry: MacGregor,

Bailey, MacMartin. The kilt, devised for workers   35
To wear among the dusty clattering looms.
Weavers, carders, spinners. The loader,

The docker, the navvy. The planter, the picker, the sorter
Sweating at her machine in a litter of cotton
As slaves in calico headrags sweated in fields:

George Herbert,° your descendant is a Black   40
Lady in South Carolina, her name is Irma
And she inspected my shirt. Its color and fit

And feel and its clean smell have satisfied
Both her and me. We have culled its cost and quality
Down to the buttons of simulated bone,   45

The buttonholes, the sizing, the facing, the characters
Printed in black on neckband and tail. The shape,
The label, the labor, the color, the shade. The shirt.

[1990]

31. Ossian: Legendary Gaelic poet, hero of a cycle of traditional tales and poems that place him in the third century C.E. The hoax involved Scottish author James Macpherson (1736–1796), who published two epic poems that he said were translations of works written by Ossian but were in fact mostly composed by Macpherson himself.
40. George Herbert: English metaphysical poet (1593–1633).

BILLY COLLINS   [b. 1941]

Nostalgia

Remember the 1340s? We were doing a dance called the Catapult.
You always wore brown, the color craze of the decade,
and I was draped in one of those capes that were popular,
the ones with unicorns and pomegranates in needlework.
Everyone would pause for beer and onions in the afternoon,   5

and at night we would play a game called "Find the Cow."
Everything was hand-lettered then, not like today.

Where has the summer of 1572 gone? Brocade and sonnet
marathons were the rage. We used to dress up in the flags
of rival baronies and conquer one another in cold rooms
    of stone.
Out on the dance floor we were all doing the Struggle
while your sister practiced the Daphne all alone in her room.
We borrowed the jargon of farriers for our slang.
These days language seems transparent, a badly broken code.

The 1790s will never come again. Childhood was big.
People would take walks to the very tops of hills
and write down what they saw in their journals without
    speaking.
Our collars were high and our hats were extremely soft.
We would surprise each other with alphabets made
    of twigs.
It was a wonderful time to be alive, or even dead.

I am very fond of the period between 1815 and 1821.
Europe trembled while we sat still for our portraits.
And I would love to return to 1901 if only for a moment,
time enough to wind up a music box and do a few
    dance steps,
or shoot me back to 1922 or 1941, or at least let me
recapture the serenity of last month when we picked
berries and glided through afternoons in a canoe.

Even this morning would be an improvement over
    the present.
I was in the garden then, surrounded by the hum of bees
and the Latin names of flowers, watching the early light
flash off the slanted windows of the greenhouse
and silver the limbs on the rows of dark hemlocks.

As usual, I was thinking about the moments of the past,
letting my memory rush over them like water
rushing over the stones on the bottom of a stream.
I was even thinking a little about the future, that place
where people are doing a dance we cannot imagine,
a dance whose name we can only guess.

[1991]

RICHARD GARCIA   [b. 1941]

Why I Left the Church

Maybe it was
because the only time
I hit a baseball
it smashed the neon cross
on the church across   5
the street. Even
twenty-five years later
when I saw Father Harris
I would wonder
if he knew it was me.   10
Maybe it was the demon-stoked
rotisseries of purgatory
where we would roast
hundreds of years
for the smallest of sins.   15
Or was it the day
I wore my space helmet
to catechism? Clear plastic
with a red-and-white
inflatable rim.   20
Sister Mary Bernadette
pointed toward the door
and said, "Out! Come back
when you're ready."
I rose from my chair   25
and kept rising
toward the ceiling
while the children
screamed and Sister
kept crossing herself.   30
The last she saw of me
was my shoes disappearing
through cracked plaster.
I rose into the sky and beyond.
It is a good thing   35
I am wearing my helmet,
I thought as I floated
and turned in the blackness
and brightness of outer space,

my body cold on one side and hot
on the other. It would   40
have been very quiet
if my blood had not been
rumbling in my ears so loud.
I remember thinking,
Maybe I will come back   45
when I'm ready.
But I won't tell
the other children
what it was like.
I'll have to make something up.   50

[1993]

SIMON J. ORTIZ   [b. 1941]

Speaking

I take him outside
under the trees,
have him stand on the ground.
We listen to the crickets,
cicadas, million years old sound.
Ants come by us.   5
I tell them,
"This is he, my son.
This boy is looking at you.
I am speaking for him."   10

The crickets, cicadas,
the ants, the millions of years
are watching us,
hearing us.
My son murmurs infant words,   15
speaking, small laughter
bubbles from him.
Tree leaves tremble.
They listen to this boy
speaking for me.   20

[1977]

TOI DERRICOTTE   [b. 1941]

A Note on My Son's Face

I

Tonight, I look, thunderstruck
at the gold head of my grandchild.
Almost asleep, he buries his feet
between my thighs;
his little straw eyes   5
close in the near dark.
I smell the warmth of his raw
slightly foul breath, the new death
waiting to rot inside him.
Our breaths equalize our heartbeats;   10
every muscle of the chest uncoils,
the arm bones loosen in the nest
of nerves. I think of the peace
of walking through the house,
pointing to the name of this, the name of that,   15
an educator of a new man.

Mother. Grandmother. Wise
Snake-woman who will show the way;
Spider-woman whose black tentacles
hold him precious. Or will tear off his head,   20
her teeth over the little husband,
the small fist clotted in trust at her breast.

This morning, looking at the face of his father,
I remembered how, an infant, his face was too dark,
nose too broad, mouth too wide.   25
I did not look in that mirror
and see the face that could save me
from my own darkness.
Did he, looking in my eye, see
what I turned from: 30
my own dark grandmother
bending over gladioli in the field,
her shaking black hand defenseless
at the shining cock of flower?

I wanted that face to die,   35
to be reborn in the face of a white child.
I wanted the soul to stay the same,

for I loved to death,
to damnation and God-death,
the soul that broke out of me.
I crowed: My Son! My Beautiful!   40
But when I peeked in the basket,
I saw the face of a black man.

Did I bend over his nose
and straighten it with my fingers
like a vine growing the wrong way?   45
Did he feel my hand in malice?

Generations we prayed and fucked
for this light child,
the shining god of the second coming;
we bow down in shame   50
and carry the children of the past
in our wallets, begging forgiveness.

II

A picture in a book,
a lynching.
The bland faces of men who watch   55
a Christ go up in flames, smiling,
as if he were a hooked
fish, a felled antelope, some
wild thing tied to boards and burned.
His charring body   60
gives off light—a halo
burns out of him.
His face scorched featureless;
the hair matted to the scalp
like feathers.   65
One man stands with his hand on his hip,
another with his arm
slung over the shoulder of a friend,
as if this moment were large enough
to hold affection.   70

III

How can we wake
from a dream
we are born into,
that shines around us,
the terrible bright air?   75

Having awakened,
having seen our own bloody hands,
how can we ask forgiveness,
bring before our children the real   80
monster of their nightmares?

The worst is true.
Everything you did not want to know.

[1989]

SHARON OLDS   [b. 1942]

I Go Back to May 1937

I see them standing at the formal gates of their colleges,
I see my father strolling out
under the ochre sandstone arch, the
red tiles glinting like bent
plates of blood behind his head, I   5
see my mother with a few light books at her hip
standing at the pillar made of tiny bricks with the
wrought-iron gate still open behind her, its
sword-tips black in the May air,
they are about to graduate, they are about to get married,   10
they are kids, they are dumb, all they know is they are
innocent, they would never hurt anybody.
I want to go up to them and say Stop,
don't do it—she's the wrong woman,
he's the wrong man, you are going to do things   15
you cannot imagine you would ever do,
you are going to do bad things to children,
you are going to suffer in ways you never heard of,
you are going to want to die. I want to go
up to them there in the late May sunlight and say it,   20
her hungry pretty blank face turning to me,
her pitiful beautiful untouched body,
his arrogant handsome blind face turning to me,
his pitiful beautiful untouched body,
but I don't do it. I want to live. I   25
take them up like the male and female
· paper dolls and bang them together
at the hips like chips of flint as if to

strike sparks from them, I say
Do what you are going to do, and I will tell about it.   30

[1987]

MARILYN HACKER   [b. 1942]

Villanelle

Every day our bodies separate,
explode torn and dazed.
Not understanding what we celebrate

we grope through languages and hesitate
and touch each other, speechless and amazed;   5
and every day our bodies separate

us further from our planned, deliberate
ironic lives. I am afraid, disphased,
not understanding what we celebrate

when our fused limbs and lips communicate   10
the unlettered power we have raised.
Every day our bodies' separate

routines are harder to perpetuate.
In wordless darkness we learn wordless praise,
not understanding what we celebrate;   15

wake to ourselves, exhausted, in the late
morning as the wind tears off the haze,
not understanding how we celebrate
our bodies. Every day we separate.

[1974]

ELLEN BRYANT VOIGT   [b. 1943]

Dooryard Flower

Because you're sick I want to bring you flowers,
flowers from the landscape that you love —
because it is your birthday and you're sick
I want to bring outdoors inside,
the natural and wild, picked by my hand,   5

but nothing is blooming here but daffodils,
archipelagic in the short green
early grass, erupted
bulbs planted decades before we came,
the edge of where a garden once was kept   10
extended now in a string of islands I straddle
as in a fairy tale, harvesting,
not taking the single blossom from a clump
but thinning where they're thickest, tall-stemmed
from the mother patch, dwarf to the west, most   15
fully opened, a loosened whorl,
one with a pale spider luffing her thread,
one with a slow beetle chewing the lip, a few
with what's almost a lion's face, a lion's mane,
and because there is a shadow on your lungs, your liver,   20
and elsewhere, hidden,
some of those with delicate green
streaks in the clown's ruff (*corolla* —
actually made from adapted leaves), and more
right this moment starting to unfold, I've gathered   25
my two fists full, I carry them like a bride,
I am bringing you the only glorious thing
in the yards and fields between my house and yours,
none of the tulips budded yet, the lilac
a sheaf of sticks, the apple trees   30
withheld, the birch unleaved —
it could still be winter here, were it not
for green dotted with gold, but you won't wait
for dogtoothed violets, trillium under the pines,
and who could bear azaleas, dogwood, early profuse rose   35
of somewhere else when you're assaulted here, early May,
not any calm narcissus, orange *corona*
on scalloped white, not even its slender stalk
in a fountain of leaves, no stiff cornets of the honest
jonquils, gendered parts upthrust in brass and cream: 40
just this common flash in anyone's yard,
scrambled cluster of petals
crayon-yellow, as in a child's drawing of the sun,
I'm bringing you a sun, a children's choir, host
of transient voices, first bright   45
splash in the gray exhausted world, a feast
of the dooryard flower we call butter-and-egg.

                                                              [2002]

LOUISE GLÜCK   [b. 1943]

The Wild Iris

At the end of my suffering
there was a door.

Hear me out: that which you call death
I remember.

Overhead, noises, branches of the pine shifting.   5
Then nothing. The weak sun
flickered over the dry surface.

It is terrible to survive
as consciousness
buried in the dark earth.   10

Then it was over: that which you fear, being
a soul and unable
to speak, ending abruptly, the stiff earth
bending a little. And what I took to be
birds darting in low shrubs.   15

You who do not remember
passage from the other world
I tell you I could speak again: whatever
returns from oblivion returns
to find a voice: 20

from the center of my life came
a great fountain, deep blue
shadows on azure seawater.

[1992]

JAMES TATE   [b. 1943]

The Wheelchair Butterfly

O sleepy city of reeling wheelchairs
where a mouse can commit suicide if he can

concentrate long enough
on the history book of rodents
in this underground town   5

of electrical wheelchairs!
The girl who is always pregnant and bruised
like a pear

rides her many-stickered bicycle
backward up the staircase   10
of the abandoned trolleybarn.

Yesterday was warm. Today a butterfly froze
in midair; and was plucked like a grape
by a child who swore he could take care

of it. O confident city where   15
the seeds of poppies pass for carfare,

where the ordinary hornets in a human's heart
may slumber and snore, where bifocals bulge

in an orange garage of daydreams,
we wait in our loose attics for a new season   20

as if for an ice-cream truck.
An Indian pony crosses the plains

whispering Sanskrit prayers to a crater of fleas.
Honeysuckle says: I thought I could swim.

The Mayor is urinating on the wrong side   25
of the street! A dandelion sends off sparks:
beware your hair is locked!

Beware the trumpet wants a glass of water!
Beware a velvet tabernacle!

Beware the Warden of Light has married   30
an old piece of string!

[1969]

QUINCY TROUPE   [b. 1943]

Poem for the Root Doctor of Rock n Roll

For Chuck Berry°

& it all came together on the mississippi river
chuck, you there riding the rocking-blue sound wave
duck-walking the poetry of hoodoo down
                  & you were the mojo-hand
of juju crowing, the gut-bucket news — running it down   5
for two records sold to make a penny
back then in those first days, "majoring in mouth" —
a long, gone, lean lightning rod
              picking the edge, charging the wires
                      of songs, huckle-bucking "roll over   10
beethoven", playing "devil's music", till white devils stole it from you
& called it their own, "rock n roll"
                  devils like elvis & pat boone
who never duck-walked back in the alley with you
& bo diddley, little richard & the fatman from new orleans   15
all yall slapping down songs meaner than the smell
of toejam & rot-gut whiskey breath
back there, in them back rooms
              of throw down

back there, where your song lyrics grew, like fresh corn   20
you, chuck berry, an authentic american genius of barbecue sauce
& deep fried catfish licks, jack-salmon guitar
                 honky-tonk rhythms
jangling warm, vibrating sounds, choo-chooing train
whistles fiddling & smoking down the tracks of the blues   25
motivating through "little queenie", "maybelline"
decked out in red on sarah & finney
alarms rolling off your whipping tongue
in the words of "johnny b good"
you clued us in, back to the magical hookup of ancestors   30
their seamless souls threading your breath
             their blood in your sluicing strut
& to much "monkey business", the reason for their deaths, cold &
  searing

Chuck Berry: Charles Edward Anderson "Chuck" Berry (b. 1926), American guitarist, singer, and songwriter, one of the pioneers of rock and roll music.

your spirit reaching down to the bones of your roots
deep in the "show me" blood of missouri soil   35
            your pruned, hawk-look, profiling
where you rode your white cadillac of words, cruising
the highways of language (what we speak & hear even now)
breathing inside your cadences
            you shaped & wheeled the music   40
duck-walking the length of the stage
duck-walked your zinging metaphors of everyday
slip-slide & strut, vibrating your hummingbird wings
your strumming style, the cutting edge
& you were what was to come   45

so hail, hail, chuck berry, root doctor of "rock n roll"
authentic american genius
            tonguing deep in river syllables
hail, hail, chuck berry, laying down the motivating juju
you great, american, mojo hand   50

root doctor, spirit, of american, "rock n roll"

[1984]

EAVAN BOLAND   [b. 1944]

The Pomegranate

The only legend I have ever loved is
the story of a daughter lost in hell.
And found and rescued there.
Love and blackmail are the gist of it.
Ceres° and Persephone the names.   5
And the best thing about the legend is

---

5. Ceres: Roman name of Demeter, the goddess of crops and harvest. Her daughter Persephone was kidnapped by Pluto (or Hades) and taken to the underworld. Demeter, grieving and angry, refused to let seeds germinate or crops grow. To save the human race from extinction, Zeus finally ordered Pluto to release Persephone. Pluto told her she was free to leave but tricked her by offering a pomegranate seed; anyone who eats food in the underworld must return there. Zeus therefore arranged a compromise: Persephone would spend a third of each year in the land of the dead with Pluto (winter, when Demeter went into mourning); but she would be with her mother for the other two-thirds of each year (spring and summer).

I can enter it anywhere. And have.
As a child in exile in
a city of fogs and strange consonants,
I read it first and at first I was   10
an exiled child in the crackling dusk of
the underworld, the stars blighted. Later
I walked out in a summer twilight
searching for my daughter at bed-time.
When she came running I was ready   15
to make any bargain to keep her.
I carried her back past whitebeams
and wasps and honey-scented buddleias.
But I was Ceres then and I knew
winter was in store for every leaf   20
on every tree on that road.
Was inescapable for each one we passed.
And for me.
           It is winter
and the stars are hidden.   25
I climb the stairs and stand where I can see
my child asleep beside her teen magazines,
her can of Coke, her plate of uncut fruit.
The pomegranate! How did I forget it?
She could have come home and been safe   30
and ended the story and all
our heart-broken searching but she reached
out a hand and plucked a pomegranate.
She put out her hand and pulled down
the French sound for apple° and   *pomme* 35
the noise of stone° and the proof   *granite*
that even in the place of death,
at the heart of legend, in the midst
of rocks full of unshed tears
ready to be diamonds by the time   40
the story was told, a child can be
hungry. I could warn her. There is still a chance.
The rain is cold. The road is flint-coloured.
The suburb has cars and cable television.
The veiled stars are above ground.   45
It is another world. But what else
can a mother give her daughter but such
beautiful rifts in time?
If I defer the grief I will diminish the gift.

The legend will be hers as well as mine.   50
She will enter it. As I have.
She will wake up. She will hold
the papery flushed skin in her hand.
And to her lips. I will say nothing.

[1994; 1995]

ANNE WALDMAN   [b. 1945]

Icy Rose

(To The Delicately Winter Coming On)

       all day feeling space
       my face is empty space
       & nighttime too

the space   the space   the space   the space

      & nighttime too   5
      I'm going blank

        Blank.

Where has that last sentence (speaking — you were speaking — gone?
& where have the birds really gone?
& where is the Ice Age now?   10
& who does this poet think he is?   or she is?

She is a far cry from Womanhood

                  O
          T-T-T-TAKE ME BACK!

                                   I stammer   15

     I go down under the moon
     I dance with the big brown bear
                 I kiss the foot

     Down to 6 below last night
     I ran thru the snow like a young puppy   20

I got the Dashboard Blues
I threw in the towel

I reacted like a Crazy Lady
                    — well —
                                — well —   25
                        not exactly

YOU SEE ALL THIS FREEDOM?????????????
                    You see where it gets you?
You see what I mean????

                        mean?   30
o calm down   cough up   curl under   crawl in
creep along   crouch down   come on
                    COME ON
there's nothing to fear except fear itself
                    Get off my fear itself!   35
                        (it fears itself)
Rather
            think of Copernicus
                    De Revolutionibus Orbium Coelestium
            & Liu Shui   40
                    (flowing water)
& you: My Boldest Dream
                    it's so easy
                    makes me sleepy
            but WHO ARE YOU?   45
                        & why do you dress so strange?
            & who are your parents?
                    & whence have you come?

                                    [1971]

LARRY LEVIS   [1946–1996]

The Poem You Asked For

My poem would eat nothing.
I tried giving it water
but it said no,

worrying me.
Day after day,   5
I held it up to the light,

turning it over,
but it only pressed its lips
more tightly together.

It grew sullen, like a toad   10
through with being teased.
I offered it all my money,

my clothes, my car with a full tank.
But the poem stared at the floor.
Finally I cupped it in   15

my hands, and carried it gently
out into the soft air, into the
evening traffic, wondering how

to end things between us.
For now it had begun breathing,   20
putting on more and

more hard rings of flesh.
And the poem demanded the food,
it drank up all the water,

beat me and took my money,   25
tore the faded clothes
off my back,

said Shit,
and walked slowly away,
slicking its hair down.   30

Said it was going
over to your place.

[1972]

LINDA HOGAN   [b. 1947]

The History of Red

First
there was some other order of things
never spoken
but in dreams of darkest creation.

Then there was black earth,   5
lake, the face of light on water.
Then the thick forest all around
that light,
and then the human clay
whose blood we still carry   10
rose up in us
who remember caves with red bison
painted in their own blood,
after their kind.

A wildness   15
swam inside our mothers,
desire through closed eyes,
a new child
wearing the red, wet mask of birth,
delivered into this land   20
already wounded,
stolen and burned
beyond reckoning.

Red is this yielding land
turned inside out   25
by a country of hunters
with iron, flint and fire.
Red is the fear
that turns a knife back
against men, holds it at their throats,   30
and they cannot see the claw on the handle,
the animal hand
that haunts them
from some place inside their blood.

So that is hunting, birth,   35
and one kind of death.
Then there was medicine, the healing of wounds.

Red was the infinite fruit
of stolen bodies.
The doctors wanted to know   40
what invented disease
how wounds healed
from inside themselves
how life stands up in skin,
if not by magic.   45

They divined the red shadows of leeches
that swam in white bowls of water;
they believed stars
in the cup of sky,
They cut the wall of skin   50
to let
what was bad escape
but they were reading the story of fire
gone out
and that was science.   55

As for the animal hand on death's knife,
knives have as many sides
as the red father of war
who signs his name
in the blood of other men.   60

And red was the soldier
who crawled
through a ditch
of human blood in order to live.
It was the canal of his deliverance.   65
It is his son who lives near me.
Red is the thunder in our ears
when we meet.
Love, like creation,
is some other order of things.   70

Red is the share of fire
I have stolen
from root, hoof, fallen fruit.
And this was hunger.

Red is the human house   75
I come back to at night
swimming inside the cave of skin

that remembers bison.
In that round nation
of blood   80
we are all burning,
red, inseparable fires
the living have crawled
and climbed through   85
in order to live
so nothing will be left
for death at the end.

This life in the fire, I love it,
I want it,   90
this life.

[1993]

AI   [b. 1947]

Why Can't I Leave You?

You stand behind the old black mare,
dressed as always in that red shirt,
stained from sweat, the crying of the armpits,
that will not stop for anything,
stroking her rump, while the barley goes unplanted.   5
I pick up my suitcase and set it down,
as I try to leave you again.
I smooth the hair back from your forehead.
I think with your laziness and the drought too,
you'll be needing my help more than ever.   10
You take my hands, I nod
and go to the house to unpack,
having found another reason to stay.

I undress, then put on my white lace slip
for you to take off, because you like that   15
and when you come in, you pull down the straps
and I unbutton your shirt.
I know we can't give each other any more
or any less than what we have.
There is safety in that, so much   20
that I can never get past the packing,

the begging you to please, if I can't make you happy,
come close between my thighs
and let me laugh for you from my second mouth.

[1972]

YUSEF KOMUNYAKAA   [b. 1947]

Facing It

My black face fades,
hiding inside the black granite.
I said I wouldn't,
dammit: No tears.
I'm stone. I'm flesh.   5
My clouded reflection eyes me
like a bird of prey, the profile of night
slanted against morning. I turn
this way — the stone lets me go.
I turn that way — I'm inside   10
the Vietnam Veterans Memorial
again, depending on the light
to make a difference.
I go down the 58,022 names,
half-expecting to find   15
my own in letters like smoke.
I touch the name Andrew Johnson;
I see the booby trap's white flash.
Names shimmer on a woman's blouse
but when she walks away   20
the names stay on the wall.
Brushstrokes flash, a red bird's
wings cutting across my stare.
The sky. A plane in the sky.
A white vet's image floats   25
closer to me, then his pale eyes
look through mine. I'm a window.
He's lost his right arm
inside the stone. In the black mirror
a woman's trying to erase names: 30
No, she's brushing a boy's hair.

[1988]

JANE KENYON   [1947–1995]

Let Evening Come

Let the light of late afternoon
shine through chinks in the barn, moving
up the bales as the sun moves down.

Let the cricket take up chafing
as a woman takes up her needles   5
and her yarn. Let evening come.

Let dew collect on the hoe abandoned
in long grass. Let the stars appear
and the moon disclose her silver horn.

Let the fox go back to its sandy den.   10
Let the wind die down. Let the shed
go black inside. Let evening come.

To the bottle in the ditch, to the scoop
in the oats, to air in the lung
let evening come.   15

Let it come, as it will, and don't
be afraid. God does not leave us
comfortless, so let evening come.

[1996]

HEATHER McHUGH   [b. 1948]

What He Thought

for Fabbio Doplicher

We were supposed to do a job in Italy
and, full of our feeling for
ourselves (our sense of being
Poets from America) we went
from Rome to Fano, met   5
the mayor, mulled
a couple matters over (what's
cheap date, they asked us; what's
flat drink). Among Italian literati

we could recognize our counterparts: 10
the academic, the apologist,
the arrogant, the amorous,
the brazen and the glib — and there was one

administrator (the conservative), in suit
of regulation gray, who like a good tour guide   15
with measured pace and uninflected tone narrated
sights and histories the hired van hauled us past.
Of all, he was most politic and least poetic,
so it seemed. Our last few days in Rome
(when all but three of the New World Bards had flown)   20
I found a book of poems this
unprepossessing one had written: it was there
in the *pensione* room (a room he'd recommended)
where it must have been abandoned by
the German visitor (was there a bus of *them?*)   25
to whom he had inscribed and dated it a month before.
I couldn't read Italian, either, so I put the book
back into the wardrobe's dark. We last Americans

were due to leave tomorrow. For our parting evening then
our host chose something in a family restaurant, and there   30
we sat and chatted, sat and chewed,
till, sensible it was our last
big chance to be poetic, make
our mark, one of us asked
                         "What's poetry?   35
Is it the fruits and vegetables and
marketplace of Campo dei Fiori, or
the statue there?" Because I was

the glib one, I identified the answer
instantly, I didn't have to think —"The truth   40
is both, it's both," I blurted out. But that
was easy. That was easiest to say. What followed
taught me something about difficulty,
for our underestimated host spoke out,
all of a sudden, with a rising passion, and he said: 45

The statue represents Giordano Bruno,
brought to be burned in the public square
because of his offense against
authority, which is to say
the Church. His crime was his belief   50
the universe does not revolve around

the human being: God is no
fixed point or central government, but rather is
poured in waves through all things. All things
move. "If God is not the soul itself, He is   55
the soul of the soul of the world." Such was
his heresy. The day they brought him
forth to die, they feared he might
incite the crowd (the man was famous
for his eloquence). And so his captors   60
placed upon his face
an iron mask, in which
he could not speak. That's
how they burned him. That is how
he died: without a word, in front   65
of everyone.

        And poetry —

              (we'd all
put down our forks by now, to listen to
the man in gray; he went on   70
softly) —

        poetry is what

he thought, but did not say.

                         [1994]

LESLIE MARMON SILKO   [b. 1948]

Prayer to the Pacific

I traveled to the ocean
           distant
                  from my southwest land of sandrock
                  to the moving blue water
           Big as the myth of origin.   5
Pale
pale water in the yellow-white light of
                sun   floating west
                     to China
                where ocean herself was born.   10
Clouds that blow across the sand are wet.

Squat in the wet sand and speak to the Ocean:
      I return to you   turquoise   the red coral you sent us,
            sister spirit of Earth.
Four round stones in my pocket   I carry back the ocean   15
           to suck and to taste.

Thirty thousand years ago
         Indians came riding across the ocean
         carried by giant sea turtles.

Waves were high that day   20
       great sea turtles waded   slowly out
              from the gray sundown sea.

Grandfather Turtle rolled in the sand   four times
          and disappeared
              swimming into the sun.   25

And so from that time
      immemorial,
          as the old people say,
rain clouds drift from the west
          gift from the ocean.   30

Green leaves in the wind
Wet earth on my feet
      swallowing raindrops
          clear from China.

                         [1981]

SEKOU SUNDIATA   [1948–2007]

Blink Your Eyes

Remembering Sterling A. Brown

I was on my way to see my woman
but the Law said I was on my way
thru a red light red light red light
and if you saw my woman
you could understand,   5
I was just being a man
It wasn't about no light
it was about my ride

and if you saw my ride
you could dig that too, you dig?
Sunroof stereo radio black leather   10
bucket seats sit low you know,
the body's cool, but the tires are worn.
Ride when the hard time come, ride
when they're gone, in other words   15
the light was green.

I could wake up in the morning
without a warning
and my world could change:
blink your eyes.   20
All depends, all depends on the skin,
all depends on the skin you're living in.

Up to the window comes the Law
with his hand on his gun
what's up? what's happening?   25
I said I guess
that's when I really broke the law.
He said *a routine, step out the car*
a routine, assume the position.
Put your hands up in the air   30
you know the routine, like you just don't care.
License and registration.
Deep was the night and the light
from the North Star on the car door, deja vu
we've been through this before,   35
why did you stop me?
Somebody had to stop you.
I watch the news, you always lose.
You're unreliable, that's undeniable.
This is serious, you could be dangerous.   40

I could wake up in the morning
without a warning
and my world could change:
blink your eyes.
All depends, all depends on the skin,   45
all depends on the skin you're living in.

New York City, they got laws
can't no bruthas drive outdoors,
in certain neighborhoods, on particular streets

near and around certain types of people.   50
They got laws.
All depends, all depends on the skin,
all depends on the skin you're living in.

[1995]

AGHA SHAHID ALI   [1949–2001]

I Dream It Is Afternoon
When I Return to Delhi

At Purana Qila I am alone, waiting
for the bus to Daryaganj. I see it coming,
but my hands are empty.
"Jump on, jump on," someone shouts,
"I've saved this change for you   5
for years. Look!"
A hand opens, full of silver rupees.
"Jump on, jump on." The voice doesn't stop.
There's no one I know. A policeman,
handcuffs silver in his hands,   10
asks for my ticket.

I jump off the running bus,
sweat pouring from my hair.
I run past the Doll Museum, past
headlines on the Times of India   15
building, PRISONERS BLINDED IN A BIHAR
JAIL, HARIJAN VILLAGES BURNED BY LANDLORDS.
Panting, I stop in Daryaganj,
outside Golcha Cinema.

Sunil is there, lighting   20
a cigarette, smiling. I say,
"It must be ten years, you haven't changed,
it was your voice on the bus!"
He says, "The film is about to begin,
I've bought an extra ticket for you,"   25
and we rush inside:

Anarkali is being led away,
her earrings lying on the marble floor.
Any moment she'll be buried alive.

"But this is the end," I turn   30
toward Sunil. He is nowhere.
The usher taps my shoulder, says
my ticket is ten years old.

Once again my hands are empty.
I am waiting, alone, at Purana Qila.   35
Bus after empty bus is not stopping.
Suddenly, beggar women with children
are everywhere, offering
me money, weeping for me.

[1987]

VICTOR HERNÁNDEZ CRUZ   [b. 1949]

Problems with Hurricanes

A campesino looked at the air
And told me:
With hurricanes it's not the wind
or the noise or the water.
I'll tell you he said: 5
it's the mangoes, avocados
Green plantains and bananas
flying into town like projectiles.

How would your family
feel if they had to tell
The generations that you   10
got killed by a flying
Banana.

Death by drowning has honor
If the wind picked you up
and slammed you   15
Against a mountain boulder
This would not carry shame
But
to suffer a mango smashing
Your skull   20
or a plantain hitting your
Temple at 70 miles per hour
is the ultimate disgrace.

The campesino takes off his hat —   25
As a sign of respect
towards the fury of the wind
And says:
Don't worry about the noise   30
Don't worry about the water
Don't worry about the wind —
If you are going out
beware of mangoes
And all such beautiful   35
sweet things.

                                                              [1991]

RAY A. YOUNG BEAR   [b. 1950]

From the Spotted Night

In the blizzard
while chopping wood
the mystical whistler
beckons my attention.   5
Once there were longhouses
here. A village.
In the abrupt spring floods
swimmers retrieved our belief.
So their spirit remains.   10
From the spotted night
distant jets transform
into fireflies who float
towards me like incandescent
snowflakes.   15
The leather shirt
which is suspended
on a wire hanger
above the bed's headboard
is humanless; yet when one   20
stands outside the house,
the strenuous sounds
of dressers and boxes
being moved can be heard.
We believe someone wears

the shirt and rearranges
the heavy furniture,   25
although nothing
is actually changed.
Unlike the Plains Indian shirts
which repelled lead bullets,
ricocheting from them   30
in fiery sparks,
this shirt is the means;
this shirt *is* the bullet.

[1990]

CAROLYN FORCHÉ   [b. 1950]

The Colonel

What you have heard is true. I was in his house. His wife carried a tray of coffee and sugar. His daughter filed her nails, his son went out for the night. There were daily papers, pet dogs, a pistol on the cushion beside him. The moon swung bare on its black cord over the house. On the television was a cop show. It was in English. Broken bottles were embedded in the walls around the house to scoop the kneecaps from a man's legs or cut his hands to lace. On the windows there were gratings like those in liquor stores. We had dinner, rack of lamb, good wine, a gold bell was on the table for calling the maid. The maid brought green mangoes, salt, a type of bread. I was asked how I enjoyed the country. There was a brief commercial in Spanish. His wife took everything away. There was some talk then of how difficult it had become to govern. The parrot said hello on the terrace. The colonel told it to shut up, and pushed himself from the table. My friend said to me with his eyes: say nothing. The colonel returned with a sack used to bring groceries home. He spilled many human ears on the table. They were like dried peach halves. There is no other way to say this. He took one of them in his hands, shook it in our faces, dropped it into a water glass. It came alive there. I am tired of fooling around he said. As for the rights of anyone, tell your people they can go fuck themselves. He swept the ears to the floor with his arm and held the last of his wine in the air. Something for your poetry, no? he said. Some of the ears on the floor caught this scrap of his voice. Some of the ears on the floor were pressed to the ground.

[1978]

MEDBH McGUCKIAN   [b. 1950]

On Ballycastle Beach

If I found you wandering round the edge
Of a French-born sea, when children
Should be taken in by their parents,
I would read these words to you,
Like a ship coming in to harbour,   5
As meaningless and full of meaning
As the homeless flow of life
From room to homesick room.

The words and you would fall asleep,
Sheltering just beyond my reach   10
In a city that has vanished to regain
Its language. My words are traps
Through which you pick your way
From a damp March to an April date,
Or a mid-August misstep; until enough winter   15
Makes you throw your watch, the heartbeat
Of everyone present, out into the snow.

My forbidden squares and your small circles
Were a book that formed within you
In some pocket, so permanently distended,   20
That what does not face north, faces east.
Your hand, dark as a cedar lane by nature,
Grows more and more tired of the skidding light,
The hunched-up waves, and all the wet clothing,
Toys and treasures of a late summer house.   25

Even the Atlantic has begun its breakdown
Like a heavy mask thinned out scene after scene
In a more protected time — like one who has
Gradually, unnoticed, lengthened her pre-wedding
Dress. But, staring at the old escape and release   30
Of the water's speech, faithless to the end,
Your voice was the longest I heard in my mind,
Although I had forgotten there could be such light.

[1998]

JOHN YAU   [b. 1950]

Chinese Villanelle

I have been with you, and I have thought of you
Once the air was dry and drenched with light
I was like a lute filling the room with description

We watched glum clouds reject their shape
We dawdled near a fountain, and listened
I have been with you, and I have thought of you   5

Like a river worthy of its gown
And like a mountain worthy of its insolence . . .
Why am I like a lute left with only description

How does one cut an axe handle with an axe   10
What shall I do to tell you all my thoughts
When I have been with you, and thought of you

A pelican sits on a dam, while a duck
Folds its wings again; the song does not melt
I remember you looking at me without description   15

Perhaps a king's business is never finished,
Though "perhaps" implies a different beginning
I have been with you, and I have thought of you
Now I am a lute filled with this wandering description

[1979]

JORIE GRAHAM   [b. 1950]

To the Reader

I swear to you she wanted back into the shut, the slow,

a ground onto which to say This is my actual life, Good Morning,
onto which to say That girl on her knees who is me
is still digging that square yard of land up
to catalogue and press onto the page *all she could find in it*
and name, somewhere late April, where they believe in ideas,   5
Thursday, a little of what persists and all the rest.

Before that, dreams. The dream of being warm
and staying warm. The dream of the upper hand like a love song,
the dream of the right weapon and then the perfect escape.   10

Then the dream of the song of having *business* here.

Then the dream of you two sitting on the couch, of the mood
of armies (hand of God), of the city burning in the distance.

The dream of before and after (are we getting closer?) the dream   15
of *finally after days*. . . .

(Miss _____ lets out a shattering scream.)

I swear to you this begins with that girl on a day after sudden rain
and then out of nowhere sun (as if to expose *what* of the hills—
the white glare of x, the scathing splendor of y,
the wailing interminable _____?) that girl having run   20
down from the house and up over the fence not like an animal
but like a thinking, link by link, and over

into the allotted earth—for Science Fair—into the *everything* of
one square yard of earth. Here it begins
to slip. She took the spade and drew the lines. Right through   25
the weedbeds, lichen, moss, keeping the halves of things that landed *in*
by chance, new leaves, riffraff the wind blew in—

Here is the smell of earth being cut, the smell of the four lines.
Here is the brownsweet of the abstract where her four small furrows
say the one word over.   30
She will take the ruler and push it down till it's all the way in.
She will slide its razor edge along through colonies, tunnels,
through powdered rock and powdered leaf,

and everything on its way to the one right destination
like a cloak coming off, shoulders rising,   35
(after one has abandoned the idea of x;
after one has accorded to the reader the y)—
her hole in the loam like a saying in the midst of the field of patience,
fattening the air above it with detail,
an embellishment on the April air,   40
the rendezvous of hands and earth—

Say we leave her there, squatting down, haunches up,
pulling the weeds up with tweezers,
pulling the thriving apart into the true,
each seedpod each worm on the way down retrieved into a   45
plastic bag (shall I compare thee), Say we

leave her there, where else is there to go? A word,
a mouth over water? Is there somewhere
neither there nor here?
Where do we continue living now, in what terrain?   50
Mud, ash, _____, _____. We want it to stick to us,
hands not full but not clean. What is wide-meshed enough
yet lets nothing through, the bunch of ribbon,
her hair tied up that the wind be seen?

If, for instance, this was the place instead,   55

where the gods fought the giants and monsters
(us the ideal countryside, flesh, interpretation),

if, for instance, this were not a chosen place but a place
blundered into, a place which is a meadow with a hole in it,

and some crawl through such a hole to the other place   60

and some use it to count with and buy with

and some hide in it and see Him go by

and to some it is the hole on the back of the man running

through which what's coming towards him is coming into him, growing
    larger,

a hole in his chest through which the trees in the distance are seen   65
growing larger shoving out sky shoving out storyline

until it's close it's all you can see this moment this hole in his back

in which now a girl with a weed and a notebook appears.

                                                    [1987]

JOY HARJO   [b. 1951]

She Had Some Horses

She had some horses.

She had horses who were bodies of sand.
She had horses who were maps drawn of blood.
She had horses who were skins of ocean water.
She had horses who were the blue air of sky.   5

She had horses who were fur and teeth.
She had horses who were clay and would break.
She had horses who were splintered red cliff.

She had some horses.

She had horses with long, pointed breasts.   10
She had horses with full, brown thighs.
She had horses who laughed too much.
She had horses who threw rocks at glass houses.
She had horses who licked razor blades.

                                                                   15
She had some horses.

She had horses who danced in their mothers' arms.
She had horses who thought they were the sun and their
bodies shone and burned like stars.
She had horses who waltzed nightly on the moon.
She had horses who were much too shy, and kept quiet   20
in stalls of their own making.

She had some horses.

She had horses who liked Creek Stomp Dance songs.
She had horses who cried in their beer.   25
She had horses who spit at male queens who made
them afraid of themselves.
She had horses who said they weren't afraid.
She had horses who lied.
She had horses who told the truth, who were stripped
bare of their tongues.   30

She had some horses.

She had horses who called themselves, "horse."
She had horses who called themselves, "spirit," and kept
their voices secret and to themselves.
She had horses who had no names.   35
She had horses who had books of names.

She had some horses.

She had horses who whispered in the dark, who were afraid to speak.
She had horses who screamed out of fear of the silence, who
carried knives to protect themselves from ghosts.   40
She had horses who waited for destruction.
She had horses who waited for resurrection.

She had some horses.

She had horses who got down on their knees for any saviour.
She had horses who thought their high price had saved them.   45
She had horses who tried to save her, who climbed in her
bed at night and prayed as they raped her.

She had some horses.

She had some horses she loved.
She had some horses she hated.   50
These were the same horses.

[1983]

GARRETT KAORU HONGO   [b. 1951]

Yellow Light

One arm hooked around the frayed strap
of a tar-black, patent-leather purse,
the other cradling something for dinner:
fresh bunches of spinach from a J-Town *yaoya*,°   *vegetable stand or seller*
sides of split Spanish mackerel from Alviso's,   5
maybe a loaf of Langendorf;° she steps
off the hissing bus at Olympic and Fig,
begins the three-block climb up the hill,
passing gangs of schoolboys playing war,
Japs against Japs, Chicanas chalking sidewalks   10
with the holy double-yoked crosses of hopscotch,
and the Korean grocer's wife out for a stroll
around this neighborhood of Hawaiian apartments
just starting to steam with cooking
and the anger of young couples coming home   15
from work, yelling at kids, flicking on
TV sets for the Wednesday Night Fights.

If it were May, hydrangeas and jacaranda
flowers in the streetside trees would be

6. **Langendorf:** A well-known bakery in California.

blooming through the smog of late spring.   20
Wisteria in Masuda's front yard would be
shaking out the long tresses of its purple hair.
Maybe mosquitoes, moths, a few orange butterflies
settling on the lattice of monkey flowers
tangled in chain-link fences by the trash.   25

But this is October, and Los Angeles
seethes like a billboard under twilight.
From used-car lots and the movie houses uptown,
long silver sticks of light probe the sky.
From the Miracle Mile, whole freeways away,   30
a brilliant fluorescence breaks out
and makes war with the dim squares
of yellow kitchen light winking on
in all the side streets of the Barrio.

She climbs up the two flights of flagstone   35
stairs to 201-B, the spikes of her high heels
clicking like kitchen knives on a cutting board,
props the groceries against the door,
fishes through memo pads, a compact,
empty packs of chewing gum, and finds her keys.   40

The moon then, cruising from behind
a screen of eucalyptus across the street,
covers everything, everything in sight,
in a heavy light like yellow onions.

[1982]

DAVID MURA   [b. 1952]

Grandfather-in-Law

It's nothing really, and really, it could have been worse, and of course, he's
        now several years dead,
and his widow, well, if oftentimes she's somewhat distracted, overly
        cautious when we visit —
after all, Boston isn't New York — she seems, for some reason, enormously
        proud that there's now a writer in the family,

and periodically, sends me clippings about the poet laureate, Thoreau,
    Anne Sexton's daughter, Lowell, New England literary lore —
in which I fit, if I fit at all, simply because I write in English — as if color
    of skin didn't matter anymore.   5
Still, years ago, during my first visit to Boston, when we were all asleep,
    he, who used to require that my wife memorize lines of Longfellow or
    Poe and recite them on the phone,
so that, every time he called, she ran outdoors and had to be coaxed
    back, sometimes with threats, to talk to Pops
(though she remembers too his sly imitations of Lincoln, ice cream at
    Brighams, burgers and fries, all the usual grandfatherly treats),
he, who for some reason was prejudiced against Albanians — where on
    earth did he find them I wondered —   10
who, in the thirties, would vanish to New York, catch a show, buy a suit,
    while up north,
the gas and water bills pounded the front door (his spendthrift ways
    startled me with my grandfather's resemblance),
who for over forty years came down each morning, "How's the old goat?"
    with a tie only his wife could knot circling his neck,
he slipped into my wife's room — we were unmarried at the time — and
    whispered so softly she thought
he almost believed she was really asleep, and was saying this like a wish
    or spell, some bohunk miscalculated Boston sense of duty: 15
"Don't make a mistake with your life, Susie. Don't make a mistake . . ."
Well. The thing that gets me now, despite the dangling rantings I've let
    go, is that, at least at that time,
he was right: There was, inside me, some pressing, raw unpeeled
    persistence, some libidinous desire for dominance
that, in the scribbled first drafts of my life, seemed to mark me as wastrel
    and rageful, bound to be unfaithful,
to destroy, in some powerful, nuclear need, fissioned both by childhood
    and racism, whatever came near —   20
And I can't help but feel, forgiving him now, that if she had listened, if
    she had been awake,
if this flourishing solace, this muscled-for-happiness, shared by us now,
    had never awakened,
he would have become for me a symbol of my rage and self-destruction,
    another raw, never healing wound,
and not this silenced grandfatherly presence, a crank and scoundrel, red-
    necked Yankee who created the delicate seed of my wife, my child.

[1989]

RITA DOVE   [b. 1952]

The Satisfaction Coal Company

1

What to do with a day.
Leaf through *Jet*. Watch T.V.
Freezing on the porch
but he goes anyhow, snow too high   5
for a walk, the ice treacherous.
Inside, the gas heater takes care of itself;
he doesn't even notice being warm.

Everyone says he looks great.
Across the street a drunk stands smiling   10
at something carved in a tree.
The new neighbor with the floating hips
scoots out to get the mail
and waves once, brightly,
storm door clipping her heel on the way in.

2   15
Twice a week he had taken the bus down Glendale hill
to the corner of Market. Slipped through
the alley by the canal and let himself in.
Started to sweep
with terrible care, like a woman   20
brushing shine into her hair,
same motion, same lullaby.
No curtains — the cop on the beat
stopped outside once in the hour
to swing his billy club and glare.   25

It was better on Saturdays
when the children came along:
he mopped while they emptied
ashtrays, clang of glass on metal
then a dry scutter. Next they counted   30
nailheads studding the leather cushions.
Thirty-four! they shouted,
that was the year and
they found it mighty amusing.

But during the week he noticed more —
lights when they gushed or dimmed
at the Portage Hotel, the 10:32   35
picking up speed past the B & O switchyard,
floorboards trembling and the explosive
kachook kachook kachook kachook
and the oiled rails ticking underneath.   40

3

They were poor then but everyone had been poor.
He hadn't minded the sweeping,
just the thought of it — like now
when people ask him what he's thinking
and he says *I'm listening.*   45

Those nights walking home alone,
the bucket of coal scraps banging his knee,
he'd hear a roaring furnace
with its dry, familiar heat. Now the nights
take care of themselves — as for the days,   50
there is the canary's sweet curdled song,
the wino smiling through his dribble.
Past the hill, past the gorge
choked with wild sumac in summer,
the corner has been upgraded.   55
Still, he'd like to go down there someday
to stand for a while, and get warm.

[1986]

NAOMI SHIHAB NYE   [b. 1952]

The Small Vases from Hebron°

Tip their mouths open to the sky.
Turquoise, amber,
the deep green with fluted handle,

Hebron: An ancient city in the West Bank area of Israel, a sacred place for both
Muslims and Jews. It has been a focus of tension between Israelis and Palestini-
ans since the 1967 Arab-Israeli war.

pitcher the size of two thumbs,
tiny lip and graceful waist.
Here we place the smallest flower
which could have lived invisibly
in loose soil beside the road,
sprig of succulent rosemary,
bowing mint.

They grow deeper in the center of the table.

Here we entrust the small life,
thread, fragment, breath.
And it bends. It waits all day.
As the bread cools and the children
open their gray copybooks
to shape the letter that looks like
a chimney rising out of a house.

And what do the headlines say?

Nothing of the smaller petal
perfectly arranged inside the larger petal
or the way tinted glass filters light.
Men and boys, praying when they died,
fall out of their skins.
The whole alphabet of living,
heads and tails of words,
sentences, the way they said,
"Ya'Allah!" when astonished,
or "ya'ani" for "I mean" —
a crushed glass under the feet
still shines.
But the child of Hebron sleeps
with the thud of her brothers falling
and the long sorrow of the color red.

[1998]

ALICE FULTON   [b. 1952]

You Can't Rhumboogie in a Ball and Chain

for Janis Joplin°

You called the blues' loose black belly lover
and in Port Arthur they called you pig-face.
The way you chugged booze straight, without a glass,
your brass-assed language, slingbacks with jeweled heel,
proclaimed you no kin to their muzzled blood.   5
No Chiclet-toothed Baptist boyfriend for you.

Strung-out, street hustling showed men wouldn't buy you.
Once you clung to the legs of a lover,
let him drag you till your knees turned to blood,
mouth hardened to a thin scar on your face,   10
cracked under songs, screams, never left to heal.
Little Girl Blue, soul pressed against the glass.

That voice rasping like you'd guzzled fiberglass,
stronger than the four armed men behind you.
But a pale horse lured you, docile, to heel: 15
warm snow flanks pillowed you like a lover.
Men feared the black holes in your body and face,
knew what they put in would return as blood.

Craving fast food, cars, garish as fresh blood,
diners with flies and doughnuts under glass,   20
Formica bars and a surfer's gold face,
in nameless motels, after sign-off, you
let TV's blank bright stare play lover,
lay still, convinced its cobalt rays could heal.

Your songs that sound ground under some stud's heel,   25
swallowed and coughed up in a voice like blood:
translation unavailable, lover!
No prince could shoe you in unyielding glass,
stories of exploding pumpkins bored you
who flaunted tattooed breast and hungry face.   30

Janis Joplin: Blues singer in the 1960s (1943–1970). Born and raised in Port
Arthur, Texas, her life was blessed by an innate musical talent and cursed by alcohol and drugs. She died of an overdose at age twenty-seven.

That night needing a sweet-legged sugar's face,
a hot, sky-eyed Southern comfort to heal
the hurt of senior proms for all but you,
plain Janis Lyn, self-hatred laced your blood.   35
You knew they worshiped drained works, emptied glass,
legend's last gangbang the wildest lover.

Like clerks we face your image in the glass,
suggest lovers, as accessories, heels.
"It's your shade, this blood dress," we say. "It's you."

[1983]

ALBERTO RÍOS   [b. 1952]

Indentations in the Sugar

As they have no difficulty with walls,
Neither do they have the services of a table,
And so the dead do not stay
Longer than twenty minutes,
The time it takes to make coffee   5
Mid-morning.
Sometimes we find a broken cup,
And we remember them, through the years
Their eyeglasses growing thicker.
But theirs was a preparation for the long   10
Look from there to here,
So that small things like cups
Up close are hard to handle.
And they do look,
Our features bending and parting   15
In the fat manner of that circus
Mirror in front of which we all stood
In our turn, making two-foot mouths.
Sometimes the glasses are not thick enough
So that they walk through us   20
To get to the other side of the kitchen,
Imagining they have a small need
Putting a hand through ours
Reaching for a stirring spoon.

For us it is bursitis or the thrill   25
Feel of coolness.
Their twenty-minute visits are finally
A courtesy of the centuries,
And they are impatient to go.
They shake their heads about things.   30
It's this kitchen, they say;
      The spoons are not good spoons.
We don't hear them.
It is the open window.

                [1990]

MARY RUEFLE   [b. 1952]

Naked Ladies

Rousseau° wanted: a cottage on the Swiss shore,
a cow and a rowboat.

Stevens° wanted a crate from Ceylon full of jam
and statuettes.

My neighbors are not ashamed of their poverty   5
but would love to be able to buy a white horse,
a stallion that would transfigure the lot.

Darwin° was dying by inches from not having anyone to talk to
about worms, and the vireo outside my window wants nothing less
than a bit of cigarette-wool for her nest.   10

The unattainable is apparently rising on the tips of forks
the world over . . .

So-and-so is wearing shoes for the first time

---

1. Rousseau: Jean-Jacques Rousseau (1712–1778, born in Geneva), a political
philosopher and early participant in the Romantic movement in Europe.
3. Stevens: Wallace Stevens (1879–1955), American poet (see pp. 117 and 354).
8. Darwin: Charles Darwin (1809–1882), English naturalist, the originator of
modern evolutionary theory.

and Emin Pasha,° in the deepest acreage of the Congo,
wanted so badly to catch a red mouse! Catch one he did   15
shortly before he died, cut in the throat by slavers who
wanted to kill him. *At last!* runs the diary

and it is just this *at last* we powder up and call progress.

So the boys chipped in and bought Bohr° a gram of radium
for his 50th birthday.   20

Pissarro° wanted white frames for his paintings
as early as 1882, and three francs for postage, second place.

Who wants to hear once more the sound of their mother throwing
Brussels sprouts into the tin bowl?

Was it *ping* or was it *ting*?   25

What would you give to smell again the black sweetpeas
choking the chain-link fence?

Because somebody wants your money.

The medallions of monkfish in a champagne sauce . . .

The long kiss conjured up by your body in a cast . . .   30

The paradisiacal vehicle of the sweet-trolley rolling in
as cumulous meringue is piled on your tongue
and your eye eats the amber glaze of a crème brûlée . . .

The forgiveness of sins, a new wife, another passport,
the swimming pool, the rice bowl   35

full of rice, the teenage mutant ninja turtles escaping
as you turn the page . . .

Oh brazen sex at the barbecue party!

Desire is a principle of selection. Who wanted *feet* in the first place?

Who wanted to stand up? Who felt like walking?   40

[2002]

14. **Emin Pasha:** Eduard Schnitzer (1840–1892), better known as "Emin Pasha,"
a German physician, explorer, naturalist, collector, and government administrator, who led an expedition into the African interior in an effort to claim the terri-
tory for Germany.
19. **Bohr:** Niels Bohr (1885–1962), a Danish physicist who made fundamental
contributions to understanding atomic structure and was one of the team that
worked on developing the first atomic bomb during World War II.
21. **Pissarro:** Camille Pissarro (1830–1903), a French Impressionist painter.

OFELIA ZEPEDA   [b. 1952]

Pulling Down the Clouds

Ñ-ku'ibaḍkaj 'ant 'an ols g cewagĭ.
With my harvesting stick I will hook the clouds.
'Ant o. 'i-waññ'io k o 'i-huḍiñ g cewagĭ.
With my harvesting stick I will pull down the clouds.
Ñ-ku'ibaḍkaj 'ant o 'i-siho g cewagĭ.   5
With my harvesting stick I will stir the clouds.

With dreams of distant noise disturbing his sleep,
the smell of dirt, wet, for the first time in what seems like months.
The change in the molecules is sudden,
they enter the nasal cavity.   10

He contemplates that smell.
What is that smell?
It is rain.
Rain somewhere out in the desert.
Comforted in this knowledge he turns over   15
and continues his sleep,
dreams of women with harvesting sticks
raised toward the sky.

[1995]

GARY SOTO   [b. 1952]

Mexicans Begin Jogging

At the factory I worked
In the fleck of rubber, under the press
Of an oven yellow with flame,
Until the border patrol opened
Their vans and my boss waved for us to run.   5
"Over the fence, Soto," he shouted,
And I shouted that I was American.
"No time for lies," he said, and pressed
A dollar in my palm, hurrying me
Through the back door.   10

Since I was on his time, I ran
And became the wag to a short tail of Mexicans —

Ran past the amazed crowds that lined
The street and blurred like photographs, in rain.
I ran from that industrial road to the soft   15
Houses where people paled at the turn of an autumn sky.
What could I do but yell *vivas*
To baseball, milkshakes, and those sociologists
Who would clock me
As I jog into the next century   20
On the power of a great, silly grin.

[1981]

JIMMY SANTIAGO BACA   [b. 1952]

Family Ties

Mountain barbecue.
They arrive, young cousins singly,
older aunts and uncles in twos and threes,
like trees. I play with a new generation
of children, my hands in streambed silt   5
of their lives, a scuba diver's hands, dusting
surface sand for buried treasure.
Freshly shaved and powdered faces
of uncles and aunts surround taco
and tamale tables. Mounted elk head on wall,   10
brass rearing horse cowboy clock
on fireplace mantle. Sons and daughters
converse round beer and whiskey table.
Tempers ignite on land grant issues.
Children scurry round my legs.   15
Old bow-legged men toss horseshoes on lawn,
other farmhands from Mexico sit on a bench,
broken lives repaired for this occasion.
I feel no love or family tie here. I rise
to go hiking, to find abandoned rock cabins   20
in the mountains. We come to a grass clearing,
my wife rolls her jeans up past ankles,
wades ice cold stream, and I barefooted,
carry a son in each arm and follow.
We cannot afford a place like this.   25
At the party again, I eat bean and chile

burrito, and after my third glass of rum,
we climb in the car and my wife drives
us home. My sons sleep in the back,
dream of the open clearing,   30
they are chasing each other with cattails
in the sunlit pasture, giggling,
as I stare out the window
at no trespassing signs white flashing past.

[1989]

JUDITH ORTIZ COFER   [b. 1952]

Cold as Heaven

Before there is a breeze again
before the cooling days of Lent, she may be gone.
My grandmother asks me to tell her
again about the snow.
We sit on her white bed   5
in this white room, while outside
the Caribbean sun winds up the world
like an old alarm clock. I tell her
about the enveloping blizzard I lived through
that made everything and everyone the same;   10
how we lost ourselves in drifts so tall
we fell through our own footprints;
how wrapped like mummies in layers of wool
that almost immobilized us, we could only
take hesitant steps like toddlers   15
toward food, warmth, shelter.
I talk winter real for her,
as she would once conjure for me to dream
at sweltering siesta time,
cool stone castles in lands far north.   20
Her eyes wander to the window,
to the teeming scene of children
pouring out of a yellow bus, then to the bottle
dripping minutes through a tube
into her veins. When her eyes return to me,   25
I can see she's waiting to hear more
about the purifying nature of ice,

how snow makes way for a body,
how you can make yourself an angel
by just lying down and waving your arms   30
as you do when you say
good-bye.

[1995]

ANITA ENDREZZE   [b. 1952]

The Girl Who Loved the Sky

Outside the second grade room,
the jacaranda tree blossomed
into purple lanterns, the papery petals
drifted, darkening the windows.
Inside, the room smelled like glue.   5
The desks were made of yellowed wood,
the tops littered with eraser rubbings,
rulers, and big fat pencils.
Colored chalk meant special days.
The walls were covered with precise   10
bright tulips and charts with shiny stars
by certain names. There, I learned
how to make butter by shaking a jar
until the pale cream clotted
into one sweet mass. There, I learned   15
that numbers were fractious beasts
with dens like dim zeros. And there,
I met a blind girl who thought the sky
tasted like cold metal when it rained
and whose eyes were always covered   20
with the bruised petals of her lids.

She loved the formless sky, defined
only by sounds, or the cool umbrellas
of clouds. On hot, still days
we listened to the sky falling   25
like chalk dust. We heard the noon
whistle of the pig-mash factory,
smelled the sourness of home-bound men.

I had no father; she had no eyes;
we were best friends. The other girls   30
drew shaky hop-scotch squares
on the dusty asphalt, talked about
pajama parties, weekend cook-outs,
and parents who bought sleek-finned cars.
Alone, we sat in the canvas swings,   35
our shoes digging into the sand, then pushing,
until we flew high over their heads,
our hands streaked with red rust
from the chains that kept us safe.

I was born blind, she said, an act of nature.   40
Sure, I thought, like birds born
without wings, trees without roots.
I didn't understand. The day she moved
I saw the world clearly; the sky
backed away from me like a departing father.   45
I sat under the jacaranda, catching
the petals in my palm, enclosing them
until my fist was another lantern
hiding a small and bitter flame.

[1988]

RAY GONZÁLEZ   [b. 1952]

Praise the Tortilla, Praise Menudo, Praise Chorizo

I praise the tortilla in honor of El Panzón,
who hit me in school every day and made me see
how the bruises on my arms looked like
the brown clouds on my mother's tortillas.
I praise the tortilla because I know   5
they can fly into our hands like
eager flesh of the one we love,
those soft yearnings we delight in biting
as we tear the tortilla and wipe the plate clean.

I praise the menudo as visionary food that it is,   10
the tripas y posole tight flashes of color
we see as the red caldo smears across our notebooks
like a vision we have not had in years,
our lives going down like the empty bowl
of menudo exploding in our stomachs   15
with the chili piquin of our poetic dreams.

I praise the chorizo and smear it
across my face and hands,
the dayglow brown of it painting me
with the desire to find out   20
what happened to la familia,
why the chorizo sizzled in the pan
and covered the house with a smell
of childhood we will never have again,
the chorizo burrito hot in our hands,   25
as we ran out to play and show the vatos
it's time to cut the chorizo,
tell it like it is before la manteca runs down
our chins and drips away.

                                                        [1992]

MARK DOTY   [b. 1953]

Tiara

Peter died in a paper tiara
cut from a book of princess paper dolls;
he loved royalty, sashes

and jewels. I don't know,
he said, when he woke in the hospice,   5
I was watching the Bette Davis film festival

on Channel 57 and then —
At the wake, the tension broke
when someone guessed

the casket closed because   10
he was *in there in a big wig
and heels*, and someone said,

You know he's always late,
he probably isn't here yet —
he's still fixing his makeup.   15

And someone said he asked for it.
Asked for it —
when all he did was go down

into the salt tide
of wanting as much as he wanted,   20
giving himself over so drunk

or stoned it almost didn't matter who,
though they were beautiful,
stampeding into him in the simple,

ravishing music of their hurry.   25
I think heaven is perfect stasis
poised over the realms of desire,

where dreaming and waking men lie
on the grass while wet horses
roam among them, huge fragments   30

of the music we die into
in the body's paradise.
Sometimes we wake not knowing

how we came to lie here,
or who has crowned us with these temporary,   35
precious stones. And given

the world's perfectly turned shoulders,
the deep hollows blued by longing,
given the irreplaceable silk

of horses rippling in orchards,   40
fruit thundering and chiming down,
given the ordinary marvels of form

and gravity, what could he do,
what could any of us ever do
but ask for it?   45

[1991]

RICHARD JONES   [b. 1953]

Cathedral

Songbirds live
in the old cathedral,
caged birds bought at the street market
and freed as a kind of offering.
Now doves and finches and parakeets   5
nest in the crooks of the nave's highest arches,
roosting on the impossibly high
sills of stained glass windows,
looking down into the valley of the altar
as if from cliffs.   10

Twice a day, you'll hear them singing:
at dawn
when the blue light
of angels' wings
and the yellow light of halos   15
flood into their nests to wake them;
and during mass
when the organ fills
the valley below with thunder.
These birds love thunder,   20
never having seen a drop of rain.
They love it when the people below stand up
and sing. They fly
in mad little loops
from window to window,   25
from the tops of arches
down toward the candles and tombs,
making the sign of the cross.

If you look up during mass
to the world's light falling   30
through the arms of saints,
you can see birds flying
through blue columns of incense
as if it were simple wood smoke
rising from a cabin's chimney   35
in a remote and hushed forest.

[1994]

JANE HIRSHFIELD   [b. 1953]

At Night

it is best
to focus your eyes
a little off to one side;
it is better to know things
drained of their color, to fathom   5
the black horses cropping
at winter grass,
their white jaws that move
in steady rotation, a sweet sound.

And when they file off to shelter
under the trees   10
you will find the pale circles of snow
pushed aside, earth opening
its single, steadfast gaze:
towards stars ticking by, one by one, overhead,
the given world flaming precisely out of its frame.   15

[1988]

LORNA DEE CERVANTES   [b. 1954]

Freeway 280

Las casitas° near the gray cannery,   *little houses*
nestled amid wild abrazos° of climbing roses   *bear hugs*
and man-high red geraniums
are gone now. The freeway conceals it
all beneath a raised scar.   5

But under the fake windsounds of the open lanes,
in the abandoned lots below, new grasses sprout,
wild mustard remembers, old gardens
come back stronger than they were,
trees have been left standing in their yards.   10
Albaricoqueros, cerezos, nogales° . . .   *apple, cherry, walnut trees*
Viejitas° come here with paper bags to gather greens.   *old women*
Espinaca, verdolagas, yerbabuena° . . .   *spinach, purslane, mint*

I scramble over the wire fence   15
that would have kept me out.
Once, I wanted out, wanted the rigid lanes
to take me to a place without sun,
without the smell of tomatoes burning
on swing shift in the greasy summer air.

                                                                      20
Maybe it's here
en los campos extraños de esta ciudad°
where I'll find it, that part of me
mown under
like a corpse   25
or a loose seed.

                                                            [1981]

21. en . . . ciudad: In the strange fields of this city.

THYLIAS MOSS   [b. 1954]

The Lynching

They should have slept, would have
but had to fight the darkness, had
to build a fire and bathe a man in
flames. No

other soap's as good when   5
the dirt is the skin. Black since
birth, burnt by birth. His father
is not in heaven. No parent

of atrocity is in heaven. My father chokes
in the next room. It is night, darkness   10
has replaced air. We are white like
incandescence

yet lack light. The God in my father
does not glow. The only lamp
is the burning black man. Holy   15
burning, holy longing, remnants of

a genie after greed. My father
baptizes by fire same as Jesus will.

Becomes a holy ghost when
he dons his sheet, a clerical collar   20

out of control, Dundee Mills percale,
fifty percent cotton, dixie, confederate
and fifty percent polyester, man-made, man-
ipulated, unnatural, mulatto fiber, warp

of miscegenation.   25
After the bath, the man is hung as if
just his washed shirt, the parts
of him most capable of sin removed.

Charred, his flesh is bark, his body
a trunk. No sign of roots. I can't leave   30
him. This is limbo. This is the life after
death coming if God is an invention as were

slaves. So I spend the night, his thin moon-begot
shadow as mattress; something smoldering
keeps me warm. Patches of skin fall onto me   35
in places I didn't know needed mending.

[1991]

LOUISE ERDRICH   [b. 1954]

A Love Medicine

Still it is raining lightly
in Wahpeton. The pickup trucks
sizzle beneath the blue neon
bug traps of the dairy bar.

Theresa goes out in green halter and chains   5
that glitter at her throat.
This dragonfly, my sister,
she belongs more than I
to this night of rising water.

The Red River swells to take the bridge.
She laughs and leaves her man in his Dodge.   10
He shoves off to search her out.
He wears a long rut in the fog.

And later, at the crest of the flood,   15
when the pilings are jarred from their sockets
and pitch into the current,
she steps against the fistwork of a man.
She goes down in wet grass
and his boot plants its grin   20
among the arches of her face.

Now she feels her way home in the dark.
The white-violet bulbs of the streetlamps
are seething with insects,
and the trees lean down aching and empty.   25
The river slaps at the dike works, insistent.

I find her curled up in the roots of a cottonwood.
I find her stretched out in the park, where all night
the animals are turning in their cages.
I find her in a burnt-over ditch, in a field   30
that is gagging on rain,
sheets of rain sweep up down
to the river held tight against the bridge.

We see that now the moon is leavened and the water,
as deep as it will go,
stops rising. Where we wait for the night to take us   35
the rain ceases. *Sister, there is nothing
I would not do.*

[1984]

KIM ADDONIZIO   [b. 1954]

The Sound

Marc says the suffering that we don't see
still makes a sort of sound — a subtle, soft
noise, nothing like the cries or screams that we
might think of — more the slight scrape of a hat doffed
by a quiet man, ignored as he stands back   5
to let a lovely woman pass, her dress
just brushing his coat. Or else it's like a crack
in an old foundation, slowly widening, the stress

and slippage going on unnoticed by
the family upstairs, the daughter leaving
for a date, her mother's resigned sigh   10
when she sees her. It's like the heaving
of a stone into a lake, before it drops.
It's shy, it's barely there. It never stops.

[1994]

DONALD REVELL   [b. 1954]

Mignonette

The metaphors are what has really happened. When
the stars go, it's a person going, or an old
religion folding like a lawn chair, only less
dramatic, less whatever you would call a girl
with cancer or a star that fell. The metaphors   5

are at the convent where she had so many friends,
so many things to talk about, and they are the blue
green of an ocean, only more like stars. The white
embroidery, her body white and smooth beneath
it, folded in a chair is wonderful to think   10

of when the moon's in Cancer. She would dream about
the lawn or of the convent moon where men betray
themselves. A lawn could only think of dreaming. Think
about a girl you saw by moonlight, dancing on
the lawn. You see a window seat from where you see   15

a chair in which a girl is dying. Cancer kills,
and only stars can help her. Mignonette, the love
of whom is dancing on the lawn like convent stars,
could never have religion, white as she could be
for anyone who talked to her or sat beside   20

her in the little chair, not even now with stars
about to fall and cancer. Metaphors are what
a girl depends on at a time like this, because
the way they work is musical, and music makes
you feel good, even if you're not religious. Life   25

is any convent, any constellation or
a chair to die in, dreaming of the way a lawn
can look. You looked at her again to see
a proof of something, but you didn't find it, didn't
betray yourself. The metaphors are what you said   30

would happen: stars around a chair, the cancer of
a girl who dances on the lawn and likes to talk
about religion when the moon's up. What you said
is that you dreamed of watching. Music dreamed. The silk,
what is so white around her folded body, watched.   35

[1983]

CORNELIUS EADY   [b. 1954]

My Mother,
If She Had Won Free Dance Lessons

Would she have been a person
With a completely different outlook on life?
There are times when I visit
And find her settled on a chair
In our dilapidated house,   5
The neighborhood crazy lady
Doing what the neighborhood crazy lady is supposed to do,
Which is absolutely nothing

And I wonder as we talk our sympathetic talk,
Abandoned in easy dialogue,   10
I, the son of the crazy lady,
Who crosses easily into her point of view
As if yawning
Or taking off an overcoat.
Each time I visit   15
I walk back into our lives

And I wonder, like any child who wakes up one day to find themself
Abandoned in a world larger than their
    Bad dreams,
I wonder as I see my mother sitting there,   20
Landed to the right-hand window in the living room,

Pausing from time to time in the endless loop of our dialogue
To peek for rascals through the
Venetian blinds,

I wonder a small thought.   25
I walk back into our lives.
Given the opportunity,
How would she have danced?
Would it have been as easily

As we talk to each other now,
The crazy lady   30
And the crazy lady's son,
As if we were old friends from opposite coasts
Picking up the thread of a long conversation,

Or two ballroom dancers
Who only know   35
One step?

What would have changed
If the phone had rung like a suitor,
If the invitation had arrived in the mail
Like Jesus, extending a hand?   40

[1986]

MARILYN CHIN   [b. 1955]

Turtle Soup

for Ben Huang

You go home one evening tired from work,
and your mother boils you turtle soup.
Twelve hours hunched over the hearth
(who knows what else is in that cauldron).

You say, "Ma, you've poached the symbol of long life;   5
that turtle lived four thousand years, swam
the Wei, up the Yellow, over the Yangtze.
Witnessed the Bronze Age, the High Tang,
grazed on splendid sericulture."
(So, she boils the life out of him.)   10

"All our ancestors have been fools.
Remember Uncle Wu who rode ten thousand miles
to kill a famous Manchu and ended up
with his head on a pole? Eat, child,
its liver will make you strong."   15

"Sometimes you're the life, sometimes the sacrifice."
Her sobbing is inconsolable.
So, you spread that gentle napkin
over your lap in decorous Pasadena.

Baby, some high priestess has got it wrong.   20
The golden decal on the green underbelly
says "Made in Hong Kong."

Is there nothing left but the shell
and humanity's strange inscriptions,
the songs, the rites, the oracles?   25

[1987]

CATHY SONG   [b. 1955]

Girl Powdering Her Neck

From a Ukiyo-e Print by Utamaro

The light is the inside
sheen of an oyster shell,
sponged with talc and vapor,
moisture from a bath.

A pair of slippers   5
are placed outside
the rice-paper doors.
She kneels at a low table
in the room,
her legs folded beneath her   10
as she sits on a buckwheat pillow.

Her hair is black
with hints of red,
the color of seaweed
spread over rocks.   15

Utamaro Kitagawa (1753–1806), *Girl Powdering Her Neck*
(Musée Guimet, Paris).

Morning begins the ritual
wheel of the body,
the application of translucent skins.
She practices pleasure:
the pressure of three fingertips   20
applying powder.
Fingerprints of pollen
some other hand will trace.

The peach-dyed kimono   25
patterned with maple leaves
drifting across the silk,
falls from right to left
in a diagonal, revealing
the nape of her neck   30
and the curve of a shoulder
like the slope of a hill
set deep in snow in a country
of huge white solemn birds.
Her face appears in the mirror,
a reflection in a winter pond,   35
rising to meet itself.

She dips a corner of her sleeve
like a brush into water
to wipe the mirror;
she is about to paint herself.   40
The eyes narrow
in a moment of self-scrutiny.
The mouth parts
as if desiring to disturb
the placid plum face;   45
break the symmetry of silence.
But the berry-stained lips,
stenciled into the mask of beauty,
do not speak.

                                                                   50
Two chrysanthemums
touch in the middle of the lake
and drift apart.

                                                        [1983]

KIMIKO HAHN   [b. 1955]

Mother's Mother

. . . There is no mother tongue.
— *Elaine Showalter*

The mother draws the shade down halfway
so the sunlight does not blind the pages
and she reads the story, *mukashi mukashi aruhi,*°
which is the way every story begins
whether about a boy riding a tortoise beneath the sea   5
or a girl born from a bamboo stalk.
Her daughter does not speak Japanese
though she can write her name in the *kana*°
that resembles tv antennae

キ ミ コ°

and she knows not everyone speaks the same language: 10
see you, ciao, adios, sayonara. She knows
her mother knows more than one way to say things
and Japanese, which is also how she *looks,*
is the language her mother was taught,
like the island of Japan,   15
almost as far from this little house on the island of Maui.

The chickens are so loud grandma.
Ursuai ne.°
So dusty.
Kitanai°
So—   20

She wants to learn every word her grandma knows.
She wants to be like her grandma
who she sees her mother loves and does not want to leave.
She wants to stay with her grandma also   25
and knows from her mother's shoulders they will not see her again.

3. mukashi mukashi aruhi: Once upon a time.
8. kana: A general term for the syllabic Japanese scripts *hiragana* and *katakana,* which were adapted from the logographic characters of Chinese origin known in Japan as *Kanji* and are easier to master.
9. キ ミ コ: Ki - mi - ko.
18. Ursuai ne: Annoying, isn't it?
20. Kitanai: Dirty, filthy.

If there is no mother tongue for women
there is for immigrant children
who play on the black volcanic beaches,
on the sharp coral reefs, in the salty rain, the plantation houses,   30
the fields of burning cane, the birds-of-paradise.
Who see the shark fins in the sunlight and linger on the blanket.

There is a mother's tongue and it is conveyed
by this mother to her daughters
who will carry the words at least in song   35
because when mother dies there will be no one else
unless there is an aunt or cousin
to correct the tense or word choice
with such affection and cause.

そうよね。°

The same cause found in domestic arts and survival.   40
When the mother dies the daughter
or the daughter-in-law, or even the son,
becomes that figure in part
and the words the older woman knew
are the words this person will parent   45
despite lineage and its repressive roots.
Its often awful branches.
The root words and radicals the daughter memorizes.

永   シ°

So when I toss my hair from my eyes I feel
it's mother tossing her head and when I cough   50
it is her cough I hear.
And when I tell my child to say *mama*
it may be that I am speaking to myself
as much as I am speaking to the small mouth
a few inches from my face.   55

[1999]

39. そうよね。: That's just the way it is, isn't it?
48. 永 シ: It is endless (the process of learning Japanese characters).

HOMAGE TO MY HIPS

these hips are big hips.
they need space to
move around in.
they don't fit into little
petty places. these hips
are free hips.
they don't like to be held back.
these hips have never been enslaved,
they go where they want to go
they do what they want to do.
these hips are mighty hips.
these hips are magic hips.
i have known them
to put a spell on a man and
spin him like a top!

Lucille Clifton

LI-YOUNG LEE   [b. 1957]

The Gift

To pull the metal splinter from my palm
my father recited a story in a low voice.
I watched his lovely face and not the blade.
Before the story ended, he'd removed
the iron sliver I thought I'd die from.   5

I can't remember the tale,
but hear his voice still, a well
of dark water, a prayer.
And I recall his hands,
two measures of tenderness   10
he laid against my face,
the flames of discipline
he raised above my head.

Had you entered that afternoon
you would have thought you saw a man   15
planting something in a boy's palm,
a silver tear, a tiny flame.
Had you followed that boy
you would have arrived here,
where I bend over my wife's right hand.   20

Look how I shave her thumbnail down
so carefully she feels no pain.
Watch as I lift the splinter out.
I was seven when my father
took my hand like this,   25
and I did not hold that shard
between my fingers and think,
Metal that will bury me,
christen it Little Assassin,
Ore Going Deep for My Heart.   30
And I did not lift up my wound and cry,
Death visited here!
I did what a child does
when he's given something to keep.
I kissed my father.   35

[1986]

MARTÍN ESPADA   [b. 1957]

The Saint Vincent de Paul
Food Pantry Stomp

Madison, Wisconsin, 1980

Waiting for the carton of food
given with Christian suspicion
even to agency-certified charity cases
like me,
thin and brittle   5
as uncooked linguini,
anticipating the factory-damaged cans
of tomato soup, beets, three-bean salad
in a welfare cornucopia,
I spotted a squashed dollar bill   10
on the floor, and with
a Saint Vincent de Paul food pantry stomp
pinned it under my sneaker,
tied my laces meticulously,
and stuffed the bill in my sock   15
like a smuggler of diamonds,
all beneath the plaster statue wingspan
of Saint Vinnie,
who was unaware
of the dance   20
named in his honor
by a maraca shaker
in the salsa band
of the unemployed.

[1990]

WANG PING   [b. 1957]

Syntax

She walks to a table
She walk to table

She is walking to a table
She walk to table now

What difference does it make
What difference it make   5

In Nature, no completeness
No sentence really complete thought

Language, like woman,
Look best when free, undressed.   10

[1999]

LUCIA PERILLO   [b. 1958]

Long Time Too Long

A long time, too long, since we have done — this:
abandoned our tools while the sun's still high
and retraced our trail up the attic steps.
The grass still wants mowing as the quilts sigh
back over the bed; the nightshade tendril
winds another turn round the tomato.   5
But this is work too, this letting clothes fall
in such harsh yellow light that what to do
with what lies underneath them must all be
relearned. Let the vines choke our one good rose,   10
let the spade stand, the Mason jars empty:
we're sweating enough at each other's lips.
Leave the fallen plums to the white-faced wasps,
beating their drunk wings against the windows.

[1999]

CARL PHILLIPS   [b. 1959]

To the Tune of a Small, Repeatable,
and Passing Kindness

In the cove of hours-like-a-dream this
is, it isn't so much
that we don't enjoy watching

a view alter rather little, and each time
in the same shift-of-a-cloud
fashion. It's the   5

swiftness with which we
find it easier, as our cast
lines catch more and more at nothing,

to lose heart—   10
            All afternoon, it's
been with the fish as with

lovers we'd come to think of as
mostly forgotten, how
anymore they less often themselves   15

surface than sometimes
will the thought of them—less
often, even, than that, their names . . .

But now the fish bring to mind
—of those lovers—   20
the ones in particular

who were knowable
only in the way a letter written
in code that resists

being broken fully can be   25
properly called a letter we
understand: *If*

you   a minute   could you   when
said I might   however   30
what if   haven't I loved

—who?
            As I remember it, I'd lie
in general alone, after, neither in

want nor—at first—sorry inside   35
the almost-dark I'd
wake to. The only stirring

the one of last light getting
scattered, as if for
my consideration. All over the room.

                                                    [2002]

BOB HICOK   [b. 1960]

Plus Shipping

*Inspired by Kokopelli,° Golfer-Pelli is a fun-loving
symbol for our times.*
— from one of the 400 mail-order catalogs
we received last year

Certainly it was a premonition of a Navajo warrior that men
in plaid would take up sticks and club a ball into a hole's

submission. And that a god of prosperity and joy, flute
player, source of the wind's conversational obsessions,

secretly longed to represent the beef-fatted, tax-sheltered,   5
divot-spewing tribe in their hunger for real estate

made green and blemish-free, acres of fertilized eternity.
It happened like this: someone named Stan or Rita

spanked their cell-phone open in Manhattan traffic, called
Lou Ellen or Robbie and went on at an ecstatic pitch   10

about a program they saw on the Learning Channel last night
that documented cave paintings in Arizona of this guy

with hair like spiders and a body twisted as if
he'd swallowed a hurricane, and wouldn't it make a hot

knickknack if we put him in knickers with a seven iron   15
in his hands? And later, after the market research,

after paying one company to come up with a name, another
to design the eyes, hips, the casual-yet-indigenous-gestalt

needed to represent a sport built around the prophecy
of leisure, Stan or Rita will confess to something like   20

inspiration, a little zing, a small frisson disrupting
their preoccupation with fear that screamed low

cost, high profit. And I wouldn't mind if I were ten
or drunk most of the time, if I'd missed

Kokopelli: A prehistoric Native American fertility deity, usually depicted as a
humpbacked flute player.

even half the commercials utilizing the dramatic skills   25
of Super Bowl quarterbacks, the winks of senators

who reached for president but fell one scandal short,
wouldn't care if I could forget Michael Jackson

trying to sell his crotch, Elizabeth Taylor
hustling the diamonds of her scent, if just once   30

someone would stand before a camera and simply say
I've made this offensive thing but won't leave you alone

until you send me ten bucks. Golfer-Pelli's destined
for mantles, to fill that hole between vase and clock

where space bleeds, needing the bandage of artifact.   35
And what of the Buddha alarm clock, Shiva° spice rack,

the shoe polisher in which red and green fuzzy wheels
pop from Muhammad's ears and spin your leather clean?

Give it time and you'll get your crack at each
and more, for as we eat and sleep there's someone   40

flipping through a magazine, strolling the open veins
of ruins, touching forgotten texts, sculpted faces

of a people centuries gone, who can't help but think
there's beauty and sorrow and money in every one of these.

[1998]

36. Shiva: The third deity of the Hindu triad of great gods.

DENISE DUHAMEL   [b. 1961]

One Afternoon when Barbie Wanted to Join the Military

It was a crazy idea, she admits now,
but camouflage was one costume she still hadn't tried.
Barbie'd gone mod with go-go boots° during Vietnam.

3. go-go boots: Low-heeled, knee-length women's fashion boot, worn initially in the mid-sixties with miniskirts.

Throughout Panama° she was busy playing with a Frisbee
the size of a Coke bottle cap. And while troops
were fighting in the Gulf,
she wore a gown inspired by Ivana Trump.°
When Mattel told her, hell no — she couldn't go,
Barbie borrowed GI Joe's° fatigues,
safety pinning his pants's big waist
to better fit her own.
She settled on his olive tank.
But Barbie thought it was boring.
"Why don't you try running over something small?"
coaxed GI Joe, who sat naked behind the leg
of a human's living room chair.
Barbie saw imaginary bunnies
hopping through the shag carpet.
"I can't," she said.
GI Joe suggested she gun down the enemy,
who was sneaking up behind her.
Barbie couldn't muster up the rage
for killing, even if it was only play.
Maybe if someone tried to take her parking space
or scratched her red Trans Am.
Maybe if someone had called her a derogatory name.
But what had this soldier from the other side done?
GI Joe, seeing their plan was a mistake,
asked her to return his clothes,
making Barbie promise not to tell anyone.
As she slipped back into her classic baby blue
one-piece swimsuit, she realized
this would be her second secret.
She couldn't tell about the time
she posed nude for *Hustler*.
A young photographer who lived in the house
dipped her legs in a full bottle of Johnson's Baby Oil,
then swabbed some more on her torso.

---

4. Panama: U.S. invasion of Panama on 20 December 1989 in order to remove military dictator Manuel Noriega.

7. Ivana Trump: A former Czechoslovakian Olympic skier and fashion model (b. 1949) who was married to magnate Donald Trump from 1977 to 1991.

9. GI Joe: An American soldier. *G. I.* is an abbreviation for *government issue,* used for equipment designed or provided for members of the U.S. armed forces. The poem refers to the GI Joe toy action figure.

Barbie lounged on the red satin lining
of the kid's Sunday jacket. He dimmed   40
the lights and lit a candle
to create a glossy centerfold mood.
"Lick your lips," he kept saying,
forgetting Barbie didn't have a tongue.
She couldn't pout. She couldn't even bite   45
the maraschino cherry he dangled in front of her mouth.
Luckily there was no film in his sister's camera,
so the boy's pictures never came out.
Luckily GI Joe wasn't in the real Army
or he said he would risk being court-martialed—   50
he wasn't supposed to lend his uniform
to anyone, especially a girl.
Just then a human hand deposited Ken from the sky.
Somewhere along the way he'd lost his sandals.
"What have you two been up to?" he asked.   55
Barbie didn't have the kind of eyes that could shift away
so she lost herself in the memory of a joke
made by her favorite comedian Sandra Bernhard,°
who said she liked her dates to be androgynous
because if she was going to be with a man   60
she didn't want to have to face that fact.
Barbie was grateful for Ken's plastic flat feet
and plastic flat crotch. No military
would ever take him, even if there was a draft.
As GI Joe bullied Ken into a headlock,   65
Barbie told the boys to cut it out. She threatened
that if he kept it up, GI Joe would
never get that honorable discharge.

[1997]

58. **Sandra Bernhard:** American comedian and actress (b. 1955).

TOM ANDREWS   [1961–2001]

The Hemophiliac's Motorcycle

For the sin against the holy ghost is ingratitude.
— *Christopher Smart,* Jubilate Agno°

May the Lord Jesus Christ bless the hemophiliac's motorcycle, the smell
   of knobby tires,
Bel-Ray oil mixed with gasoline, new brake and clutch cables and
   handlebar grips,
the whole bike smothered in WD40 (to prevent rust, and to make the
   bike shine),
may He divine that the complex smell that simplified my life was
   performing the work of the spirit,
a window into the net of gems, linkages below and behind the given
   material world,   5
my little corner of the world's danger and sweet risk, a hemophiliac
   dicing on motocross tracks
in Pennsylvania and Ohio and West Virginia each Sunday from April
   through November,
the raceway names to my mind then a perfect sensual music, Hidden
   Hills, Rocky Fork, Mt. Morris, Salt Creek,
and the tracks themselves part of that music, the double jumps and off-
   camber turns, whoop-de-doos and fifth-gear downhills,
and me with my jersey proclaiming my awkward faith — "Powered By
   Christ," it said above a silk-screened picture of a rider in a radical
   cross-up,   10
the bike flying sideways off a jump like a ramp, the rider leaning his
   whole body into a left-hand corner —
may He find His name glorified in such places and smells,
and in the people, Mike Bias, Charles Godby, Tracy Woods, David and
   Tommy Hill, Bill Schultz° —
their names and faces snowing down to me now as I look upward to the
   past —

Epigraph: In 1756 Christopher Smart (1722–1771) was seized by an urge to pray
publicly, sometimes forcing passers-by to kneel with him. He was placed in an
institution, where he began pouring out innovative poetry, including *Jubilate Agno
(Rejoice in the Lamb).* It is, in part, a liturgy of worship, joining the material and
spiritual universe in prayers of praise and thanksgiving. The most famous section
is on his cat Jeoffry (see p. 32).
13. Mike Bias . . . Bill Schultz: Motocross racers.

friends who taught me to look at the world luminously in front of my
   eyes,   15
to find for myself the right rhythm of wildness and precision, when to
   hold back and when to let go,
each of them with a style, a thumbprint, a way of tilting the bike this
   way or that out of a berm shot, or braking heavily into a corner,
may He hear a listening to the sure song of His will in those years,
for they flooded me with gratitude that His informing breath was
   breathed into me,
gratitude that His silence was the silence of all things, His presence
   palpable everywhere in His absence,   20
gratitude that the sun flashed on the Kanawha River, making it shimmer
   and wink,
gratitude that the river twisted like a wrist in its socket of bottomland,
   its water part of our speech
as my brother and I drifted in inner tubes fishing the Great White Carp,
gratitude that plump squirrels tight-walked telephone lines and trellises
   of honeysuckle vines
and swallows dove and banked through the limbs of sycamore trees,
   word-perfect and sun-stunned   25
in the middle of the afternoon, my infusion of factor VIII° sucked in and
   my brother's dialysis sucked in and out—
both of us bewildered by the body's deep swells and currents and eerie
   backwaters,
our eyes widening at the white bursts on the mountain ash, at
   earthworms inching into oil-rainbowed roads—
gratitude that the oak tops on the high hills beyond the lawns fingered
   the denim sky
as cicadas drilled a shrill voice into the roadside sumac and
   peppergrass,   30
gratitude that after a rain catbirds crowded the damp air, bees spiraling
   from one exploding blossom to another,
gratitude that at night the star clusters were like nun buoys moored to a
   second sky, where God made room for us all,
may He adore each moment alive in the whirring world,
as now sitting up in this hospital bed brings a bright gladness for the
   human body, membrane of web and dew
I want to hymn and abide by, splendor of tissue, splendor of cartilage
   and bone,   35
splendor of the taillike spine's desire to stretch as it fills with blood
after a mundane backward plunge on an iced sidewalk in Ann Arbor,

26. factor VIII: An enzyme essential to blood clotting.

splendor of fibrinogen and cryoprecipitate, loosening the blood pooled
    in the stiffened joints
so I can sit up oh sit up in radiance, like speech after eight weeks of
    silence,
and listen for Him in the blood-rush and clairvoyance of the healing
    body,   40
in the sweet impersonal luck that keeps me now
from bleeding into the kidney or liver, or further into the spine,
listen for Him in the sound of my wife and my father weeping and
    rejoicing,
listen as my mother kneels down on the tiled floor like Christopher
    Smart
praying with strangers on a cobbled London street, kneels here in broad
    daylight   45
singing a "glorious hosanna from the den"
as nurses and orderlies and patients rolling their IV stands behind them
    like luggage
stall and stare into the room and smile finally and shuffle off, having
    heard God's great goodness lifted up
on my mother's tongue, each face transformed for a moment by ridicule
or sympathy before disappearing into the shunt-light of the hallway,   50
listen for Him in the snap and jerk of my roommate's curtain as he
    draws it open
to look and look at my singing mother and her silent choir
and to wink at me with an understanding that passeth peace, this kind,
    skeletal man
suffering from end-stage heart disease who loves science fiction and
    okra,
who on my first night here read aloud his grandson's bar mitzvah speech
    to me,   55
". . . In my haftorah portion, the Lord takes Ezekiel to a valley full of
    bones,
the Lord commands him to prophesy over the bones so they will become
    people . . . ,"
and solemnly recited the entire text of the candlelighting ceremony,
"I would like to light the first candle in memory of Grandma Ruth, for
    whom I was named,
I would like Grandma Dot and Grandpa Dan to come up and light the
    second candle,   60
I would like Aunt Mary Ann and my Albuquerque cousins Alanna and
    Susanna to come up and light the third candle . . . ,"
his voice rising steadily through the vinegary smell and brutal hush
    in the room,

may the Lord hear our listening, His word like matchlight cupped to a
  cigarette
the instant before the intake of breath, like the smoke clouds pooled in
  the lit tobacco
before flooding the lungs and bloodstream, filtering into pith and
  marrow,   65
may He see Himself again in the hemophiliac's motorcycle
on a certain Sunday in 1975 — Hidden Hills Raceway, Gallipolis, Ohio,
a first moto holeshot and wire-to-wire win, a miraculously benign
  sideswipe early on in the second moto
bending the handlebars and front brake lever before the possessed
  rocketing up through the pack
to finish third after passing Brian Kloser on his tricked-out Suzuki
  RM125   70
midair over the grandstand double jump —
may His absence arrive like that again here in this hygienic room,
not with the rush of a peaked power band and big air over the jumps
but with the strange intuitive calm of that race, a stillness somehow
  poised
in the body even as it pounded and blasted and held its line across the
  washboard track,   75
may His silence plague us like that again,
may He bless our listening and our homely tongues.

                                                              [1994]

VIRGIL SUÁREZ   [b. 1962]

Tea Leaves, *Caracoles*, Coffee Beans

My mother, who in those Havana days believed in divination,
found her tea leaves at *El Volcán,* the Chinese market/apothecary,

brought the leaves in a precious silk paper bundle, unwrapped
them as if unwrapping her own skin, and then boiled water

to make my dying grandmother's tea; while my mother read   5
its leaves, I simply saw *leaves floating* in steaming water,

vapor kissed my skin, my nose became moist as a puppy's.
My mother did this because my grandmother, her mother-in-law,

believed in all things. Her appetite for knowledge was vast,
the one thing we all agreed she passed down to me, the skinny   10

kid sent to search for *caracoles,* these snail shells
that littered the underbrush of the empty lot next door.

My mother threw them on top of the table, cleaned them of dirt,
kept them in a mason jar and every morning before breakfast,

read them on top of the table, their way of falling, some up,   15
some down, their ridges, swirls of creamy lines, their broken

edges. . . . Everything she read looked bad, for my grandmother,
for us, for staying in our country, this island of suspended

disbelief. My mother read coffee beans too, with their wrinkled,
fleshy green and red skin. Orange-skinned beans she kept aside.   20

Orange meant death, and my mother didn't want to accept it.
I learned mostly of death from the way a sparrow fell

when I hit it in the chest with my slingshot and a lead pellet
I made by melting my toy soldiers. The sparrow's eyes

always hid behind droopy eyelids, which is how my grandmother   25
died, by closing her eyes to the world; truth became this fading

light, a tunnel, as everybody says, but instead of heaven
she went into the ground, to that one place that still nourishes

the tea leaves, *caracoles,* and the coffee beans, which, if I didn't
know better, I'd claim shone; those red-glowing beans   30

in starlight were the eyes of the dead looking out through
the darkness as those of us who believed in such things walked

through life with a lightness of feet, spirit, a vapor-aura
that could be read or sung.

[2005]

TIMOTHY LIU   [b. 1965]

Thoreau

My father and I have no place to go.
His wife will not let us in the house —
afraid of catching AIDS. She thinks
sleeping with men is more than a sin,
my father says, as we sit on the curb   5

in front of someone else's house.
Sixty-four years have made my father
impotent. Silver roots, faded black
dye mottling his hair make him look
almost comical, as if his shame   10
belonged to me. Last night we read
Thoreau in a steak house down the road
and wept: *If a man does not keep pace*
with his companions, let him travel
to the music that he hears, however   15
measured or far away. The orchards
are gone, his village near Shanghai
bombed by the Japanese, the groves
I have known in Almaden — apricot,
walnut, peach and plum — hacked down.   20

[1995]

SHERMAN ALEXIE   [b. 1966]

Postcards to Columbus

Beginning at the front door of the White House, travel west
for 500 years, pass through small towns and house fires, ignore
hitchhikers and stranded motorists, until you find yourself
back at the beginning of this journey, this history and country

folded over itself like a Mobius strip. Christopher Columbus   5
where have you been? Lost between Laramie and San Francisco
or in the reservation HUD house, building a better mousetrap?
Seymour saw you shooting free throws behind the Tribal School

in a thunderstorm. Didn't you know lightning strikes the earth
800 times a second? But, Columbus, how could you ever imagine   10
how often our lives change? *Electricity is lightning pretending*
to be permanent and when the Indian child pushes the paper clip

into the electrical outlet, it's applied science, insane economics
of supply and demand, the completion of a 20th century circuit.
Christopher Columbus, you are the most successful real estate agent   15
who ever lived, sold acres and acres of myth, a house built on stilts

above the river salmon travel by genetic memory. Beneath the burden
of 15,000 years my tribe celebrated this country's 200th birthday
by refusing to speak English and we'll honor the 500th anniversary
of your invasion, Columbus, by driving blindfolded cross-country   20

naming the first tree we destroy *America*. We'll make the first guardrail
we crash through our national symbol. Our flag will be a white sheet
stained with blood and piss. Columbus, can you hear me over white
   noise
of your television set? Can you hear ghosts of drums approaching?

[1993]

HONORÉE FANONNE JEFFERS   [b. 1967]

Outlandish Blues (The Movie)

*. . . newly arrived Africans were classified in the North American
lexicon as "outlandish" in that they were "strangers to the
English language" and had yet to learn their new roles.*
— Michael A. Gomez

Where else can you sail across a blue sea
into a horizon emptied of witnesses?
This is the cathartic's truth, the movie mind's eye,
a vibrant ship voyage where the slaves luckily escape,

where the horizon empties of witnesses,   5
and the food and the water and the mercy run low
on this photogenic voyage where slaves luckily will escape,
but not before sailors throw a few souls in the ocean.

Before the food, water and mercy run low,
watch the celluloid flashes of sexy, tight bodies   10
that the sailors throw into the mouths of waiting fish,
bodies branded with the Cross, baptized with holy water,

tight-packed bodies flashing across the screen,
Hollywood flat stomachs pressed to buttocks pressed to shoulders
first branded with the Cross, baptized with holy water   15
and then covered with manufactured filth.

The stomachs press to buttocks press to shoulders
and of course, there is no pleasure in the touch —
under the filth we can see the taut black beauty
and we guiltily consider the following: 20

Are we sure there was no pleasure in those touches?
Are we sure most kidnapped Africans were not full grown?
We guiltily consider the following:
Were these really children picked for long lives of work?

Are we sure these were not full grown Africans   25
instead of children stolen or sold from their parents,
picked for long lives of work to be squeezed from them?
Must we think on coins passed between white and black hands?

These were children stolen or sold from their parents
though we don't see any of that on the movie screen.   30
We don't see coins passed between white and black hands.
We don't see any boys and girls raped by the sailors.

We don't see much of their lives on the screen,
only the clean Bible one of the male slaves is given.
We don't see any boys and girls raped by the sailors,   35
only prayers for redemption the slave definitely receives.

There are close-ups of the Bible given to a slave
but no questions about the God he sees in his dreams.
Who gives him the redemption I'm sure he receives?
Who will he call on — the God of his parents?   40

Who is the God he sees in his dreams?
Who placed him in the gut of this three-hour nightmare?
Who will he call on — the God of his parents
or his Bible's Savior, a man who walks on water?

Who placed him in the gut of this three-hour nightmare?   45
Certainly not the God of cathartic truth
or even the Bible's Savior, a man walking across water,
just right on over blues cast like bait upon the sea.

[2003]

ALLISON JOSEPH   [b. 1967]

On Being Told I Don't Speak Like a Black Person

Emphasize the "h," you hignorant ass,
was what my mother was told
when colonial-minded teachers
slapped her open palm with a ruler
in that Jamaican schoolroom.   5
Trained in England, they tried
to force their pupils to speak
like Eliza Doolittle° after
her transformation, fancying themselves
British as Henry Higgins,   10
despite dark, sun-ripened skin.
Mother never lost her accent,
though, the music of her voice
charming everyone, an infectious lilt
I can imitate, not duplicate.   15
No one in the States told her
to eliminate the accent,
my high school friends adoring
the way her voice would lift
when she called me to the phone,   20
A-ll-i-son, it's friend Cathy.
Why don't you sound like her?,
they'd ask. I didn't sound
like anyone or anything,
no grating New Yorker nasality,   25
no fastidious British mannerisms
like the ones my father affected
when he wanted to sell someone
something. And I didn't sound
like a Black American,   30
college acquaintances observed,
sure they knew what a black person

8–10. Eliza Doolittle . . . Henry Higgins: Flower-girl with a strong Cockney (working-class) accent in George Bernard Shaw's play *Pygmalion* and the musical based on it, *My Fair Lady.* Henry Higgins, a linguistics professor, takes on the challenge of teaching her how to speak (and act and dress) like a proper British lady.

was supposed to sound like.
Was I supposed to sound lazy,
dropping syllables here, there,   35
not finishing words but
slurring the final letter so that
each sentence joined the next,
sliding past the listener?
Were certain words off limits,   40
too erudite, too scholarly
for someone with a natural tan?
I asked what they meant,
and they stuttered, blushed,
said you know, Black English,   45
applying what they'd learned
from that semester's text.
Does everyone in your family
speak alike?, I'd question,
and they'd say don't take this the   50
wrong way, nothing personal.

Now I realize there's nothing
more personal than speech,
that I don't have to defend
how I speak, how any person,   55
black, white, chooses to speak.
Let us speak. Let us talk
with the sounds of our mothers
and fathers still reverberating
in our minds, wherever our mothers   60
or fathers come from:
Arkansas, Belize, Alabama,
Brazil, Aruba, Arizona.
Let us simply speak
to one another,   65
listen and prize the inflections,
differences, never assuming
how any person will sound
until her mouth opens,
until his mouth opens,   70
greetings familiar
in any language.

[1999]

Biographical Notes on the Authors
[Arranged Alphabetically]

This section offers brief biographical sketches of the 196 known authors of the poems included in this book. For fuller biographical information, the most convenient print sources are the *Dictionary of Literary Biography* (Detroit: Gale, 1978–), currently at 329 volumes; and *Contemporary Authors*, also published by Gale (original series, 248 volumes; new revised series, currently 155 volumes). Biographical information for many authors can also be found on the Internet. The Academy of American Poets Web site (poets.org) is particularly valuable and convenient; we are indebted to it for many of the entries. The Modern American Poetry Web site (http://www.english.uiuc.edu/maps/) also is excellent and very convenient. The Bedford/St. Martin's LitLinks site (http://bcs.bedfordstmartins.com/litlinks/Pages/Main.aspx) is another useful resource. Sites for many individual authors — personal home pages for some contemporary poets and sites maintained by scholars or fans of writers old and new — are available as well. Poets often work with and are influenced by each other. Whenever poets represented in this anthology appear within a biographical entry, their names are in small capitals as a reminder that their biographical notes will shed further light on the author at hand.

Kim Addonizio (b. 1954) was born in Washington, D.C. She received her B.A. and M.A. from San Francisco University. She has published several volumes of poetry, a collection of stories, and a book on the pleasures of writing poetry, and she coedited *Dorothy Parker's Elbow: Tattoos on Writers, Writers on Tattoos*. She was a founding editor of *Five Fingers Review*. She has received numerous honors, including fellowships from the National Endowment for the Arts and a Pushcart Prize, and she was named a finalist for the National Book Award. She teaches in the M.F.A. program at Goddard College.

Ai (b. 1947), who has described herself as one-half Japanese, one-eighth Choctaw, one-fourth black, and one-sixteenth Irish, was born Florence Anthony in Albany, Texas, and grew up in Tucson, Arizona. She legally changed her name to "Ai," which means "love" in Japanese. She received a B.A. in Japanese from the University of Arizona and an M.F.A. from the University of California at Irvine. She is the author of half a dozen books of poetry, among them *Vice* (1999), which won the National Book Award for poetry. She has taught at Wayne State University, George Mason University, and the University of Kentucky, and she currently teaches at Oklahoma State University and lives in Stillwater, Oklahoma.

Sherman Alexie (b. 1966), of Spokane/Coeur d'Alene Indian descent, was born on the Spokane Indian Reservation in Wellpinit, Washington. He earned his B.A. from Washington State University in Pullman. He has published ten books of poetry and several novels and collections of short fiction, including *The Lone Ranger and Tonto Fistfight in Heaven*

(1993). He wrote the script for the film *Smoke Signals* on the basis of one of his short stories. "Postcards to Columbus" reflects Alexie's concern about the devaluation of his native culture.

Agha Shahid Ali (1949–2001) was born in New Delhi and grew up Muslim in Kashmir. He was educated at the University of Kashmir, Srinagar, and at the University of Delhi. He earned a Ph.D. from Pennsylvania State University in 1984 and an M.F.A. from the University of Arizona in 1985. He was a poet (author of eight books of poetry), critic (author of *T. S. Eliot as Editor,* 1986), translator (*The Rebel's Silhouette: Selected Poems* by Faiz Ahmed Faiz, 1992), and editor (*Ravishing Disunities: Real Ghazals in English,* 2000). He held teaching positions at the University of Delhi and at several colleges and universities in the United States. "I Dream It Is Afternoon When I Return to Delhi" shows Ali's use of Western formal cultural principles in work that focuses on his own cultural background.

Tom Andrews (1961–2001) was born and grew up in West Virginia. He graduated from Hope College and earned his M.F.A. at the University of Virginia. He published three books of poems and a memoir, *Codeine Diary* (1998), about his coming to terms with his hemophilia and his determined refusal to let it circumscribe his life. He edited collections of essays on WILLIAM STAFFORD and CHARLES WRIGHT. "The Hemophiliac's Motorcycle" is written as a single sentence and displays the same spirit of celebration one finds in CHRISTOPHER SMART's *Jubilate Agno.*

Matthew Arnold (1822–1888) was born in the small English village of Laleham and raised at Rugby School, where his

father was headmaster. He attended Oxford University and, in 1857, was elected professor of poetry at Oxford, a position he held for ten years, writing mostly literary criticism. He also worked for thirty-five years as an inspector of schools and made two lecture tours of the United States.

John Ashbery (b. 1927) grew up on a farm near Rochester, New York. He graduated from Harvard University and received his M.A. from Columbia University. He studied in France for two years and then stayed on, writing art criticism. Returning to New York, he taught, edited *Art News,* and wrote for *Newsweek.* He is the author of twenty-five books of poetry, including *Some Trees* (1956), which was selected by W. H. AUDEN for the Yale Younger Poets Series, and *Self-Portrait in a Convex Mirror* (1975), which received the Pulitzer Prize for poetry, the National Book Critics Circle Award, and the National Book Award. His most recent books are *A Worldly Country* (2005) and *Where Shall I Wander* (2007). He has also published literary criticism, a book of art criticism, a collection of plays, and a novel.

Margaret Atwood (b. 1939) was born in Ottawa and grew up in northern Ontario, Quebec, and Toronto. She began writing while attending high school in Toronto. She received her undergraduate degree from Victoria College at the University of Toronto and her master's degree from Radcliffe College. She won the E. J. Pratt Medal for her privately printed book of poems, *Double Persephone* (1961), and has published fifteen more collections of poetry. She is perhaps best known for her twelve novels, which include *The Handmaid's Tale* (1983), *The Robber Bride* (1994), and *The Blind Assassin* (2000, winner of the Booker Prize). She has also published nine collections of short stories, six children's books, and five books of nonfiction, and edited several anthologies. Her work has been translated into more than thirty languages, including Farsi, Japanese, Turkish, Finnish, Korean, Icelandic, and Estonian.

W.[ystan] H.[ugh] Auden (1907–1973) was born in York, England. He went to private school and then to Oxford University, where he began to write poetry. He supported himself by teaching and publishing and wrote books based on his travels to Iceland, Spain, and China. He also wrote (with Chester Kallman) several librettos, including the one for Igor Stravinsky's *The Rake's Progress* (1951). He lived in the United States from 1939 until his death and became a U.S. citizen in 1946. His work combines lively intelligence, quick wit, careful craftsmanship, and social concern.

Jimmy Santiago Baca (b. 1952) was born in Sante Fe, New Mexico, of Chicano and Apache heritage. Abandoned by his parents at the age of two, he lived with one of his grandparents for several years before being placed in an orphanage. He lived on the streets as a youth and was imprisoned for six years for drug possession. In prison, he taught himself to read and write and began to compose poetry. A fellow inmate convinced him to submit some of his poems for publication. He has since published a dozen books of poetry, a memoir, a collection of stories and essays, a play, and a screenplay, with a novel forthcoming. He lives outside Albuquerque in a one-hundred-year-old adobe house.

Jim Barnes (b. 1933), born in Oklahoma of Choctaw and Welsh heritage, worked for ten years as a lumberjack. He studied at Southeastern Oklahoma State

University and received his M.A. and Ph.D. from the University of Arkansas. He has published many books of poetry, most recently *Visiting Picasso* (2006); several books of translations and criticism; and over 500 poems in more than 100 journals, including *The Chicago Review, The American Scholar, Prairie Schooner,* and *Georgia Review.* He is the founding editor of the Chariton Review Press and editor of *The Chariton Review.* He taught at Truman State University from 1970 to 2003, then at Brigham Young University, and presently lives in Santa Fe.

John Berryman (1914–1972) was born John Smith in McAlester, Oklahoma; he took the name of his stepfather after his father's suicide. He attended a private school in Connecticut, Columbia College, and Clare College, Cambridge. He taught at Wayne State University, Harvard University, Princeton University, and the University of Minnesota. His early work was traditional, highly crafted, and admired, but only later, when he was in his forties, did his poetry emerge as boldly original and innovative. *77 Dream Songs,* published in 1964 and awarded a Pulitzer Prize, unveiled the alter egos "Henry" and "Mr. Bones" in a sequence of sonnet-like poems whose unusual diction, difficult syntax, leaps in language and tone, and mixture of lyricism and comedy reached depths of the human spirit and psyche. He added to the sequence in the following years until they totaled nearly four hundred in *The Dream Songs* (1969). Berryman suffered throughout his life from mental and emotional difficulties and commited suicide by jumping off a bridge in Minneapolis.

Elizabeth Bishop (1911–1979), born in Worcester, Massachusetts, was raised in Nova Scotia by her grandparents after her father died and her mother was committed to an asylum. She attended Vassar College, intending to study medicine, but was encouraged by MARIANNE MOORE to be a poet. From 1935 to 1937 she traveled in France, Spain, northern Africa, Ireland, and Italy and then settled in Key West, Florida, for four years, after which she lived in Rio de Janeiro for almost twenty years. She wrote slowly and carefully and produced a small body of poetry (totaling only around one hundred poems), technically sophisticated, formally varied, witty, and thoughtful, revealing in precise, true-to-life images her impressions of the physical world. She served as Consultant in Poetry at the Library of Congress from 1949 to 1950.[1]

William Blake (1757–1827) was born and lived in London. His only formal schooling was in art — he studied for a year at the Royal Academy and was apprenticed to an engraver. He worked as a professional engraver, doing commissions and illustrations, assisted by his wife, Catherine Boucher. Blake started writing poetry at the age of eleven and later engraved and hand-printed his own poems, in very small batches, with his own hand-colored illustrations. His early work showed a strong social conscience, and his later work turned increasingly mythic and prophetic.

1. The first appointment of a Consultant in Poetry at the Library of Congress was made in 1937. The title was changed to Poet Laureate Consultant in Poetry in 1986. Appointments are made for one year, beginning in September, and sometimes have been renewed for a second year.

Robert Bly (b. 1926) was born in Madison, Minnesota, and served in the navy during World War II. He studied at St. Olaf College for a year before going to Harvard University. He lived in New York for a few years, then earned an M.A. from the University of Iowa Writers' Workshop. He received a Fulbright grant in 1956 to travel to Norway and began to translate Norwegian poetry into English. In 1966 he founded (with David Ray) American Writers Against the Vietnam War. He has published more than thirty books of poetry, many books of translations, and a number of nonfiction books and has edited numerous collections of poetry. A best-selling author, he is also a challenging critic of contemporary consumerist culture (his controversial 1990 best-seller *Iron John* was a key book in the "men's movement"). "Driving to Town Late to Mail a Letter" is an example of his ability to discover a moment of epiphany in the most common of situations. He now lives on a farm near the small town of Moose Lake, Minnesota.

Louise Bogan (1897–1970) was born in Maine and educated in Boston. For thirty-eight years she was the poetry editor at the *New Yorker*. She was reclusive and disliked talking about herself, and for that reason details about her private life are scarce. The majority of her poetry was written in the earlier half of her life and published in the *New Republic*, the *Nation*, *Poetry*, *Scribner's*, *Atlantic Monthly*, and in several volumes of collected verse. Her poetry is notable for its strict adherence to lyrical forms while maintaining a high emotional pitch. "Women," like much of her verse, explores the perpetual disparity of heart and mind.

Eavan Boland (b. 1944) was born in Dublin and educated there and in London and New York. She has taught at Trinity College and University College, Dublin; Bowdoin College; and the University of Iowa. She is currently Melvin and Bill Lane Professor in the Humanities at Stanford University. An influential figure in Irish poetry, Boland has published a dozen volumes of poetry, including *The Journey and Other Poems* (1987), *Night Feed* (1994), *The Lost Land* (1998), *Code* (2001), and *New Collected Poems* (2005), and has edited several other books including *Three Irish Poets: An Anthology* (2003) and *Irish Writers on Writing* (2007). Her poems and essays have appeared in magazines such as the *New Yorker*, the *Atlantic*, *Kenyon Review*, and *American Poetry Review*. She is a regular reviewer for the *Irish Times*.

Anne Bradstreet (c. 1612–1672), born in Northampton, England, was educated by tutors, reading chiefly religious writings and the Bible. In 1628 she married Simon Bradstreet, a brilliant young Puritan educated at Cambridge. They were among the earliest settlers of the Massachusetts Bay Colony, in 1630, and her father and husband were leading figures in its governance. She wrote regularly in both prose and verse throughout her busy and difficult years in Massachusetts.

Gwendolyn Brooks (1917–2000), born in Topeka, Kansas, was raised in Chicago and wrote her first poems at age seven. She began studying poetry at the Southside Community Art Center. Her second collection of poems, *Annie Allen* (1949), earned the first Pulitzer Prize given to an African American poet. She served as Consultant in Poetry at the Library of Congress from 1985 to 1986 and worked in community programs and poetry workshops in Chicago to encourage young African American writers.

Sterling A. Brown (1901–1989) was born in Washington, D.C., and educated at Dunbar High School, Williams College, and Harvard University. He taught for more than fifty years at Howard University. Like many other black poets of the period, he expresses his concerns about race in America. His first book of poems, *Southern Road* (1932), was well received by critics, and Brown became part of the artistic tradition of the Harlem Renaissance. Brown was deeply interested in African American music and dialect. He became one of the great innovators in developing poetry related to jazz. His work is known for its frank, unsentimental portraits of black people and their experiences and its successful incorporation of African American folklore and contemporary idiom.

Elizabeth Barrett Browning (1806–1861) was born in Durham, England, and studied with her brother's tutor. Her first book of poetry was published when she was thirteen, and she soon became the most famous female poet to that point in English history. A riding accident at the age of sixteen left her a semi-invalid in the house of her possessive father, who had forbidden any of his eleven children to marry. She and ROBERT BROWNING were forced to elope (she was thirty-nine at the time); they lived in Florence, Italy, where she died fifteen years later. Her best-known book of poems was *Sonnets from the Portuguese*, a sequence of forty-four sonnets recording the growth of her love for Robert.

Robert Browning (1812–1889) was the son of a bank clerk in Camberwell, then a suburb of London. As an aspiring poet in 1844, he admired ELIZABETH BARRETT's poetry and began a correspondence with her that led to one of the world's most famous romances. Their courtship lasted until 1846 when they were secretly wed and ran off to Italy, where they lived until Elizabeth's death in 1861. The years in Florence were among the happiest for both of them. To her he dedicated *Men and Women*, which contains his best poetry. Although she was the more popular poet during her lifetime, his reputation grew upon his return to London after her death, assisted somewhat by public sympathy for him. The late 1860s were the peak of his career: he and TENNYSON were mentioned together as the foremost poets of the age.

Charles Bukowski (1920–1994), born in Andernach, Germany, came to the United States at age three and grew up in poverty in Los Angeles. He drifted extensively, but for much of his life made his home in San Pedro, working for many years in the U.S. Postal Service. He was familiar with the people of the streets, skid row residents, hustlers, and a transient lifestyle. He began writing in childhood, and published his first story at age twenty-four and his first poetry when he was thirty-five. In addition to his many books of poetry, he published novels and short stories written in a style reminiscent of that of Ernest Hemingway. He is very popular in Europe. The strong sense of immediacy in his writing and its refusal to embrace standard formal structures reflect the influence of the Beat movement.

Robert Burns (1759–1796) was born in Ayrshire in southwestern Scotland, the son of a poor farming family. His formal education lasted only to about his ninth year, when he was needed to work on the farm, but he read widely and voraciously whenever he could find time. His first book of poems, published in 1785, sold out within a month. Despite living in poverty, he poured out a flood of his finest poems in the early 1790s. Burns is regarded as Scotland's national bard for his ability to depict with loving accuracy the life of his fellow rural Scots. His use of dialect brought a stimulating, much-needed freshness and raciness into English poetry, but his greatness extends beyond the limits of dialect: his poems are written about Scots, but, in tune with the rising humanitarianism of his day, they apply to a multitude of universal problems.

George Gordon, Lord Byron (1788–1824) was one of the great Romantic poets, although he is best known for his lighthearted and humorous verse, such as *Don Juan*. He was born in London and raised in Scotland; he studied at Harrow and at Trinity College, Cambridge. He inherited the title of sixth baron Byron (with estate) at age ten. The last few years of his life were spent in Italy, and he died in Greece after joining the Greek forces in their war for independence.

Lorna Dee Cervantes (b. 1954) was born in San Francisco and grew up in San Jose. There she studied at San Jose City College and San Jose State University. She is the author of two volumes of poetry, *Emplumada* (1981) — winner of an American Book Award — and *From the Cables of Genocide: Poems on Love and Hunger* (1991). She is also coeditor of *Red Dirt*, a cross-cultural poetry journal, and her work has been included in many anthologies. Cervantes, who considers herself "a Chicana writer, a feminist writer, a political writer," lives in Colorado and is a professor at the University of Colorado at Boulder.

Marilyn Chin (b. 1955) is a first-generation Chinese American, born in Hong Kong and raised in Portland, Oregon. She is the author of three volumes of poetry, *Dwarf Bamboo* (1987), *The Phoenix Gone, The Terrace Empty* (1994), and *Rhapsody in Plain Yellow* (2002). She also is a coeditor of *Dissident Song: A Contemporary Asian American Anthology* (1991) and has translated poems by the modern Chinese poet Ai Qing and cotranslated poems by the Japanese poet Gozo Yoshimasu. She has received numerous awards for her poetry, including a Stegner fellowship, the PEN/Josephine Miles Award, and four Pushcart Prizes. She is codirector of the M.F.A. program at San Diego State University.

Lucille Clifton (b. 1936) was born in Depew, New York, and studied at Howard University. She has published many books of poetry, including *Blessing the Boats: New and Selected Poems 1988–2000* (2000), which won the National Book Award. She has also published a memoir and more than twenty books for children. She has taught at several colleges and worked in the Office of Education in Washington, D.C. She has served as poet laureate for the State of Maryland and is currently Distinguished Professor of Humanities at St. Mary's College of Maryland. Her poems typically reflect her ethnic pride, womanist principles, and race and gender consciousness.

Judith Ortiz Cofer (b. 1952) was born in Hormigueros, Puerto Rico. Her family moved to Paterson, New Jersey, in 1955. For the next decade, she grew up

moving between those two very different worlds. She graduated from Augusta College in Georgia, married and had a daughter, completed a graduate degree, and began teaching English. But, she says, something was missing from her life: She realized that she needed to write. Her first book of poetry, *Reaching for the Mainland* (1987), was followed by several others including, most recently, *A Love Story Beginning in Spanish: Poems* (2006). She has also published novels for adults, a memoir — *Silent Dancing: A Partial Remembrance of a Puerto Rican Childhood* (1990) — and a book about writing, *Woman in Front of the Sun: On Becoming a Writer* (2000). She has written several award-winning books for young adults, including *An Island Like You: Stories of the Barrio* (1996). She is Regents' and Franklin Professor of English and Creative Writing at the University of Georgia and lives with her husband on the family farm near Louisville, Georgia.

Samuel Taylor Coleridge (1772–1834) was born in Devonshire and sent to school in London after his father's death. He went to Jesus College, Cambridge, in 1791, and dropped out twice without a degree. In 1798 Coleridge and WILLIAM WORDSWORTH published *Lyrical Ballads*, which initiated the Romantic movement in English poetry and established both of their reputations. After 1802 Coleridge became addicted to opium, used as a treatment for physical discomfort and seizures. He and his wife were separated, his friendship with Wordsworth broke up, and his poetic output stopped. From 1816 to his death he lived under constant medical supervision, but still published a journal and wrote several plays, pieces of criticism, and philosophical and religious treatises.

Billy Collins (b. 1941), born and raised in New York City, is the author of numerous collections of poems, most recently *The Trouble with Poetry* (2005). Perhaps no poet since ROBERT FROST has managed to combine high critical acclaim with such broad popular appeal. The typical Collins poem opens on a clear and hospitable note but soon takes an unexpected turn; poems that begin in irony may end in a moment of lyric surprise. Collins sees his poetry as "a form of travel writing" and considers humor "a door into the serious." Collins is Distinguished Professor of Literature at Lehman College of the City University of New York and a writer-in-residence at Sarah Lawrence College. He was appointed Poet Laureate Consultant in Poetry at the Library of Congress from 2001 to 2003.

Jayne Cortez (b. 1936) was born in Arizona, grew up in the Watts section of Los Angeles, and now lives in New York City. A poet and performance artist, she has published ten books of poetry and made a number of recordings, often performing her poetry with the jazz group the Firespitters. Her poems have been translated into twenty-eight languages. In 1964 she founded the Watts Repertory Company, and in 1972 she formed her own publishing company, Bola Press.

Hart Crane (1899–1932), born in Garrettsville, Ohio, began writing verse in his early teenage years. Though he never attended college, he read widely on his own. An admirer of T. S. ELIOT, Crane combined the influences of European literature and traditional versification with a particularly American sensibility derived from WALT WHITMAN. His major work, the book-length poem *The Bridge* (1930), expresses in ecstatic terms a vision of the historical and spiritual significance of America. Like Eliot, Crane used the landscape of the modern, industrialized city to create a powerful new symbolic literature. He committed suicide in 1932, at the age of thirty-three, by jumping from the deck of a steamship sailing back to New York from Mexico.

Stephen Crane (1871–1900), born in Newark, New Jersey, was the fourteenth and youngest child of a Methodist minister. He started to write stories at the age of eight and at sixteen was writing feature articles for the *New York Tribune*. He attended Lafayette College and Syracuse University and then returned to New York where he lived in poverty as a freelance writer and journalist. His experience in the Bowery slums supplied details for his first, self-published novel, *Maggie: A Girl of the Streets* (1893), a pioneer work of the naturalistic movement. His most famous novel, *The Red Badge of Courage*, a realistic depiction of the Civil War from the point of view of an ordinary soldier, was published in 1895 and was a resounding success. His achievements as a novelist won him assignments as a special newspaper correspondent and enabled him to travel widely, reporting on the Spanish-American and Greco-Turkish wars. In addition to several volumes of essays and short stories, he published two collections of poems, *The Black Riders* (1895) and *War Is Kind* (1899). He settled briefly in England and died from tuberculosis in Badenweiler, Germany, a few months before his twenty-ninth birthday.

Robert Creeley (1926–2005) was born in Arlington, Massachusetts, attended Harvard University, then lived in France and Spain before joining the faculty of Black Mountain College (an experimental arts college in North Carolina) in 1954, where he edited the *Black Mountain Review*. His influence helped to define an emerging countertradition to the literary establishment. He published more than sixty books of poetry in the United States and abroad. In 1967 he began teaching at the State University of New York, Buffalo, where from 1989 to 2003 he was Samuel P. Capen Professor of Poetry and Humanities. "Time" illustrates his technique of fracturing lines to convey tension, anxiety, and fragmentation of the psyche.

Victor Hernández Cruz (b. 1949) was born in Aguas Buenas, Puerto Rico, and moved to New York City with his family at the age of five. His first book of poetry was published when he was seventeen. A year later, he moved to California's Bay Area and published his second book. In 1971 Cruz visited Puerto Rico and reconnected with his ancestral heritage; eighteen years later, he returned to Puerto Rico to live. He now divides his time between Puerto Rico and New York. He is the author of five collections of poetry, including *Maraca: New and Selected Poems 1965–2000* (2001). He is a cofounder of the East Harlem Gut Theatre in New York and the Before Columbus Foundation and has taught at the University of California at Berkeley and San Diego, San Francisco State College, and the University of Michigan. Much of his work explores the relation between the English language and his native Spanish, playing with grammatical and syntactical conventions within both languages to create his own bilingual idiom.

Countee Cullen (1903–1946) was born either in Louisville, Kentucky; Baltimore, Maryland; or (as he himself claimed) New York City. He was adopted by the Reverend Frederick A. Cullen and his wife and grew up, as he put it, "in the conservative atmosphere of a Methodist parsonage." He studied at New York University and Harvard University. A forerunner of the Harlem Renaissance movement, he was in the 1920s the most popular black literary figure in America. From the 1930s until his death, he wrote less and worked as a junior high school French teacher. For many years after his death, his reputation was eclipsed by that of other Harlem Renaissance writers, particularly LANGSTON HUGHES and Zora Neale Hurston; recently, however, there has been a resurgence of interest in his life and work.

E. E. Cummings (1894–1962) was born in Cambridge, Massachusetts, where his father was a Unitarian minister and a sociology lecturer at Harvard University. He graduated from Harvard and then served as an ambulance driver during World War I. *The Enormous Room* (1922) is an account of his confinement in a French prison camp during the war. After the war, he lived in rural Connecticut and Greenwich Village, with frequent visits to Paris. In his work, Cummings experimented radically with form, punctuation, spelling, and syntax, abandoning traditional techniques and structures to create a new, highly idiosyncratic means of poetic expression. At the time of his death in 1962, he was the second most widely read poet in the United States, after ROBERT FROST.

Toi Derricotte (b. 1941) was born and raised in Detroit. She earned a B.A. in special education from Wayne State University and an M.A. in English literature from New York University. She is the author of several collections of poetry as well as a memoir, *The Black Notebooks* (1997). With poet CORNELIUS EADY, she cofounded Cave Canem, which offers workshops and retreats for African American poets. Among many honors she has received is the Distinguished Pioneering of the Arts Award from the United Black Artists. Derricotte teaches creative writing at the University of Pittsburgh.

Emily Dickinson (1830–1886) was born in Amherst, Massachusetts, and lived there her entire life, rarely leaving. She briefly attended a women's seminary but became homesick and left before a year was out. Dickinson never married and became reclusive later in life, forgoing even the village routines and revelries she enjoyed. She wrote over 1,700 fresh, often unconventional, carefully crafted poems, marked by striking images, surprising figures of speech, metrical irregularities, frequent slant rhymes, and unique punctuation. Only five were published during her lifetime. Not until 1955 was there a complete edition of her poems attempting to present them as originally written.

John Donne (1572–1631) was born in London to a prosperous Catholic family (through his mother he was related to Sir Thomas More and the playwright John Heywood). Donne studied at Oxford University for several years but did not take a degree. He fought with Sir Walter Raleigh in two naval strikes against Spain. In 1601 Donne's promising political career was permanently derailed by his precipitous marriage to Anne More without her father's consent. He was briefly imprisoned, lost a very promising position with Sir Thomas Egerton, and spent years seeking further political employment before finally being convinced by King James

in 1615 to become a priest of the Church of England. His life was described by Isaac Walton later in the century as being divided into two parts. In Phase I he was "Jack Donne" of Lincoln's Inn: When young, Donne employed a sophisticated urban wit that created in his earlier poetry a sort of jaded tone. "The Flea" presumably appeared during this stage of his life and illustrates its characteristics well (a typical **metaphysical poem** — see the glossary). In Phase II he was John Donne, dean of St. Paul's: After Donne took holy orders in 1615, his poetry became markedly less amorous and more religious in tone. His *Holy Sonnets* (of which "Death, be not proud" is one) are as dense and complex as his earlier work, with his talent now directed toward exploration of his relationship with God.

Hilda Doolittle [H. D.] (1886–1961) was born in Bethlehem, Pennsylvania. She went to private schools in Philadelphia and then dropped out of Bryn Mawr after a year because of ill health. She moved to England, where an old friend (and fiancé for a time), EZRA POUND, encouraged her to write and sent some of her poetry to a journal. H. D. became a leader of Pound's Imagist group but eventually moved away from it. From 1933 to 1934 she visited Sigmund Freud as a patient and later wrote *Tribute to Freud* (1956). Besides poetry, she wrote novels and translated Greek.

Mark Doty (b. 1953) is the author of seven collections of poetry and three memoirs — *Heaven's Coast* (1996), about the loss of his partner, Wally Roberts; *Firebird* (1999), a gay coming-of-age story, a chronicle of a gradual process of finding in art a place of personal belonging; and *Dog Years* (2007), about the relationships between humans and the dogs they love. He has taught at Brandeis University, Sarah Lawrence College, Vermont College, and the University of Iowa Writers' Workshop. He now lives in New York City and Houston, Texas, where he teaches at the University of Houston.

Rita Dove (b. 1952) was born in Akron, Ohio; her father was the first research chemist to break the race barrier in the tire industry. She graduated from Miami University in Oxford, Ohio, with a degree in English; after a year at Tübingen University in Germany on a Fulbright fellowship, she joined the University of Iowa Writers' Workshop, where she earned her M.F.A. in 1977. She has taught at Tuskegee Institute and Arizona State University and now is on the faculty of the University of Virginia. She was appointed Poet Laureate Consultant in Poetry at the Library of Congress in 1993, making her the youngest person — and the first African American — to receive this highest official honor in American letters. She is the author of numerous collections of poetry, including *Thomas and Beulah* (1986), a book-length sequence loosely based on the lives of her grandparents which was awarded the Pulitzer Prize in 1987. "The Satisfaction Coal Company" is from that book ("he" is Thomas; "they" are Thomas and Beulah); it reflects Dove's concern for those living workaday lives and her celebration of their worth and dignity.

Michael Drayton (1563–1631) was born a year before Shakespeare and in the same county, Warwickshire, England. He wrote sonnets, pastorals, odes, verse epistles, satires, and historical epics. His masterpiece is a topographical work on England titled *Poly-Olbion*, a poem

celebrating all the counties of England and Wales. He was an influential writer of religious poetry as well. "Since there's no help, come let us kiss and part" is the sixty-first in a sequence of sonnets addressed to "Idea," the embodiment of the Platonic idea of virtue and beauty.

Denise Duhamel (b. 1961) was born in Woonsocket, Rhode Island. She received her B.F.A. from Emerson College and her M.F.A. from Sarah Lawrence College. She has published many collections of poetry, most recently *Two and Two* and *Mille et un sentiments,* both in 2005. She was winner of the Crab Orchard Poetry Prize for her collection *The Star-Spangled Banner* (1999). She has been anthologized widely and has been included in four volumes of *The Best American Poetry*. She teaches creative writing at Florida International University.

Paul Laurence Dunbar (1872–1906) was the first African American to gain national eminence as a poet. Born and raised in Dayton, Ohio, he was the son of ex-slaves. He was an outstanding student. The only African American in his class, he was both class president and class poet. Although he lived to be only thirty-three years old, Dunbar was prolific, writing short stories, novels, librettos, plays, songs, and essays as well as the poetry for which he became well known. He was popular with both black and white readers of his day. His style encompasses two distinct voices — the standard English of the classical poet and the evocative dialect of the turn-of-the-century black community in America.

Robert Duncan (1919–1988) was born in Oakland, California, and raised by adoptive parents who were devout theosophists and instilled in him a life-long interest in occult spirituality. He entered the University of California at Berkeley in 1936 and moved into leftist politics and a bohemian lifestyle. He was drafted in 1941 but was discharged after declaring his homosexuality. His 1944 essay "The Homosexual in Society" compared the situation faced by homosexuals in modern society with that of blacks and Jews. Influenced by a variety of poets, Duncan credited a long correspondence with DENISE LEVERTOV with helping him find a new poetics — a magical, mystical blend of the experimental with the traditional. His first book, *Heavenly City, Earthly City*, was published in 1947, the same year he met Charles Olson, whose literary theories helped shape Duncan's "grand collage" concept of verse. He returned to San Francisco in 1948, becoming part of the San Francisco Renaissance and cultivating the role of a guru, discoursing on literature, spiritualism, and sexual diversity. He became affiliated with Olson's Black Mountain movement and taught at Black Mountain College in 1956. His reputation as a poet was established by three major collections: *The Opening of the Field* (1960), *Roots and Branches* (1964), and *Bending the Bow* (1968). He was awarded the Harriet Monroe Memorial Prize in 1961, a Guggenheim fellowship in 1963, the Levinson Prize in 1964, and the National Poetry Award in 1985.

Cornelius Eady (b. 1954) was born and raised in Rochester, New York, and attended Monroe Community College and Empire State College. He began writing as a teenager. His poems are his biography, their subjects ranging from blues musicians to the witnessing of his father's death. He has published six volumes of poetry. With poet TOI DERRICOTTE, he co-founded Cave Canem, which offers workshops and retreats for African American poets, and with composer Diedre Murray he has collaborated on two highly acclaimed music-dramas. Formerly the director of the Poetry Center at the State University of New York, Stony Brook, he is currently associate professor of English and director of the creative writing program at the University of Notre Dame.

Russell Edson (b. 1935) was born in Connecticut and currently resides in Stamford, Connecticut. He is one of the most important writers of prose poetry in America, having written exclusively in that form before it became fashionable. Often simultaneously visionary, funny, and horrifying, his poems commonly fuse and confuse the banal and the bizarre. He handset his first books, before New Directions gathered his poems and published them in a collection titled *The Very Thing That Happens* (1964). Since then he has published ten more books of poetry — most recently *The Rooster's Wife: Poems*, in 2005 — as well as a novel, *The Song of Percival Peacock* (1992), and a book of plays, *The Falling Sickness* (1975).

T.[homas] S.[tearns] Eliot (1888–1965) was born and raised in St. Louis. He went to prep school in Massachusetts and to Harvard University, where he earned an M.A. in philosophy in 1910 and started his doctoral dissertation. He studied at the Sorbonne, Paris, and then at Marburg, Germany, in 1914. The war forced him to Oxford, where he married and abandoned philosophy for poetry. After teaching and working in a bank, he became an editor at Faber and Faber and editor of the journal *Criterion* and was the dominant force in

English poetry for several decades. He became a British citizen and a member of the Church of England in 1927. He won the Nobel Prize in literature in 1948. He also wrote plays, essays, and a series of poems on cats that became the basis of a musical by Andrew Lloyd Weber. The poems included in this anthology show Eliot's use of collage techniques to embody the fragmentation he saw in culture and individual psyches in his day.

Elizabeth I (1533–1603) was queen of England from 1558 to 1603. In addition to being well educated and a skillful politician and ruler, she wrote extensively, mostly speeches and translations but also a few original poems in the forms and manner typical of her time. Though the attribution of "When I was fair and young" has been questioned, it is credited to her in the most recent collection of her works.

Anita Endrezze (b. 1952) was born in Long Beach, California, of Yaqui and European ancestry, and earned her M.A. from Eastern Washington University. She is a poet, writer, and painter (in watercolor and acrylics) who also works in fiber and creates handmade books. She is a member of Atlatl, a Native American arts service organization. In addition to four volumes of poetry, she has published a children's novel, short stories, and nonfiction. She lives in Everett, Washington, where she is a storyteller, teacher, and writer.

Louise Erdrich (b. 1954) was born in Minnesota to a French Ojibwe mother and a German-born father. She grew up near the Turtle Mountain Reservation in North Dakota and is a member of the Turtle Mountain Band of Chippewa. Her grandfather was tribal chief of the reservation. She was among the first women admitted to Dartmouth College, where she began writing; she also studied at Johns Hopkins University. She has published eleven novels, four children's books, three collections of poetry, and two books of nonfiction. She lives in Minneapolis and is the owner of Birchbark Books, a small independent bookstore.

Martín Espada (b. 1957) was born in Brooklyn, New York, and has an eclectic résumé: radio journalist in Nicaragua, welfare rights paralegal, advocate for mental patients, night desk clerk in a transient hotel, attendant in a primate nursery, groundskeeper at a minor league ballpark, bindery worker in a printing plant, bouncer in a bar, and practicing lawyer in Chelsea, Massachusetts. Author of eight books of poetry, his most recent is *The Republic of Poetry* (2006). His book *Alabanza: New and Selected Poems, 1982–2002* (2003) received the Paterson Award for Sustained Literary Achievement and was named an American Library Association Notable Book of the Year. He is an essayist, editor, and translator as well as a poet. He presently teaches at the University of Massachusetts, Amherst.

Carolyn Forché (b. 1950) was born in Detroit, attended Michigan State University, and earned an M.F.A. from Bowling Green State University. She achieved immediate success as a writer, winning the Yale Younger Poets Prize in 1976. Her work underwent a remarkable shift following a year spent on a Guggenheim fellowship in El Salvador, where she worked with human rights activist Archbishop Oscar Humberto Romero and with Amnesty International. The shock of witnessing countless atrocities in Central America led her to begin writing what she calls "poetry of witness." The volume *The Country Between Us* (1981) stirred immediate controversy because of its overtly political topics and themes. "The Colonel," a prose poem in which the speaker conveys a horrific story with chilling flatness, is probably the most disturbing and memorable poem in the book. She is the author of four books of poetry, most recently *Blue Hour* (2004), and the editor of *Against Forgetting: Twentieth-Century Poetry of Witness* (1993). She has also translated several books of poetry. She is currently a faculty member at George Mason University in Virginia.

Robert Frost (1874–1963) was born in San Francisco and lived there until he was eleven. When his father died, the family moved to Massachusetts, where Robert did well in school, especially in the classics, but he dropped out of both Dartmouth College and Harvard University. He went unrecognized as a poet until 1913, when he was first published in England, where he had moved with his wife and four children. Upon returning to the United States, he quickly achieved success with more publications and became the most celebrated poet in mid-twentieth-century America. He held a teaching position at Amherst College and received many honorary degrees as well as an invitation to recite a poem at John F. Kennedy's inauguration. Although his work is principally associated with the life and landscape of New England, and although he was a poet of traditional verse forms and meters, he is also a quintessentially modern poet in his adherence to language as it is actually spoken, in the psychological complexity of his portraits, and in the degree to which his work is infused with layers of ambiguity and irony.

Alice Fulton (b. 1952) was born and grew up in Troy, New York. Winner of many fellowships and awards, she is the author of seven books of poetry (most recently *Cascade Experiment: Selected Poems*, 2004) and a collection of essays. She has taught at the University of California, Los Angeles; Ohio State University; the University of North Carolina, Wilmington; and for eighteen years at the University of Michigan. She was a member of the American delegation at the 1988 Chinese-American Writers' Conference, held in Beijing, Xian, Leshan, Wuhan, and Shanghai. Fulton currently teaches at Cornell University. "You Can't Rhumboogie in a Ball and Chain" is a **sestina** (see the glossary). The poem's form with its repetition is particularly interesting in light of the obsessive nature of its content.

Richard Garcia (b. 1941) was born in San Francisco, a first-generation American (his mother was from Mexico, his father from Puerto Rico). While still in high school, he had a poem published by City Lights in a Beat anthology. After publishing his first collection in 1972, however, he did not write poetry again for twelve years, until an unsolicited letter of encouragement from poet Octavio Paz inspired him to resume. Since then, his work has appeared widely in literary magazines such as the *Kenyon Review, Parnassus,* and the *Gettysburg Review,* as well as three later books, *The Flying Garcias* (1991), *Rancho Notorious* (2001), and *The Persistence of Objects* (2006). He is also the author of a bilingual children's book, *My Aunt Otilia's Spirits* (1987). For twelve years he was the poet-in-residence at Children's Hospital Los Angeles, where he conducted poetry and art workshops for hospitalized children. He teaches creative writing in the Antioch University Los Angeles M.F.A. program and the Idyllwild Summer Poetry Program.

Allen Ginsberg (1926–1997) was born in Newark, New Jersey, and graduated from Columbia University, after several suspensions, in 1948. Several years later, Ginsberg left for San Francisco to join other poets of the Beat movement. His poem "Howl," the most famous poem of the movement, was published in 1956 by Lawrence Ferlinghetti's City Lights Books; the publicity of the ensuing censorship trial brought the Beats to national attention. Ginsberg was co-founder with ANNE WALDMAN of the Jack Kerouac School of Disembodied Poetics at the Naropa Institute in Boulder, Colorado. In his later years he became a distinguished professor at Brooklyn College.

Louise Glück (b. 1943) was born in New York City and educated at Sarah Lawrence College and Columbia University. She has published numerous collections of poetry, including *The Triumph of Achilles* (1985), which received the National Book Critics Circle Award and the Poetry Society of America's Melville Kane Award; *Ararat* (1990), which received the Rebekah Johnson Bobbitt National Prize for Poetry; *The Wild Iris* (1992), which received the Pulitzer Prize and the Poetry Society of America's William Carlos Williams Award; and most recently *Averno,* a finalist for the 2006 National Book Award in Poetry. She has also published a collection of essays, *Proofs and Theories: Essays on Poetry* (1994), which won the PEN/Martha Albrand Award for Nonfiction. In 2003 she became the Library of Congress's twelfth Poet Laureate Consultant in Poetry. She is a writer-in-residence at Yale University.

Ray González (b. 1952) received his M.F.A. in creative writing from Southwest Texas State University. He has published nine books of poetry, including *The Heat of Arrivals* (which won the 1997 Josephine Miles Book Award) and *The Hawk Temple at Tierra Grande,* winner of a 2003 Minnesota Book Award in Poetry. He is the author of two books of nonfiction — *Memory Fever* (1999), a memoir about growing up in the Southwest, and *The Underground Heart* (2002), which received the 2003 Carr P. Collins/Texas Institute of Letters Award for Best Book of Nonfiction — and two collections of short stories — *The Ghost of John Wayne* (2001) and *Circling the Tortilla Dragon* (2002) — and is editor of twelve anthologies. He has served as poetry editor for *The Bloomsbury Review* for twenty-five years. He teaches creative writing at the University of Minnesota.

Jorie Graham (b. 1950) was born in New York City, but grew up in Italy. She attended New York University as an undergraduate and received an M.F.A. from the University of Iowa Writers' Workshop. She is the author of numerous collections of poetry, including *The Dream of the Unified Field: Selected Poems 1974–1994,* which won the 1996 Pulitzer Prize for poetry. Her most recent book is *Overlord* (2005). She has also edited two anthologies, *Earth Took of Earth: 100 Great Poems of the English Language* (1996) and *The Best American Poetry 1990.* She has taught at the University of Iowa and is currently the Boylston Professor of Rhetoric and Oratory at Harvard University. Her use of formal constraints with daring innovations, illustrated in "To the Reader," has influenced many contemporary poets.

Thomas Gray (1716–1771) was born in London and educated at Eton and at Cambridge University, where he studied literature and history. In November 1741 his father died, and Gray moved with his mother and aunt to the village of Stoke Poges in Buckinghamshire, where he wrote his first important poems, the "Ode on the Spring," "Ode on a Distant Prospect of Eton College," and "Hymn to Adversity," and began his masterpiece, "Elegy Written in a Country Churchyard," called the most famous and diversified of all graveyard poems. These poems solidified his reputation as one of the most important English poets of the eighteenth century. In 1757 he was named poet laureate but refused the position. In 1762 he applied for the Regius Professorship of Modern History at Cambridge but was rejected; however, he was given the position in 1768, when the successful candidate was killed. A painfully shy and private person, he never delivered any lectures as a professor.

Marilyn Hacker (b. 1942) was born in New York City. She is the author of ten books of poetry, including *Presentation Piece* (1974), which was the Lamont Poetry Selection of the Academy of American Poets and a National Book Award winner, and *Selected Poems, 1965–1990* (1994), which received the Poets' Prize. Her most recent collection is *Desesperanto: Poems 1999–2002* (2003). She was editor of the *Kenyon Review* from 1990 to 1994 and has received numerous honors and awards. She lives in New York City and Paris. Often labeled a neo–formalist, Hacker often handles traditional forms in fresh ways, as "Villanelle" illustrates.

Kimiko Hahn (b. 1955) was born in Mt. Kisco, New York, to two artists, a Japanese American mother from Hawaii and a German American father from Wisconsin. She majored in English and East Asian studies at the University of Iowa and received an M.A. in Japanese literature at Columbia University. She is the author of seven volumes of poetry, including *The Unbearable Heart* (1996), which received an American Book Award, and *The Narrow Road to the Interior* (2006). In 1995 she wrote ten portraits of women for a two-hour HBO special titled *Ain't Nuthin' but a She-Thing.* She has taught at Parsons School of Design, the Poetry Project at St. Mark's Church, and Yale University. She lives in New York and is a Distinguished Professor in the English Department at Queens College/CUNY.

Donald Hall (b. 1928) was born and raised in Connecticut, studied at Harvard, Oxford, and Stanford, and taught at the University of Michigan. For the past thirty years, he has lived on Eagle Pond Farm in rural New Hampshire, in the house where his grandmother and mother were born. He was married for twenty-three years to the poet JANE KENYON, who died in 1995. He has written eighteen books of poetry, beginning with *Exiles and Marriages* in 1955. His most recent collection is *White Apples and the Taste of Stone: Selected Poems 1946–2006* (2006). He has also published twenty books of prose in a variety of genres: short stories, including *Willow Temple: New and Selected Stories* (2003); autobiographical works, such as *The Best Day the Worst Day: Life with Jane Kenyon* (2005); a collection of essays about poetry, *Breakfast Served Any Time All Day* (2003); numerous books for children (*Ox-Cart Man* was awarded the Caldecott Medal in 1979); and two books about life in New Hampshire, collected in *Eagle Pond* (2007). In 2006, he was named Poet Laureate Consultant in Poetry to the Library of Congress.

Thomas Hardy (1840–1928) was born in a cottage in Higher Bockhampton, Dorset, near the regional market town of Dorchester in southwestern England. Apprenticed at age sixteen to an architect, he spent most of the next twenty years restoring old churches. He had always had an interest in literature and started writing novels in his thirties, publishing more than a dozen. In 1896 Hardy gave up prose and turned to poetry, writing until his death at age eighty-eight. He had a consistently bleak, even pessimistic, outlook on life. Many of his works stress the dark effects of "hap" (happenstance, coincidence) in the world, which is a central motif in "The Convergence of the Twain."

Joy Harjo (b. 1951) was born in Tulsa, Oklahoma. Her mother was of Cherokee-French descent and her father was Creek. She moved to the Southwest and began writing poetry in her early twenties. She then earned her B.A. at the University of New Mexico and her M.F.A. from the University of Iowa Writers' Workshop. Harjo has published numerous volumes of poetry, including *In Mad Love and War* (1990), which received an American Book Award and the Delmore Schwartz Memorial Award. She also performs her poetry and plays saxophone with her band, Poetic Justice. She is professor of English at the University of New Mexico, Albuquerque. Of "She Had Some Horses" Harjo has said, "This is the poem I'm asked most about and the one I have the least to say about. I don't know where it came from."

Michael S. Harper (b. 1938) was born in Brooklyn and grew up surrounded by jazz. When his family moved to Los Angeles, he worked at all kinds of jobs, from the post office to professional football. He studied at the City College of Los Angeles; California State University, Los Angeles; and the University of Iowa Writers' Workshop. He has written more than ten books of poetry, most recently *Selected Poems* (2002), and edited or co-edited several collections of African American poetry. He is University Professor and professor of English at Brown University, where he has taught since 1970. He lives in Barrington, Rhode Island.

Robert Hayden (1913–1980) was raised in a poor neighborhood in Detroit and had an emotionally tumultuous childhood. Because of impaired vision, he was unable to participate in sports and spent his time reading instead. He graduated from high school in 1932 and attended Detroit City College (later Wayne State University). His first book of poems, *Heart-Shape in the Dust*, was published in 1940. After working for newspapers and on other projects, he studied under W. H. AUDEN in the graduate creative writing program at the University of Michigan. He taught at Fisk University and at the University of Michigan. His poetry gained international recognition in the 1960s, and he was awarded the grand prize for poetry at the First World Festival of Negro Arts in Dakar, Senegal, in 1966 for his book *Ballad of Remembrance*. In 1976 he became the first black American to be appointed as Consultant in Poetry at the Library of Congress.

Samuel Hazo (b. 1928), of Lebanese and Syrian heritage, is a highly influential Arab American writer of verse, educator, and advocate on behalf of poetry. He is the author of numerous collections of poetry, fiction, and essays. He is founder, director, and president of the International Poetry Forum in Pittsburgh and McAnulty Distinguished Professor of English Emeritus at Duquesne University. He is the recipient of the 1986 Hazlett Memorial Award for Excellence in the Arts. In 1993 he was chosen to be the first state poet of the Commonwealth of Pennsylvania, a position he still holds.

H. D., *see* **Doolittle, Hilda.**

Seamus Heaney (b. 1939) grew up on a small farm near Castledawson, County Derry, Northern Ireland. He was educated at St. Columb's College, a Catholic boarding school in the city of Derry, and then at Queen's University, Belfast. As a young English teacher in Belfast in the early 1960s, he joined a poetry workshop and began writing verse. Subsequently he became a major force in contemporary Irish literature. The author of many volumes of poetry, translations, and essays as well as two plays, he is well known for his bestselling verse translation of *Beowulf* (2000). He held the chair of professor of poetry at Oxford University from 1989 to 1994. He was awarded the Nobel Prize in literature in 1995.

George Herbert (1593–1633) was the fifth son in an ancient and wealthy Welsh family. He studied at Cambridge, graduating with honors, and was elected public orator of the university. He served in Parliament for two years but fell out of political favor and become rector of Bemerton near Salisbury. Herbert was a model Anglican priest and an inspiring preacher. All of his poetry, religious in nature, was published posthumously in 1633. "Easter-wings" is among the earliest of concrete poems (see the glossary), and "The Pulley" is a fine example of **metaphysical wit** (see the glossary).

Mary (Sidney) Herbert, Countess of Pembroke (1561–1621) was an important literary patron and writer of the Elizabethan period. In addition to editorial work and translations, she wrote a number of original poems. She also contributed 107 poetic renderings of psalms to a series of 150 begun by her brother Sir Philip Sidney, each written in a different stanzaic and metrical pattern. "Psalm 100 *Jubilate Deo*" is from that volume.

Robert Herrick (1591–1674), the son of a well-to-do London goldsmith, was apprenticed to his uncle (also a goldsmith), studied at Cambridge University, then lived for nine years in London, where he hobnobbed with a group of poets that included BEN JONSON. Under familial pressure to do something more worthwhile, Herrick became an Anglican priest. He was given the parish of Dean Prior, Devonshire—a rural place that at first he hated—and there he quietly wrote poems about imagined mistresses and pagan rites (as in his well-known "Corinna's Going A-Maying") and deft but devout religious poems. When he returned to London in 1648, having been ejected from his pulpit by the Puritan revolution, he published his poetry in a volume with two titles, *Hesperides* for the secular poems, *Noble Numbers* for those with sacred subjects. Probably his most famous poem is "To the Virgins, to Make Much of Time," a short lyric on the traditional **carpe diem** theme (see the glossary).

Bob Hicok (b. 1960), in addition to writing poetry, spent years as an automotive die designer and computer system administrator in Ann Arbor, Michigan. His first collection of poetry, *The Legend of Light* (1995), won the Felix Pollack Prize in Poetry and was named a "notable book of the year" by the American Library Association's *Booklist* magazine. He has published four more books: *Plus Shipping* (1998); *Animal Soul* (2001), a finalist for the National Book Critics Circle Award; *Insomnia Diary* (2004); and *This Clumsy Living* (2007). He currently teaches in the M.F.A. program at Virginia Tech.

Conrad Hilberry (b. 1928) grew up in Michigan. He earned his B.A. at Oberlin College and his M.A. and Ph.D. at the University of Wisconsin and taught at Kalamazoo College until his recent retirement. Hilberry has published ten collections of poetry, most recently *The Fingernail of Luck* (2005), and has been poetry editor of *Passages North* and of the anthology *Poems from the Third Coast* (1976). Hillberry has been praised for his mastery of tone, through which he achieves subtleties of implication in his work, as is evidenced in "Player Piano."

Geoffrey Hill (b. 1932) is a major presence in contemporary British poetry. Born in Bromsgrove, Worcestershire, he attended the local grammar school there before going on to study English language and literature at Keble College, Oxford. He taught at Leeds University from 1954 until 1980, when he moved to Emmanuel College, Cambridge. In 1988 he became University Professor and a professor of literature and religion at Boston University. In 2006 he returned to England and now lives in Cambridge.

Jane Hirshfield (b. 1953) is the author of six books of poetry, editor and cotranslator of two anthologies of poetry by women, and author of a collection of essays, *Nine Gates: Entering the Mind of Poetry* (1997). A graduate of Princeton University, she studied Soto Zen from 1974 to 1982, including three years of monastic practice, the influence of which is apparent in her work. She has said, "For me, poetry, like Zen practice, is a path toward deeper and more life. There are ways to wake up into the actual texture of one's own existence, to widen it, to deepen and broaden it, and poetry is one of the things that does that." She teaches at Bennington College and lives in the San Francisco Bay area.

Linda Hogan (b. 1947), a poet, novelist, essayist, playwright, and activist widely considered to be one of the most influential and provocative Native American figures in the contemporary American literary landscape, was born in Denver. Because her father, who was from the Chickasaw Nation, was in the army and was transferred frequently during Hogan's childhood, she lived in various locations while she was growing up, but considers Oklahoma to be her true home. In her late twenties, while working with orthopedically handicapped children, she began writing during her lunch hours, although she had no previous experience as a writer and little experience reading literature. She pursued her writing by commuting to the University of Colorado, Colorado Springs, for her undergraduate degree and earning an M.A. in English and creative writing at the University of Colorado, Boulder, in 1978. She has published more than a dozen books — poetry, novels, and nonfiction — and received numerous awards for her work. She is an emeritus professor in the University of Colorado English department.

Garrett Kaoru Hongo (b. 1951) was born in Volcano, Hawaii, grew up on Oahu and in Los Angeles, and did graduate work in Japanese language and literature at the University of Michigan. His second book of poetry, *The River of Heaven* (1988), was the Lamont Poetry Selection of the Academy of American Poets and a finalist for the Pulitzer Prize. He has also written *Volcano: A Memoir of Hawai'i* (1995) and edited collections of Asian American verse. He currently teaches at the University of Oregon, Eugene, where he directed the creative writing program from 1989 to 1993. His work often uses rich textures and sensuous detail to comment on conditions endured by Japanese Americans during World War II and thereafter.

Gerard Manley Hopkins (1844–1889) was born in London, the eldest of eight children. His father was a ship insurer who also wrote a book of poetry. Hopkins studied at Balliol College, Oxford, and, after converting to Catholicism, taught in a school in Birmingham. In 1868 he became a Jesuit and burned all of his early poetry, considering it "secular" and worthless. He then worked as a priest and teacher in working-class London, Glasgow, and Merseyside, and later as professor of classics at University College, Dublin. Hopkins went on to write many poems on spiritual themes, but he published little during his lifetime; his poems were not known until they were published by his friend Robert Bridges in 1918. They convey a spiritual sensuality, celebrating the wonder of nature both in their language and in their rhythms (which he called "sprung rhythm"; see the glossary under **accentual meter**).

A. E. Housman (1859–1936) was born in Fockbury, Worcestershire. A promising student at Oxford University, he failed his final exams (because of emotional turmoil possibly caused by his suppressed homosexual love for a fellow student) and spent the next ten years feverishly studying and writing scholarly articles while working as a clerk at the patent office. Housman was rewarded with the chair of Latin at University College, London, and later at Cambridge University. His poetry, like his scholarship, was meticulous, impersonal in tone, and limited in output: two slender volumes — *A Shropshire Lad* (1896) and *Last Poems* (1922) — during his lifetime, and a small book titled *More Poems* (1936) after his death. His poems often take up the theme of doomed youths acting out their brief lives in the context of agricultural communities and activities, especially the English countryside and traditions he loved.

Langston Hughes (1902–1967) was born in Joplin, Missouri, and grew up in Lincoln, Illinois, and Cleveland, Ohio. During high school he began writing poetry. He attended Columbia University for a year, then held odd jobs as an assistant cook, a launderer, and a busboy and traveled to Africa and Europe working as a seaman. In 1924 he moved to Harlem. Hughes's first book of poetry, *The Weary Blues*, was published in 1926. He finished his college education at Lincoln University in Pennsylvania three years later. He wrote novels, short stories, plays, songs, children's books, essays, and memoirs as well as poetry, and is also known for his engagement with the world of jazz and the influence it had on his writing. His life and work were enormously important in shaping the artistic contributions of the Harlem Renaissance of the 1920s.

Randall Jarrell (1914–1965) was born in Nashville, Tennessee, and earned his B.A. and M.A. at Vanderbilt University. From 1937 to 1939 he taught at Kenyon College, where he met JOHN CROWE RANSOM and ROBERT LOWELL, and afterward he taught at the University of Texas. He served in the air force during World War II. Jarrell's reputation as a poet was established in 1945 with the publication of his second book, *Little Friend, Little Friend,* which documents the intense fears and moral struggles of young soldiers. Other volumes followed, all characterized by great technical skill, empathy with others, and deep sensitivity. Following the war, Jarrell began teaching at the University of North Carolina, Greensboro, and remained there, except for occasional absences to teach elsewhere, until his death. Besides poetry, he wrote a satirical novel, several children's books, numerous poetry reviews — collected in *Poetry and the Age* (1953) — and a translation of Goethe's *Faust.*

Honorée Fanonne Jeffers (b. 1967) has published fiction in addition to two books of poetry, *The Gospel of Barbecue* (2000), which won the 1999 Stan and Tom Wick Prize for Poetry and was a finalist for the 2001 Paterson Poetry Prize, and *Outlandish Blues* (2003). She is currently working on a third book of poetry, *Red Clay Suite,* and her first book of collected fiction. She has won the 2002 Julia Peterkin Award for Poetry and awards from the Barbara Deming Memorial Fund and the Rona Jaffe Foundation. Her poetry has been published in the anthologies *At Our Core: Women Writing about Power, Dark Eros,* and *Identity Lessons* and in many journals, including *Callaloo, The Kenyon Review,* and *Prairie Schooner.* She teaches at the University of Oklahoma.

Robinson Jeffers (1887–1962) was born in Pittsburgh, where his father was a professor of Old Testament literature and biblical history at Western Theology Seminary. He began to learn Greek from his father at the age of five, and his early lessons were followed by travel in Europe, which included schooling in Zurich, Leipzig, and Geneva. He moved with his family to southern California in 1903. After graduating from Occidental College in 1906 and pursuing graduate studies in medicine and forestry, Jeffers decided to concentrate on poetry. In 1914 he settled in Carmel, California, and built a stone cottage and a forty-foot stone tower on land overlooking Carmel Bay and facing Point Lobos, where he lived the rest of his life (Tor House and Hawk Tower are open to the public — see www.torhouse.org). Much of Jeffers's verse celebrates the awesome beauty of the Carmel–Big Sur region, often contrasting the intense, rugged beauty of the landscape with the degraded and introverted condition of modern man.

Richard Jones (b. 1953) was born in London, where his father was serving in the U.S. Air Force, and studied at the University of Virginia. Jones is the author of several books of poems, including *The Blessing: New and Selected Poems,* which received the Midland Authors Award for Poetry for 2000. His most recent volume is *Apropos of Nothing* (2006). He has also published two critical anthologies and has been the editor of the literary journal *Poetry East* since 1979. He has taught at Piedmont College and the University of Virginia and presently is professor of English and director of the creative writing program at DePaul University in Chicago.

Ben Jonson (1572–1637), born in London, was the stepson of a bricklayer (his father died before he was born). He attended Westminster School and then joined the army. Jonson later worked as an actor and wrote comedies such as *Everyman in His Humor* (in which SHAKESPEARE acted the lead), *Volpone*, and *The Alchemist*. He wrote clear, elegant, "classical" poetry that contrasted with the intricate, subtle, "metaphysical" poetry of his contemporaries JOHN DONNE and GEORGE HERBERT. He was named poet laureate and was the idol of a generation of English writers, who dubbed themselves the Sons of Ben.

Allison Joseph (b. 1967) was born in London to Caribbean parents and grew up in Toronto and the Bronx. She earned her B.A. from Kenyon College and her M.F.A. from Indiana University. She is the author of five collections of poetry: *What Keeps Us Here* (winner of Ampersand Press's 1992 Women Poets Series Competition and the John C. Zacharis First Book Award), *Soul Train* (1997), *In Every Seam* (1997), *Imitation of Life* (2003), and *Worldly Pleasures* (2004). Her poems are often attuned to the experiences of women and minorities. She is an associate professor at Southern Illinois University, Carbondale, where she is editor of the *Crab Orchard Review*.

John Keats (1795–1821) was born in London. His father, a worker at a livery stable who married his employer's daughter and inherited the business, was killed by a fall from a horse when Keats was eight. When his mother died of tuberculosis six years later, Keats and his siblings were entrusted to the care of a guardian, a practical-minded man who took Keats out of school at fifteen and apprenticed him to a doctor. As soon as he qualified for medical practice, in 1815, he abandoned medicine for poetry, which he had begun writing two years earlier. In 1818, the year he contracted tuberculosis, he also fell madly in love with a pretty, vivacious young woman named Fanny Brawne, whom he could not marry because of his poverty, illness, and devotion to poetry. In the midst of such stress and emotional turmoil, his masterpieces poured out between January and September 1819: the great odes, a number of sonnets, and several longer lyric poems. In February 1820, his health failed rapidly; he went to Italy in the autumn, in hopes that the warmer climate would improve his health, and died there on February 23, 1821. His poems are rich with sensuous, lyrical beauty and emotional resonance, reflecting his delight in life as well as his awareness of life's brevity and difficulty.

Jane Kenyon (1947–1995) was born in Ann Arbor, Michigan, and grew up in the Midwest. She earned her B.A. and M.A. from the University of Michigan. She was married to poet DONALD HALL from 1972 until her death from leukemia in 1995. During her lifetime she published four books of poetry — *From Room to Room* (1978), *The Boat of Quiet Hours* (1986), *Let Evening Come* (1990), and *Constance* (1993) — and a book of translation, *Twenty Poems of Anna Akhmatova* (1985). Two additional volumes were published after her death: *Otherwise: New and Selected Poems* (1996) and *A Hundred White Daffodils: Essays, Interviews, the Akhmatova Translations, Newspaper Columns, and One Poem* (1999). At the time of her death, she was New Hampshire's poet laureate.

Galway Kinnell (b. 1927) was born in Providence, Rhode Island, and attended Princeton University and the University of Rochester. He served in the U.S. Navy and then visited Paris on a Fulbright fellowship. Returning to the United States, he worked for the Congress on Racial Equality and then traveled widely in the Middle East and Europe. He has taught in France, Australia, and Iran as well as at numerous colleges and universities in the United States. He has published many books of poetry, including *Selected Poems* (1980), for which he received both the Pulitzer Prize and the National Book Award. He has also published translations of works by Yves Bonnefoy, Yvanne Goll, François Villon, and Rainer Maria Rilke. He was the Erich Maria Remarque Professor of Creative Writing at New York University. He is now retired and lives in Vermont.

Etheridge Knight (1933–1991) was born in Corinth, Mississippi. He dropped out of school at age sixteen and served in the U.S. Army in Korea from 1947 to 1951, returning home with a shrapnel wound that caused him to fall deeper into a drug addiction that had begun during his service. In 1960 he was arrested for robbery and sentenced to eight years in an Indiana state prison. During this time he began writing poetry. His first book, *Poems from Prison* (1968), was published one year before his release. The book was a success, and Knight joined other poets in what came to be called the Black Arts Movement, the aesthetic and spiritual sister of the Black Power concept. He went on to write several more books of poetry and to receive many prestigious honors and awards. In 1990 he earned a B.A. in American poetry and criminal justice from Martin Center University in Indianapolis.

Kenneth Koch (1925–2002) was born in Cincinnati and, after service in World War II, received his B.A. from Harvard University and his Ph.D. from Columbia University. As a young poet, Koch was known for his association with the New York school of poetry, a cosmopolitan movement influenced by the Beats, French surrealism, and European avant-gardism in general. In addition to many books of poetry, including *One Train* and *On the Great Atlantic Rainway: Selected Poems, 1950–1988* (both 1994), which together won the Bollingen Prize in 1995, and *New Addresses* (2000), a finalist for the National Book Award, he wrote plays, a novel, a libretto, criticism, and several influential books on teaching creative writing to children, including *Wishes, Lies, and Dreams* (1970) and *Rose, Where Did You Get That Red?* (1973). He lived in New York City, where he was professor of English at Columbia University.

Yusef Komunyakaa (b. 1947) was born and grew up in Bogalusa, Louisiana. He earned degrees at the University of Colorado, Colorado State University, and the University of California, Irvine. His numerous books of poems include *Neon Vernacular: New and Selected Poems, 1977–1989* (1994), for which he received the Pulitzer Prize and the Kingsley Tufts Poetry Award, and *Thieves of Paradise* (1998), which was a finalist for the National Book Critics Circle Award. Other publications include *Blues Notes: Essays, Interviews & Commentaries* (2000), *The Jazz Poetry Anthology* (coedited with J. A. Sascha Feinstein, 1991), and a translation (with Martha Collins) of *The Insomnia of Fire* by Nguyen Quang Thieu (1995). He has taught at the University of New Orleans, Indiana University, and Princeton University.

Ted Kooser (b. 1939) was born in Ames, Iowa. He received his B.A. from

Iowa State University and his M.A. in English from the University of Nebraska, Lincoln. He is the author of ten collections of poetry, including *Sure Signs* (1980), *One World at a Time* (1985), *Weather Central* (1994), *Winter Morning Walks: One Hundred Postcards to Jim Harrison* (2000, winner of the 2001 Nebraska Book Award for poetry), and *Delights & Shadows* (2004). His fiction and nonfiction books include *Local Wonders: Seasons in the Bohemian Alps* (2002, winner of the Nebraska Book Award for Nonfiction in 2003) and *Braided Creek: A Conversation in Poetry* (2003), written with fellow poet and longtime friend Jim Harrison. His honors include two National Endowment for the Arts fellowships in poetry, a Pushcart Prize, the Stanley Kunitz Prize, and a Merit Award from the Nebraska Arts Council. He served as the United States Poet ,Laureate Consultant in Poetry to the Library of Congress from 2004 to 2006. He lives on acreage near the village of Garland, Nebraska, and is a visiting professor in the English department of the University of Nebraska, Lincoln.

Maxine Kumin (b. 1925) was born in Philadelphia and received her B.A. and M.A. at Radcliffe College. She has published eleven books of poetry, including *Up Country: Poems of New England* (1972), for which she received the Pulitzer Prize. She is also the author of a memoir, *Inside the Halo and Beyond: The Anatomy of a Recovery* (2000); four novels; a collection of short stories; more than twenty children's books; and four books of essays. She has taught at the University of Massachusetts, Columbia University, Brandeis University, and Princeton University, and has served as Consultant in Poetry to the Library of Congress and as poet laureate of New Hampshire, where she lives.

Stanley Kunitz (1905–2006) was among the most beloved of poets. His life in poetry spanned more than three-quarters of a century, during which time he was always at the center of the poetry world. Born in Worcester, Massachusetts, Kunitz earned his B.A. and M.A. at Harvard University. His work often explored the consequences of traumatic events on a person's life, many times his own. He was quoted as saying that poetry was for him the single most important thing one could do with one's life. His first two books garnered little attention, but after serving in World War II, he continued to write and received great recognition. His *Selected Poems, 1928–1958* won the Pulitzer Prize, and in 1995 he received the National Book Award for *Passing Through: The Later Poems, New and Selected* (1995). His work has often been called an extension of the vision of JOHN KEATS. In 2000, at age ninety-five, he was named Poet Laureate Consultant in Poetry to the Library of Congress. He taught for many years at Columbia University and divided his time between New York City and Provincetown, Massachusetts, where he tended his magnificent garden.

Philip Larkin (1922–1985) was born into a working-class family in Coventry, England. He received a scholarship to attend Oxford University. With his second volume of poetry, *The Less Deceived* (1955), Larkin became the preeminent poet of his generation and a leading voice of what came to be called "The Movement," a group of young English writers who rejected the prevailing fashion for neo-Romantic writing exemplified by W. B. YEATS and DYLAN THOMAS. Like THOMAS HARDY, a major influence on his work, Larkin focused on intense personal emotion but strictly avoided sentimentality or self-pity. In addition to writing poetry, Larkin was a highly respected jazz critic. He worked as a librarian in the provincial city of Hull, where he died in 1985.

Li-Young Lee (b. 1957) was born in Jakarta, Indonesia, to Chinese parents. His father, who had been personal physician to Mao Tse-tung, relocated his family to Indonesia, where he helped found Gamaliel University. In 1959 the Lee family fled the country to escape anti-Chinese sentiment, and they settled in the United States in 1964. Lee studied at the University of Pittsburgh, the University of Arizona, and the Brockport campus of the State University of New York. He has taught at several universities, including Northwestern University and the University of Iowa. He is the author of four collections of poetry—*Rose* (1986), which won the Delmore Schwartz Memorial Poetry Award; *The City in Which I Love You* (1991), the 1990 Lamont Poetry selection; *Book of My Nights* (2001); and *Behind My Eyes* (2008)—and a memoir, *The Winged Seed: A Remembrance* (1995), which received an American Book Award from the Before Columbus Foundation. In his poems one often senses a profound sense of exile, the influence of his father's presence, and a rich spiritual sensuality.

Denise Levertov (1923–1997) was born in Ilford, Essex. Her mother was Welsh and her father was a Russian Jew who became an Anglican priest. She was educated at home and claimed to have decided to become a writer at the age of five. Her first book, *The Double Image* (1946), brought her recognition as one of a group of poets dubbed the "New Romantics"—her poems often blend the sense of an objective observer with the sensibility

of a spiritual searcher. She moved to the United States after marrying the American writer Mitchell Goodman. There she turned to free-verse poetry, and with her first American book, *Here and Now* (1956), she became an important voice in the American avant-garde. In the 1960s, she became involved in the movement protesting the Vietnam war. Levertov went on to publish more than twenty collections of poetry, four books of prose, and three volumes of poetry in translation. From 1982 to 1993, she taught at Stanford University. She spent the last decade of her life in Seattle.

Philip Levine (b. 1928) was born in Detroit and received his degrees from Wayne State University and the University of Iowa. He is the author of sixteen books of poetry, including *The Simple Truth* (1994), which won the Pulitzer Prize. He has also published a collection of essays, *The Bread of Time: Toward an Autobiography* (1994), edited *The Essential Keats* (1987), and coedited and translated two books of poetry, by Spanish poet Gloria Fuertes and Mexican poet Jamie Sabines. He divides his time between Fresno, California, and New York City, where he taught at New York University.

Larry Levis (1946–1996) grew up on a farm near Fresno, California. He earned his B.A. from Fresno State College (now California State University), an M.A. from Syracuse University, and a Ph.D. from the University of Iowa. He published six collections of poetry— several of them receiving major awards—and a collection of short fiction. He taught at the University of Missouri, the University of Utah, and Virginia Commonwealth University. Levis died of a heart attack at the age of forty-nine. PHILIP LEVINE wrote that he had years earlier recognized Levis as "the most gifted and determined young poet I have ever had the good fortune to have in one of my classes."

Timothy Liu (b. 1965) was born in San Jose, California, to parents who had immigrated from the Chinese mainland. He studied at Brigham Young University, the University of Houston, and the University of Massachusetts, Amherst. He is the author of several books of poetry — including *Vox Angelica*, which won the 1992 Norma Farber First Book Award from the Poetry Society of America and *Of Thee I Sing* (2004), selected by *Publishers Weekly* as a 2004 Book-of-the-Year — and the editor of *Word of Mouth: An Anthology of Gay American Poetry* (2000). He is an associate professor at William Paterson University and lives in Manhattan.

Audre Lorde (1934–1992) was born in New York City to West Indian parents. She grew up in Manhattan and attended Roman Catholic schools. While she was still in high school, her first poem appeared in *Seventeen* magazine. She earned her B.A. from Hunter College in New York City and her M.A. in library science from Columbia University. In 1968 she left her job as head librarian at the University of New York to become a lecturer and creative writer. She accepted a poet-in-residence position at Tougaloo College in Mississippi, where she discovered a love of teaching; published her first volume of poetry, *The First Cities* (1968); and met her long-term partner, Frances Clayton. Many other volumes of poetry followed, several winning major awards. She also published four volumes of prose, among them *The Cancer Journals* (1980), which chronicled her struggles with cancer, and *A Burst of Light* (1988),

which won a National Book Award. In the 1980s, Lorde and writer Barbara Smith founded Kitchen Table: Women of Color Press. She was also a founding member of Sisters in Support of Sisters in South Africa, an organization that worked to raise awareness about women under apartheid. She was the poet laureate of New York from 1991 to 1992.

Richard Lovelace (1618–1657) was born into a prominent family in Kent, England, and went to Oxford, where his dashing appearance and wit made him a social and literary favorite. He fought in the English civil war on the Royalist side and was imprisoned and exiled. Later he fought in France against the Spanish and was again imprisoned on his return to England. After his release he spent ten years in poverty and isolation before his death. He was a leader of the "Cavalier poets," followers of King Charles I who were soldiers and courtiers but also wrote well-crafted, light-hearted lyric poetry. "To Lucasta, Going to the Wars" is an excellent example of the type.

Robert Lowell (1917–1978) was born in Boston into a prominent New England family. He attended Harvard University and then Kenyon College, where he studied under JOHN CROWE RANSOM. At Louisiana State University he studied with Robert Penn Warren and Cleanth Brooks as well as Allen Tate. He was always politically active — a conscientious objector during World War II and a Vietnam protestor — and suffered from manic depression. Lowell's reputation was established early: his second book, *Lord Weary's Castle*, was awarded the Pulitzer Prize for poetry in 1947. In the mid-1950s he began to write more directly from personal experience and loosened his adherence to traditional meter and form. The result was a watershed collection of the "confessional" school, *Life Studies* (1959), which changed the landscape of modern poetry, much as T. S. ELIOT's *The Waste Land* had done three decades earlier. He died suddenly from a heart attack at age sixty.

Christopher Marlowe (1564–1593) was born in Canterbury the same year as WILLIAM SHAKESPEARE. The son of a shoemaker, he needed the help of scholarships to attend King's School, Canterbury, and Corpus Christi College, Cambridge. He was involved in secret political missions for the government. He was one of the most brilliant writers of his generation in narrative poetry, lyric poetry, and drama (his best-known play is *Doctor Faustus*). He died after being stabbed in a bar fight, reportedly over his bill, at the age of twenty-nine. "The Passionate Shepherd to His Love" is among the most famous of Elizabethan songs.

Andrew Marvell (1621–1678) was born in Hull, Yorkshire, and educated at Trinity College, Cambridge. After traveling in Europe, he worked as a tutor and in a government office (as assistant to JOHN MILTON) and later became a member of Parliament for Hull. Marvell was known in his lifetime as a writer of rough satires in verse and prose. His "serious" poetry, like "To His Coy Mistress," was not published until after his death. It is a famous exploration of the **carpe diem** theme (see the glossary).

Medbh McGuckian (b. 1950) was born in Belfast and educated at a Dominican convent and at Queens University, Belfast. She has published more than a dozen books of poetry, including *The Flower Master* (1982), *Venus and the Rain* (1984), *On Ballycastle Beach* (1988), *Marconi's Cottage* (1992), *Captain Lavender* (1995), *Selected Poems 1978–1994* (1997), *Shelmalier* (1998), *Drawing Ballerinas* (2001), and *The Book of the Angel* (2004). Among the prizes she has won are the British National Poetry Competition, the Cheltenham Award, the Alice Hunt Bartlett Prize, the Rooney Prize, and the American Ireland Fund Literary Award. She has been writer-in-residence at Queen's University and at the University of Ulster; visiting fellow at the University of California, Berkeley; and writer-fellow at Trinity College Dublin.

Heather McHugh (b. 1948) was born to Canadian parents in San Diego and grew up in Virginia. She is a graduate of Radcliffe College and the University of Denver. McHugh has published numerous books of poetry, including *Eyeshot* (2003) and *Hinge & Sign: Poems 1968–1993* (1994), which won both the *Boston Book Review*'s Bingham Poetry Prize and the Pollack-*Harvard Review* Prize, was a finalist for the National Book Award, and was named a "notable book of the year" by the *New York Times Book Review*. She has also written a book of prose, *Broken English: Poetry and Partiality* (1993), and two books of translations. She teaches as a core faculty member in the M.F.A. Program for Writers at Warren Wilson College and as Milliman Writer-in-Residence at the University of Washington, Seattle.

Claude McKay (1890–1948), the son of poor farm workers, was born in Sunny Ville, Jamaica. He was educated by his older brother, who possessed a library of English novels, poetry, and scientific texts. At age twenty, McKay published a book of verse called *Songs* *of Jamaica*, recording his impressions of black life in Jamaica in dialect. In 1912, he traveled to the United States to attend Tuskegee Institute. He soon left to study agriculture at Kansas State University. In 1914 he moved to Harlem and became an influential member of the Harlem Renaissance. After committing himself to communism and traveling to Moscow in 1922, he lived for some time in Europe and Morocco, writing fiction. McKay later repudiated Communism, converted to Roman Catholicism, and returned to the United States. He published several books of poetry as well as an autobiography, *A Long Way from Home* (1937). He wrote a number of sonnets protesting the injustices of black life in the United States, "America" among them. They are of interest for the way they use the most Anglo of forms to contain and intensify what the poem's language is saying.

James Merrill (1926–1995) was born in New York City, son of Charles Merrill, cofounder of Merrill Lynch. At the age of eight, he was already writing poems, and at age sixteen, while he was in prep school, his father had a book of them privately printed under the title *Jim's Book*. He received his B.A. from Amherst College after service in World War II interrupted his education. He taught for a year at Bard College and spent two and a half years traveling in Europe. In 1955 he moved to the small coastal town of Stonington, Connecticut, with his companion David Jackson. He published a memoir and two novels in addition to more than two dozen books of poetry, for which he won numerous prestigious awards, including the Pulitzer Prize for *Divine Comedies* (1976), which was composed with the help of a Ouija board. Merrill

is recognized as one of the most complex and erudite of modern poets.

W. S. Merwin (b. 1927) was born in New York City and lived in New Jersey and Pennsylvania during his precollege years. He studied creative writing and foreign languages at Princeton University and became a translator, living mostly in England and France until 1968, when he returned to the United States. He is the author of more than fifteen books of poetry, including *A Mask for Janus* (1952), which was selected by W. H. AUDEN for the Yale Series of Younger Poets, and *Carrier of Ladders* (1970), which received the Pulitzer Prize. *Migration: New and Selected Poems* (2005) won the National Book Award for that year. His most recent volume is *Present Company* (2007). He has also published nearly twenty books of translation, including Dante's *Purgatorio* (2000); numerous plays; and four books of prose, including *The Lost Upland* (1992), his memoir of life in the south of France. He lives in Hawaii and is active in environmental movements.

Edna St. Vincent Millay (1892–1950) was born in Rockland, Maine, and was encouraged to write from an early age by her mother. In 1912, at her mother's urging, Millay entered her poem "Renascence" into a contest; she won fourth place, publication in *The Lyric Year*, and a scholarship to Vassar. She spent the Roaring Twenties in Greenwich Village acting, writing plays and prize-winning poetry, and living a bohemian lifestyle. In 1923 her book *The Harp Weaver* was awarded the Pulitzer Prize. Millay continued to write and take an active part in political affairs for several decades thereafter, despite a diminished literary reputation.

John Milton (1608–1674), son of a well-off London businessman, was educated at St. Paul's School and at home with private tutors. After graduating with an M.A. from Christ's College, Cambridge, he spent the next six years reading at home. Milton had written verse since his university days, but he broke off to write prose tracts in favor of Oliver Cromwell, in whose government he later headed a department. The strain of long hours of reading and writing for the revolutionary cause aggravated a genetic weakness and resulted in his total blindness around 1651. He wrote his most famous works, *Paradise Lost* (1667), *Paradise Regained* (1671), and *Samson Agonistes* (1671), by dictating them to his daughter and other amanuenses.

Marianne Moore (1887–1972) was born near St. Louis and grew up in Carlisle, Pennsylvania. After studying at Bryn Mawr College and Carlisle Commercial College, she taught at a government Indian school in Carlisle. She moved to Brooklyn, where she became an assistant at the New York Public Library. She loved baseball and spent a good deal of time watching her beloved Brooklyn Dodgers. She began to write **Imagist poetry** (see the glossary) and to contribute to the *Dial*, a prestigious literary magazine. She served as acting editor of the *Dial*, from 1925 to 1929, and later was editor for four years. Moore was widely recognized for her work, receiving among other honors the Bollingen Prize, the National Book Award, and the Pulitzer Prize.

Thylias Moss (b. 1954) was born in Cleveland, Ohio. She attended Syracuse University and received her B.A. from Oberlin College and M.F.A. from the University of New Hampshire. She is the author of numerous books of poetry, most recently *Tokyo Butter* (2006); a memoir, *Tale of a Sky-Blue Dress* (1998); two children's books; and two plays, *Talking to Myself* (1984) and *The Dolls in the Basement* (1984). Among her awards are a Guggenheim fellowship and a MacArthur Foundation fellowship. She lives in Ann Arbor, where she is a professor of English at the University of Michigan.

David Mura (b. 1952), a third-generation Japanese American, was born in Great Lakes, Illinois, and graduated from Grinnell College in Iowa; he did graduate work at the University of Minnesota and Vermont College. Mura is a poet, creative nonfiction writer, critic, playwright, and performance artist. He is the author of numerous books of poetry, including *After We Lost Our Way* (1989), which was selected by GERALD STERN as a National Poetry Series winner, and two memoirs, *Turning Japanese: Memoirs of a Sansei* (1991), which was a New York Times Notable Book of the Year, and *Where the Body Meets Memory: An Odyssey of Race, Sexuality & Identity* (1996).

Lorine Niedecker (1903–1970) was born and died in Fort Atkinson, Wisconsin. She lived much of her life in a small cabin on Black Hawk Island on Lake Koshkonong. Though celebrated by many of the most acclaimed experimental, modernist, and objectivist writers of the twentieth century, among them WILLIAM CARLOS WILLIAMS and LOUIS ZUKOFSKY, she chose to remain outside the poetry world, living an all but isolated life. Niedecker said that she spent her childhood outdoors and from that developed her keen eye and strong sense of place. In 1931 she discovered objectivist poetry, which called for sincerity and objectification, values that fit well with her own vision and influenced her poems from that time on. While living on Black Hawk Island, she worked in a local hospital cleaning the kitchen and scrubbing floors. Her books include *New Goose* (1946), *North Central* (1968), *My Life by Water* (published the year of her death), and *Blue Chicory* (published posthumously in 1976). Her book of selected poems, *The Granite Pail*, was not published until 1985.

John Frederick Nims (1913–1999) was born in Muskegon, Michigan, and studied at DePaul University, the University of Notre Dame, and the University of Chicago, where he received his Ph.D. in 1945. By that time, he had already distinguished himself as a poet and critic. He went on to teach at Harvard University, the University of Florence, the University of Toronto, the Bread Loaf School of English, Williams College, and the University of Missouri, among others. He was editor of *Poetry* magazine from 1978 to 1984. He was the author of many books of poetry and many translations, as well as several critical works and a widely used textbook, *Western Wind: An Introduction to Poetry* (1974).

Naomi Shihab Nye (b. 1952), born in St. Louis of a Palestinian father and an American mother, grew up in both the United States and Jerusalem. She received her B.A. from Trinity University in San Antonio, Texas, where she still resides with her family. She is the author of many books of poems, most recently *You and Yours* (2005), which received the Isabella Gardner Poetry Award. She has also written short stories and books for children and has edited anthologies, several of which focus on the lives of children and represent work from around the world. She is a singer-songwriter and on several occasions has traveled to the Middle East and Asia for the U.S. Information Agency, promoting international goodwill through the arts. Nye's work often attests to a universal sense of exile, from place, home, love, and one's self and the way the human spirit confronts them.

Frank (Francis Russell) O'Hara (1926–1966) was born in Baltimore and grew up in Massachusetts. He studied piano at the New England Conservatory in Boston from 1941 to 1944 and served in the South Pacific and Japan during World War II. He majored in English at Harvard, then received his M.A. in English at the University of Michigan in 1951. He moved to New York, where he worked at the Museum of Modern Art and began writing poetry seriously as well as composing essays and reviews on painting and sculpture. His first volume of poems, *A City in Winter* — thirteen poems together with two drawings by the artist Larry Rivers — was published in 1952. Other collaborations with artists followed. His first major collection of poetry was *Meditations in an Emergency* (1957). His poetry is often casual, relaxed in diction, and full of specific detail, seeking to convey the immediacy of life. He described his work as "I do this I do that" poetry because his poems often read like entries in a diary, as in the opening lines of "The Day Lady Died." He was killed at forty when he was struck by a sand buggy while vacationing on Fire Island, New York.

Sharon Olds (b. 1942) was born in San Francisco and educated at Stanford and Columbia Universities. She has written eight books of poetry (most recently *Strike Sparks: Selected Poems, 1980–2002* [2004]) and received numerous important prizes and awards. In the words of Elizabeth Frank, "she and her work are about nothing less than the joy of making — of making love, making babies, making poems, making sense of love, memory, death, the feel — the actual bodily texture — of life." She held the position of New York State Poet from 1998 to 2000. She teaches poetry workshops at New York University's graduate creative writing program, along with workshops at Goldwater Hospital in New York, a public facility for physically disabled persons.

Mary Oliver (b. 1935) was born in Cleveland and educated at Ohio State University and Vassar College. She is the author of eleven volumes of poetry, including *American Primitive* (1983), for which she won the Pulitzer Prize, and four books of prose. She holds the Catharine Osgood Foster Chair for Distinguished Teaching at Bennington College and lives in Provincetown, Massachusetts, and Bennington, Vermont. Oliver is one of the most respected of poets concerned for the natural world.

Simon J. Ortiz (b. 1941) was born and raised in the Acoma Pueblo Community in Albuquerque, New Mexico. He received his early education from the Bureau of Indian Affairs school on the Acoma reservation, later attending the University of New Mexico and completing his M.F.A. at the University of Iowa, where he was a part of the International Writing Program. Unlike most Native American contemporary writers, Ortiz is a full-blooded Native American, and his first language was Keresan. By learning English, he found a way to communicate with those outside his immediate culture. His poetry explores the significance of individual origins and journeys, which he sees as forming a vital link in the continuity of life. His many writing accomplishments include poems, short stories, essays, and children's books. Ortiz has taught Native American literature and creative writing at San Diego State University, Navajo Community College, Marin College, the Institute for the Arts of the American Indian, the University of New Mexico, and most recently the University of Toronto.

Wilfred Owen (1893–1918) was born in Oswestry, Shropshire, and went to school at Birkenhead Institute and Shrewsbury Technical School. He studied at London University but was forced to withdraw for financial reasons. After that he went to Dunsden, Oxfordshire, as a vicar's assistant. At Dunsden, Owen grew disaffected with the church and left to teach in France. He enlisted in 1915 and six months later was hospitalized in Edinburgh, where he met Siegfried Sassoon, whose war poems had just been published. Owen was sent back to the front and was killed one week before the armistice. He is the most widely recognized of the "war poets," a group of World War I writers who brought the realism of war into poetry.

Linda Pastan (b. 1932) was born in New York City, graduated from Radcliffe College, and earned an M.A. from Brandeis University. She has published many books of poetry — most recently *Queen of a Rainy Country* (2006) — and received numerous awards for them, including a Dylan Thomas Award. Her deeply emotional poetry often has grief at its center. Her work is referred to as "spare, plain-spoken" poetry, a kind of plainsong. Pastan served as poet laureate of Maryland from 1991 to 1994. She presently lives in Potomac, Maryland.

Lucia Perillo (b. 1958) has published four books of poetry: *Dangerous Life*, winner of the Norma Farber Award for the best "first book" of 1989; *The Body Mutinies* (1996), which was awarded the Revson Foundation Fellowship from PEN, the Kate Tufts Prize from Claremont University, and the Balcones Prize; *The Oldest Map with the Name America* (1999); and *Luck Is Luck*, a finalist for the Los Angeles Times Book Prize and included in the New York Public Library's list of "books to remember" for 2005. In her thirties she was diagnosed with multiple sclerosis, about which she has written with candor and intimacy in poetry and prose, including her book of essays *I've Heard the Vultures Singing: Field Notes on Poetry, Illness, and Nature* (2007). In 2000 she was awarded a MacArthur Foundation Award for her work in poetry. She has taught at Syracuse University, Saint Martin's University, and Southern Illinois University, Carbondale, and now lives in Olympia, Washington.

Carl Phillips (b. 1959) is the author of numerous books of poetry, most recently *Riding Westward* (2006) and *Quiver of Arrows: Selected Poems 1986–2006* (2007). His collection *The Rest of Love* (2004) won the Theodore Roethke Memorial Foundation Poetry Prize and the Thom Gunn Award for Gay Male Poetry, and was a finalist for the National Book Award. Phillips is also the author of a book of prose, *Coin of the Realm: Essays on the Art and Life of Poetry* (2004), and the translator of Sophocles' *Philoctetes* (2003). He is a chancellor of the Academy of American

Poets and professor of English and of African and Afro-American studies at Washington University in St. Louis, where he also teaches in the creative writing program.

Marge Piercy (b. 1936) was born in working-class Detroit and studied at the University of Michigan and Northwestern University. She has published seventeen books of poetry, seventeen novels, a collection of essays on poetry, *Parti-Colored Blocks for a Quilt* (1982), and a memoir, *Sleeping with Cats* (2002). She has been deeply involved in many of the major progressive political battles of the past fifty years, including anti-Vietnam war activities, the women's movement, and most recently the resistance to the war in Iraq.

Wang Ping (b. 1957) received her B.A. from Beijing University and came to the United States in 1985. She earned a Ph.D. at New York University. She is the author of two short story collections, *American Visa* (1994) and *The Last Communist Virgin* (2007); a novel, *Foreign Devil* (1996); two poetry collections, *Of Flesh & Spirit* (1998) and *The Magic Whip* (2003); and a cultural study, *Aching for Beauty: Footbinding in China* (2000). She is also the editor and cotranslator of the anthology *New Generation: Poetry from China Today* (1999), and her writing has appeared in many journals and anthologies. She teaches English at Macalester College in St. Paul, Minnesota.

Robert Pinsky (b. 1940) was born in Long Branch, New Jersey. He is the author of seven books of poetry, including *The Figured Wheel: New and Collected Poems, 1966–1996* (1996), which won the 1997 Lenore Marshall Poetry Prize and was a Pulitzer Prize nominee.

He has also published four books of criticism, two books of translation, a biography — *The Life of David* (2005) — several books on reading poetry, and a computerized novel, *Mindwheel*. In 1999 he coedited with Maggie Dietz *Americans' Favorite Poems: The Favorite Poem Project Anthology*. He is currently poetry editor of the weekly Internet magazine *Slate*. He teaches in the graduate writing program at Boston University, and in 1997 he was named Poet Laureate Consultant in Poetry at the Library of Congress. He lives in Newton Corner, Massachusetts.

Sylvia Plath (1932–1963) grew up in a middle-class family in Boston and showed early promise as a writer, having stories and poems published in magazines such as *Seventeen* while she was in high school. As a student at Smith College, she was selected for an internship at *Mademoiselle* magazine and spent a month working in New York in the summer of 1953. Upon her return home, she suffered a serious breakdown and attempted suicide, was institutionalized, and then returned to Smith College for her senior year in 1954. She received a Fulbright fellowship to study at Cambridge University in England, where she met the poet Ted Hughes. They were married in 1956. They lived in the United States as well as England, and Plath studied under ROBERT LOWELL at Boston University. Her marriage broke up in 1962, and from her letters and poems it appears that she was approaching another breakdown. On February 11, 1963, she committed suicide. Four books of poetry appeared during her lifetime, and her *Selected Poems* was published in 1985. The powerful, psychologically intense poetry for which she is best known (including "Daddy") was written after 1960, influenced by Lowell's "confessional" style (see **confessional poetry** in the glossary).

Edgar Allan Poe (1809–1849) was born in Boston. His parents were touring actors; both died before he was three years old, and he was taken into the home of John Allan, a prosperous merchant in Richmond, Virginia, and baptized Edgar Allan Poe. His childhood was uneventful, although he studied in England for five years (1815–1820). In 1826 he entered the University of Virginia but, because of gambling debts, stayed for only a year. He began to write and published a book of poems in 1827. He joined the army and gained an appointment to West Point, but was dismissed after six months for disobeying orders. He turned to fiction writing and journalism to support himself. He began publishing stories and was appointed editor of the *Southern Literary Messenger* in Richmond, but his job was terminated after two years because of his drinking. He achieved success as an artist and editor in New York City (1837), then in Philadelphia (1838–1844), and again in New York (1844–1849), but failed to satisfy his employers and to secure a livelihood, and thus lived in or close to poverty his entire life. He is famous for his horror tales and is credited with inventing the detective story, as well as for writing poetry with a prominent use of **rhythms, alliteration,** and **assonance** (see the glossary) that gives it a strongly musical quality.

Alexander Pope (1688–1744) was born in London to a successful textile merchant and spent his childhood in the country, stunted by tuberculosis of the spine (his height never exceeded four and a half feet). Pope was also limited by his Catholicism, which prevented him from going to university, voting, or holding public office. He instead turned to writing and gained considerable fame for his satire *The Rape of the Lock* and his translations of Homer. Fame also brought ridicule and vehement attacks from critics holding different political views, and Pope struck back with nasty satires on his detractors. Later in his career, he wrote a good deal of ethical and philosophical verse.

Ezra Pound (1885–1972) was born in Idaho but grew up outside Philadelphia; he attended the University of Pennsylvania for two years and graduated from Hamilton College. He taught for two years at Wabash College, then left for Europe, living for the next few years in London, where he edited *Little Review* and founded several literary movements — including the **Imagists** (see the glossary) and the Vorticists. After moving to Italy, he began his major work, the *Cantos,* and became involved in fascist politics. During World War II he did radio broadcasts from Italy in support of Mussolini, for which he was indicted for treason in the United States. Judged mentally unfit for trial, he remained in an asylum in Washington, D.C., until 1958, when the charges were dropped. Pound spent his last years in Italy. He is generally considered the poet most responsible for defining and promoting a modernist aesthetic in poetry.

Dudley Randall (1914–2000) was born in Washington, D.C., and lived most of his life in Detroit. His first published poem appeared in the *Detroit Free Press* when he was thirteen. He worked for Ford Motor Company and then for the U.S. Postal Service and served in the South Pacific during World War II.

He graduated from Wayne State University in 1949 and then from the library school at the University of Michigan. In 1965 Randall established the Broadside Press, one of the most important publishers of modern black poetry. "Ballad of Birmingham," written in response to the 1963 bombing of a church in which four girls were killed, has been set to music and recorded. It became an anthem for many in the civil rights movement.

John Crowe Ransom (1888–1974) was born in Pulaski, Tennessee, the son of a preacher. He studied at Vanderbilt University and then at Christ Church College, Oxford, on a Rhodes scholarship. After service in World War I, he taught first at Vanderbilt and later at Kenyon College, where he edited the *Kenyon Review.* He published three volumes of highly acclaimed poetry, but after 1927 principally devoted himself to critical writing. He was a guiding member of the Fugitives, a group of writers who sought to preserve a traditional aesthetic ideal that was firmly rooted in classical values and forms. As a critic, he promulgated the highly influential New Criticism, which focused attention on texts as self-sufficient entities, to be analyzed through rigorous methodologies intended to reveal their depth, subtleties, and intricacies of technique and theme.

Donald Revell (b. 1954) was born in the Bronx. He is a graduate of Harper College, with graduate degrees from the State University of New York at both Binghamton and Buffalo. He is the author of ten books of poetry, most recently *Pennyweight Windows: New and Selected Poems* (2005) and *A Thief of Strings* (2007). He has also published translation and criticism as well as books on creative writing and on the creative process, and is poetry editor of the *Colorado Review.* He was the winner of the 2004 Lenore Marshall Award and two-time winner of the PEN Center USA Award in poetry. Since 1994, he has been a professor of English at the University of Utah.

Adrienne Rich (b. 1929) was born in Baltimore, the elder daughter of a forceful Jewish intellectual who encouraged and critiqued her writing. While she was at Radcliffe College in 1951, W. H. AUDEN selected her book *A Change of World* for the Yale Younger Poets Award. She became involved in radical politics, especially in the opposition to the Vietnam war, and taught inner-city minority youth. She had felt a tension as she modeled her early poetry on that of male writers, and in the 1970s Rich became a feminist, freeing herself from her old models and becoming an influential figure in contemporary American literature. She is the author of nearly twenty volumes of poetry — including *Diving into the Wreck* (1973), *Dark Fields of the Republic* (1995), and *The School Among the Ruins: Poems 2000–2004* (2004), which won the Book Critics Circle Award — and several books of nonfiction prose. She was awarded a MacArthur Foundation Fellowship in 1994 and in 1999 received the Lifetime Achievement Award from the Lannan Foundation.

Alberto Ríos (b. 1952) was born to a Guatemalan father and an English mother in Nogales, Arizona, on the Mexican border. He earned a B.A. in English and one in psychology and an M.F.A. at the University of Arizona. In addition to seven books of poetry, he has published two collections of short stories, and a memoir, *Capirotada: A Nogales Memoir* (1999). His work often fuses realism, surrealism, and magical realism, as exemplified by "Indentations in the Sugar." Since 1994 he has been Regents Professor of English at Arizona State University, where he has taught since 1982.

Edwin Arlington Robinson (1869–1935) was born in Head Tide, Maine, and grew up in the equally provincial Maine town of Gardiner, the setting for much of his poetry. He was forced to leave Harvard University after two years because of his family's financial difficulties. He published his first two books of poetry in 1896 and 1897 ("Richard Cory" appeared in the latter). For the next quarter-century Robinson chose to live in poverty and write his poetry, relying on temporary jobs and charity from friends. President Theodore Roosevelt, at the urging of his son Kermit, used his influence to get Robinson a sinecure job in the New York Custom House in 1905, giving him time to write. He published numerous books of mediocre poetry in the next decade. The tide turned for him with *The Man Against the Sky* (1916); the numerous volumes that followed received high praise and sold well. He was awarded three Pulitzer Prizes: for *Collected Poems* in 1921, *The Man Who Died Twice* in 1924, and *Tristram* in 1927. Robinson was the first major American poet of the twentieth century, unique in that he devoted his life to poetry and willingly paid the price in poverty and obscurity.

Theodore Roethke (1908–1963) was the son of a commercial greenhouse operator in Saginaw, Michigan. As a child, he spent much time in the greenhouse, and the impressions of nature he formed there later influenced the subjects and imagery of his verse. Roethke graduated from the University of Michigan and studied at Harvard University. Although he published only eight books of poetry, they were held in high regard by critics, some of whom considered him among the best poets of his generation. *The Waking* was awarded the Pulitzer Prize in 1954; *Words for the Wind* (1958) received the Bollingen Prize and the National Book Award. He taught at many colleges and universities and gained a reputation as an exceptional teacher of poetry writing, although his career was interrupted several times by serious mental breakdowns.

Christina Rossetti (1830–1894), born in London into a literary family (her brother Dante Gabriel Rossetti was one of the Pre-Raphaelite group), began writing poetry at an early age. Ill health saved her from a career as a governess; instead she nursed her ailing father and worked at the St. Mary Magdalen Home for Fallen Women. Rossetti had a strong Anglican religiosity that led her to give up theater and opera and turn down two offers of marriage. She wrote six collections of poetry, as well as short stories, nursery rhymes, and religious essays.

Mary Ruefle (b. 1952) was born near Pittsburgh but spent her early life moving around the United States and Europe as the daughter of a military officer. She graduated from Bennington College with a literature major. She has published ten books of poetry, including *Memling's Veil* (1982); *The Adamant* (1989), winner of the 1988 Iowa Poetry Prize; *A Little White Shadow* (2006); and *Indeed I Was Pleased with the World* (2007). Among awards she has received

are a Guggenheim fellowship, an American Academy of Arts and Letters Award in Literature, and a Whiting Foundation Writer's Award. She lives in Vermont, where she is a professor in the Vermont College M.F.A. program.

Sonia Sanchez (b. 1934) was born Wilsonia Driver in Birmingham, Alabama. In 1943 she moved to Harlem with her sister to live with their father and his third wife. She earned a B.A. in political science from Hunter College in 1955 and studied poetry writing with Louise Bogan at New York University. In the 1960s she became actively involved in the social movements of the times, and she has continued to be a voice for social change. She has published more than a dozen books of poetry, many plays, and several books for children, and she has edited two anthologies of literature. She began teaching in the San Francisco area in 1965 and was a pioneer in developing black studies courses at what is now San Francisco State University, from 1968 to 1969. She was the first Presidential Fellow at Temple University, where she began teaching in 1977, and held the Laura Carnell Chair in English there until her retirement in 1999. She lives in Philadelphia.

Anne Sexton (1928–1974) was born in Newton, Massachusetts, and dropped out of Garland Junior College to get married. After suffering nervous breakdowns following the births of her two children, she was encouraged to enroll in writing programs. Studying under Robert Lowell at Boston University, she was a fellow student of Sylvia Plath. Like the work of other "confessional" poets, Sexton's poetry includes an intimate view of her life and emotions. She made the experience of being a woman a central issue in her poetry, bringing into it such subjects as menstruation, abortion, and drug addiction. She published at least a dozen books of poetry—*Live or Die* was awarded the Pulitzer Prize for poetry in 1966—as well as four children's books coauthored with MAXINE KUMIN. Sexton's emotional problems continued, along with a growing addiction to alcohol and sedatives, and she committed suicide in 1974.

William Shakespeare (1564–1616) was born in Stratford-upon-Avon, England, where his father was a glovemaker and bailiff, and he presumably went to grammar school there. He married Anne Hathaway in 1582, and sometime before 1592 he left for London to work as a playwright and actor. Shakespeare joined the Lord Chamberlain's Men (later the King's Men), an acting company for which he wrote thirty-five plays, before retiring to Stratford around 1612. In addition to being a skillful dramatist, he was perhaps the finest lyric poet of his day, as exemplified by songs scattered through his plays, two early nondramatic poems (*Venus and Adonis* and *The Rape of Lucrece*), and the sonnet sequence expected of all noteworthy writers in the Elizabethan age. Shakespeare's sonnets were probably written in the 1590s, although they were not published until 1609.

Percy Bysshe Shelley (1792–1822) was born into a wealthy aristocratic family in Sussex County, England. He was educated at Eton and then went on to Oxford University, but was expelled after six months for writing a defense of atheism, the first price he would pay for his nonconformity and radical (for his time) commitment to social justice.

The following year he eloped with Harriet Westbrook, daughter of a tavern keeper, despite his belief that marriage was a tyrannical and degrading social institution (she was sixteen, he eighteen). He became a disciple of the radical social philosopher William Godwin, fell in love with Godwin's daughter, Mary Wollstonecroft Godwin (the author, later, of *Frankenstein*), and went to live with her in France. Two years later, after Harriet committed suicide, they married and moved to Italy, where they shifted about restlessly and Shelley was generally short on money and in poor health. In such trying circumstances he wrote his greatest works. He died at age thirty, when the boat he was in was overturned by a sudden storm.

Sir Philip Sidney (1554–1586) was born into an important aristocratic family in Elizabethan England. He attended Shrewsbury School and Oxford University, although he left without a degree and completed his education through extended travel on the Continent. He was the epitome of the well-rounded courtier idealized in his era, excelling as a soldier, writer, literary patron, and diplomat. He was the author of an important work of prose fiction (*Arcadia*), a landmark essay in literary criticism (*The Defense of Poesy*), and an important sonnet cycle (*Astrophil and Stella*, which includes "Loving in truth, and fain in verse my love to show"). His poetry has been labeled "news from the heart."

Leslie Marmon Silko (b. 1948) was born in Albuquerque of mixed Pueblo, Mexican, and white ancestry and grew up on the Laguna Pueblo Reservation in New Mexico. She earned her B.A. (with honors) from the University of

New Mexico. In a long and productive writing career (she was already writing stories in elementary school), she has published poetry, novels, short stories, essays, letters, and film scripts. She taught creative writing first at the University of New Mexico and later at the University of Arizona. She has been named a Living Cultural Treasure by the New Mexico Humanities Council and has received the Native Writers' Circle of the Americas Lifetime Achievement Award. Her work is a graphic telling of the life of native peoples, maintaining its rich spiritual heritage while exposing the terrible consequences of European domination.

Charles Simic (b. 1938) was born in Belgrade, Yugoslavia. In 1953 he, his mother, and his brother joined his father in Chicago, where he lived until 1958. His first poems were published when he was twenty-one. In 1961 he was drafted into the U.S. Army, and in 1966 he earned his B.A. from New York University. His first book of poems, *What the Grass Says*, was published in 1967. Since then he has published more than sixty books of poetry, translations, and essays, including *The World Doesn't End: Prose Poems* (1990), for which he received the Pulitzer Prize for poetry. Since 1973 he has lived in New Hampshire, where he is a professor of English at the University of New Hampshire. In 2007, he was named Poet Laureate Consultant in Poetry to the Library of Congress.

Edith Sitwell (1887–1964) was born into an aristocratic and literary family in late Victorian England. She both shocked and amused people by her writing, eccentric behavior, and dramatic Elizabethan dress. Influenced by Baudelaire and the symbolists, T. S. Eliot's poetry, Stravinsky's music, and abstract art, Sitwell introduced verbal and rhythmic innovations that contrasted sharply with then-current verse.

Christopher Smart (1722–1771) was born in Shipbourne, Kent. He attended the Durham School and was later educated at Pembroke College, Cambridge, where he won prizes for his poetry. After college, Smart lived in London, editing and writing copy for periodicals and composing songs for the popular theater. In 1752 he published his first collection, *Poems on Several Occasions*. In the 1750s Smart developed a form of religious mania that compelled him to continuous prayer. From 1756 on, he was confined, with one brief intermission, in St. Luke's Hospital until 1763 and then in Mr. Potter's Madhouse in Bethnal Green. During his confinement, he wrote what many see as his most original and lasting works—*A Song to David* and *Jubilate Agno*, with its well-known homage to his cat, Jeoffry. Smart ranks as one of the most respected and influential religious poets in English literature.

Gary Snyder (b. 1930) was born in San Francisco and grew up in Oregon and Washington. He studied anthropology at Reed College and Oriental languages at the University of California, Berkeley, where he became associated with the Beat movement; however, his poetry often deals with nature rather than the urban interests more typical of Beat poetry. He has published sixteen books of poetry and prose, including *Turtle Island* (1974), which won the Pulitzer Prize for poetry. Snyder is active in the environmental movement and spent a number of years in Japan devoting extensive study to Zen Buddhism. He taught for many years at the University of California, Davis.

Cathy Song (b. 1955) was born in Hawaii and lived in the small town of Wahiawa on Oahu. She left Hawaii for the East Coast, earning a B.A. from Wellesley College and an M.A. in creative writing from Boston University. Her first book, *Picture Bride,* was chosen by Richard Hugo for the Yale Series of Younger Poets in 1982. Since then she has published three other books of poetry: *Frameless Windows, Squares of Light* (1988), *School Figures* (1994), and *The Land of Bliss* (2001). She lives in Honolulu and teaches at the University of Hawaii at Manoa.

Gary Soto (b. 1952) grew up in Fresno, California. He earned his B.A. from California State University, Fresno, and M.F.A. from the University of California, Irvine. He worked his way through college at jobs such as picking grapes and chopping beets. Much of his poetry comes out of and reflects his working background, that of migrant workers and tenant farmers in the fields of southern California, and provides glimpses into the lives of families in the barrio. Soto's language comes from earthy, gritty, raw everyday American speech. His first book, *The Elements of San Joaquin,* won the 1976 United States Award from the International Poetry Forum. He has published ten collections of poetry, three novels, four essay collections, and numerous young adult and children's books and has edited three anthologies. He lives in Berkeley, California.

Edmund Spenser (1552–1599), a contemporary of WILLIAM SHAKESPEARE, was the greatest English nondramatic poet of his time. Best known for his romantic and national epic *The Faerie Queene,* Spenser wrote poems of a number of other types as well and was important as an innovator in metrics and forms (as in his development of the special form of sonnet that bears his name — see **Spenserian sonnet** in the glossary). "One day I wrote her name upon the strand" is number 75 in *Amoretti,* a sequence of sonnets about a courtship addressed to a woman named Elizabeth, probably Elizabeth Boyle, who became his second wife.

William Stafford (1914–1995) was born in Hutchinson, Kansas, and studied at the University of Kansas and then at the University of Iowa Writers' Workshop. In between, he was a conscientious objector during World War II and worked in labor camps. In 1948 Stafford moved to Oregon, where he taught at Lewis and Clark College until he retired in 1980. His first major collection of poems, *Traveling through the Dark,* was published when Stafford was forty-eight. It won the National Book Award in 1963. He went on to publish more than sixty-five volumes of poetry and prose and came to be known as a very influential teacher of poetry. From 1970 to 1971 he was Consultant in Poetry at the Library of Congress.

Gertrude Stein (1874–1946) was born in Allegheny, Pennsylvania. After attending Radcliffe College, Harvard University, and Johns Hopkins Medical School, she moved to France in 1903 and became a central figure in the Parisian art world. An advocate of the avant-garde, her salon became a gathering place for the "new moderns." What Henri Matisse and Pablo Picasso achieved in the visual arts, Stein attempted in her writing. Her first published book, *Three Lives* (1909), the stories of three working-class women, has been called a minor masterpiece. A number of other books followed, including *The Autobiography of Alice B. Toklas* (1933), actually Stein's own autobiography.

Gerald Stern (b. 1925) was born in Pittsburgh and studied at the University of Pittsburgh and Columbia University. Stern came late to poetry: he was forty-six when he published his first book. Since then he has published sixteen collections of poems. Stern has often been compared to WALT WHITMAN and JOHN KEATS for his exploration of the self and the sometimes ecstatic exuberance of his verse. He taught at Columbia University, New York University, Sarah Lawrence College, the University of Pittsburgh, and the University of Iowa Writers' Workshop, among others, until his retirement in 1995. He now lives in Easton, Pennsylvania, and New York City.

Wallace Stevens (1879–1955) was born in Reading, Pennsylvania, and attended Harvard University for three years. He tried journalism and then attended New York University Law School, after which he worked as a legal consultant. He spent most of his life working as an executive for the Hartford Accident and Indemnity Company, spending his evenings writing some of the most imaginative and influential poetry of his time. Although now considered one of the major American poets of the twentieth century, he did not receive widespread recognition until the publication of his *Collected Poems* just a year before his death.

Mark Strand (b. 1934) was born on Prince Edward Island, Canada, and studied at Antioch College, Yale University, the University of Florence, and the University of Iowa. He is the author of many collections of poetry, including *Reasons for Moving* (1968), *The Story of Our Lives* (1973), *Selected Poems* (1980), *The Continuous Life* (1990), *Blizzard of One* (1998)—which won the Pulitzer Prize for poetry—*Dark Harbor* (1993), and *Man and Camel* (2006). He has also published two books of prose, several volumes of translation (of works by Rafael Alberti and Carlos Drummond de Andrade, among others), several monographs on contemporary artists, and three books for children. He served as Poet Laureate Consultant in Poetry to the Library of Congress from 1990 to 1991 and is a former chancellor of the Academy of American Poets. He teaches English and comparative literature at Columbia University in New York.

Virgil Suárez (b. 1962) was born in Havana, Cuba. Eight years later he left with his parents for Spain, where they lived until they came to the United States in 1974. He is the author of six collections of poetry, five novels, and a volume of short stories and the editor of several best-selling anthologies. His work often reflects the impact of the diaspora on the everyday life of Cuban and other exiles. He is professor of creative writing at Florida State University.

Sekou Sundiata (1948–2007) was born and raised in Harlem. His work is deeply influenced by the music, poetry, and oral traditions of African American culture. A self-proclaimed radical in the 1970s, for the past several decades he used poetry to comment on the life and times of our culture. His work, which encompasses print, performance, music, and theater, received praise for its fusion of soul, jazz, and hiphop grooves with political insight, humor, and rhythmic speech. He regularly recorded and performed on tour with artists such as Craig Harris and Vernon Reid.

Jonathan Swift (1667–1745) was born in Ireland of English parents and educated at Kilkenny College and Trinity College, Dublin. He worked in England for a decade as a private secretary and for four years as a political writer, but spent the rest of his life in Ireland, as dean of St. Patrick's Cathedral in Dublin. Although he is best known for his satires in prose (such as *Gulliver's Travels* and "A Modest Proposal"), Swift's original ambition was to be a poet, and he wrote occasional verse throughout his life.

James Tate (b. 1943), a native of Kansas City, Missouri, studied at the University of Missouri and Kansas State College during his undergraduate years. He then earned his M.F.A. at the University of Iowa Writers' Workshop in 1967, the same year his first poetry collection, *The Lost Pilot*, was published (it was selected by Dudley Fitts for the Yale Series of Younger Poets). He is the author of numerous books of poetry, including *Selected Poems* (1991), which won the Pulitzer Prize and the William Carlos Williams Award. Tate's poems often include highly unusual juxtapositions of imagery, tone, and context, as is evident in "The Wheelchair Butterfly." Tate has taught at the University of Iowa, the University of California, Berkeley, and Columbia University and now teaches at the University of Massachusetts, Amherst.

Edward Taylor (c. 1642–1729) was born in England and emigrated to the colonies, where he became a clergyman in Westfield, a frontier village in what is now Massachusetts. Taylor regarded his poems as sacramental acts of private devotion and asked that they never be published. When he died, his manuscripts were placed in the Yale University library, and two centuries passed before his work was discovered. The selection of his poems published in 1939 established him as a writer of genuine power, perhaps unsurpassed in America until William Cullen Bryant appeared a century and a half later.

Alfred, Lord Tennyson (1809–1892) was born in Somersby, Lincolnshire, and grew up there in the tense atmosphere of his unhappy father's rectory. He went to Trinity College, Cambridge, but was forced to leave because of family and financial problems, so he returned home to study and practice the craft of poetry. His early volumes, published in 1830 and 1832, received bad reviews, but his *In Memoriam* (1850), an elegy on his close friend Arthur Hallam, who died of a seizure, won acclaim. He was unquestionably the most popular poet of his time (the "poet of the people") and arguably the greatest of the Victorian poets. He succeeded WILLIAM WORDSWORTH as poet laureate, a position he held from 1850 until his death.

Dylan Thomas (1914–1953) was born in Swansea, Wales, and after grammar school became a journalist. He worked as a writer for the rest of his life. His first book of poetry, *Eighteen Poems*, appeared in 1934 and was followed by *Twenty-five Poems* (1936), *Deaths and Entrances* (1946), and *Collected Poems* (1952). His poems are often rich in textured rhythms and images. He also wrote prose, chiefly short stories collectively appearing as *Portrait of the Artist as a Young Dog* (1940), and a number of film scripts and radio plays. His most famous work, *Under Milk Wood*, written as a play for voices, was first performed in New York on May 14, 1953. Thomas's radio broadcasts and his lecture tours and poetry readings in the United States brought him fame and popularity. Alcoholism contributed to his early death in 1953.

Jean Toomer (1894–1967) was born in Washington, D.C., of mixed French, Dutch, Welsh, black, German, Jewish, and Native American blood (according to him). Although he passed for white during certain periods of his life, he was raised in a predominantly black community and attended black high schools. He began college at the University of Wisconsin but transferred to the College of the City of New York. He spent several years publishing poems and stories in small magazines. In 1921 he took a teaching job in Georgia and remained there four months; the experience inspired *Cane* (1923), a book of prose poetry describing the Georgian people and landscape that became a central work of the Harlem Renaissance. He later experimented in communal living and both studied and tried to promulgate the ideas of Quakerism and the Russian mystic George Gurdjieff. From 1950 on he published very little, writing mostly for himself.

Quincy Troupe (b. 1943) was born in New York City and grew up in St. Louis, Missouri. He is the author of sixteen books, including eight volumes of poetry, most recently *The Architecture of Language* (2006). He is recipient of two American Book Awards, for his collection of poetry *Snake-Back Solos* (1980) and his nonfiction book *Miles the Autobiography* (1989). In 1991 he received the prestigious Peabody Award for writing and coproducing the seven-part Miles Davis Radio Project aired on National Public Radio in 1990. *Transcircularities: New and Selected Poems* (2002) received the Milt Kessler Award

for 2003 and was finalist for the Paterson Poetry Prize. Troupe has taught at the University of California, Los Angeles; Ohio University; the College of Staten Island (CUNY); Columbia University (in the graduate writing program); and the University of California, San Diego, where he is now professor emeritus of creative writing and American and Caribbean literature. He is the founding editorial director for *Code* magazine and former artistic director of "Arts on the Cutting Edge," a reading and performance series at the Museum of Contemporary Art, San Diego. He was the first official poet laureate of the State of California, appointed to the post in 2002 by Governor Gray Davis.

Ellen Bryant Voigt (b. 1943) was born in Danville, Virginia, and studied at Converse College, the University of South Carolina, and the University of Iowa, where she earned an M.F.A. in music and literature. She is a pianist as well as a writer; her highly tuned musical ear is evident in the rich textures of sound in her poetry. She is the author of six collections of poetry, most recently *Messenger: New and Selected Poems 1976–2006* (2007), and *The Flexible Lyric* (1999), a collection of craft essays. She has taught at Goddard College, where she founded the writing program, and at M.I.T., and now teaches at Warren Wilson College in North Carolina, where she is the founding director of the writing program. She lives in Cabot, Vermont, where she served as the Vermont State Poet from 1999 to 2003.

Derek Walcott (b. 1930), born on the eastern Caribbean island of St. Lucia, moves between the African heritage of his family and the English cultural heritage of his reading and education. Both of his parents were educators who immersed themselves in the arts. His early training was in painting, which like his poetry was influenced by his Methodist religious training. He attended St. Mary's College and the University of the West Indies in Jamaica. His first book, *Twenty-Five Poems* (1948), appeared when he was eighteen, and he has published prolifically since then: more than twenty books of poetry, at least twenty plays, and a book of nonfiction. His work, which explores both the isolation of the artist and regional identity, is known for blending Caribbean, English, and African traditions. He was awarded the Nobel Prize for literature in 1992, the academy citing him for "a poetic oeuvre of great luminosity, sustained by a historical vision, the outcome of a multicultural achievement." He teaches creative writing at Boston University every fall and lives the rest of the year in St. Lucia.

Anne Waldman (b. 1945) was born in Millville, New Jersey, and grew up in Greenwich Village. She is associated with the bohemian poetics of the Lower East Side in New York and with "Beat poetics." She attended Bennington College, cofounded the literary magazine *Angel Hair*, and for ten years directed the St. Mark's Church Poetry Project in New York City. She became a Buddhist, guided by the Tibetan Chogyam Trungpa Rinpoche, who would also become ALLEN GINSBERG's guru. She and Ginsberg worked together to create the Jack Kerouac School of Disembodied Poetics, at Trungpa's Naropa Institute in Boulder, Colorado. Both an author and a performance artist, she has published more than forty books and gives exuberant, highly physical readings of her own work. She now lives in Boulder and New York City.

James Welch (b. 1940) was born in Browning, Montana. His father was a member of the Blackfoot tribe, his mother of the Gros Ventre tribe. He attended schools on the Blackfoot and Fort Belknap reservations and took a degree from the University of Montana, where he studied under Richard Hugo. Welch has published many books of poetry, fiction, and nonfiction. His hard, spare poems often evoke the bleakest side of contemporary Native American life. He received a Lifetime Achievement Award for literature from the Native Writers' Circle in 1997. He makes his home on a farm outside Missoula, Montana.

Walt Whitman (1819–1892) was born in rural Long Island, the son of a farmer and carpenter. He attended grammar school in Brooklyn and took his first job as a printer's devil for the *Long Island Patriot*. Attending the opera, dabbling in politics, participating in street life, and gaining experience as student, printer, reporter, writer, carpenter, farmer, seashore observer, and teacher provided the bedrock for his future poetic vision of an ideal society based on the realization of self. Although Whitman liked to portray himself as uncultured, he read widely in the King James Bible, SHAKESPEARE, Homer, Dante, Aeschylus, and Sophocles. He worked for many years in the newspaper business and began writing poetry only in 1847. In 1855, at his own expense, Whitman published the first edition of *Leaves of Grass,* a thin volume of twelve long untitled poems. Written in a highly original and innovative **free verse,** influenced significantly by music, with a wide-ranging subject matter, the work seemed strange to most of the poet's contemporaries — but they did recognize its value: Ralph

Waldo Emerson wrote to him shortly after Whitman sent him a copy, "I greet you at the beginning of a great career." He spent much of the remainder of his life revising and expanding this book. *Leaves of Grass* today is considered a masterpiece of world literature, marking the beginning of modern American poetry, and Whitman is widely regarded as America's national poet.

Richard Wilbur (b. 1921) was born in New York City and grew up in rural New Jersey. He attended Amherst College and began writing poetry during World War II while fighting in Italy and France. Afterward, he studied at Harvard University and then taught there and at Wellesley College, Wesleyan University, and Smith College. He has published many books of poetry, including *Things of This World* (1956), for which he received the Pulitzer Prize for poetry and the National Book Award, and *New and Collected Poems* (1988), which also won a Pulitzer Prize. He has always been respected as a master of formal constraints, comparing them to the genie in the bottle: the restraints stimulate the imagination to achieve results unlikely to be reached without them. He has also published translations of French plays, two books for children, a collection of prose pieces, and editions of WILLIAM SHAKESPEARE and EDGAR ALLAN POE. In 1987 he was appointed Poet Laureate Consultant in Poetry at the Library of Congress. He now lives in Cummington, Massachusetts.

Nancy Willard (b. 1936) was raised in Ann Arbor, Michigan, and educated at the University of Michigan and Stanford University. She is a noted writer of books for children. *A Visit to William Blake's Inn: Poems for Innocent and Experienced Travelers* (1981) was the first book of poetry to win the prestigious Newbery Medal, which recognizes the most distinguished American children's book published the previous year. She is an excellent poet, essayist, and novelist. Her work in all genres frequently leads to experiencing the common in a most uncommon way. She teaches at Vassar College and lives in Poughkeepsie, New York.

William Carlos Williams (1883–1963) was born in Rutherford, New Jersey; his father was an English emigrant and his mother was of mixed Basque descent from Puerto Rico. While in high school in New York City, he decided to be both a writer and a doctor. He graduated from the medical school at the University of Pennsylvania, where he was a friend of EZRA POUND and HILDA DOOLITTLE. After an internship in New York, writing poems between seeing patients, Williams practiced general medicine in Rutherford (he was ALLEN GINSBERG's pediatrician). His first book of poems was published in 1909, and he subsequently published poems, novels, short stories, plays, criticism, and essays. Initially one of the principal poets of the **Imagist** movement (see the glossary), Williams sought later to invent an entirely fresh—and distinctly American—poetic whose subject matter was centered on the everyday circumstances of life and the lives of common people. Williams, like WALLACE STEVENS, became one of the major poets of the twentieth century and exerted great influence upon poets of his own and later generations.

Nellie Wong (b. 1934) was born and raised in Oakland, California's Chinatown section. Since she began writing in the 1970s, she has spoken out against the oppression of all people, in particular workers, women, minorities, and immigrants, and has worked steadily with community-based and international organizations to achieve racial justice. She is known as both a poet and a feminist human rights activist. She is the author of three poetry volumes and the coeditor of an anthology of political essays, *Voices of Color* (1999). She has taught creative writing at several colleges in the Bay area. Until her retirement, she worked as senior analyst in the Office of Affirmative Action/Equal Opportunity at the University of San Francisco. She lives in San Francisco and continues to speak at conferences nationwide on issues of race, gender, class, literature, labor, and community organizing.

William Wordsworth (1770–1850) was born and raised in the Lake District of England. Both his parents died by the time he was thirteen. He studied at Cambridge, toured Europe on foot, and lived in France for a year during the first part of the French Revolution. He returned to England, leaving behind a lover, Annette Vallon, and their daughter, Caroline, from whom he was soon cut off by war between England and France. He met SAMUEL TAYLOR COLERIDGE, and in 1798 they published *Lyrical Ballads,* the first great work of the English Romantic movement. He changed poetry forever by his decision to use common language in his poetry instead of heightened **poetic diction** (see the glossary). In 1799 he and his sister Dorothy moved to Grasmere, in the Lake District, where he married Mary Hutchinson, a childhood friend. His greatest works were produced between 1797 and 1808. He continued to write for the next forty years but never regained the heights of his

early verse. In 1843 he was named poet laureate, a position he held until his death in 1850.

Charles Wright (b. 1935) was born in Pickwick Dam, Tennessee, and grew up in Tennessee and North Carolina. He studied at Davidson College, served a four-year stint in Italy as a captain in the U.S. Army Intelligence Corps, and then continued his education at the University of Iowa Writers' Workshop and at the University of Rome on a Fulbright fellowship. He has published many books of poetry — including *Black Zodiac,* which won the Pulitzer Prize for poetry in 1997 — two volumes of criticism, and a translation of Eugenio Montale's poetry. His most recent collection, *Scar Tissue* (2007), was the international winner of the Griffin Poetry Prize. Wright's poems have been labeled impressionistic, combining images from the natural world, Catholicism, and the rural South. He taught at the University of California, Irvine, for almost twenty years and now is Souder Family Professor of English at the University of Virginia.

James Wright (1927–1980) grew up in Martin's Ferry, Ohio. He attended Kenyon College, where his study under JOHN CROWE RANSOM sent his early poetry in a formalist direction. After spending a year in Austria on a Fulbright fellowship, he returned to the United States and earned an M.A. and a Ph.D. at the University of Washington, studying under THEODORE ROETHKE and STANLEY KUNITZ. He went on to teach at the University of Minnesota, Macalester College, and Hunter College. His working-class background and the poverty that he saw during the Depression stirred a sympathy for the poor and "outsiders" of various sorts that shaped the tone and content of his poetry. He published numerous books of poetry; his *Collected Poems* received the Pulitzer Prize in 1972.

Lady Mary Wroth (c. 1587–c. 1651), niece of SIR PHILIP SIDNEY and MARY SIDNEY HERBERT, was one of the best and most prolific women writers of the English Renaissance and an important literary patron. Her husband's early death left her deeply in debt. She wrote *Pamphilia to Amphilanthus*, the only known English sonnet sequence on love themes by a woman of her time; seventy-four poems that appeared in *Urania* (the first full-length work of prose fiction by a woman); and several other pieces. BEN JONSON said that reading her sonnets had made him "a better lover and a much better poet."

Sir Thomas Wyatt (1503–1542) was born in Kent and educated at St. John's College, Cambridge. He spent most of his life as a courtier and diplomat, serving King Henry VIII as ambassador to Spain and as a member of several missions to Italy and France. These travels introduced Wyatt to Italian writers of the High Renaissance, whose work he translated, thus introducing the sonnet form into English. He was arrested twice and charged with treason, sent to the Tower of London, and acquitted in 1541. Aristocratic poets at the time rarely published their poems themselves: works circulated in manuscript and in published collections ("miscellanies") gathered by printers. The most important of these is a volume published by Richard Tottel in 1557 titled *Songs and Sonnets* but more commonly known as *Tottel's Miscellany*, which includes ninety-seven of Wyatt's sonnets and delightful lyrics.

John Yau (b. 1950) was born in Lynn, Massachusetts, a year after his parents emigrated from China. He received a B.A. from Bard College and an M.F.A. from Brooklyn College, where he studied with JOHN ASHBERY. He has published over fifty books and pamphlets — among them artists' books, a great deal of art criticism, an anthology of fiction, and at least ten volumes of poetry, including *Corpse and Mirror* (1983), a National Poetry Series book selected by John Ashbery, and most recently, *Paradiso Diaspora* (2006).

William Butler Yeats (1865–1939) was born in Sandymount, Dublin, to an Anglo-Irish family. On leaving high school in 1883, he decided to be an artist, like his father, and attended art school, but soon gave it up to concentrate on poetry. His first poems were published in 1885 in the *Dublin University Review*. Religious by temperament but unable to accept orthodox Christianity, Yeats throughout his life explored esoteric philosophies in search of a tradition that would substitute for a lost religion. He became a member of the Theosophical Society and the Order of the Golden Dawn, two groups interested in Eastern occultism, and later developed a private system of symbols and mystical ideas. Through the influence of Lady Gregory, a writer and promoter of literature, he became interested in Irish nationalist art, helping to found the Irish National Theatre and the famous Abbey Theatre. He was actively involved in Irish politics, especially after the Easter Rising of 1916. He continued to write and to revise earlier poems, leaving behind at his death a body of verse that, in its variety and power, placed him among the greatest twentieth-century poets of the English language. He was awarded the Nobel Prize for Literature in 1923.

Al Young (b. 1939) was born in Ocean Springs, Mississippi, and lived for a decade in the South, then moved to Detroit. He attended the University of Michigan and the University of California, Berkeley. Young has been a professional guitarist and singer, a disk jockey, a medical photographer, and a warehouseman, and has written eight books of poetry (most recently *Coastal Nights and Inland Afternoons: Poems, 2001–2006*), five novels, memoirs, essays, and film scripts. He has edited a number of books, including *Yardbird Lives!* (1978) and *African American Literature: A Brief Introduction and Anthology* (1995). In the 1970s and 1980s, Young cofounded the journals *Yardbird Reader* and *Quilt* with poet-novelist Ishmael Reed. From 2005 to 2007 he served as California's poet laureate.

Ray A. Young Bear (b. 1950) was born and raised in the Mesquakie Tribal Settlement near Tama, Iowa. His poetry has been influenced by his maternal grandmother, Ada Kapayou Old Bear, and his wife, Stella L. Young Bear. He attended Pomona College in California as well as Grinnell College, the University of Iowa, Iowa State University, and Northern Iowa University. He has taught creative writing and Native American literature at the Institute of American Indian Art, Eastern Washington University, the University of Iowa, and Iowa State University. Young Bear and his wife cofounded the Woodland Song and Dance Troupe of Arts Midwest in 1983. Young Bear's group has performed traditional Mesquakie music in the United States and the Netherlands. Author of four books of poetry, a collection of short stories, and a novel,

he has contributed to contemporary Native American poetry and the study of it for nearly three decades.

Ofelia Zepeda (b. 1952) was born and raised in Stanfield, Arizona, near the Tohono O'odham and Pima reservations. She received her undergraduate education and her Ph.D. at the University of Arizona, where she now teaches in the linguistics department and the American Indian studies program. She is considered the foremost authority in Tohono O'odham language and literature. Zepeda has published two volumes of poetry as well as literary anthologies and the only pedagogical textbook on the Tohono O'odham language, *A Papago Grammar*. She has worked to improve her tribe's literacy in their native language, and she directs the American Indian Language Development Institute for Native American teachers. For her work Zepeda received a MacArthur Foundation Fellowship in 1999.

Paul Zimmer (b. 1934) was born in Canton, Ohio, and educated at Kent State University. He is the author of more than a dozen poetry collections, including *The Great Bird of Love*, which was selected for the National Poetry Series in 1998. His most recent collection is *Crossing to Sunlight Revisited: New and Selected Poems* (2007). He has become well known for his many poems in the voice of the persona "Zimmer," a kind of Buster Keaton everyman. Zimmer directed the university presses at the University of Georgia, the University of Iowa, and the University of Pittsburgh and was instrumental in the foundation of an influential poetry series at each.

Louis Zukofsky (1904–1978) was the son of immigrant Russian Jews and grew up on the Lower East Side of Manhattan. His "Poem Beginning 'The'" brought him to the attention of EZRA POUND, at whose behest he was invited to edit a special issue of *Poetry* magazine, for which he coined the term "Objectivist" poetry. He became a leading member of the Objectivist group, together with WILLIAM CARLOS WILLIAMS, Charles Reznikoff, George Oppen, and Carl Rakosi. Widely considered an important forerunner of contemporary avant-garde writing, he was an accomplished writer of fiction, a ceaseless experimenter in poetry and theory, and one of the most influential poets and critics of his era.

Groupings of Poems by Form and Type

Accentual Meter

Thomas Hardy, "The Convergence of the Twain" (p. 98).

Elizabeth Bishop, "The Fish" (p. 153)

Allegory

Edward Taylor, "Housewifery" (p. 24)

Ballad: Literary

John Keats, "La Belle Dame sans Merci" (p. 55)

Dudley Randall, "Ballad of Birmingham" (p. 160)

Ballad: Popular

"Lord Randal" (p. 1)

Ballad Stanza

John Keats, "La Belle Dame sans Merci" (p. 55)

W. H. Auden, "As I Walked Out One Evening" (p. 149)

Dudley Randall, "Ballad of Birmingham" (p. 160)

Blank Verse

William Wordsworth, "Lines Composed a Few Miles above Tintern Abbey" (p. 38)

Alfred, Lord Tennyson, "Ulysses" (p. 62)

William Butler Yeats, "The Second Coming" (p. 103)

Robert Frost, "Birches" (p. 113)

Robert Frost, "'Out, Out —'" (p. 115)

Wallace Stevens, "Sunday Morning" (p. 118)

William Stafford, "Traveling through the Dark" (p. 161)

Catalog Poetry

Christopher Smart, from *Jubilate Agno* (p. 32)

Walt Whitman, from *Song of Myself* (p. 72)

Walt Whitman, "When Lilacs Last in the Dooryard Bloom'd" (p. 85)

Langston Hughes, "The Negro Speaks of Rivers" (p. 142)

Kenneth Koch, "Thank You" (p. 175)

Jayne Cortez, "Into This Time" (p. 217)

Joy Harjo, "She Had Some Horses" (p. 265)

Concrete Poetry

George Herbert, "Easter-wings" (p. 14)

Confessional Poetry

Robert Lowell, "Skunk Hour" (p. 166)

Sylvia Plath, "Daddy" (p. 205)

Couplets: Tetrameter

Andrew Marvell, "To His Coy Mistress" (p. 23)

A. E. Housman, "Loveliest of trees, the cherry now" (p. 101)

Couplets: Pentameter

Ben Jonson, "On My First Son" (p. 12)

Anne Bradstreet, "To My Dear and Loving Husband" (p. 22)

Robert Browning, "My Last Duchess" (p. 70)

Jean Toomer, "Reapers" (p. 139)

Couplets: Heroic

Ben Jonson, "On My First Son" (p. 12)

Jonathan Swift, "A Description of the Morning" (p. 25)

Alexander Pope, from "An Essay on Criticism" (p. 26)

Couplets: Other

Gerard Manley Hopkins, "Spring and Fall" (p. 100)

Gwendolyn Brooks, "We Real Cool" (p. 165)

Dramatic Monologue

Alfred, Lord Tennyson, "Ulysses" (p. 62)

Robert Browning, "My Last Duchess" (p. 70)

T. S. Eliot, "The Love Song of J. Alfred Prufrock" (p. 129)

Elegy

Ben Jonson, "On My First Son" (p. 12)

John Milton, "Lycidas" (p. 16)

Thomas Gray, "Elegy Written in a Country Churchyard" (p. 28)

Walt Whitman, "When Lilacs Last in the Dooryard Bloom'd" (p. 85)

John Crowe Ransom, "Bells for John Whiteside's Daughter" (p. 135)

Frank O'Hara, "The Day Lady Died" (p. 178)

Geoffrey Hill, "In Memory of Jane Fraser" (p. 203)

Free Verse (see Open Form)

Haiku

Gary Snyder, "Hitch Haiku" (p. 200)

Imagist Poetry

William Carlos Williams, "The Red Wheelbarrow" (p. 122)

William Carlos Williams, "This Is Just to Say" (p. 123)

H. D. [Hilda Doolittle], "Garden" (p. 124)

Lorine Niedecker, "My Life by Water" (p. 145)

Language Poetry

Gertrude Stein, "Susie Asado" (p. 117)

Louis Zukofsky, from " 'A' 15" (p. 146)

John Ashbery, "Worsening Situation" (p. 184)

Anne Waldman, "Icy Rose" (p. 246)

Wang Ping, "Syntax" (p. 298)

Carl Phillips, "To the Tune of a Small, Repeatable, and Passing Kindness" (p. 299)

Litany

Maxine Kumin, "Credo" (p. 174)

Joy Harjo, "She Had Some Horses" (p. 265)

Narrative

Alfred, Lord Tennyson, "The Lady of Shalott" (p. 64)

Robert Frost, "'Out, Out —'" (p. 115)

Langston Hughes, "Theme for English B" (p. 142)

Elizabeth Bishop, "In the Waiting Room" (p. 155)

William Stafford, "Traveling through the Dark" (p. 161)

Randall Jarrell, "The Death of the Ball Turret Gunner" (p. 164)

Galway Kinnell, "The Bear" (p. 185)

Li-Young Lee, "The Gift" (p. 297)

Glossary of Poetic Terms

This selective glossary is intended to help readers who seek a better understanding of poetic terms and techniques. It often provides examples and explanations in addition to definitions, and it can be used as a reference, as needed, or it can be read straight through. Becoming more aware of the tools and techniques poets work with can help one experience a poem more richly and fully. We have drawn numerous illustrations from John Frederick Nims's "Love Poem" (p. 158), because it provides particularly clear and memorable examples of many figures of speech.

For a more complete, book-length guide to literary terminology, see Ross Murfin and Supryia Ray, *The Bedford Glossary of Critical and Literary Terms* (3rd ed., 2009); M. H. Abrams, *A Glossary of Literary Terms* (8th ed., 2005); or William Harmon, *A Handbook to Literature* (10th ed., 2006), all excellent resources on which we have drawn frequently. The most authoritative work is the massive *New Princeton Encyclopedia of Poetry and Poetics,* ed. Alex Preminger and T. V. Brogan (3rd ed., 1993). Several glossaries of literary terms are available on the Internet.

Accent   The stress, or greater emphasis, given to some syllables of words relative to that received by adjacent syllables.

Accentual meter   A metrical system in which the number of accented, or stressed, syllables per line is regular (all lines having the same number, or the corresponding lines of different stanzas having the same number), while the number of unstressed syllables in lines varies randomly. Accentual meter with two accented syllables in each half-line, linked by a system of alliteration, was the principle of Old English poetry (up to the eleventh century), and some modern poets — e.g., W. H. Auden — have sought to revive it. Gerard Manley Hopkins developed a unique variety of accentual verse he called *sprung rhythm* (see pp. 99–101).

Accentual-syllabic verse   Verse whose meter takes into account both the number of syllables per line and the pattern of accented and unaccented syllables. The great majority of metrical poems in English are accentual-syllabic. Cf. **quantitative verse.**

Alexandrine   A poetic line with six iambic feet (iambic hexameter).

Allegory   A form or manner, usually narrative, in which objects, persons, and actions make coherent sense on a literal level but also are equated in a sustained and obvious way with (usually) abstract meanings that lie outside the story. A classic example in prose is John Bunyan's *The Pilgrim's Progress;* in narrative poetry, Edmund Spenser's *The Faerie Queene.* Edward Taylor's "Housewifery" (p. 24), though not narrative, is allegorical in approach.

Alliteration   The repetition of identical consonant sounds in the stressed syllables of words relatively near each other (in the same line or adjacent lines, usually). Alliteration is most common at the beginnings of words or syllables ("as the grass was green") but can involve consonants within words and syllables as well ("green and care*f*ree, *f*amous among the barns"). Alliteration applies to sounds, not spelling: "And honoured among *f*oxes and *ph*easants" (examples from Dylan Thomas, "Fern Hill," p. 162). Cf. **consonance.**

Allusion   A figure of speech that echoes or makes brief reference to a literary or artistic work or a historical figure, event, or object; for example, the references to Lazarus and Hamlet in "The Love Song of J. Alfred Prufrock" (p. 129). It is usually a way of placing one's poem within, or alongside, a whole other context that is evoked in a very economical fashion. See also **intertextuality.**

Ambiguity   In expository prose, an undesirable doubtfulness or uncertainty of meaning or intention, resulting from imprecision in use of words or construction of sentences. In poetry, the desirable condition of admitting more than one possible meaning, resulting from the capacity of language to function on levels other than the literal. Related terms sometimes employed are "ambivalence" and "polysemy."

Anapest   A metrical foot consisting of three syllables, with two unaccented syllables followed by an accented one (˘˘´). In "anapestic meter," anapests are the predominant foot in a line or poem. The following line from William Cowper's "The Poplar Field" (1784) is in anapestic meter: "Ănd thĕ whís | pĕriňg soúnd | ŏf thĕ cóol | čolŏnnáde."

Anaphora   Repetition of the same word or words at the beginning of two or more lines, clauses, or sentences. For examples, see the portion of Christopher Smart's *Jubilate Agno* included in the anthology (p. 32); Walt Whitman employs it extensively in "Song of Myself" (p. 72) and "When Lilacs Last in the Dooryard Bloom'd" (p. 85).

Anticlimax   An arrangement of details such that one of lesser importance appears after one or ones of greater importance, where an even greater one is expected; for example, "Not louder shrieks to pitying heaven are cast, / When husbands or when lapdogs breathe their last" (Alexander Pope, "The Rape of the Lock," [1714]).

Antithesis   A figure of speech in which contrasting words, sentences, or ideas are expressed in balanced, parallel grammatical structures; for example, "She had some horses she loved. / She had some horses she hated" (Joy Harjo, "She Had Some Horses," p. 265) illustrates antithesis.

Apostrophe   A figure of speech in which an absent person, an abstract quality, or a nonhuman entity is addressed as though present. It is a particular type of personification. See, as examples, Ben Jonson, "On My First Son" (p. 12) and John Keats, "Ode on a Grecian Urn" (p. 57).

Approximate rhyme   See **slant rhyme.**

Archetype   An image, symbol, character type, or plot line that occurs frequently enough in literature, religion, myths, folktales, and fairy tales to be recognizable as an element of universal experience and thus to evoke a deep emotional response. In "Spring and Fall" (p. 100) Gerard Manley Hopkins develops the archetypes in his title, those of spring (archetype for birth and youth) and fall (archetype for old age and the approach of death).

Assonance   The repetition of identical or similar vowel sounds in words relatively near each other (usually within a line or in adjacent lines) whose consonant sounds differ. It can be initial ("*a*pple . . . *a*nd h*a*ppy *a*s") or, more commonly, internal ("gr*ee*n and car*e*fr*ee*," "T*i*me held m*e* gr*ee*n and d*y*ing") (examples from Dylan Thomas, "Fern Hill," p. 162).

Aubade   A dawn song, ordinarily expressing the regret of two lovers that day has come to separate them.

Ballad   A poem that tells a story and was meant to be recited or sung; originally a folk art, transmitted orally from person to person and generation to generation. Many of the popular ballads were not written down and published until the eighteenth century, though their origins may have been centuries earlier. See "Lord Randal" (p. 1) for an example of a popular Scottish ballad.

Ballad stanza   A quatrain in iambic meter rhyming *abcb* with (usually) four feet in the first and third lines, three in the second and fourth. See, for example, Robert Burns, "A Red, Red Rose" (p. 36).

Blank verse   Lines of unrhymed iambic pentameter. It is the most widely used verse form of poetry in English because it is the closest to the natural rhythms of English speech. Shakespeare's plays as well as Milton's *Paradise Lost* and *Paradise Regained,* Wordsworth's *Prelude,* and countless other long poems were composed in blank verse because it is well suited to narrative, dialogue, and reflection. For a poem based on blank verse but using it freely, see Robert Frost's "Birches" (p. 113).

Cacophony   A harsh or unpleasant combination of sounds. An example can be found in Alexander Pope's "An Essay on Criticism," lines 368–69: "But when loud surges lash the sounding shore, / The hoarse, rough verse should like the torrent roar" (p. 26). Cf. **euphony.**

Caesura   A pause or break within a line of verse, usually signaled by a mark of punctuation.

Carpe diem   "Seize the day," a Latin phrase from an ode by Horace. It is the label for a theme common in literature, especially sixteenth- and seventeenth-century English love poetry, that life is short and fleeting and that therefore we must make the most of present pleasures. See Robert Herrick, "To the Virgins, to Make Much of Time" (p. 13) and Andrew Marvell, "To His Coy Mistress" (p. 23).

Chaucerian stanza   A seven-line iambic stanza rhyming *ababbcc,* sometimes having an alexandrine (hexameter) closing line. See, for example, Sir Thomas Wyatt, "They flee from me" (p. 2).

Closed form   Any structural pattern or repetition of meter, rhyme, or stanza. Cf. **open form.**

Compression   The dropping of a syllable to make a line fit the meter, sometimes marked with an apostrophe (e.g., William Shakespeare, Sonnet 73 [p. 7], line 13: "This thou perceiv'st"). One common device is elision, the dropping of a vowel at the beginning or end of a word (e.g., John Donne, "A Valediction: Forbidding Mourning" [p. 9], lines 7 and 28: " 'Twere profanation of our joys" and "To move, but doth, if th' other do").

Conceit   A figure of speech that establishes a striking or far-fetched analogy between seemingly very dissimilar things, either the exaggerated, unrealistic comparisons of love poems (such as those used in Shakespeare's Sonnet 18 [p. 7] and parodied in Sonnet 130 [p. 8]) or the complex analogies of metaphysical wit (as in John Donne's "The Flea," p. 10).

Concrete poem   A poem shaped in the form of the object the poem describes or discusses. See, for example, George Herbert's "Easter-wings" (p. 14).

Confessional poetry   Poetry about personal, private issues that usually speaks directly, without the use of a persona. See, for example, Robert Lowell, "Skunk Hour" (p. 166) and Sylvia Plath, "Daddy" (p. 205).

Connotation   The shared or communal range of emotional implications and associations a word may carry in addition to its dictionary definitions. Cf. **denotation.**

Consonance   The repetition of consonant sounds in words whose vowels are different. In perfect examples, all the consonants are alike — *live, love; chitter, chatter; reader, rider;* but words in which all the consonants following the main vowels are identical also are considered consonance — *dive, love; swatter, chitter; sound, bond; gate* and *mat, set, pit.*

Convention   A rule, method, practice, or characteristic established by usage; a customary feature.

Couplet   Two consecutive lines of poetry with the same end rhyme. English (Shakespearean) sonnets end with a couplet (see pp. 7–9); for an entire poem in tetrameter couplets, see Andrew Marvell, "To His Coy Mistress" (p. 23). See also **heroic couplets.**

Dactyl   A metrical foot consisting of three syllables, an accented one followed by two unaccented ones ($\smile\smile$). In "dactylic meter," dactyls are the predominant foot of a line or poem. The following lines from Thomas Hardy's "The Voice" (1914) are in dactylic meter: "Wómăn mŭch | mǐssed, hŏw yŏu | cáll tŏ m̆e, | cáll tŏ m̆e, / Sáyĭng tȟat | nów yŏu ăre | nót aš yŏu | wére."

Denotation   The basic meanings of a word; its dictionary definitions.

Diction   Choice of words; the kind of words, phrases, and figurative language used to make up a work of literature. See also **poetic diction.**

Dimeter   A line of verse consisting of two metrical feet.

Double rhyme   A rhyme in which the accented, rhyming syllable is followed by one or more identical, unstressed syllables: *thrilling* and *killing, marry* and *tarry.* Formerly known as "feminine rhyme."

Dramatic irony   A situation in which a reader or audience knows more than the speakers or characters, either about the outcome of events or the discrepancy between a meaning intended by a speaker or character and that recognized by the reader or audience.

Dramatic monologue   A poem with only one speaker, overheard in a dramatic moment (usually addressing another character or characters who do not speak), whose words reveal what is going on in the scene and expose significant depths of the speaker's temperament, attitudes, and values. See Robert Browning, "My Last Duchess" (p. 70) and T. S. Eliot, "The Love Song of J. Alfred Prufrock" (p. 129).

Elegy   In Greek and Roman literature, a serious, meditative poem written in "elegiac meter" (alternating hexameter and pentameter lines); since the 1600s, a sustained and formal poem lamenting the death of a particular person, usually ending with a consolation, or setting forth meditations on death or another solemn theme. See Thomas Gray's "Elegy Written in a Country Churchyard" (p. 28), John Milton's pastoral elegy "Lycidas" (p. 16), and Walt Whitman's "When Lilacs Last in the Dooryard Bloom'd" (p. 85). The adjective "elegiac" is also used to describe a general tone of sadness or a worldview that emphasizes suffering and loss. It is most often applied to Anglo-Saxon poems like *Beowulf* or *The Seafarer,* but can also be used for modern poems such as, for example, A. E. Housman's poems in *A Shropshire Lad* (1896).

Elision   See **compression.**

End rhyme   Rhyme at the ends of lines in a poem.

End-stopped line   A line in which both the grammatical structure and the thought reach completion at the end. Cf. **run-on line.**

English sonnet   A sonnet consisting of three quatrains (four-line units, typically rhyming *abab cdcd efef*) and a couplet (two rhyming lines). Usually the subject is introduced in the first quatrain, expanded in the second, and expanded still further in the third; the couplet adds a logical, pithy conclusion or gives a surprising twist. Also called the Shakespearean sonnet (see examples on pp. 7–9). Cf. **Spenserian sonnet.**

Enjambment   See **run-on line.**

Epic   A long narrative poem that celebrates the achievements of great heroes and heroines, often determining the fate of a tribe or nation, in formal language and an elevated style. Examples include Homer's *Iliad* and *Odyssey,* Virgil's *Aeneid,* and John Milton's *Paradise Lost.*

Epigram   Originally an inscription, especially an epitaph; in modern usage a short poem, usually polished and witty with a surprising twist at the end. (Its other dictionary definition, "any terse, witty, pointed statement," generally does not apply in poetry.)

Epigraph   In literature, a quotation at the beginning of a poem or on the title page or the beginning of a chapter in a book. See the epigraph from Dante at the beginning of T. S. Eliot, "The Love Song of J. Alfred Prufrock" (p. 129).

Epiphany   An appearance or manifestation, especially of a divine being; in literature, since James Joyce adapted the term to secular use in 1944, a sudden sense of radiance and revelation one may feel while perceiving a commonplace object; a moment or event in which the essential nature of a person, a situation, or an object is suddenly perceived. The term is more common in narrative than in lyric poetry. William Wordsworth, in "Ode: Intimations of Immortality" (p. 42), writes about epiphanies, although the poem itself does not depict them; Robert Bly depicts one in "Driving to Town Late to Mail a Letter" (p. 182).

Euphony   Language that strikes the ear as smooth, musical, and agreeable. An example can be found in Alexander Pope, "An Essay on Criticism," lines 366–67: "Soft is the strain when Zephyr gently blows, / And the smooth stream in smoother numbers flows" (p. 26). Cf. **cacophony.**

Exact rhyme   Rhyme in which all sounds following the vowel sound are the same: *spite* and *night*, *art* and *heart*, *ache* and *fake*, *card* and *barred*.

Exaggeration   See **hyperbole.**

Extension   Pronunciation that adds a syllable for the sake of the meter. See, for example, the second line of Edmund Spenser's sonnet "One day I wrote her name upon the strand" (p. 4): "But came the waves and washèd it away."

Falling meter   Meter using a foot (usually a trochee or a dactyl) in which the first syllable is accented, followed by unaccented syllables that give a sense of stepping down. Cf. **rising meter.**

Feminine rhyme   See **double rhyme.**

Figure of speech and **figurative language**   Uses of language that depart from standard or literal usage in order to achieve a special effect or meaning.

Fixed form   Poetry written in definite, repeating patterns of line, rhyme scheme, or stanza.

Foot   The basic unit in metrical verse, composed of (usually) one stressed and one or more unstressed syllables. See also **anapest, dactyl, iamb, spondee,** and **trochee.**

Form   (1) Genre or literary type (e.g., the lyric form); (2) patterns of meter, lines, and rhymes (stanzaic form); (3) the organization of the parts of a literary work in relation to its total effect (e.g., "The form [structure] of this poem is very effective").

Free verse   See **open form.**

Genre   A recurring type of literature; a literary form as defined by rules or conventions followed in it (e.g., tragedy, comedy, epic, lyric, pastoral, novel, short story, essay).

Haiku   A lyric form, originating in Japan, of seventeen syllables in three lines, the first and third having five syllables and the second seven, presenting an image of a natural object or scene that expresses a distinct emotion or spiritual insight. Gary Snyder incorporates haiku into "Hitch Haiku" (p. 200).

Half rhyme   See **slant rhyme.**

Heptameter   A poetic line with seven metrical feet.

Heroic couplets   Couplets in iambic pentameter, usually with a full stop at the end. See Jonathan Swift, "A Description of the Morning" (p. 25). Also called "closed couplets."

Hexameter   A poetic line with six metrical feet. See also **alexandrine.**

Hyperbole   Exaggeration; a figure of speech in which something is stated more strongly than is logically warranted. Hyperbole is often used to make a point emphatically, as when Hamlet protests that he loved Ophelia much more than her brother did: "Forty thousand brothers / Could not with all their quantity of love / Make up my sum" (5.1.272–74). See also Robert Burns, "A Red, Red Rose" (p. 36).

Iamb   A metrical foot consisting of two syllables, an unaccented one followed by an accented one (˘´). In iambic meter (the most widely used of English metrical forms), iambs are the predominant foot in a line or poem. The following line from Thomas Gray's "Elegy Written in a Country Churchyard" (p. 28) is in iambic meter: "Thĕ cúr | fĕw tólls | thĕ kńell | ŏf párt | ĭng dáy."

Image   (1) A word or group of words that refers to a sensory experience or to an object that can be known by one or more of the senses. "Imagery" signifies all such language in a poem or other literary work collectively and can include any of the senses; see, for example, the first two stanzas of T. S. Eliot's "Preludes" (p. 133). See also **synesthesia.** (2) A metaphor or other comparison. "Imagery" in this sense refers to the characteristic that several images in a poem have in common, for example, the Christian imagery in William Blake's "The Lamb" (p. 34).

Imagist poetry   Poetry that relies on sharp, concrete images, written in a highly concentrated style that is suggestive rather than discursive. See, for example, H. D.'s "Garden" (p. 124).

Implied metaphor   Metaphor in which the *to be* verb is omitted and one aspect of the comparison is implied, rather than stated directly. "A car thief is a dirty dog" is direct metaphor; "some dirty dog stole my car" contains an implied metaphor. Examples are "whose hands *shipwreck* vases," "A *wrench* in clocks and the solar system," "In *traffic* of wit expertly manoeuvre" in John Frederick Nims, "Love Poem" (p. 158).

Internal rhyme   Rhyme that occurs between words within a line, between words within lines near each other, or between a word within a line and one at the end of the same or a nearby line. Edgar Allan Poe's "Annabel Lee" (p. 61) offers many examples: "chilling / And killing," "Can ever dissever," "And the stars never rise but I see the bright eyes."

Intertextuality   The implied presence of previous texts within a literary work or as its context. Devices used to achieve this include allusion and choice of genre. An intertextual approach assumes that interpretation is incomplete until the relation of the new work to its predecessors — response, opposition, development — has been considered.

Irony   A feeling, tone, mood, or attitude arising from the awareness that what is (reality) is opposite from, and usually worse than, what seems (appearance). What a person *says* may be ironic (see **verbal irony**), or a discrepancy between what a character knows or means and what a reader or audience knows can be ironic (see **dramatic irony**), or, without centering on one person, a general situation can be seen as ironic (**situational irony**). Irony should not be confused with mere coincidence. See also **Socratic irony.**

Italian sonnet   A sonnet composed of an octave (an eight-line unit), rhyming *abbaabba,* and a sestet (a six-line unit), often rhyming *cdecde* or *cdcdcd,* although variations are frequent. The octave usually develops an idea, question, or problem; then the poem pauses, or "turns," and the sestet completes the idea, answers the question, or resolves the difficulty. Sometimes called a Petrarchan sonnet. See Gerard Manley Hopkins, "God's Grandeur" (p. 99).

Juxtaposition   Placement of things side by side or close together for comparison or contrast or to create something new from the union, without necessarily making them grammatically parallel. See, for example, Jimmy Santiago Baca, "Family Ties" (p. 278), lines 29–34: "My sons sleep in the back, / dream of the open clearing, / . . . / as I stare out the window / at no trespassing signs white flashing past."

Line   A sequence of words printed as a separate entity on a page; the basic structural unit in poetry (except prose poems).

Literal   In accordance with the primary or strict meaning of a word or words; not figurative or metaphorical.

Litotes   See **understatement.**

Lyric   Originally, a poem sung to the accompaniment of a lyre; now a short poem expressing the personal emotion and ideas of a single speaker.

Masculine rhyme   See **single rhyme.**

Metaphor   A figure of speech in which two things usually thought to be dissimilar are treated as if they were alike and have characteristics in common. "Whose *palms are bulls* in china" (John Frederick Nims, "Love Poem," p. 158). See also **implied metaphor.**

Metaphysical poetry   The work of a number of seventeenth-century poets that was characterized by philosophical subtlety and intellectual rigor; subtle, often outrageous logic; imitation of actual speech, sometimes resulting in "rough" meter and style; and far-fetched analogies. John Donne, "A Valediction: Forbidding Mourning" and "The Flea" (pp. 9 and 10) exemplify the type. See also **conceit.**

Meter   A steady beat, or measured pulse, created by a repeating pattern of accents, syllables, or both.

Metonymy   A figure of speech in which the name of one thing is substituted for that of something closely associated with it, as in commonly used phrases such as "The *White House* announced today . . ." (the name of the building is substituted for the president or the staff members who issued the announcement), "He's got *a Constable* on his wall," "The *trains* are on strike," or "*Wall Street* is in a panic." In the last line of John Frederick Nims's "Love Poem" (p. 158), "All the toys of the world would break," *toys* is substituted for "things that give happiness" (as toys do to a child). See also **synecdoche.**

Mock epic   A literary form that imitates the grand style and conventions of the epic genre, such as the opening statement of a theme, an address to the muse, long formal speeches, and epic similes, but applies them to a subject unworthy of such exalted treatment. Alexander Pope's "The Rape of the Lock" (1712, 1714) is commonly regarded as the best example of the mock epic in English. Pope uses the form for comic effect and at the same time treats seriously the great epic themes concerning human destiny and mortality. Also called "mock heroic." See also **epic.**

Monometer   A poetic line with one metrical foot.

Narrative   A story in prose or verse; an account of events involving characters and a sequence of events, told by a storyteller (narrator).

Near rhyme   See **slant rhyme.**

Octameter   A poetic line with eight metrical feet.

Octave   The first eight lines of an Italian sonnet.

Ode   A long lyric poem, serious (often intellectual) in tone, elevated and dignified in style, dealing with a single theme. The ode is generally more complicated in form than other lyric poems. Some odes retain a formal division into strophe, antistrophe, and epode, which reflects the ode's origins in the chorus of Greek tragedy. See William Wordsworth, "Ode: Intimations of Immortality" (p. 42), Percy Bysshe Shelley, "Ode to the West Wind" (p. 52), and John Keats, "Ode on a Grecian Urn" (p. 57).

Onomatopoeia   The use of words whose sounds supposedly resemble the sounds they denote (such as *thump, rattle, growl, hiss*), or a group of words whose sounds help to convey what is being described; for example, Emily Dickinson's "I heard a Fly *buzz* — when I died" (p. 95).

Open form   A form free of any predetermined metrical and stanzaic patterns. Cf. **closed form.**

Ottava rima   An eight-line stanza in iambic pentameter rhyming *ababababcc*. See William Butler Yeats, "Among School Children" (p. 105).

Overstatement   See **hyperbole.**

Oxymoron   A figure of speech combining in one phrase (usually adjective-noun) two seemingly contradictory elements, such as "loving hate" or "feather of lead, bright smoke, cold fire, sick health" (Shakespeare, *Romeo and Juliet* 1.1.176–80). Oxymoron is a type of **paradox.**

Pantoum   A poem composed of quatrains rhyming *abab* in which the second and fourth lines of each stanza serve as the first and third lines of the next, this process continuing through the last stanza (it repeats the first and third lines of the first stanza in reverse order, so the poem ends with the same line with which it began). See Nellie Wong, "Grandmother's Song" (p. 230).

Paradox   A figure of speech in which a statement initially seeming self-contradictory or absurd turns out, seen in another light, to make good sense. The closing line of John Donne's sonnet "Death, be not proud" (p. 11) contains a paradox: "Death, thou shalt die." See also **oxymoron.**

Parallelism   (1) A verbal arrangement in which elements of equal weight within phrases, sentences, or paragraphs are expressed in a similar grammatical order and structure. It can appear within a line or pair of lines ("And he was always quietly arrayed, / And he was always human when he talked"—Edwin Arlington Robinson, "Richard Cory" [p. 109]) or, more noticeably, as a series of parallel items, as in Langston Hughes's "Harlem" (p. 144). (2) A principle of poetic structure in which consecutive lines in open form are related by a line's repeating, expanding on, or contrasting with the idea of the line or lines before it, as in the poems of Walt Whitman (pp. 72–92).

Parody   Now, a humorous or satirical imitation of a serious piece of literature or writing. In the sixteenth and seventeenth centuries, poets such as George Herbert practiced "sacred parody" by adapting secular lyrics to devotional themes.

Partial rhyme   See **slant rhyme.**

Pastoral   A poem (also called an "eclogue," a "bucolic," or an "idyll") that expresses a city poet's nostalgic image of the simple, peaceful life of shepherds and other country folk in an idealized natural setting. Christopher Marlowe's "The Passionate Shepherd to His Love" (p. 6) uses some pastoral conventions, as do certain elegies (including John Milton's "Lycidas," p. 16).

Pause   See **caesura.**

Pentameter   A poetic line with five metrical feet.

Persona   Literally, the mask through which actors spoke in Greek plays. In some critical approaches of recent decades, the "character" projected by the author, the "I" of a narrative poem or novel, or the speaker whose voice is heard in a lyric poem. In this view, the poem is an artificial construct distanced from the poet's autobiographical self. Cf. **voice.**

Personification   A figure of speech in which something nonhuman is treated as if it had human characteristics or performed human actions. Sometimes it involves abstractions, as in Thomas Gray's phrase "Fair Science frowned" ("Elegy Written in a Country Churchyard," p. 28); science cannot literally frown. In other cases concrete things are given human characteristics, as in the phrase "Wearing white for Eastertide" from A. E. Housman's "Loveliest of trees, the cherry now" (p. 101). Cherry trees do not actually wear clothes—they are being given, briefly, a human attribute. Difficulty can arise when personification is redefined (incorrectly) as treating something nonhuman in terms of anything alive rather than specifically human: "the mouth of time" in Nancy Willard's "Questions My Son Asked Me, Answers I Never Gave Him" (p. 221) is metaphor, not personification, since animals as well as humans have mouths. See also **apostrophe.**

Petrarchan sonnet   See Italian sonnet.

Poem   A term whose meaning exceeds all attempts at definition. Here is a slightly modified version of an attempt at definition by William Harmon and C. Hugh Holman in *A Handbook to Literature* (1996): A poem is a literary composition, written or oral, typically characterized by imagination, emotion, sense impressions, and concrete language that invites attention to its own physical features, such as sound or appearance on the page.

Poetic diction   In general, specialized language used in or considered appropriate to poetry. In the late seventeenth and the eighteenth centuries, a refined use of language that excluded "common" speech from poetry as indecorous—and substituted elevated circumlocutions, archaic synonyms, or such forms as *ope* and *e'er.*

Prose poem   A poem printed as prose, with lines wrapping at the right margin rather than being divided through predetermined line breaks. See Carolyn Forché, "The Colonel" (p. 261).

Prosody   The principles of versification, especially of meter, rhythm, rhyme, and stanza forms.

Pun   A play on words based on similarity in sound between two words having very different meanings. Also called "paronomasia." See the puns on "heart" and "kindly" in Sir Thomas Wyatt's "They flee from me" (p. 2).

Quantitative verse   Verse whose meter is based on the length of syllables (phonetic length being a distinguishing feature of ancient Greek and Latin, whereas English is an accentual language). Classical poetry exhibits a great variety of meters, and some English poets in the late 1500s attempted to fashion English verse on this principle. In *Evangeline* Henry Wadsworth Longfellow used dactylic hexameter in imitation of Virgil's *Aeneid,* but defined it by accent, not quantity. Cf. **accentual-syllabic verse.**

Quatrain A stanza of four lines or other four-line unit within a larger form, such as a sonnet.

Refrain One or more identical or deliberately similar lines repeated through-out a poem, such as the final line of a stanza or a block of lines between stanzas or sections.

Rhyme The repetition of the accented vowel sound of a word and all succeed-ing consonant sounds. See also **exact rhyme; slant rhyme.**

Rhyme royal An alternative term for **Chaucerian stanza,** because it was used by King James I of Scotland in his poem *The Kingis Quair* ("The King's Book"), written about 1424.

Rhyme scheme The pattern of end rhymes in a poem or stanza; the recurring sequence is usually described by assigning a letter to each word-sound, the same word-sounds having the same letter (e.g., a quatrain might be *abcb*).

Rhythm The patterned "movement" of language created by the choice of words and their arrangement, usually described through such metaphors as fast or slow, smooth or halting, graceful or rough, deliberate or frenzied, syncopated or disjointed. Rhythm in poetry is affected, in addition to meter, by such factors as line length; line endings; pauses (or lack of them) within lines; spaces within, at the beginning or end of, or between lines; word choice; and combinations of sounds.

Rising meter A foot (usually an iamb or an anapest) in which the final, accented syllable is preceded by one or two unaccented syllables, thus giving a sense of stepping up. Cf. **falling meter.**

Run-on line A line whose sense and grammatical structure continue to the next line. In the following lines by William Stafford ("Traveling through the Dark," p. 161), the first line is run-on, the second end-stopped: "Traveling through the dark I found a deer / dead on the edge of the Wilson River road." Also called "enjambment." Cf. **end-stopped line.**

Sarcasm A harsh and cutting form of verbal irony, often involving apparent praise that is obviously not meant: "Oh, no, these are fine. I *prefer* my eggs thor-oughly charred."

Satire A work, or manner within a work, that combines a critical attitude with humor and wit with the intent of improving humanity or human institutions. See, for example, Bob Hicok's "Plus Shipping" (p. 301).

Scansion The division of metrical verse into feet in order to determine and label its meter. Scanning a poem involves marking its stressed syllables with an accent mark [´] and its unstressed syllables with a curved line [˘], using a vertical line to indicate the way it divides into feet, and then describing (or labeling) the type of foot used most often and the line length—that is, the number of feet in each line. See also **foot** and **line.**

Sestet   The last six lines of an Italian sonnet.

Sestina   A lyric poem consisting of six six-line stanzas and a three-line concluding stanza (or "envoy"). The six end-words of the first stanza must be used as the end-words of the other five stanzas, in a specified pattern (the first line ends with the end-word from the last line of the previous stanza, the second line with that of the first line of the previous stanza, the third line with that of the previous fifth line, the fourth line with that of the previous second line, the fifth line with that of the previous fourth line, the sixth line with that of the previous third line). The three lines of the envoy must use the end-words of lines five, three, and one from the first stanza, in that order, and must include the other three end-words within the lines. See Alice Fulton, "You Can't Rhumboogie in a Ball and Chain" (p. 273).

Shakespearean sonnet   See **English sonnet**.

Shaped poem   See **concrete poem**.

Simile   Expression of a direct similarity, using such words as *like, as,* or *than,* between two things usually regarded as dissimilar, as in "Shrinking from far *headlights pale as a dime*" (John Frederick Nims, "Love Poem," p. 158). It is important to distinguish *simile* from *comparison,* in which the two things joined by "like" or "as" are *not* dissimilar.

Single rhyme   A rhyme in which the stressed, rhyming syllable is the final syllable: *west* and *vest, away* and *today*. Formerly called "masculine rhyme."

Situational irony   The mood evoked when an action intended to have a certain effect turns out to have a different and more sinister effect. See Thomas Hardy, "The Convergence of the Twain" (p. 98).

Slant rhyme   Consonance at the ends of lines; for example, *Room* and *Storm, firm* and *Room,* and *be* and *Fly* in Emily Dickinson's "I heard a Fly buzz — when I died" (p. 95). It can also be internal, if repeated enough to form a discernible pattern.

Socratic irony   A pose of self-deprecation, or of belittling oneself, in order to tease the reader into deeper insight.

Sonnet   A fourteen-line poem usually written in iambic pentameter; originally lyrical love poems, sonnets came to be used also for meditations on religious themes, death, and nature, and are now open to all subjects. Some variations in form have been tried: Sir Philip Sidney's "Loving in truth, and fain in verse my love to show" (p. 4) is in hexameters; George Meredith wrote sixteen-line sonnets; John Milton's "On the New Forcers of Conscience under the Long Parliament," written around 1646, is a "caudate" (tailed) sonnet with a six-line coda appended; and Gerard Manley Hopkins designed "Pied Beauty" (p. 100) as a "curtal" (abbreviated) sonnet (six lines in place of the octave, then four lines, and a half-line ending in place of the sestet). See **English sonnet** and **Italian sonnet**.

Sonnet sequence   A group of sonnets so arranged as to imply a narrative progression in the speaker's experience or attitudes; used especially in the sixteenth century. Also called "sonnet cycle."

Spenserian sonnet   A variation of the English sonnet that employs the structure of three quatrains plus a couplet but joins the quatrains by linking rhymes: *abab bcbc cdcd ee*. For examples, see page 4.

Spenserian stanza   A stanza of nine iambic lines, the first eight pentameter and the ninth hexameter, rhyming *ababbcbcc*. They are used in Edmund Spenser's *The Faerie Queene* (1590, 1596) and in such Romantic narrative poems as John Keats's *The Eve of St. Agnes* (1820) and Percy Bysshe Shelley's *Adonais* (1824).

Spondee   A metrical foot made up of two stressed syllables (´´), with no unstressed syllables. Spondees could not, of course, be the predominant foot in a poem; they are usually substituted for iambic or trochaic feet as a way of increasing emphasis, as in this line from John Donne's "Batter my heart, three-personed God" (1633): "Ăš yét | bŭt knŏck, | bréathe, shĭne, | ănd séek | tŏ ménd."

Sprung rhythm   See **accentual meter.**

Stanza   A grouping of poetic lines into a section, either according to form — each section having the same number of lines and the same prosody (see Percy Bysshe Shelley's "Ode to the West Wind," p. 52) — or according to thought, creating irregular units comparable to paragraphs in prose (as in William Wordsworth's "Ode: Intimations of Immortality," p. 42).

Stress   See **accent.**

Structure   (1) The planned framework — the general plan or outline — of a literary work; (2) narrower patterns within the overall framework. Cf. **form.**

Substitution   The use of a different kind of foot in place of the one normally demanded by the predominant meter of a poem, as a way of adding variety, emphasizing the dominant foot by variation from it, speeding up or slowing down the pace, or signaling a switch in meaning.

Surrealism   An artistic movement that attempted to portray or interpret the workings of the unconscious mind, especially as realized in dreams, by an irrational, noncontextual choice and arrangement of images or objects. Now more often used to refer to anything defying the normal sense of reality.

Syllabic verse   A metrical pattern in which all lines in the poem have the same number of syllables (as in Sylvia Plath's "Metaphors," p. 204) or all first lines of stanzas have the same number, all second lines the same, and so on (see Dylan Thomas's "Fern Hill," p. 162) — while the stressed syllables are random in number and placement.

Symbol   Something that is itself and also stands for something else; a literary symbol is a prominent or repeated image or action that is present in the poem (or story or play) and can be seen, touched, smelled, heard, tasted, or experienced imaginatively but also conveys a cluster of abstract meanings beyond itself. Most critics agree that the tiger in William Blake's "The Tyger" (p. 35) and the wrecked vessel in Adrienne Rich's "Diving into the Wreck" (p. 197), for example, carry symbolic meaning.

Synecdoche   A special kind of metonymy in which a part of a thing is substituted for the whole of which it is a part, as in the commonly used phrases "give me a hand," "lend me your ears," or "many mouths to feed." See, for example, "whose *hands* shipwreck vases" and "For should your *hands* drop white and empty" (John Frederick Nims, "Love Poem," p. 158).

Synesthesia   Description of one kind of sense experience in relation to another, such as attribution of color to sounds ("blue notes") and vice versa ("a loud tie") or of taste to sounds ("sweet music"). See, for example, "With Blue—uncertain stumbling Buzz—" (Emily Dickinson, "I heard a Fly buzz—when I died," p. 95).

Tercet   A stanza of three lines, each usually ending with the same rhyme; but see **terza rima**. Cf. **triplet**.

Terza rima   A poetic form consisting of three-line stanzas (tercets) with interlinked rhymes, *aba bcb cdc ded efe*, etc., made famous by Dante's use of it in *The Divine Comedy*. Terza rima is used in Percy Bysshe Shelley's "Ode to the West Wind" (p. 52).

Tetrameter   A poetic line with four metrical feet. Robert Frost's line "The woods are lovely, dark, and deep" ("Stopping by Woods on a Snowy Evening," p. 116) is an example of iambic tetrameter.

Text   Traditionally, a piece of writing. In recent reader response criticism, "text" has come to mean the words with which the reader interacts; in this view, a poem is not an object, not a shape on the page or a spoken performance, but what is completed in the reader's mind.

Theme   The central idea embodied or explored in a literary work, for some idea-based approaches to literature; the general concept, explicit or implied, that the work incorporates and makes persuasive to the reader.

Title   The name attached to a work of literature. For poetry, a title in some cases is an integral part of a poem and needs to be considered in interpreting it; see, for example, George Herbert's "The Pulley" (p. 14). In other cases the name has been added as a means of identifying the poem and is not integral to interpretation. Sometimes the poem is untitled and the first line is used as a convenient way of referring to it, but should not be thought of as a title and does not follow the capitalization rules for titles.

Tone   The attitude, or "stance," toward the subject and toward the reader or audience implied in a literary work; the "tone of voice" it seems to project (serious or playful; exaggerated or understated; formal or informal; ironic or straightforward; or a complex mixture of more than one of these).

Transferred epithet   A figure of speech in which a modifier that ought, strictly, to apply to one word is transferred to another word that it does not strictly fit. In "The drunk clambering on his undulant floor" (John Frederick Nims, "Love Poem," p. 158), the drunk's perception, not the floor, is undulating.

Trimeter   A poetic line with three metrical feet.

Triplet   A group of three consecutive lines with the same rhyme, often used for variation in a long sequence of couplets. Cf. tercet.

Trochee   A metrical foot consisting of two syllables, an accented one followed by an unaccented one (˜). In trochaic meter, trochees are the predominant foot in a line or poem. The following lines from William Blake's introduction to *Songs of Innocence* (1789) are in trochaic meter (each line lacking the final unaccented syllable): "Pípǐng | dówn thě | válleŷs | wíld, / Pípǐng | Sóngs ǒf | pléasǎnt | glée, / Ón ǎ | clóud Ǐ | sáw ǎ | chíld, / Aňd hé | laúghǐng | sáid tǒ | mé."

Understatement   A figure of speech expressing something in an unexpectedly restrained way. Paradoxically, to de-emphasize through understatement can be a way of emphasizing, of making people react with "there must be more to it than that." When Mercutio in Shakespeare's *Romeo and Juliet,* after being stabbed by Tybalt, calls his wound "a scratch, a scratch" (3.1.92), he is understating, for the wound is serious — he calls for a doctor in the next line, and he dies a few minutes later.

Verbal irony   A figure of speech in which what is said is nearly the opposite of what is meant (such as saying "Lovely day out" when the weather actually is miserable). See Stephen Crane's "Do not weep, maiden, for war is kind" (p. 110).

Villanelle   A nineteen-line lyric poem divided into five tercets and a final four-line stanza, rhyming *aba aba aba aba aba abaa.* Line 1 is repeated to form lines 6, 12, and 18; line 3 is repeated to form lines 9, 15, and 19. See Elizabeth Bishop, "One Art" (p. 158), Dylan Thomas, "Do not go gentle into that good night" (p. 163), and John Yau, "Chinese Villanelle" (p. 263).

Voice   The supposed authorial presence in poems that do not obviously employ persona as a distancing device.

Acknowledgments

Kim Addonizio. "The Sound" from *The Philosopher's Club* (Rochester, New York: BOA Editions, 1994). Copyright © 1994 by Kim Addonizio. Used by permission of the author.

Ai. "Why Can't I Leave You?" from *Vice: New and Selected Poems*. Copyright © 1973 by Ai. Used by permission of W. W. Norton & Company, Inc.

Sherman Alexie. "Postcards to Columbus" from *Old Shirts and New Skins* (Los Angeles: American Indian Studies Center, 1993). Copyright © 1993 by Sherman Alexie. Reprinted with the permission of Nancy Stauffer Associates.

Agha Shahid Ali. "I Dream It Is Afternoon When I Return to Delhi" from *The Half-Inch Himalayas*. Copyright © 1987 by Agha Shahid Ali. Reprinted with the permission of Wesleyan University Press, www.wesleyan.edu/wespress.

Tom Andrews. "The Hemophiliac's Motorcycle" from *The Hemophiliac's Motorcycle*. Copyright © 1994 by Tom Andrews. Reprinted with the permission of the University of Iowa Press.

John Ashbery. "Worsening Situation" from *Self-Portrait in a Convex Mirror*. Copyright © 1975 by John Ashbery. Used by permission of Viking, a division of Penguin Group (USA) Inc.

Margaret Atwood, "True Stories" from *Selected Poems 1966–1984*. Copyright © 1990 by Margaret Atwood. Reprinted with the permission of Phoebe Larmore Literary Agency and Oxford University Press Canada.

W. H. Auden, "As I Walked Out One Evening." Copyright © 1940 and renewed © 1968 by W. H. Auden. "Musée des Beaux Arts." Copyright © 1940 and renewed © 1968 by W. H. Auden. From *Collected Poems* by W. H. Auden. Used by permission of Random House, Inc.

Jimmy Santiago Baca. "Family Ties" from *Black Mesa Poems*. Copyright © 1989 by Jimmy Santiago Baca. Reprinted with the permission of New Directions Publishing Corp.

Jim Barnes. "Return to La Plata, Missouri" from *American Book of the Dead: Poems*. Copyright © 1982 by Jim Barnes. Used with permission of the poet and the University of Illinois Press.

John Berryman. "Henry's Confession" from *The Dream Songs*. Copyright © 1969 by John Berryman. Reprinted with the permission of Farrar, Straus & Giroux, LLC.

Elizabeth Bishop. "The Fish," "One Art," and "In the Waiting Room" from *The Complete Poems, 1927–1979*. Copyright © 1979, 1983 by Alice Helen Methfessel. Reprinted with the permission of Farrar, Straus & Giroux, LLC.

Robert Bly. "Driving to Town Late to Mail a Letter" from *Silence in the Snowy Fields* (Middletown, Conn.: Wesleyan University Press, 1962). Copyright © 1962 by Robert Bly. Reprinted with the permission of the author.

Louise Bogan. "Women" from *Collected Poems: 1923–1953*. Copyright © 1954 by Louise Bogan. Reprinted with the permission of Farrar, Straus & Giroux, LLC.

Eavan Boland. "The Pomegranate" from *In a Time of Violence*. Copyright © 1994 by Eavan Boland. Used by permission of W. W. Norton & Company, Inc.

Gwendolyn Brooks. "We Real Cool" and "The Bean Eaters" from *Blacks*. Copyright © 1991 by Gwendolyn Brooks. Reprinted by consent of Brooks Permissions.

Alice Fulton. "You Can't Rhumboogie in a Ball and Chain" from *Dance Script with Electric Ballerina*. Copyright © 1983 by Alice Fulton. Used with permission of the University of Illinois Press.

Richard Garcia. "Why I Left the Church" from *The Flying Garcias*. Copyright © 1993. Reprinted by permission of the University of Pittsburgh Press.

Allen Ginsberg. "A Supermarket in California" from *Collected Poems 1982–1992*. Copyright © 1955 by Allen Ginsberg. Used by permission of HarperCollins Publishers.

Louise Glück. "The Wild Iris" from *The Wild Iris*. Copyright © 1992 by Louise Glück. Used by permission of HarperCollins Publishers.

Ray González. "Praise the Tortilla, Praise Menudo, Praise Chorizo" from *The Heat of Arrivals: Poems*. Copyright © 1992 by Ray González. Reprinted with the permission of BOA Editions, Ltd., www.boaeditions.org.

Jorie Graham. "To the Reader" from *The End of Beauty*. Copyright © 1987 by Jorie Graham. Used by permission of HarperCollins Publishers.

Marilyn Hacker. "Villanelle" from *Selected Poems: 1965–1990*. Copyright © 1974 by Marilyn Hacker. Used by permission of W. W. Norton & Company, Inc.

Kimiko Hahn. "Mother's Mother" from *Volatile*. Copyright ©1999 by Kimiko Hahn. Reprinted with the permission of Hanging Loose Press.

Donald Hall. "Names of Horses" from *Old and New Poems*. Copyright © 1990 by Donald Hall. Reprinted by permission of Houghton Mifflin Company. All rights reserved.

Joy Harjo. "She Had Some Horses" from *She Had Some Horses*. Copyright © 1983, 1997 by Thunder's Mouth Press. Reprinted with the permission of Seal Press, a member of Perseus Books Group.

Michael S. Harper. "Nightmare Begins Responsibility" from *Images of Kin: New and Selected Poems*. Copyright © 1977 by Michael S. Harper. Used with permission of the University of Illinois Press.

Robert Hayden. "Those Winter Sundays" from *Angle of Ascent: New and Selected Poems*. Copyright © 1966 by Robert Hayden. Used by permission of Liveright Publishing Corporation.

Samuel Hazo. "For Fawzi in Jerusalem" from *Blood Rights* (Pittsburgh: University of Pittsburgh Press, 1968). Copyright © 1968 by Samuel Hazo. Reprinted with the permission of the author.

Seamus Heaney. "Digging" from *Poems 1965–1975*. Copyright © 1980 by Seamus Heaney. Reprinted with the permission of Farrar, Straus & Giroux LLC and Faber and Faber Ltd.

Bob Hicok. "Plus Shipping" from *Plus Shipping*. Copyright © 1998 by Bob Hicok. Reprinted with the permission of BOA Editions, Ltd., www.boaeditions.org.

Conrad Hilberry. "Player Piano" from *Player Piano: Poems*. Copyright © 1999 by Conrad Hilberry. Reprinted with the permission of Louisiana State University Press.

Geoffrey Hill. "In Memory of Jane Fraser" from *Collected Poems* (Penguin Books, 1985). Copyright © 1985 by Geoffrey Hill. First published in *For the Unfallen*, copyright © 1959 by Geoffrey Hill. Reprinted with the permission of Penguin Books, Ltd. and Oxford University Press, Ltd.

David Mura. "Grandfather-in-Law" from *After We Lost Our Way* (New York: E. P. Dutton, 1989). Copyright © 1989 by David Mura. Reprinted with the permission of the author.

Lorine Niedecker. "My Life by Water" from *Collected Works*. Copyright © 1985 by Lorine Niedecker. Reprinted with the permission of the University of California Press.

John Frederick Nims. "Love Poem" from *Selected Poems*. Copyright © 1982 by the University of Chicago. Reprinted with the permission of Bonnie Nims.

Naomi Shihab Nye. "The Small Vases from Hebron" from *Fuel*. Copyright © 1998 by Naomi Shihab Nye. Reprinted with the permission of BOA Editions Ltd., ed. www.boaeditions.org.

Frank O'Hara. "The Day Lady Died," "A Step Away from Them," "Personal Poem," and "Poem" ["Lana Turner has collapsed"] from *Lunch Poems*. Copyright © 1964 by Frank O'Hara. Reprinted with the permission of City Lights Books.

Sharon Olds. "I Go Back to May 1937" from *The Gold Cell*. Copyright © 1987 by Sharon Olds. Used by permission of Alfred A. Knopf, a division of Random House, Inc.

Mary Oliver. "First Snow" from *American Primitive*. Copyright © 1978 by Mary Oliver. Reprinted with the permission of Little, Brown & Company.

Simon J. Ortiz. "Speaking" from *Woven Stone*. Copyright © 1992. Reprinted with the permission of the author.

Linda Pastan. "An Early Afterlife" from *Carnival Evening: New and Selected Poems: 1968–1998*. Copyright © 1998 by Linda Pastan. Used by permission of W. W. Norton & Company, Inc.

Lucia Perillo. "Long Time Too Long" from *The Oldest Map With the Name America*. Copyright © 1999 by Lucia Perillo. Used by permission of Random House, Inc.

Carl Phillips. "To the Tune of a Small, Repeatable, and Passing Kindness" from *Rock Harbor*. Copyright © 2002 by Carl Phillips. Reprinted with the permission of Farrar, Straus & Giroux, LLC.

Marge Piercy. "Barbie Doll" from *Circles on the Water*. Copyright © 1982 by Marge Piercy. Used by permission of Alfred A. Knopf, a division of Random House, Inc.

Wang Ping. "Syntax" from *Of Flesh & Spirit*. Copyright © 1998 by Wang Ping. Reprinted with the permission of Coffee House Press, www.coffeehousepress.org.

Robert Pinsky. "Shirt" from *The Want Bone*. Copyright © 1990 by Robert Pinsky. Reprinted by permission of HarperCollins Publishers.

Sylvia Plath. "Metaphors" from *Crossing the Water*. Copyright © 1960 by Ted Hughes. "Daddy" from *Ariel*. Copyright © 1963 by Ted Hughes. Reprinted by permission of HarperCollins Publisher, Inc. and Faber and Faber Ltd.

Ezra Pound. "The River-Merchant's Wife: A Letter" from *Personae*. Copyright © 1926 by Ezra Pound. Reprinted by permission of New Directions Publishing Corp.

Dudley Randall. "Ballad of Birmingham" from *Cities Burning*. Copyright © 1968 by Dudley Randall. Reprinted with the permission of Broadside Press.

John Crowe Ransom. "Bells for John Whiteside's Daughter" from *Selected Poems, Third Edition, Revised and Enlarged*. Copyright © 1924, 1927 by Alfred A.

Knopf, Inc., and renewed 1952, 1955 by John Crowe Ransom. Used by permission of Alfred A. Knopf, a division of Random House, Inc.

Donald Revell. "Mignonette" from *From the Abandoned Cities*. Copyright © 1983 by Donald Revell. Used by permission of HarperCollins Publishers.

Adrienne Rich. "Diving into the Wreck" from *The Fact of a Doorframe: Selected Poems 1950–2001*. Copyright © 2002 by Adrienne Rich. Copyright © 1973 by W. W. Norton & Company, 2002. Inc. Used by permission of the author and W. W. Norton & Company, Inc.

Alberto Ríos. "Indentations in the Sugar" from *Teodora Luna's Two Kisses*. Copyright © 2000 by Alberto Ríos. Used by permission of W. W. Norton & Company, Inc.

Theodore Roethke. "My Papa's Waltz" from *Collected Poems of Theodore Roethke*. Copyright © 1942 by Hearst Magazines, Inc. Used by permission of Doubleday, a division of Random House, Inc.

Mary Ruefle. "Naked Ladies" from *Apparition Hill*. Copyright © 2002 by Mary Ruefle. Reprinted with the permission of CavanKerry Press, Ltd.

Sonia Sanchez. "An Anthem" from *Under a Soprano Sky*. Copyright © 1987 by Sonia Sanchez. Reprinted with the permission of the author.

Anne Sexton. "Cinderella" from *Transformations*. Copyright © 1971 by Anne Sexton. Reprinted with the permission of Houghton Mifflin Company. All rights reserved.

Leslie Marmon Silko. "Prayer to the Pacific" from *Storyteller*, published by Seaver Books, New York, New York. Copyright © 1981 by Leslie Marmon Silko. Reprinted by permission of Seaver Books.

Charles Simic. "Begotten of the Spleen" from *Charles Simic: Selected Early Poems*. Copyright © 1999 by Charles Simic. Reprinted with the permission of George Braziller, Inc.

Edith Sitwell. "Lullaby" from *The Collected Poems of Edith Sitwell*. Copyright © 1968 by Edith Sitwell. Reprinted with the permission of David Higham Associates.

Gary Snyder. "Hitch Haiku" from *The Black Country*. Copyright © 1968 by Gary Snyder. Reprinted by permission of New Directions Publishing Corp.

Cathy Song. "Girl Powdering Her Neck" from *Picture Bride*. Copyright © 1983 by Yale University Press. Reprinted with the permission of Yale University Press.

Gary Soto. "The Elements of San Joaquin" from *New and Selected Poems*. Copyright © 1995 by Gary Soto. Reprinted with the permission of Chronicle Books LLC.

William Stafford. "Traveling through the Dark" from *The Way It Is: New and Selected Poems*. Copyright © 1962, 1998 by the Estate of William Stafford. Reprinted with the permission of Graywolf Press, Saint Paul Minnesota.

Gerald Stern. "The Dog" from *Leaving Another Kingdom: Selected Poems*. Copyright © 1990 by Gerald Stern. Reprinted with the permission of HarperCollins Publishers.

Mark Strand. "Eating Poetry" from *Selected Poems*. Copyright © 1979, 1980 by Mark Strand. Used by permission of Alfred A. Knopf, a division of Random House, Inc.

Virgil Suárez. "Tea Leaves, *Caracoles*, Coffee Beans" from *90 Miles: Selected and New Poems*. Copyright © 2005. Reprinted by permission of the University of Pittsburgh Press.

Sekou Sundiata. "Blink Your Eyes." Copyright © 1995 by Sekou Sundiata. Reprinted with permission.

James Tate. "The Wheelchair Butterfly" from *Selected Poems*. Copyright © 1991 by James Tate. Reprinted by permission of Wesleyan University Press, www.wesleyan.edu/wespress.

Dylan Thomas. "Fern Hill" from *The Poems of Dylan Thomas*. Copyright © 1945 by The Trustees for the Copyrights of Dylan Thomas. "Do not go gentle into that good night." Copyright © 1952 by Dylan Thomas. Reprinted with the permission of New Directions Publishing Corp.

Jean Toomer. "Reapers" from *Cane*. Copyright © 1923 by Boni & Liveright, renewed 1951 by Jean Toomer. Used by permission of Liveright Publishing Corporation.

Quincy Troupe. "Poem for the Root Doctor of Rock n Roll" from *Weather Reports: New and Selected Poems* (New York: Harlem River Press, 1991). Later in *Transcircularities: New and Selected Poems* (Minneapolis: Coffee House Press, 2001). Copyright © 2001 by Quincy Troupe. Reprinted with the permission of Coffee House Press, www.coffeehousepress.org.

Ellen Bryant Voigt. "Dooryard Flower" from *Shadow of Heaven*. Copyright © 2002 by Ellen Bryant Voigt. Used by permission of W. W. Norton & Company, Inc.

Derek Walcott. "Sea Grapes" from *Collected Poems 1948–1984*. Copyright © 1986 by Derek Walcott. Reprinted with the permission of Farrar, Straus & Giroux, LLC.

Anne Waldman. "Icy Rose" from *Life Notes*. Copyright © 1973 by Amy Waldman. Reprinted with the permission of the author.

James Welch. "Christmas Comes to Moccasin Flat" from *Riding the Earthboy 40* by James Welch. Copyright © 1971, 1976, 1990 by James Welch. Used by permission of Penguin, a division of Penguin Group (USA) Inc.

Richard Wilbur. "Love Calls Us to the Things of This World" from *Things of This World*. Copyright © 1956 and renewed 1984 by Richard Wilbur. Reprinted by permission of Harcourt, Inc.

Nancy Willard. "Questions My Son Asked Me, Answers I Never Gave Him" from *Household Tales of Moon and Water*. Copyright © 1978 by Nancy Willard. Reprinted by permission of Harcourt, Inc.

William Carlos Williams. "The Red Wheelbarrow," "Spring and All" and "This Is Just to Say" from *The Collected Poems: 1909–1939, Volume I*. Copyright © 1938 by New Directions Publishing Corporation. Reprinted with the permission of New Directions Publishing Corp.

Nellie Wong. "Grandmother's Song" from *Dreams in Harrison Railroad Park*. Copyright © 1977 by Nellie Wong. Reprinted with the permission of Kelsey Street Press.

Charles Wright. "March Journal" from *The World of Ten Thousand Things: Poems 1980–1990*. Copyright © 1990 by Charles Wright. Reprinted with the permission of Farrar, Straus & Giroux, LLC.

James Wright. "A Blessing" from *The Branch Will Not Break*. Copyright © 1963 by James Wright. Reprinted by permission of Wesleyan University Press, www .wesleyan.edu/wespress.

John Yau. "Chinese Villanelle" from *Radiant Silhouette: New and Selected Work 1974–1988*. Copyright © 1989 by John Yau. Reprinted with the permission of the author.

William Butler Yeats, "Leda and the Swan," "Among School Children," and "Sailing to Byzantium" from *The Collected Poems of W. B. Yeats, Volume I: The Poems, Revised*, edited by Richard J. Finneran. Copyright © 1928 by the Macmillan Publishing Company. Copyright renewed © 1956 by Georgie Yeats. Reprinted with the permission of Scribner, an imprint of Simon & Schuster Adult Publishing Group. All rights renewed.

Al Young. "A Dance for Ma Rainey" from *Heaven: Collected Poems 1956–1990* (Berkeley: Creative Arts Book Company, 1992). Copyright © 1969 and 1992 by Al Young. Reprinted with the permission of the author.

Ray A. Young Bear. "From the Spotted Night" from *The Invisible Musician*. Copyright © 1990 by Ray A. Young Bear. Reprinted with the permission of Holy Cow! Press.

Ofelia Zepeda. "Pulling Down the Clouds" from *Ocean Power: Poems from the Desert*. Copyright © 1995 by Ofelia Zepeda. Reprinted by permission of the University of Arizona Press.

Paul Zimmer. "Zimmer Imagines Heaven" from *Crossing to Sunlight: Selected Poems*. Copyright © 1983 by Paul Zimmer. Reprinted with the permission of The University of Georgia Press.

Louis Zukofsky excerpt from "'A' 15" from *AA*." Copyright © 1978 by Celia Zukofsky and Louis Zukofsky. All Louis Zukofsky material copyright Paul Zukofsky; the material may not reproduced, quoted, or used in any manner whatsoever without the explicit and specific permission of the copyright holder.

Art:

Pieter the Elder Brueghel. "Landscape with the Fall of Icarus." Musee d'Art Ancien, Musees Royaux des Beaux-Arts, Brussels, Belgium. Scala/Art Resource, NY. Reprinted with permission.

Kitagawa Utamaro. "Woman Powdering Her Neck." Musée des Arts Asiatiques-Guimet, Paris, France. Reunion des Musees Nationaux/Art Resource, NY.

Index of Authors, Titles, and First Lines